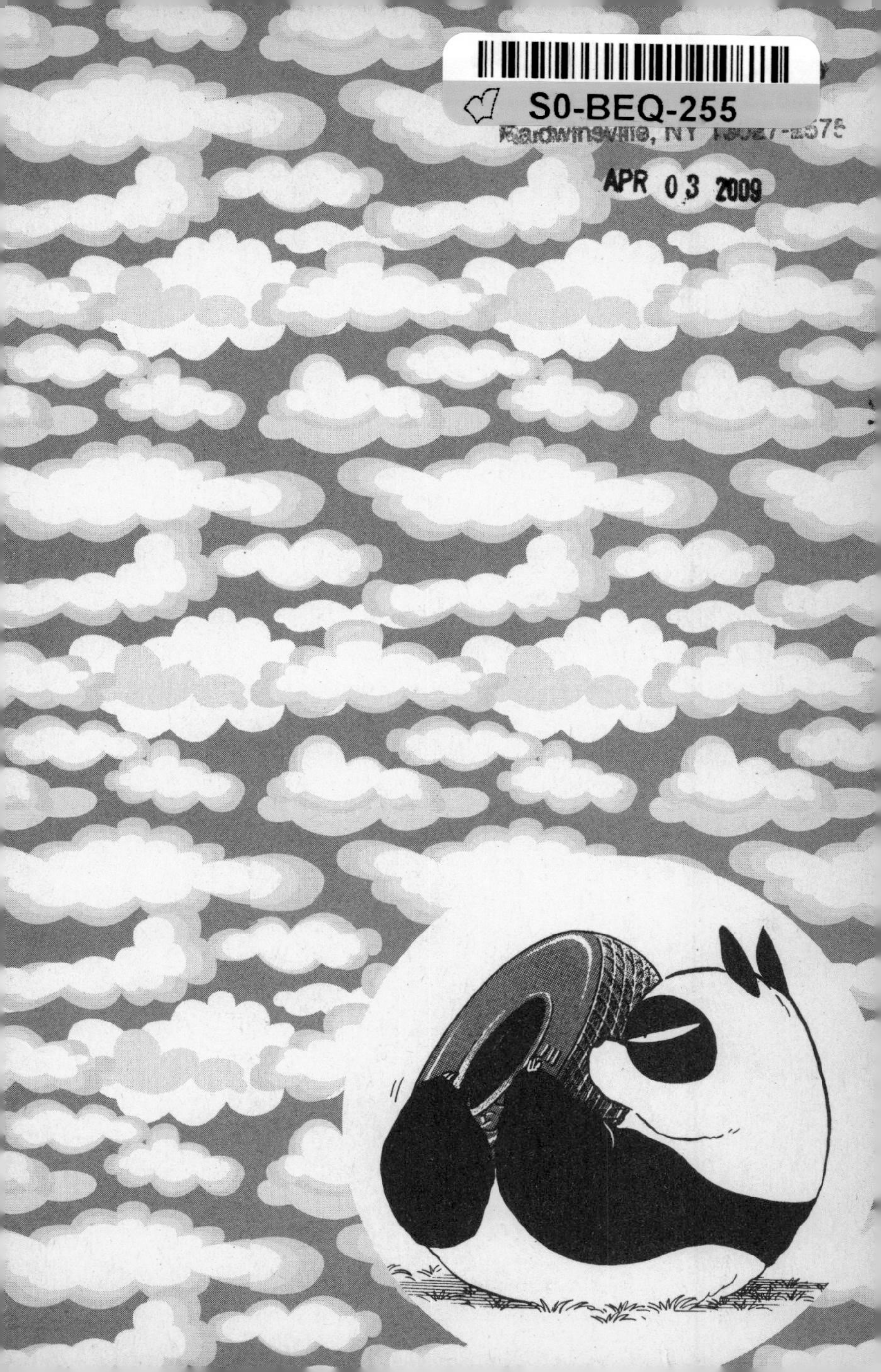

Ranma 1/2

VOL. 19
Action Edition

Story and Art by
RUMIKO TAKAHASHI

English Adaptation/Gerard Jones and Toshifumi Yoshida
Touch-Up Art & Lettering/Wayne Truman
Cover and Interior Design/Yuki Ameda
Editor (1st Edition)/Julie Davis
Editor (Action Edition)/Avery Gotoh
Supervising Editor (Action Edition)/Michelle Pangilinan

Managing Editor/Annette Roman
Director of Production/Noboru Watanabe
Vice President of Publishing/Alvin Lu
Sr. Director of Acquisitions/Rika Inouye
Vice President of Sales and Marketing/Liza Coppola
Publisher/Hyoe Narita

Printed in Canada.

Published by VIZ, LLC
P.O. Box 77010
San Francisco, CA 94107

1st Edition Published 2001

Action Edition
10 9 8 7 6 5 4 3 2 1
First Printing, July 2005

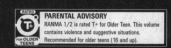

PARENTAL ADVISORY
RANMA 1/2 is rated T+ for Older Teen. This volume contains violence and suggestive situations. Recommended for older teens (16 and up).

www.viz.com

Ranma 1/2

VOL. 19

Action Edition

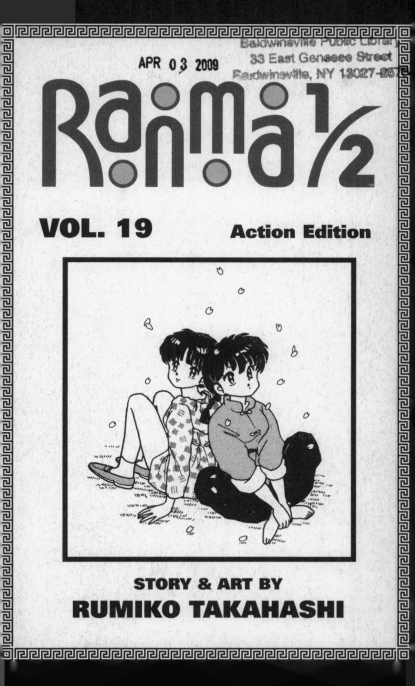

STORY & ART BY
RUMIKO TAKAHASHI

STORY THUS FAR

The Tendos are an average, run-of-the-mill Japanese family—on the surface, that is. Soun Tendo is the owner and proprietor of the Tendo Dojo, where "Anything Goes Martial Arts" is practiced. Like the name says, anything goes, and usually does.

When Soun's old friend Genma Saotome comes to visit, Soun's three lovely young daughters—Akane, Nabiki and Kasumi—are told that it's time for one of them to become the fiancée of Genma's teenage son, as per an agreement made between the two fathers years ago. Youngest daughter Akane—who says she hates boys—is quickly nominated for bridal duty by her sisters.

Unfortunately, Ranma and his father have suffered a strange accident. While training in China, both plunged into one of many "cursed" springs at the legendary martial arts training ground of Jusenkyo. These springs transform the unlucky dunkee into whoever—or whatever—drowned there hundreds of years ago.

From then on, a splash of cold water turns Ranma's father into a giant panda, and Ranma becomes a beautiful, busty young woman. Hot water reverses the effect...but only until next time. As it turns out, Ranma and Genma aren't the only ones who have taken the Jusenkyo plunge—and it isn't long before they meet several other members of the Jusenkyo "cursed."

Although their parents are still determined to see Ranma and Akane marry and assume ownership of the training hall, Ranma seems to have a strange talent for accumulating surplus fiancées...and Akane has a few stubbornly determined suitors of her own. Will the two ever work out their differences and get rid of all these "extra" people, or will they just call the whole thing off? What's a half-boy, half-girl (not to mention all-girl, *angry* girl) to do...?

CAST OF CHARACTERS

THE OTOMES

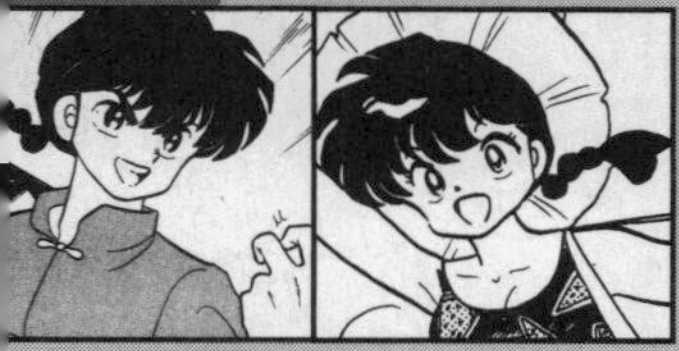

ANMA SAOTOME
lartial artist with far too many fiancées, and an go that won't let him take defeat. Changes into girl when splashed with cold water.

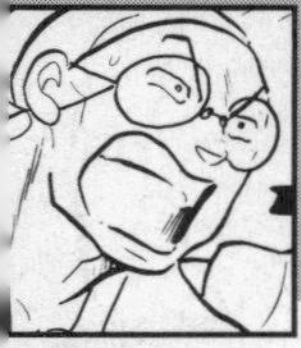

GENMA SAOTOME
Genma's father. Changes into a roly-poly, sign-talkin' panda when wet.

THE ENDOS

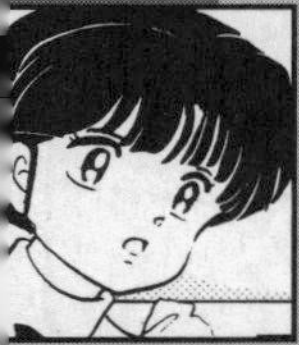

AKANE TENDO
Martial artist, tomboy, and Ranma's reluctant fiancée. Still totally in the dark about the "Ryoga/P-chan" thing.

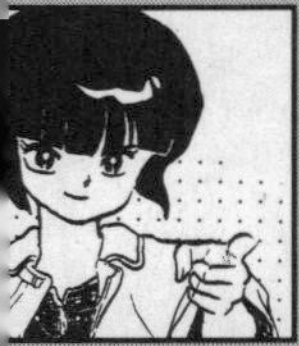

NABIKI TENDO
Middle Tendo daughter. Nothing comes close to her love of money.

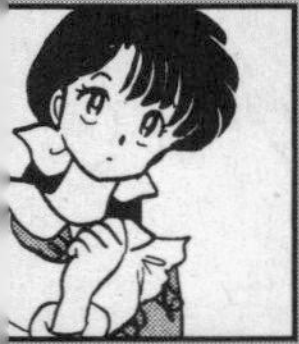

KASUMI TENDO
Eldest Tendo daughter who's the sweet-natured, stay-at-home type.

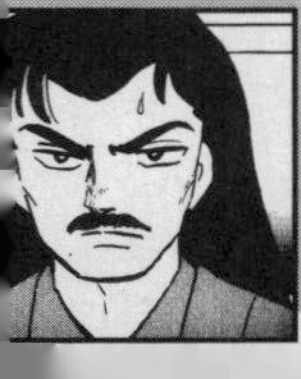

SOUN TENDO
Tendo family patriarch and former Happosai disciple. Easily excitable.

THE MASTER

HAPPOSAI
Pint-sized pervert and former (if you ask Happosai, he'll say different) master to Genma and Soun.

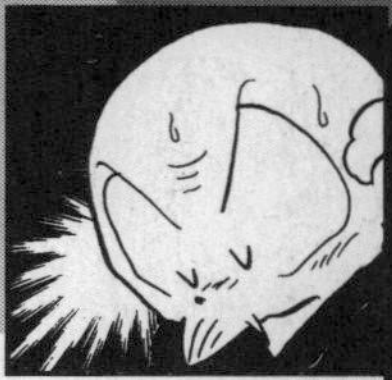

THE SUITORS

RYOGA
Martial artist with no sense of direction, a huge crush on Akane, and the rotten (or is it?) luck to change when wet into "P-chan," Akane's pet miniature black pig.

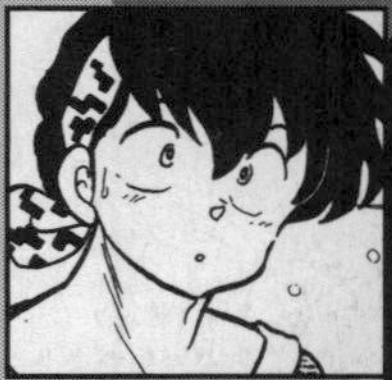

TATEWAKI KUNO
Seventeen-year-old kendo enthusiast in love with both Akane and the mysterious "pig-tailed girl" (girl-type Ranma).

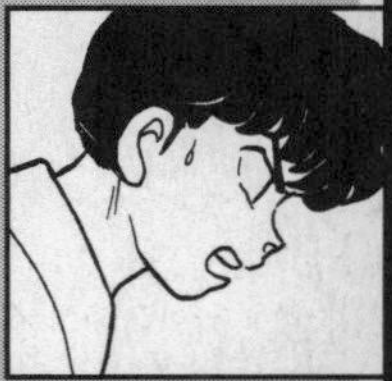

AND IN THIS CORNER...

MARIKO KONJO
Cheerleading champion of Seishun ("Seisyun") High who, heaven knows why, falls in love with Kuno and enters a "cheer-off" against Ranma to prove it.

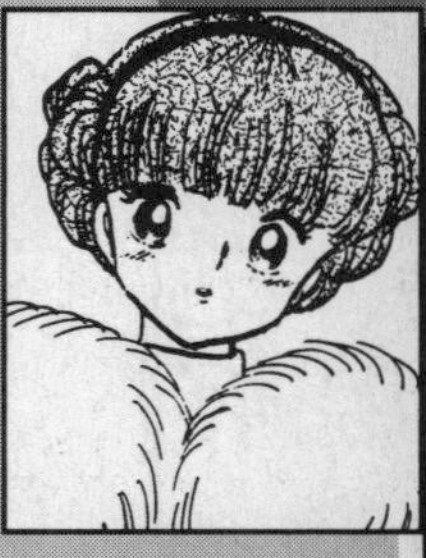

CONTENTS

Part 1

WHEN DADDY WAS STRONG

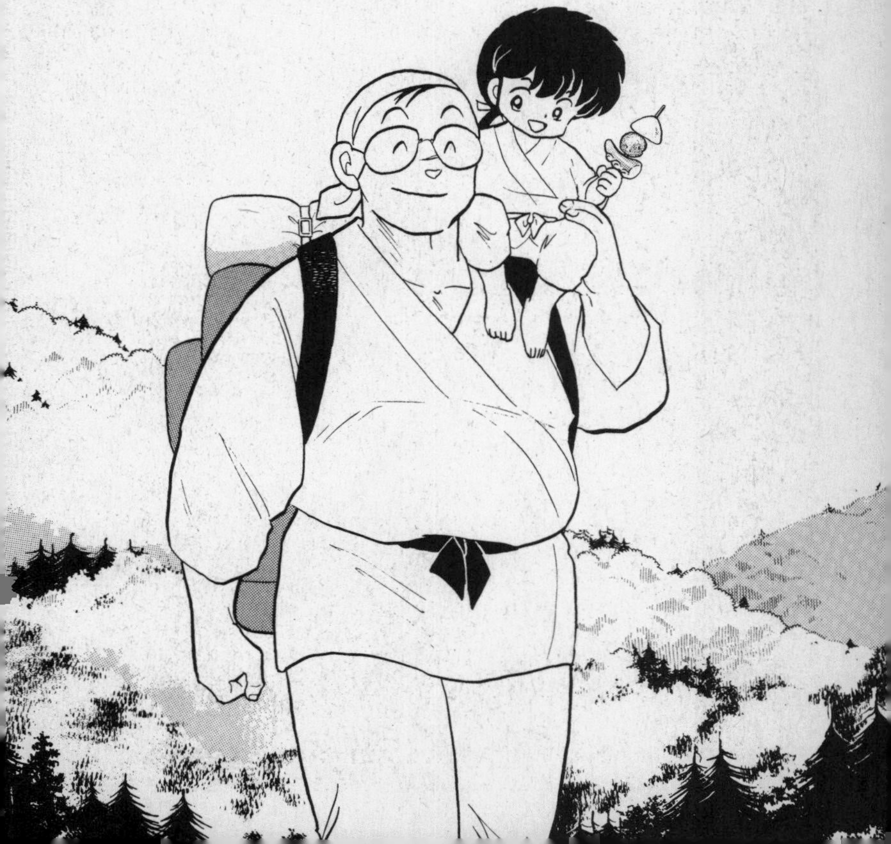

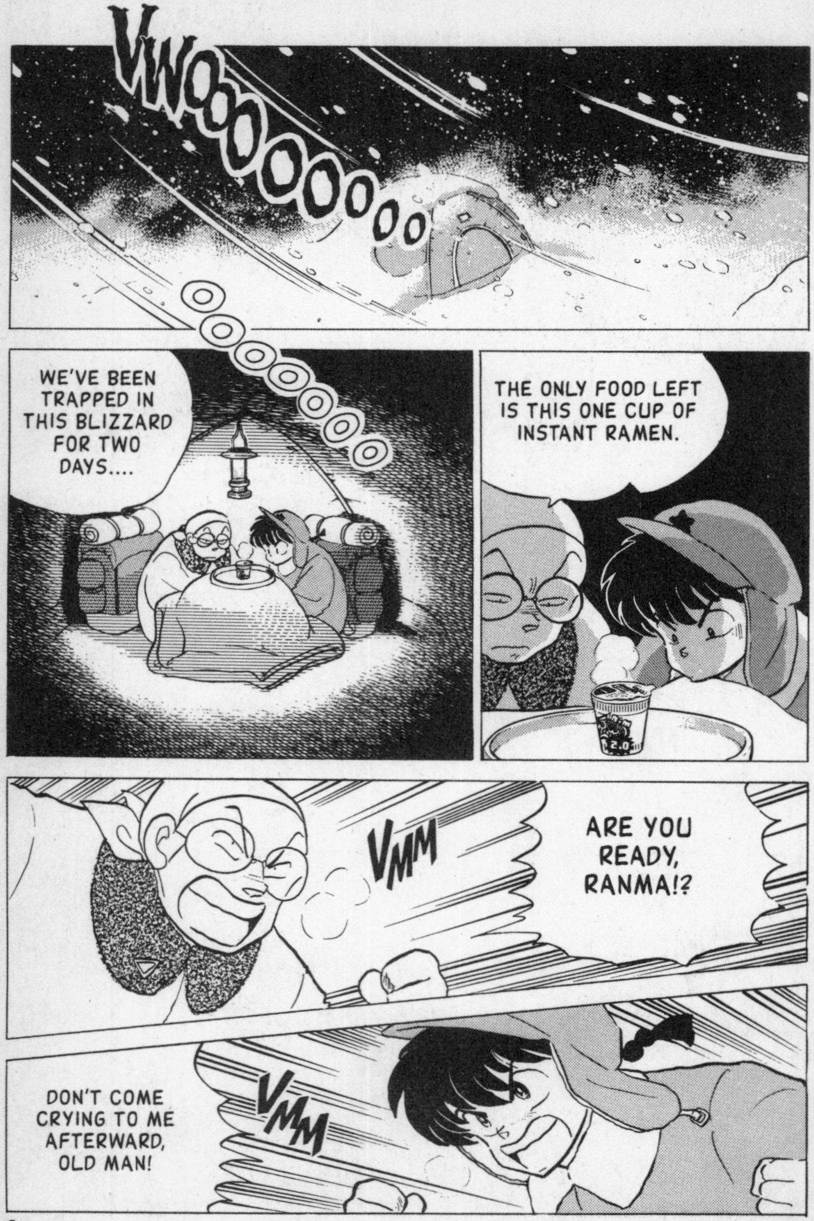
VWOOOOOOOOOOOOOOOOOOO
WE'VE BEEN TRAPPED IN THIS BLIZZARD FOR TWO DAYS....
THE ONLY FOOD LEFT IS THIS ONE CUP OF INSTANT RAMEN.
VMM
ARE YOU READY, RANMA!?
VMM
DON'T COME CRYING TO ME AFTERWARD, OLD MAN!

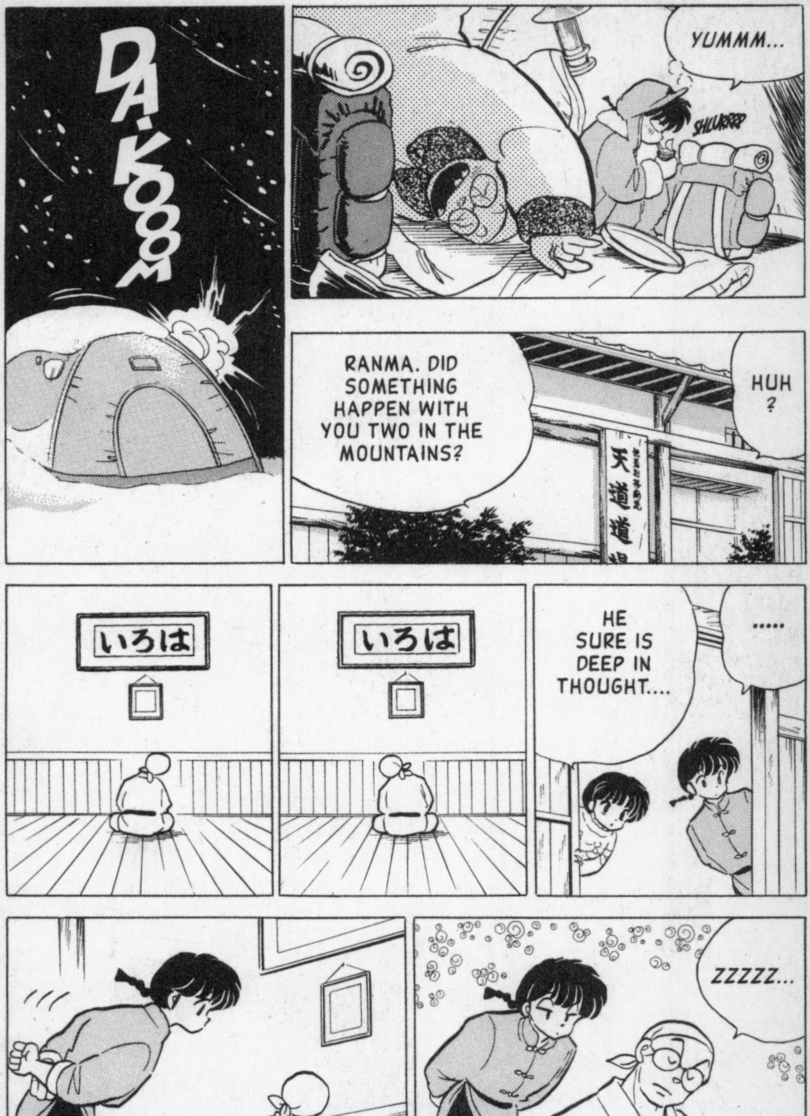
DA-KOOOM
YUMMM...
SHLURRP
RANMA. DID SOMETHING HAPPEN WITH YOU TWO IN THE MOUNTAINS?
HUH?
天道道場
いろは
いろは
HE SURE IS DEEP IN THOUGHT....
.....
ZZZZZ...

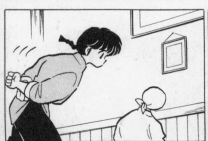

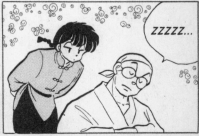

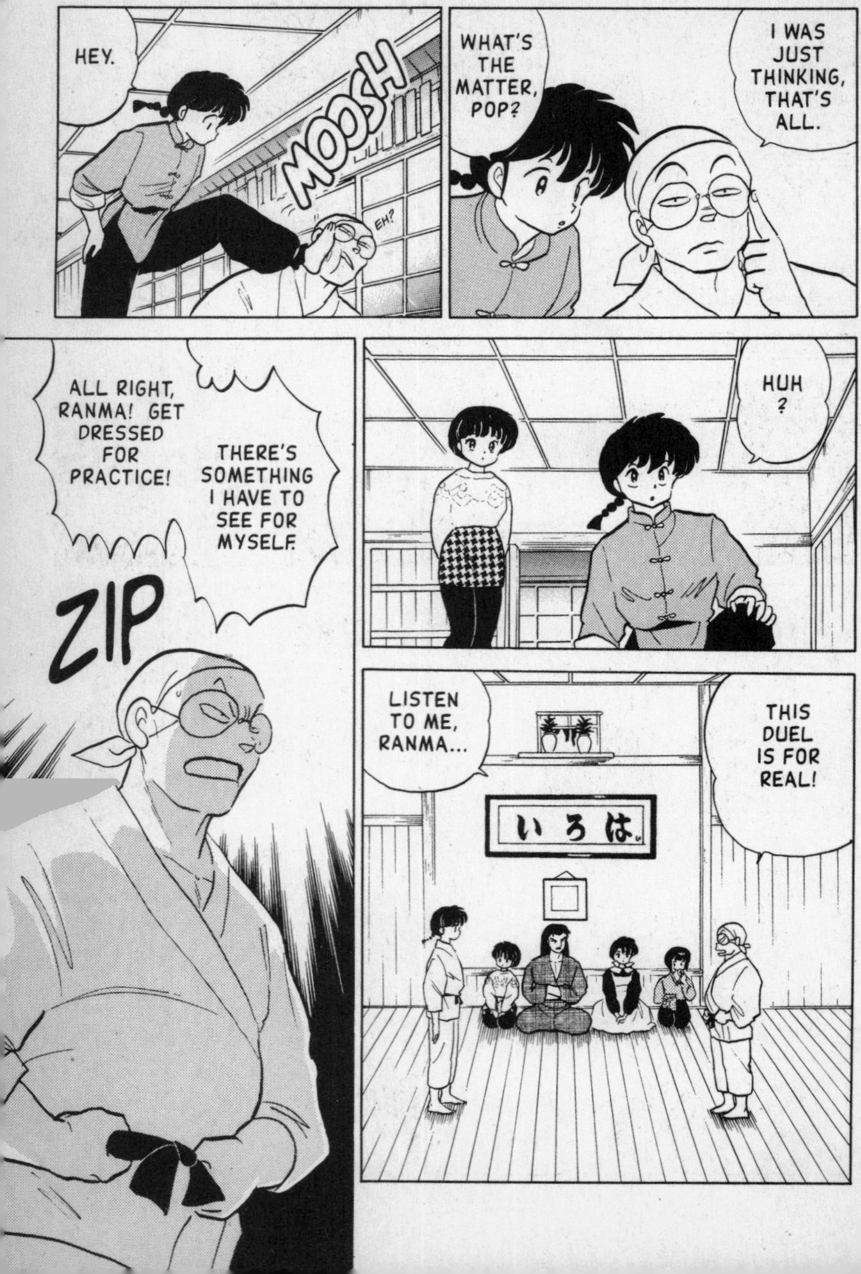
HEY.
MOOSH
EH?
WHAT'S THE MATTER, POP?
I WAS JUST THINKING, THAT'S ALL.
ALL RIGHT, RANMA! GET DRESSED FOR PRACTICE!
THERE'S SOMETHING I HAVE TO SEE FOR MYSELF.
ZIP
HUH?
LISTEN TO ME, RANMA...
いろは
THIS DUEL IS FOR REAL!

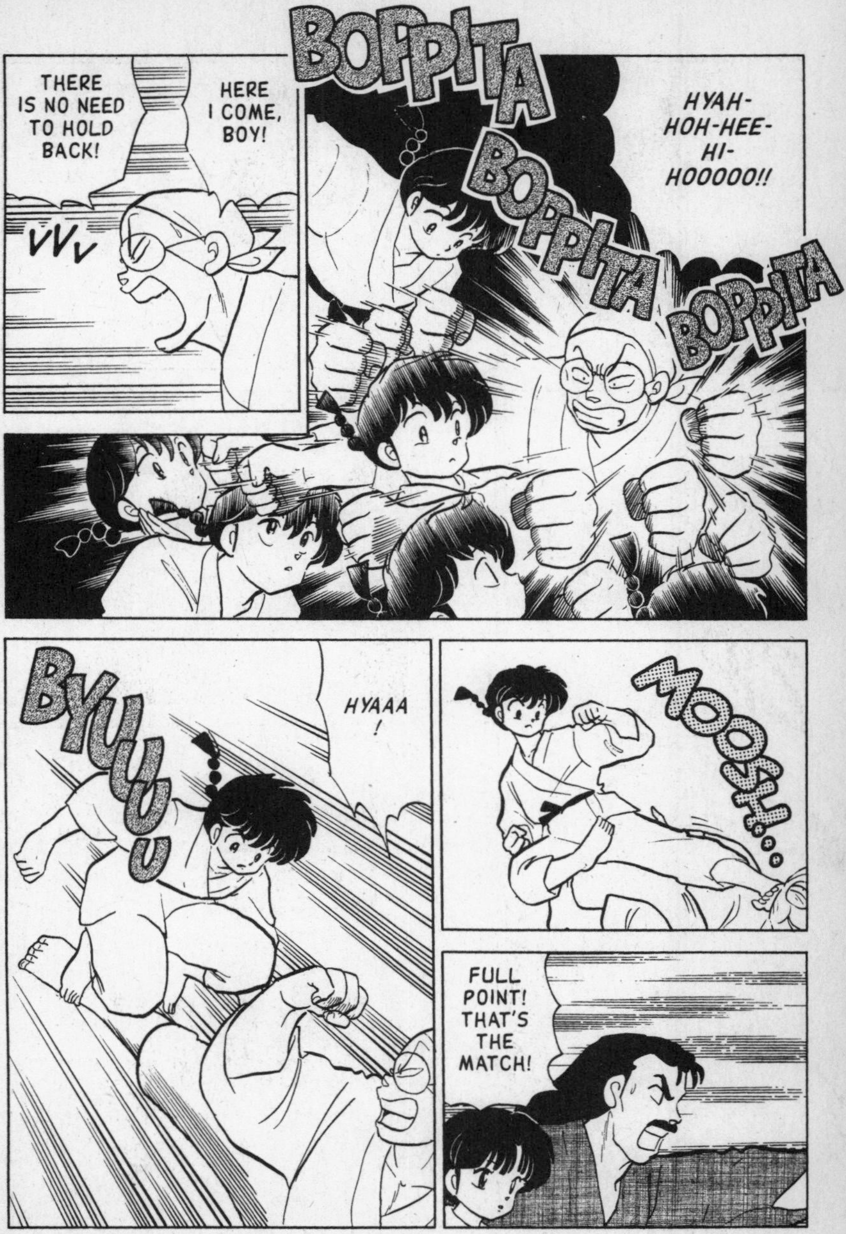
THERE IS NO NEED TO HOLD BACK!
HERE I COME, BOY!
VVV
BOPPITA BOPPITA BOPPITA BOPPITA
HYAH-HOH-HEE-HI-HOOOOO!!
BYUUUU
HYAAA!
MOOSH...
FULL POINT! THAT'S THE MATCH!

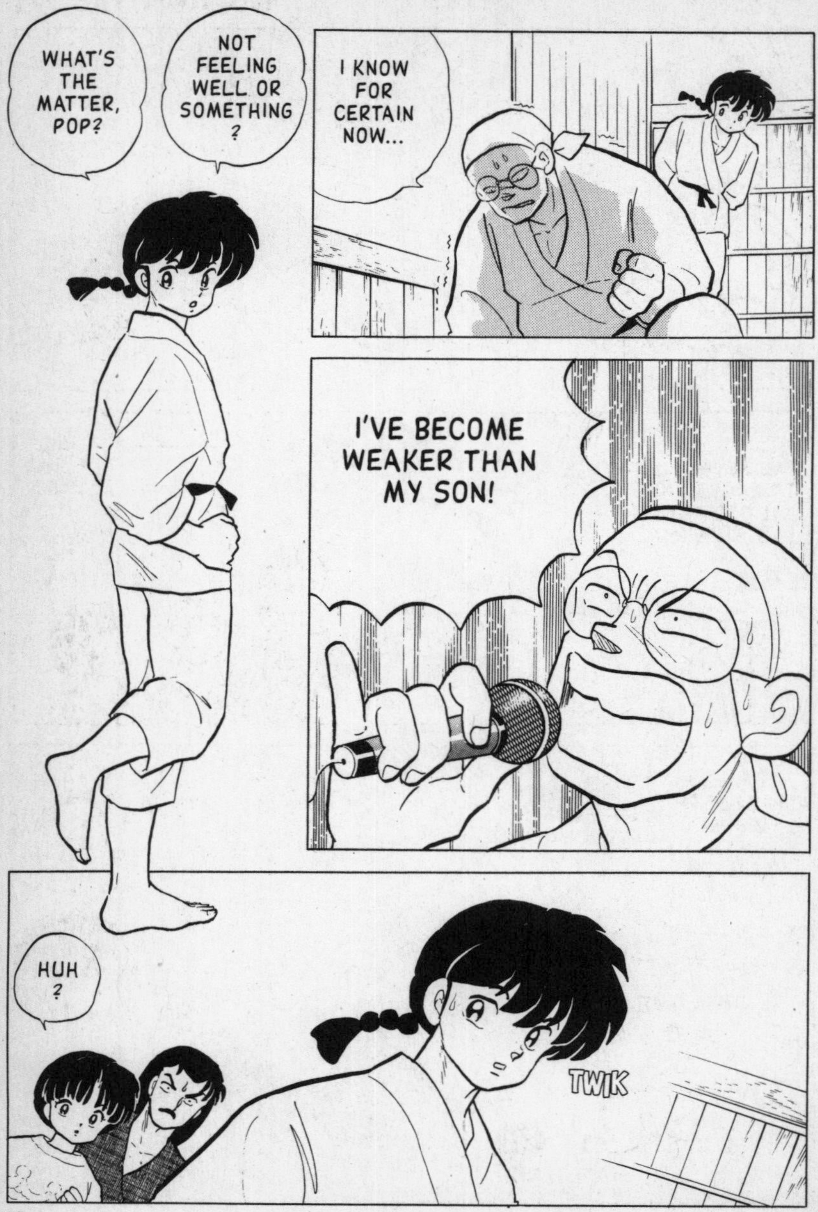
WHAT'S THE MATTER, POP?
NOT FEELING WELL OR SOMETHING?
I KNOW FOR CERTAIN NOW...
I'VE BECOME WEAKER THAN MY SON!
HUH?
TWIK

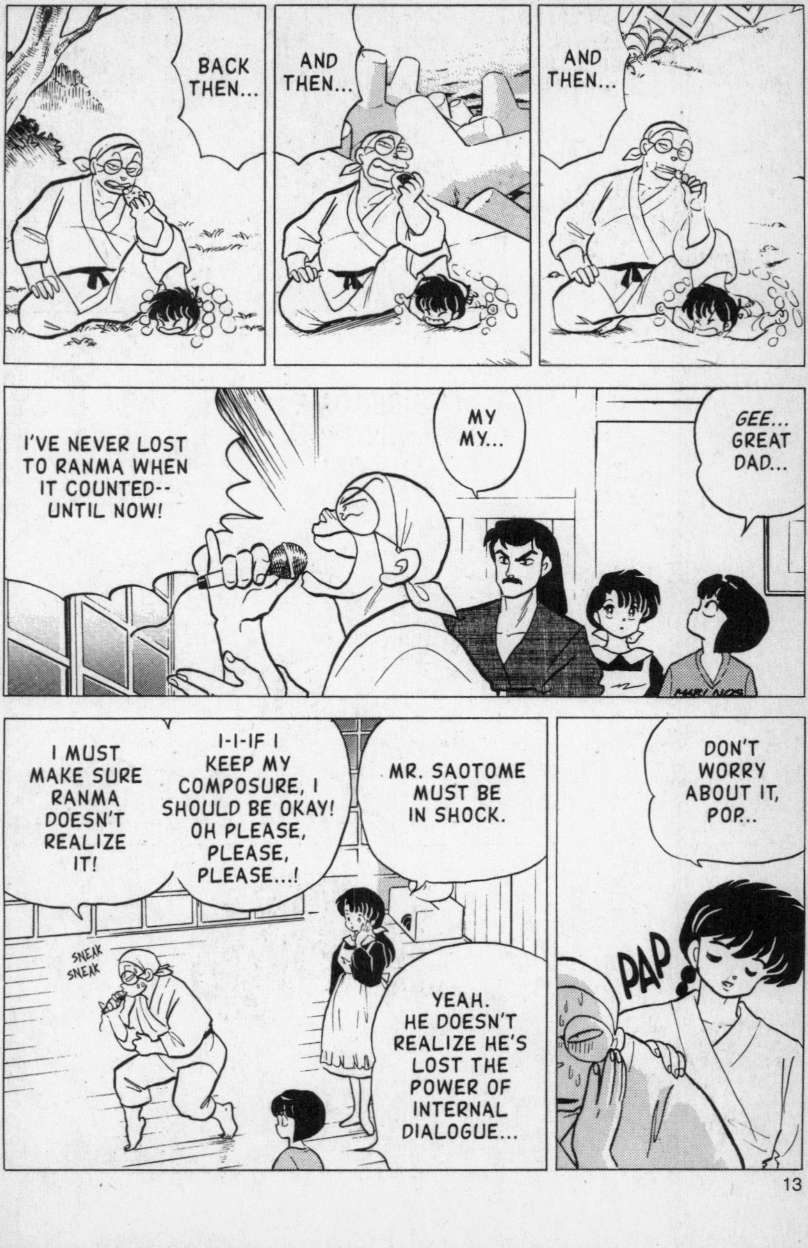
BACK THEN...
AND THEN...
AND THEN...
I'VE NEVER LOST TO RANMA WHEN IT COUNTED-- UNTIL NOW!
MY MY...
GEE... GREAT DAD...
I MUST MAKE SURE RANMA DOESN'T REALIZE IT!
I-I-IF I KEEP MY COMPOSURE, I SHOULD BE OKAY! OH PLEASE, PLEASE, PLEASE...!
MR. SAOTOME MUST BE IN SHOCK.
SNEAK SNEAK
YEAH. HE DOESN'T REALIZE HE'S LOST THE POWER OF INTERNAL DIALOGUE...
DON'T WORRY ABOUT IT, POP...
PAP

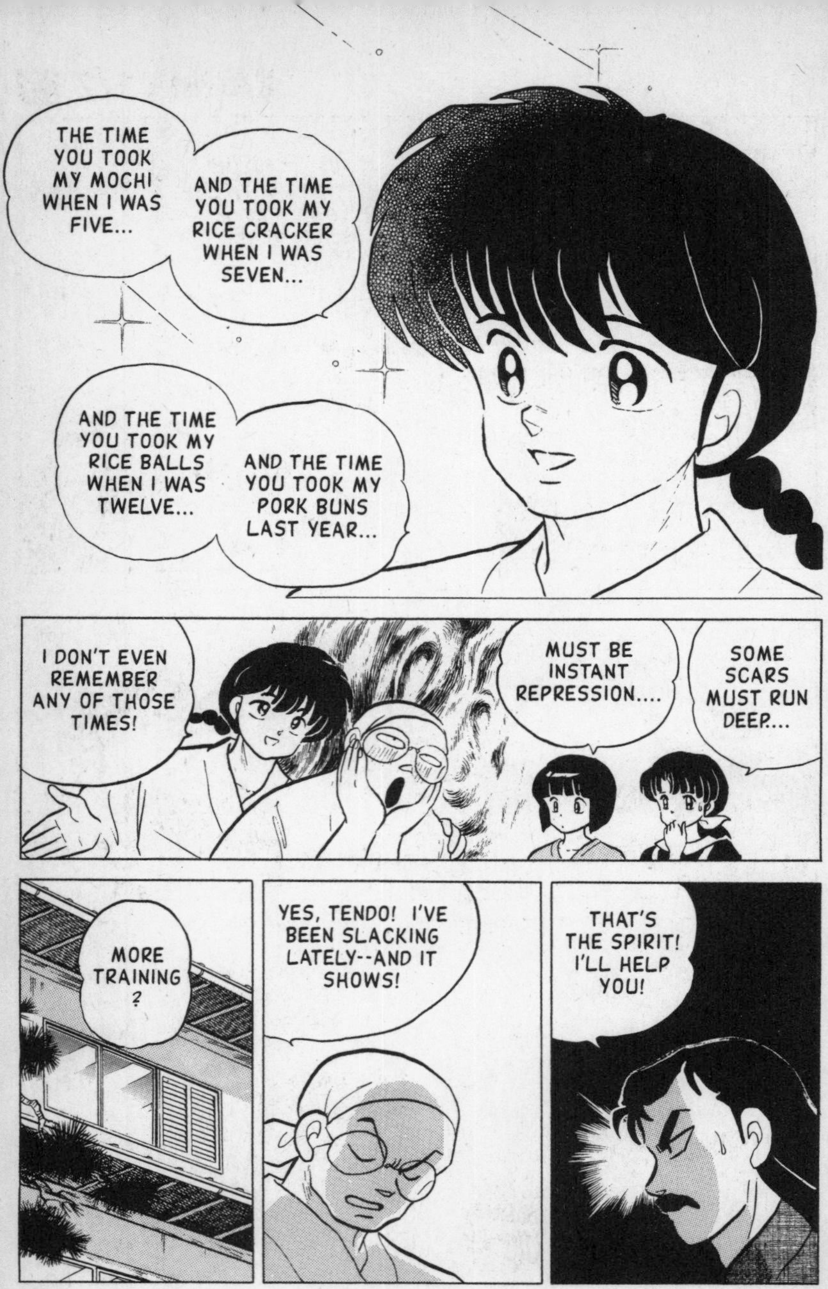
THE TIME YOU TOOK MY MOCHI WHEN I WAS FIVE...
AND THE TIME YOU TOOK MY RICE CRACKER WHEN I WAS SEVEN...
AND THE TIME YOU TOOK MY RICE BALLS WHEN I WAS TWELVE...
AND THE TIME YOU TOOK MY PORK BUNS LAST YEAR...
I DON'T EVEN REMEMBER ANY OF THOSE TIMES!
MUST BE INSTANT REPRESSION....
SOME SCARS MUST RUN DEEP....
MORE TRAINING ?
YES, TENDO! I'VE BEEN SLACKING LATELY--AND IT SHOWS!
THAT'S THE SPIRIT! I'LL HELP YOU!

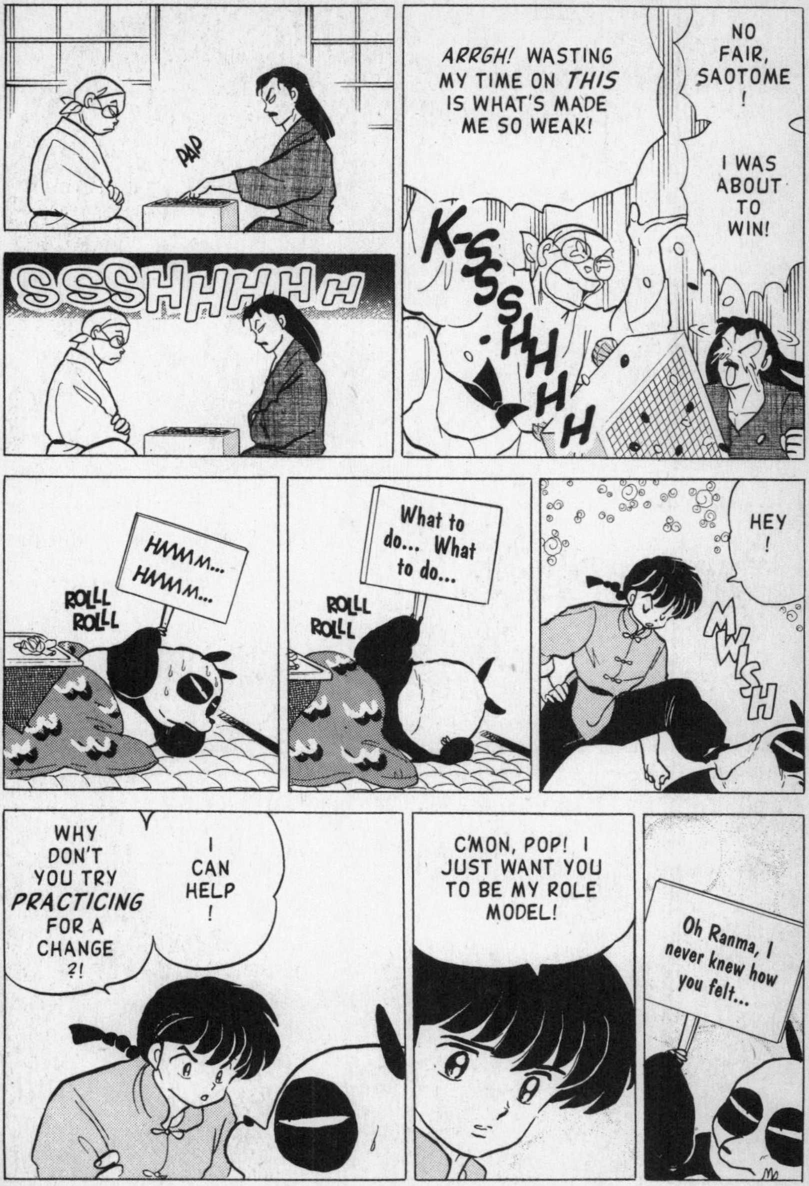
PAP
SSSHHHHHH
ARRGH! WASTING MY TIME ON THIS IS WHAT'S MADE ME SO WEAK!
NO FAIR, SAOTOME!
I WAS ABOUT TO WIN!
K-SSSHHHHH
HMMM... HMMM...
ROLLL ROLLL
What to do... What to do...
ROLLL ROLLL
HEY!
MWISH
WHY DON'T YOU TRY PRACTICING FOR A CHANGE?!
I CAN HELP!
C'MON, POP! I JUST WANT YOU TO BE MY ROLE MODEL!
Oh Ranma, I never knew how you felt...

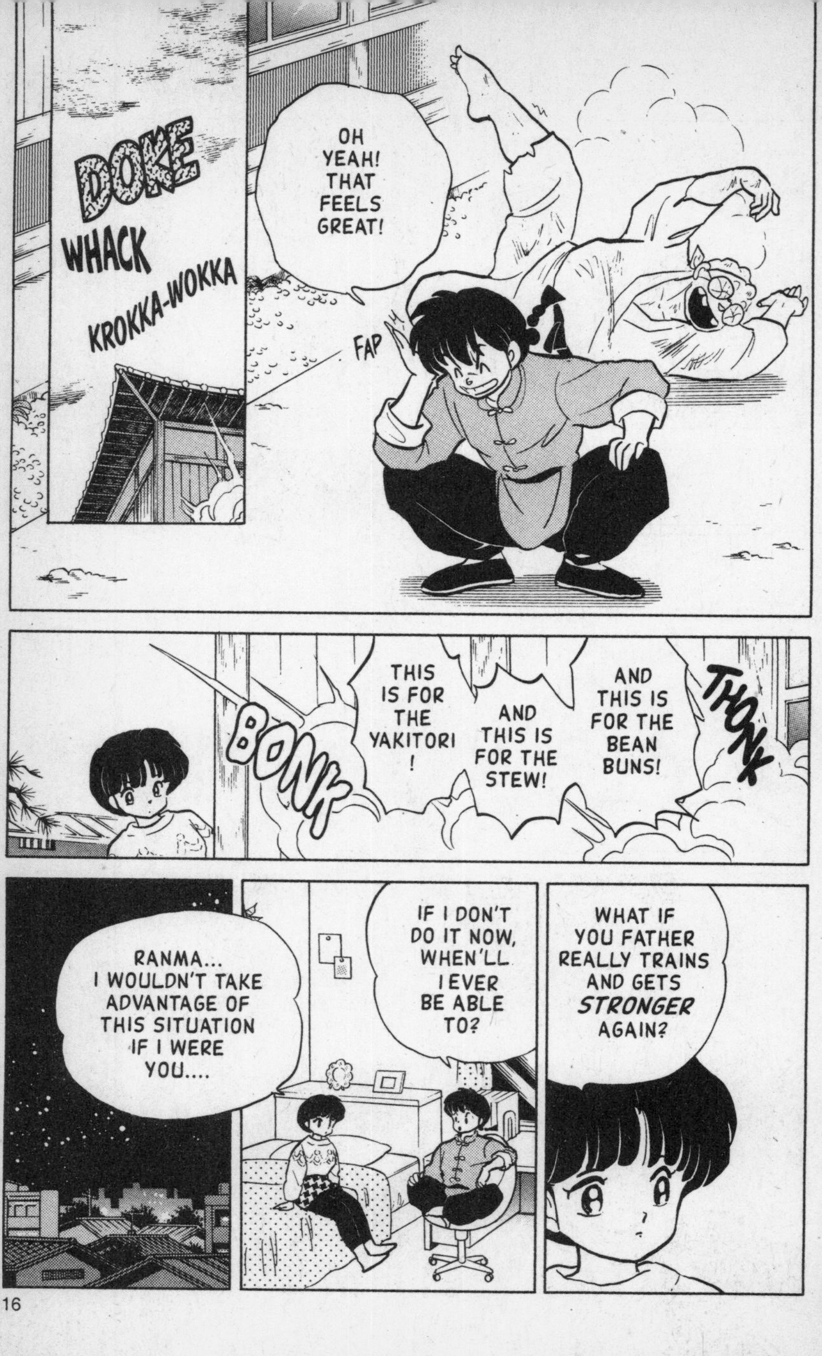
DOKE
WHACK
KROKKA-WOKKA
OH YEAH! THAT FEELS GREAT!
FAP
BONK
THIS IS FOR THE YAKITORI !
AND THIS IS FOR THE STEW!
AND THIS IS FOR THE BEAN BUNS!
THONK
RANMA... I WOULDN'T TAKE ADVANTAGE OF THIS SITUATION IF I WERE YOU....
IF I DON'T DO IT NOW, WHEN'LL I EVER BE ABLE TO?
WHAT IF YOU FATHER REALLY TRAINS AND GETS *STRONGER* AGAIN?

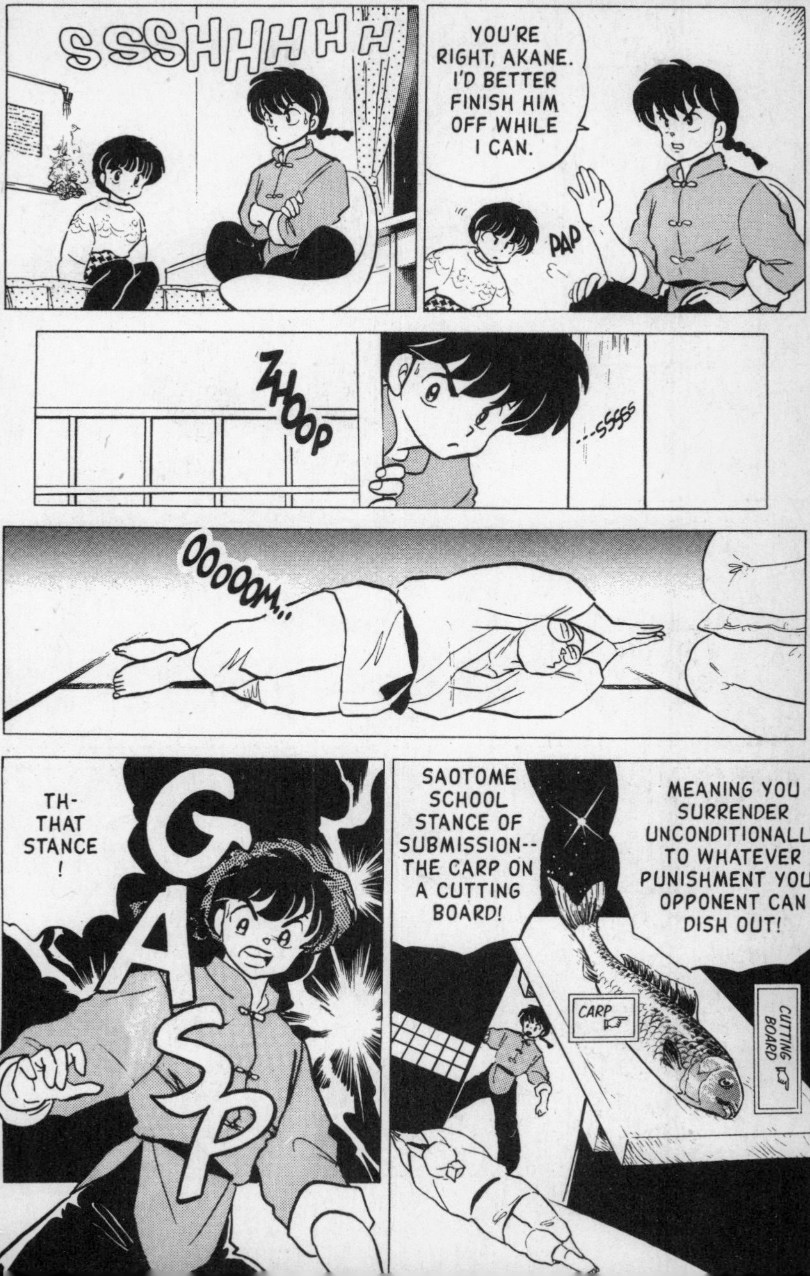
SSSHHHHH
YOU'RE RIGHT, AKANE. I'D BETTER FINISH HIM OFF WHILE I CAN.
PAP
ZHOOP
---SSSSS
OOOOOM...
TH- THAT STANCE !
GASP
SAOTOME SCHOOL STANCE OF SUBMISSION-- THE CARP ON A CUTTING BOARD!
MEANING YOU SURRENDER UNCONDITIONALLY TO WHATEVER PUNISHMENT YOUR OPPONENT CAN DISH OUT!
CARP
CUTTING BOARD

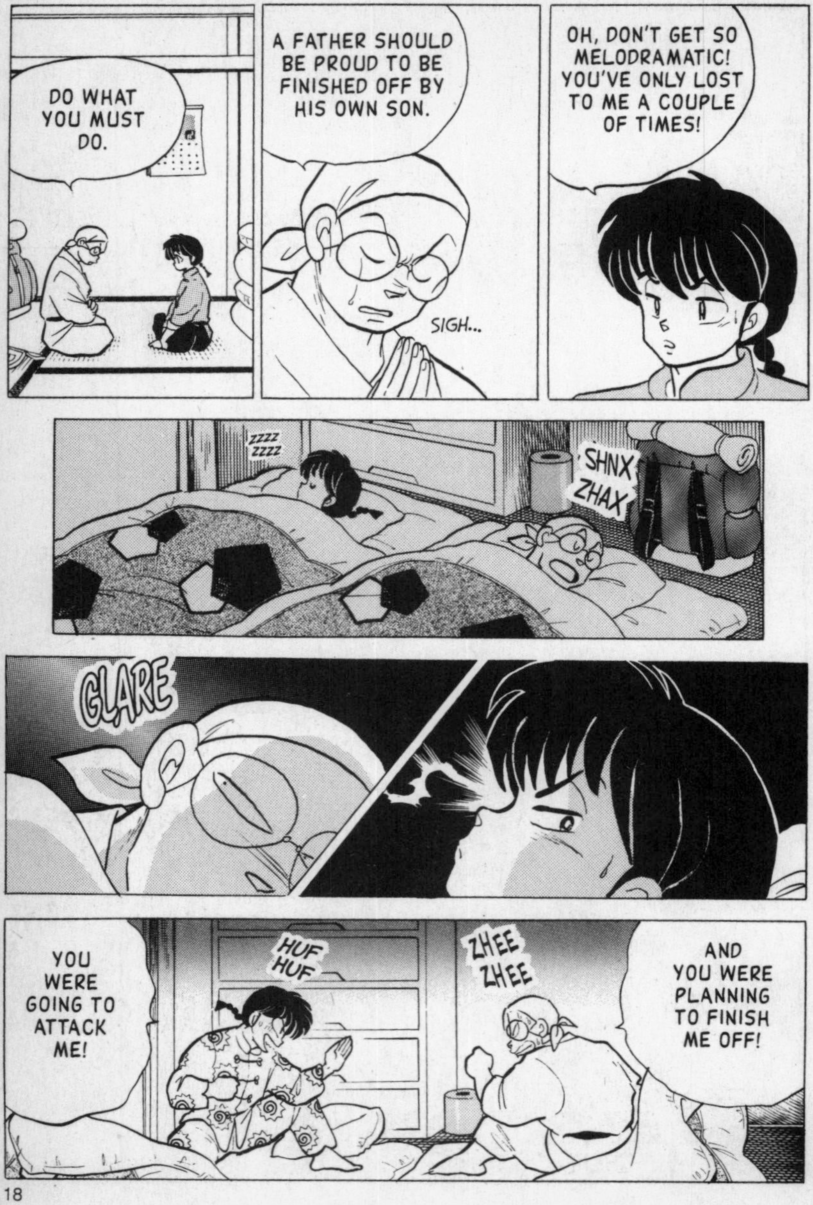
DO WHAT YOU MUST DO.
A FATHER SHOULD BE PROUD TO BE FINISHED OFF BY HIS OWN SON.
SIGH...
OH, DON'T GET SO MELODRAMATIC! YOU'VE ONLY LOST TO ME A COUPLE OF TIMES!
ZZZZ ZZZZ
SHNX ZHAX
GLARE
YOU WERE GOING TO ATTACK ME!
HUF HUF
ZHEE ZHEE
AND YOU WERE PLANNING TO FINISH ME OFF!

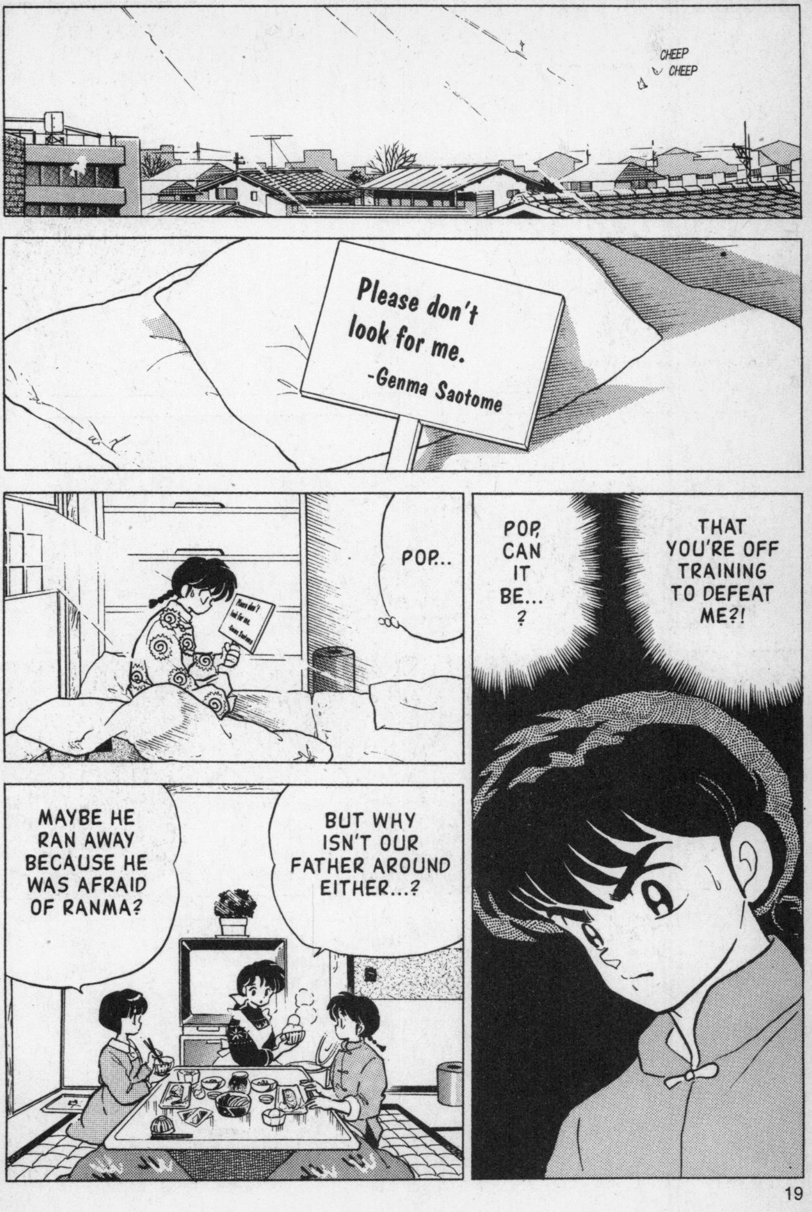
CHEEP
CHEEP
Please don't look for me.
-Genma Saotome
POP...
MAYBE HE RAN AWAY BECAUSE HE WAS AFRAID OF RANMA?
BUT WHY ISN'T OUR FATHER AROUND EITHER...?
POP, CAN IT BE...?
THAT YOU'RE OFF TRAINING TO DEFEAT ME?!

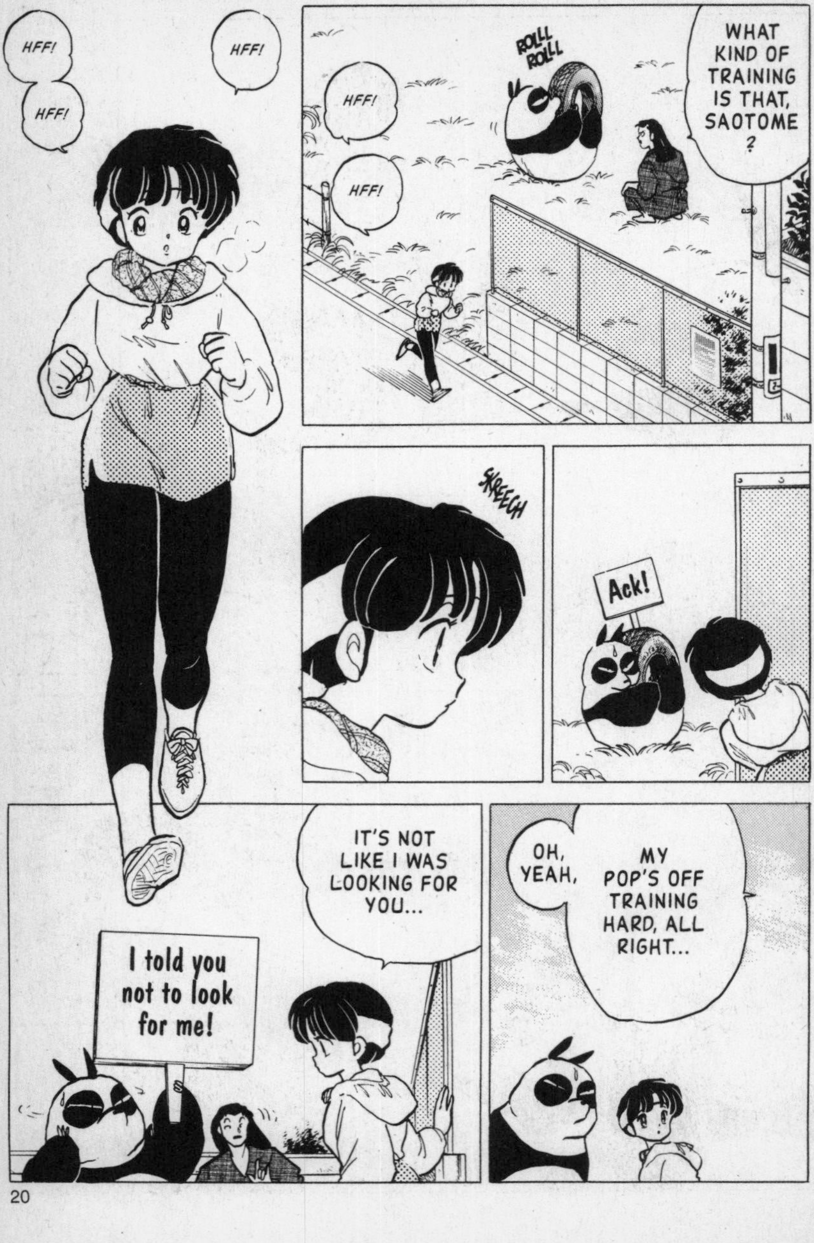
HFF!
HFF!
HFF!
HFF!
HFF!
ROLLL ROLLL
WHAT KIND OF TRAINING IS THAT, SAOTOME?
SKREECH
Ack!
I told you not to look for me!
IT'S NOT LIKE I WAS LOOKING FOR YOU...
OH, YEAH,
MY POP'S OFF TRAINING HARD, ALL RIGHT...

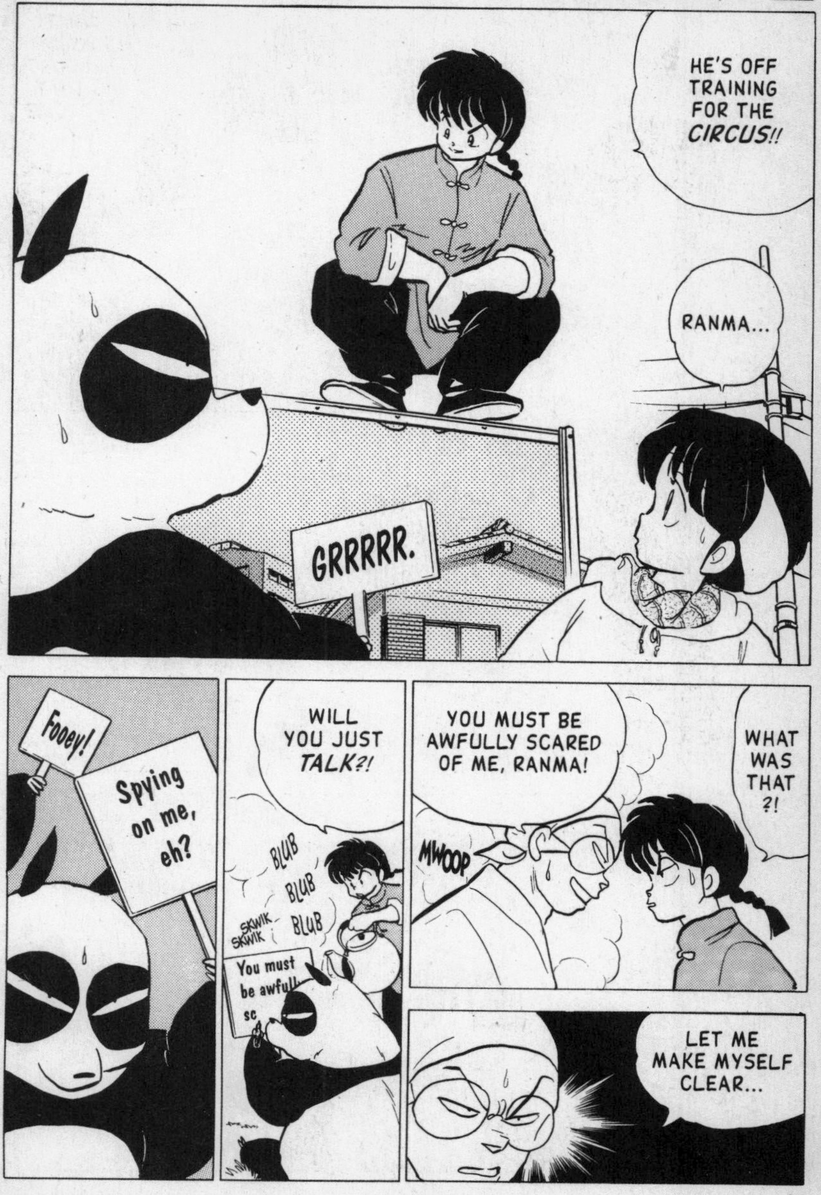
HE'S OFF TRAINING FOR THE *CIRCUS!!*
RANMA...
GRRRRR.
Fooey!
Spying on me, eh?
WILL YOU JUST *TALK?!*
BLUB
BLUB
SKWIK SKWIK
BLUB
You must be awfull sc
YOU MUST BE AWFULLY SCARED OF ME, RANMA!
WHAT WAS THAT ?!
MWOOP
LET ME MAKE MYSELF CLEAR...

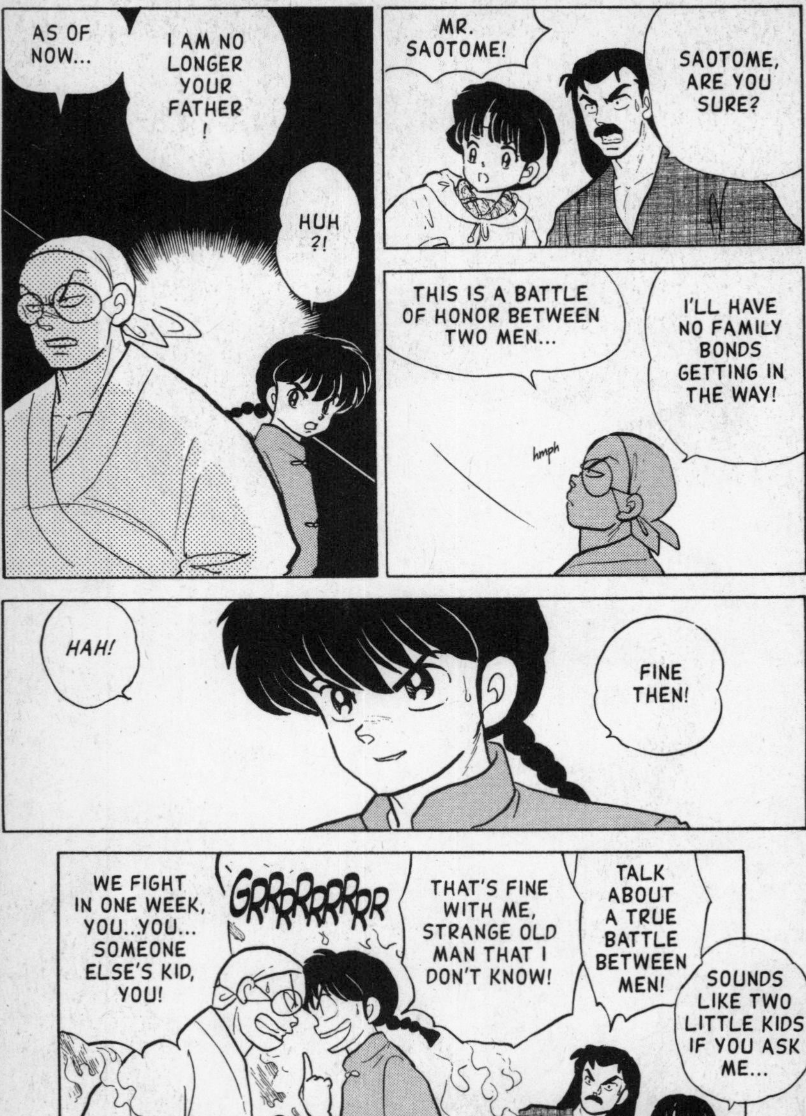
AS OF NOW...
I AM NO LONGER YOUR FATHER !
HUH ?!
MR. SAOTOME!
SAOTOME, ARE YOU SURE?
THIS IS A BATTLE OF HONOR BETWEEN TWO MEN...
I'LL HAVE NO FAMILY BONDS GETTING IN THE WAY!
hmph
HAH!
FINE THEN!
WE FIGHT IN ONE WEEK, YOU...YOU... SOMEONE ELSE'S KID, YOU!
GRRRRRRRRRR
THAT'S FINE WITH ME, STRANGE OLD MAN THAT I DON'T KNOW!
TALK ABOUT A TRUE BATTLE BETWEEN MEN!
SOUNDS LIKE TWO LITTLE KIDS IF YOU ASK ME...

Part 2

TIME TO LEAVE THE NEST

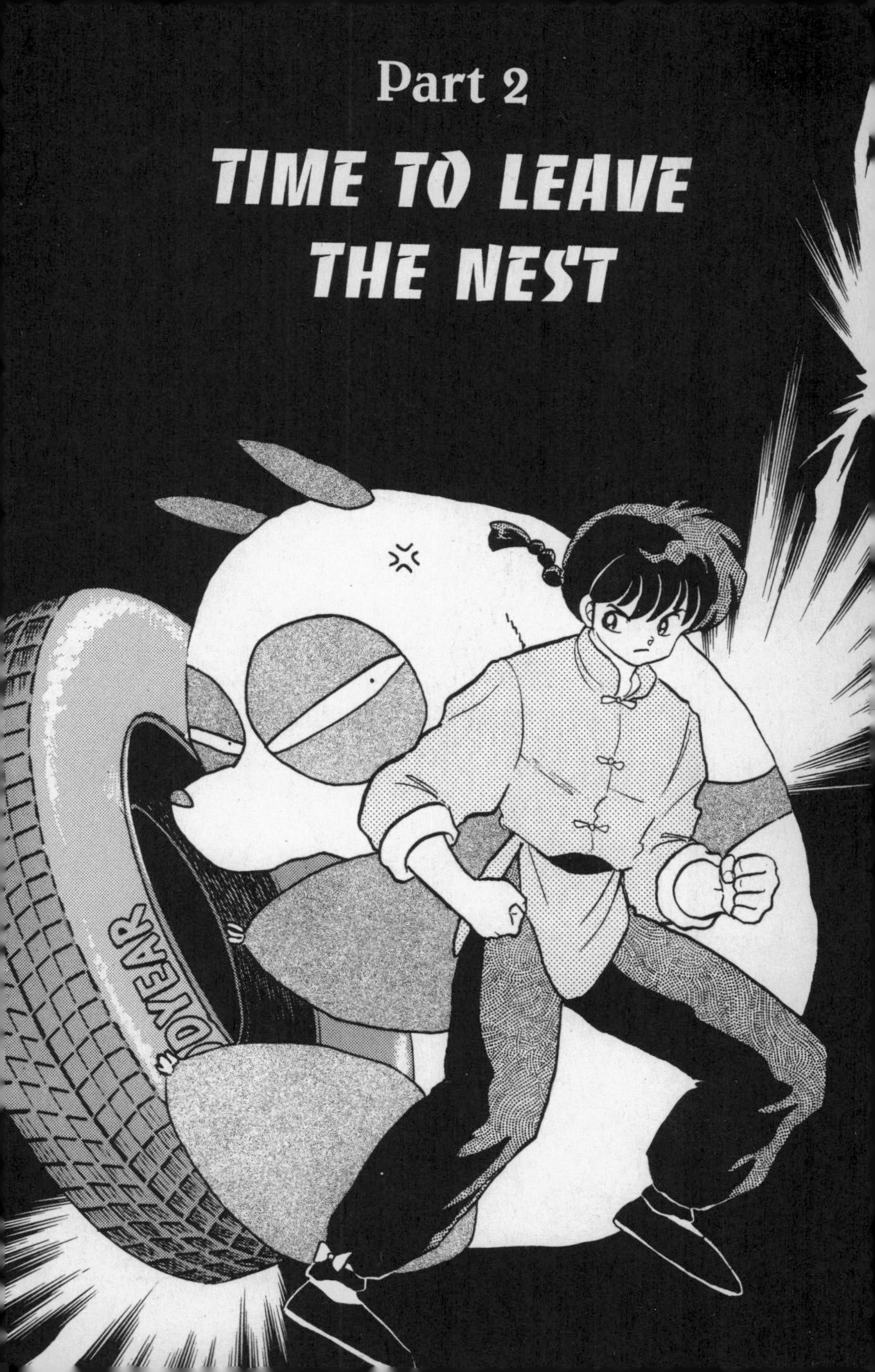

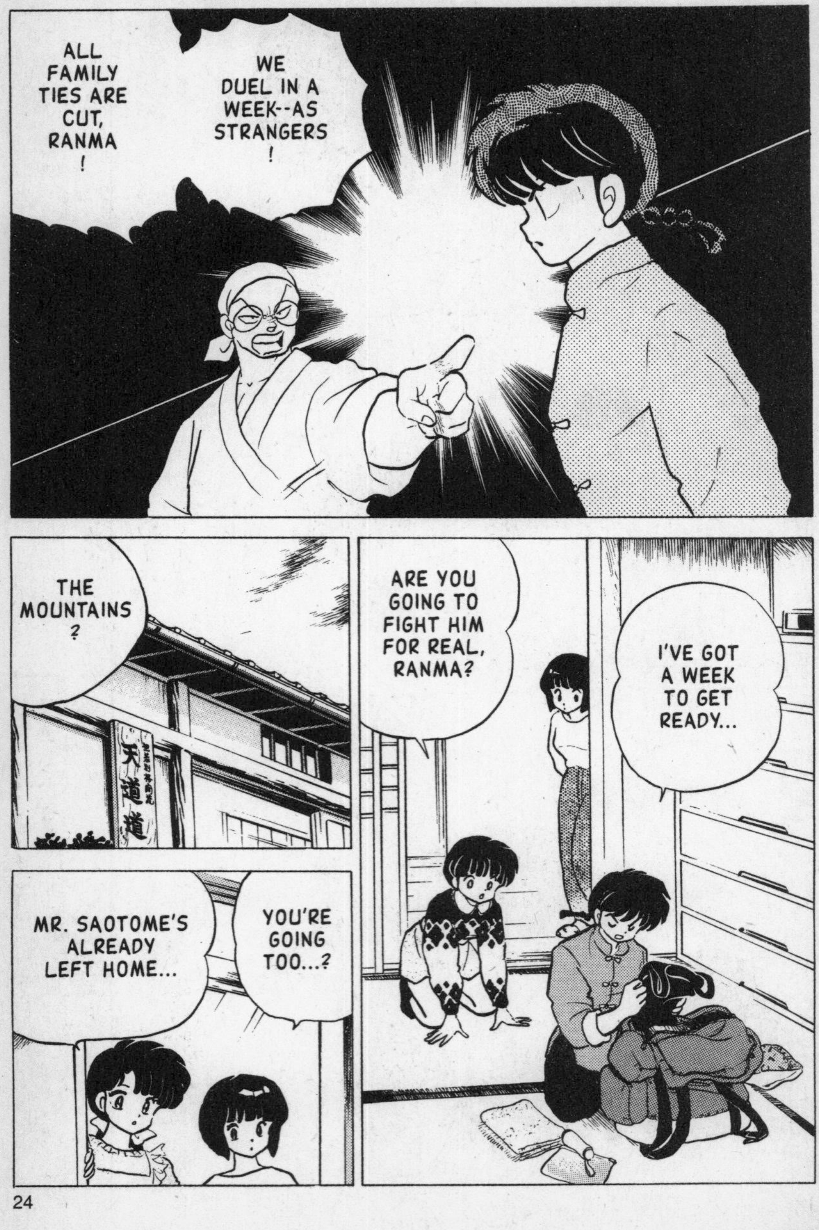
ALL FAMILY TIES ARE CUT, RANMA!
WE DUEL IN A WEEK--AS STRANGERS!
THE MOUNTAINS?
MR. SAOTOME'S ALREADY LEFT HOME...
YOU'RE GOING TOO...?
ARE YOU GOING TO FIGHT HIM FOR REAL, RANMA?
I'VE GOT A WEEK TO GET READY...

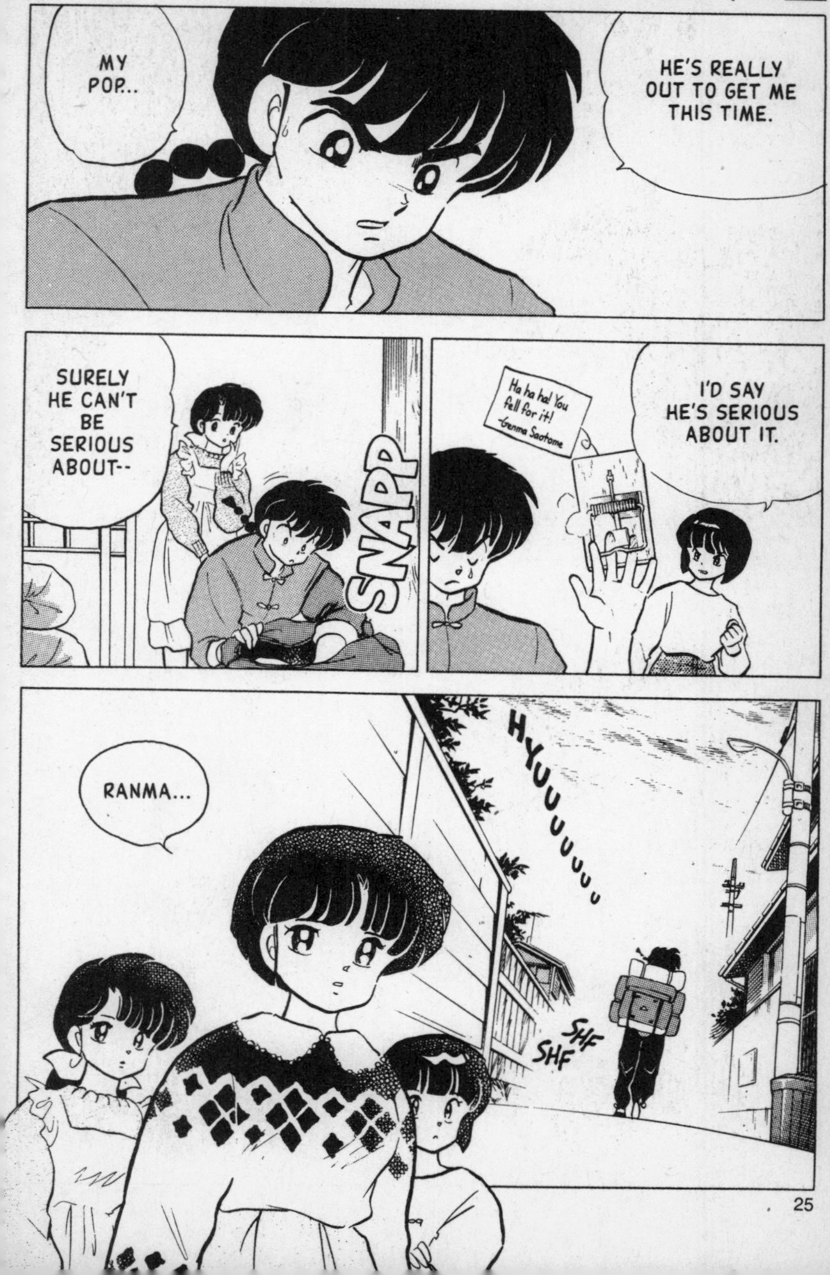
MY POP...
HE'S REALLY OUT TO GET ME THIS TIME.
SURELY HE CAN'T BE SERIOUS ABOUT--
SNAPP
Ha ha ha! You fell for it! -Genma Saotome
I'D SAY HE'S SERIOUS ABOUT IT.
RANMA...
HYUUUUUUUU
SHF SHF

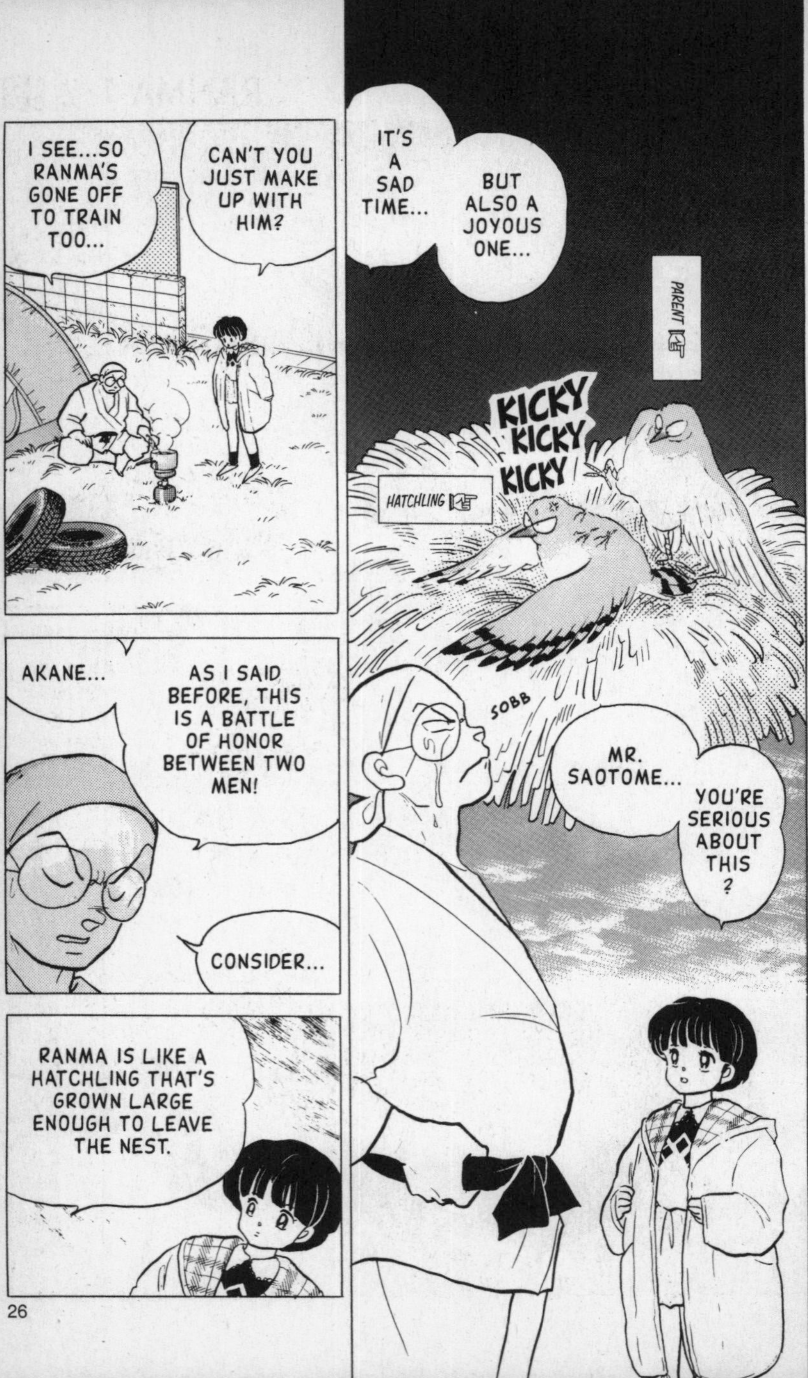
I SEE...SO RANMA'S GONE OFF TO TRAIN TOO...
CAN'T YOU JUST MAKE UP WITH HIM?
AKANE...
AS I SAID BEFORE, THIS IS A BATTLE OF HONOR BETWEEN TWO MEN!
CONSIDER...
RANMA IS LIKE A HATCHLING THAT'S GROWN LARGE ENOUGH TO LEAVE THE NEST.
IT'S A SAD TIME...
BUT ALSO A JOYOUS ONE...
PARENT
KICKY KICKY KICKY
HATCHLING
SOBB
MR. SAOTOME...
YOU'RE SERIOUS ABOUT THIS?

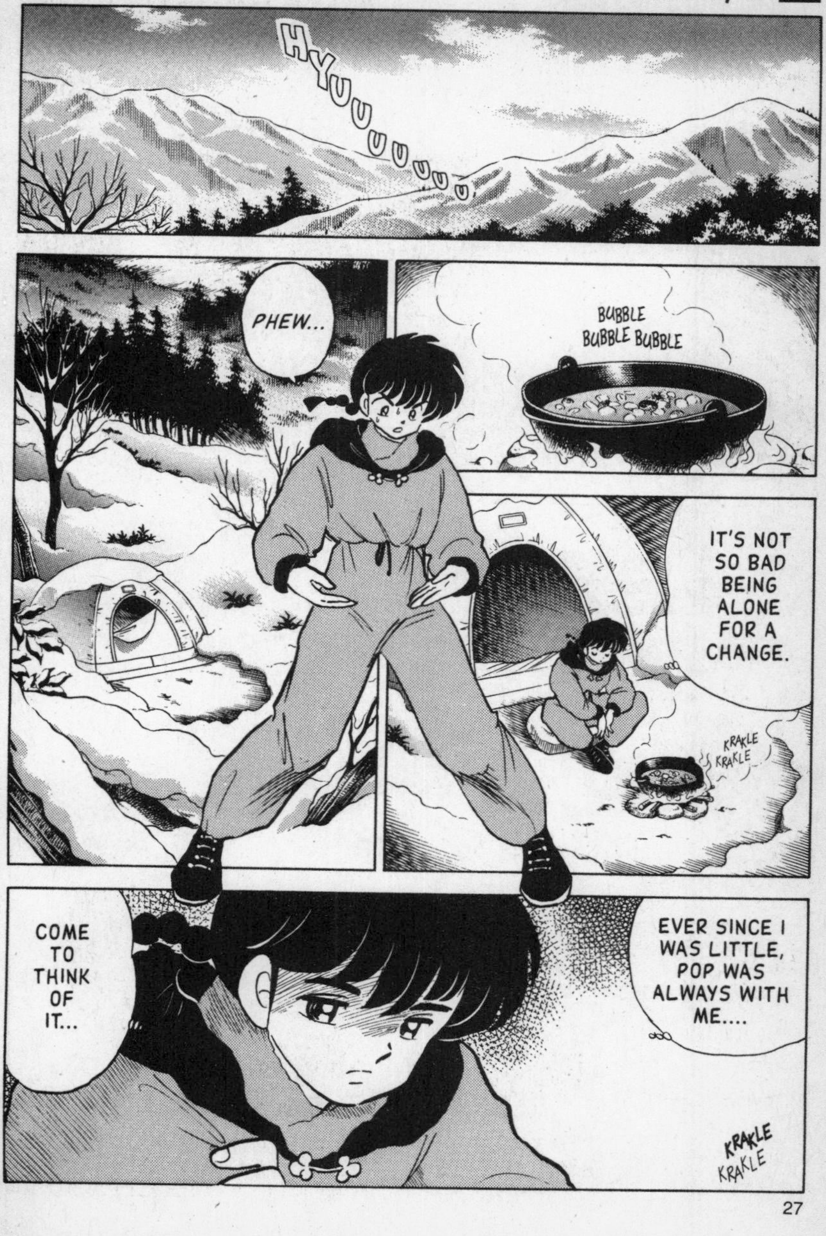
HYUUUUUUU
PHEW...
BUBBLE BUBBLE BUBBLE
IT'S NOT SO BAD BEING ALONE FOR A CHANGE.
KRAKLE KRAKLE
COME TO THINK OF IT...
EVER SINCE I WAS LITTLE, POP WAS ALWAYS WITH ME....
KRAKLE KRAKLE

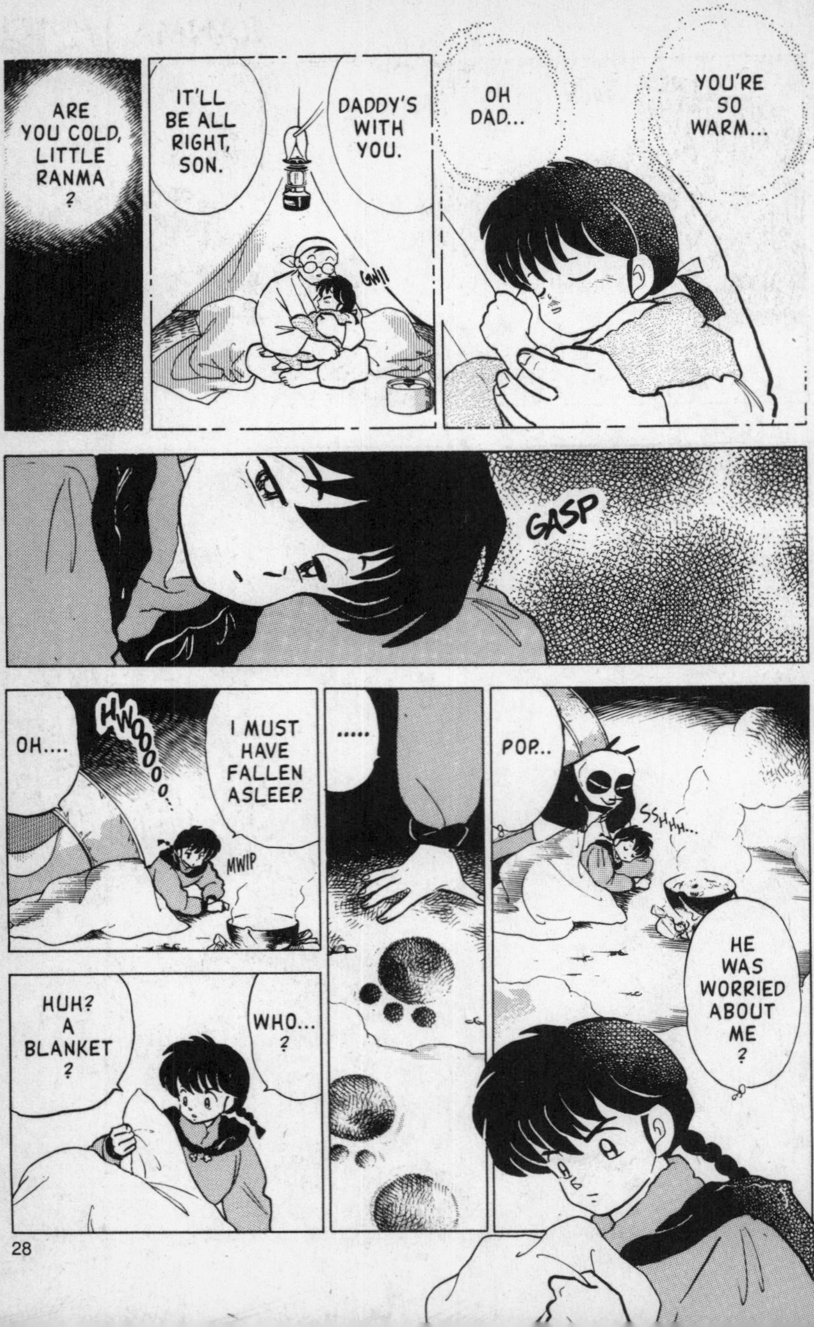

ARE YOU COLD, LITTLE RANMA?
IT'LL BE ALL RIGHT, SON.
DADDY'S WITH YOU.
GWII
OH DAD...
YOU'RE SO WARM...
GASP
OH....
HWOOOOOOO...
I MUST HAVE FALLEN ASLEEP.
MWIP
HUH? A BLANKET?
WHO...?
.....
POP...
SSHHH...
HE WAS WORRIED ABOUT ME?

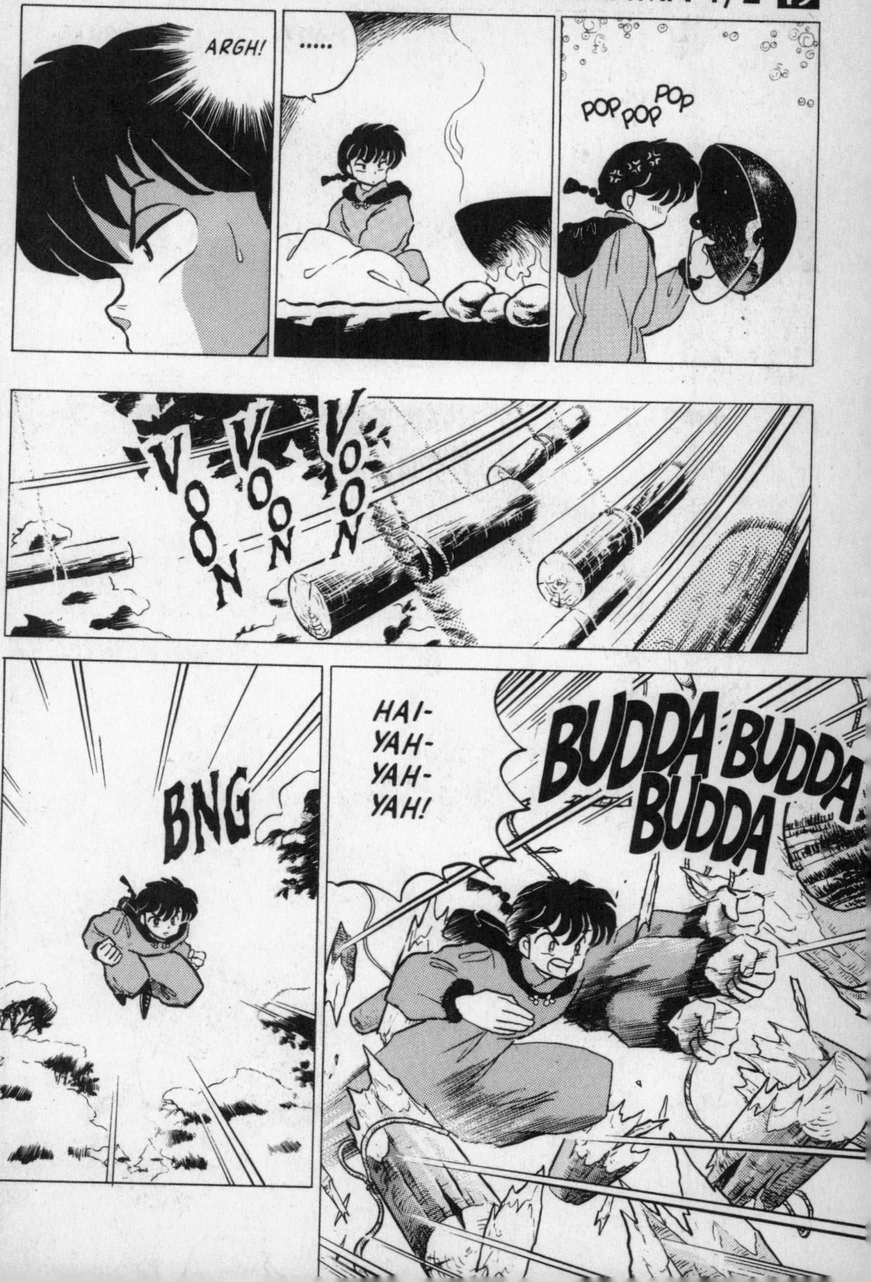
ARGH!
.....
POP POP POP
VOON
VOON
VOON
BNG
HAI-
YAH-
YAH-
YAH!
BUDDA BUDDA
BUDDA
BUDDA

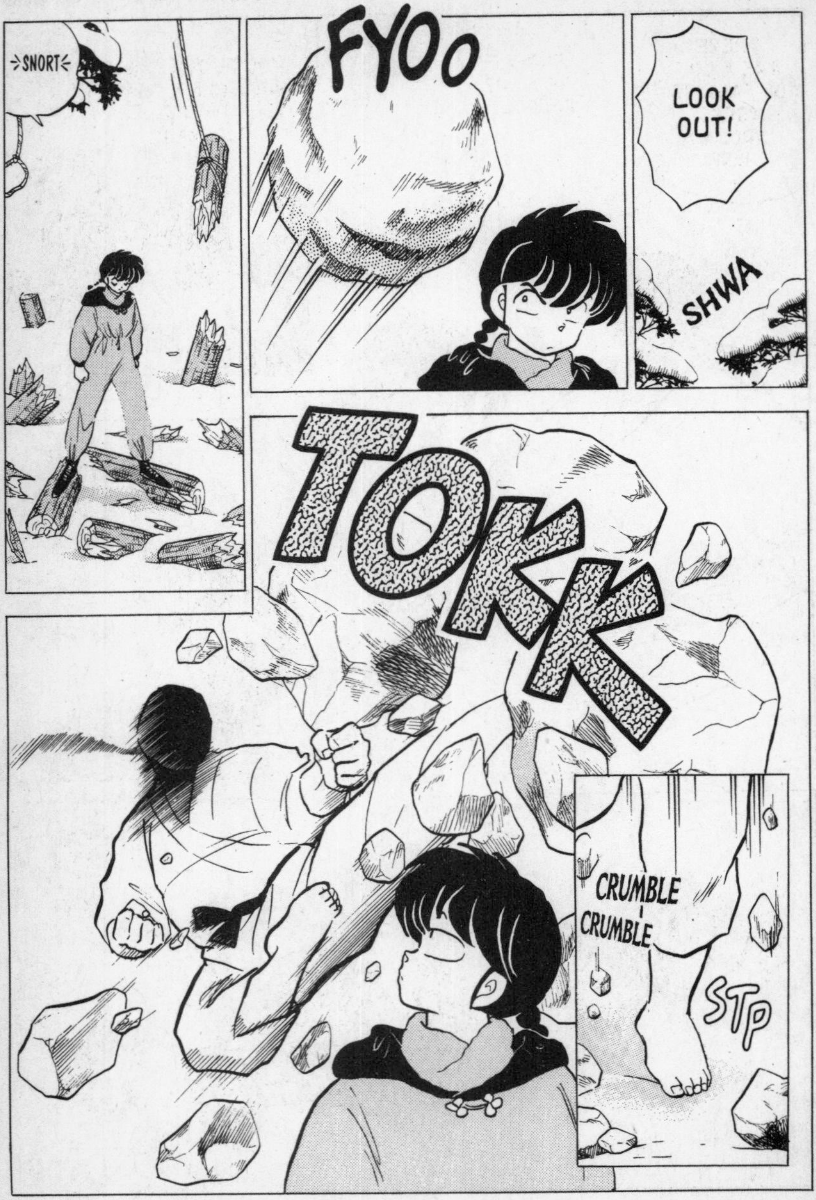
SNORT
FYOO
LOOK OUT!
SHWA
TOKK
CRUMBLE CRUMBLE
STP

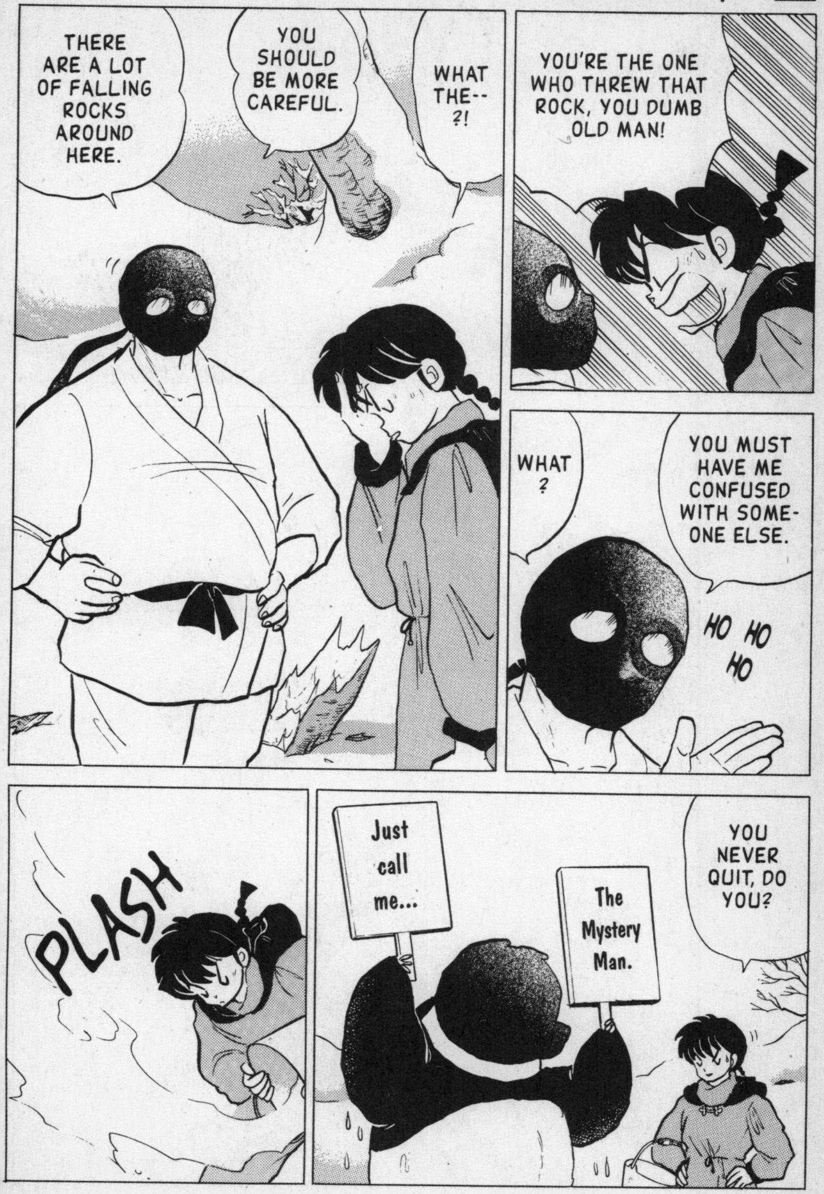
THERE ARE A LOT OF FALLING ROCKS AROUND HERE.
YOU SHOULD BE MORE CAREFUL.
WHAT THE-- ?!
YOU'RE THE ONE WHO THREW THAT ROCK, YOU DUMB OLD MAN!
WHAT ?
YOU MUST HAVE ME CONFUSED WITH SOME-ONE ELSE.
HO HO HO
PLASH
Just call me...
The Mystery Man.
YOU NEVER QUIT, DO YOU?

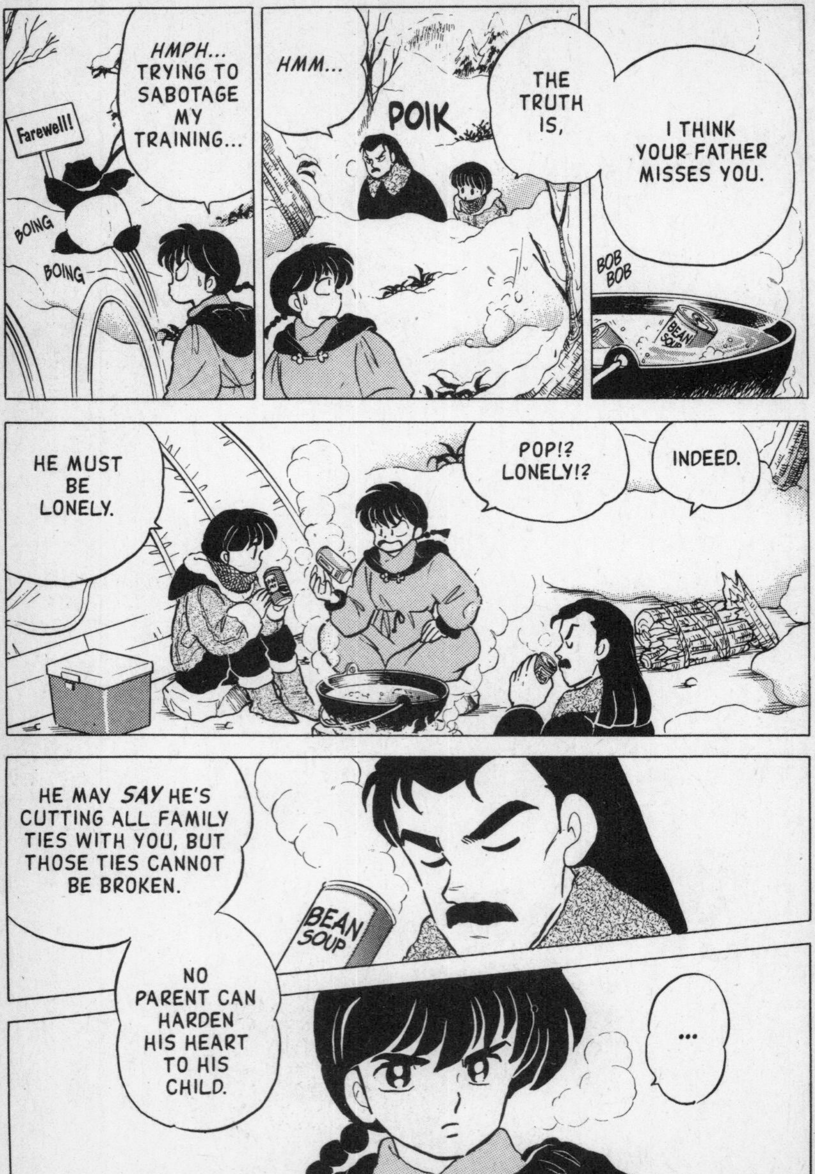
HMPH... TRYING TO SABOTAGE MY TRAINING...
Farewell!
BOING
BOING
HMM...
POIK
THE TRUTH IS,
I THINK YOUR FATHER MISSES YOU.
BOB BOB
BEAN SOUP
HE MUST BE LONELY.
POP!? LONELY!?
INDEED.
HE MAY SAY HE'S CUTTING ALL FAMILY TIES WITH YOU, BUT THOSE TIES CANNOT BE BROKEN.
BEAN SOUP
NO PARENT CAN HARDEN HIS HEART TO HIS CHILD.
...

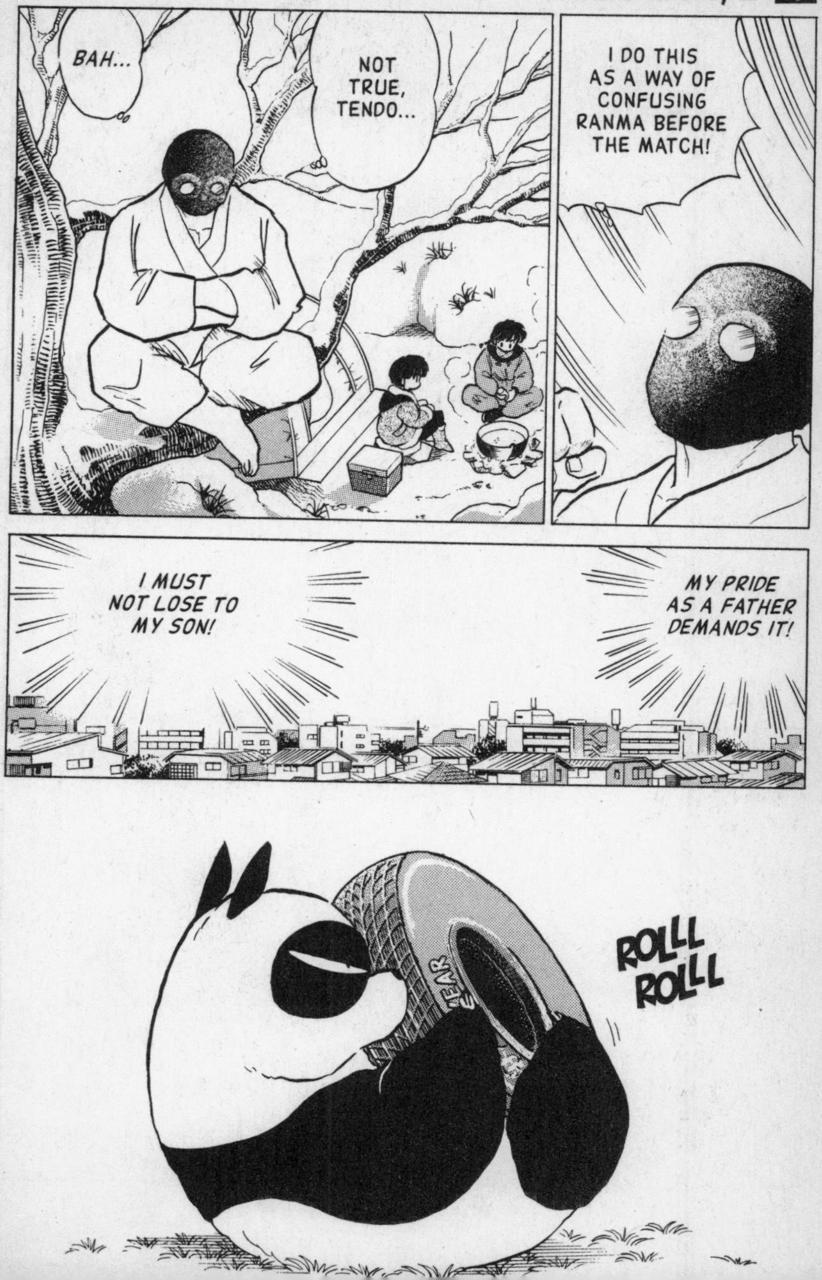
BAH...
NOT TRUE, TENDO...
I DO THIS AS A WAY OF CONFUSING RANMA BEFORE THE MATCH!
I MUST NOT LOSE TO MY SON!
MY PRIDE AS A FATHER DEMANDS IT!
ROLLL ROLLL

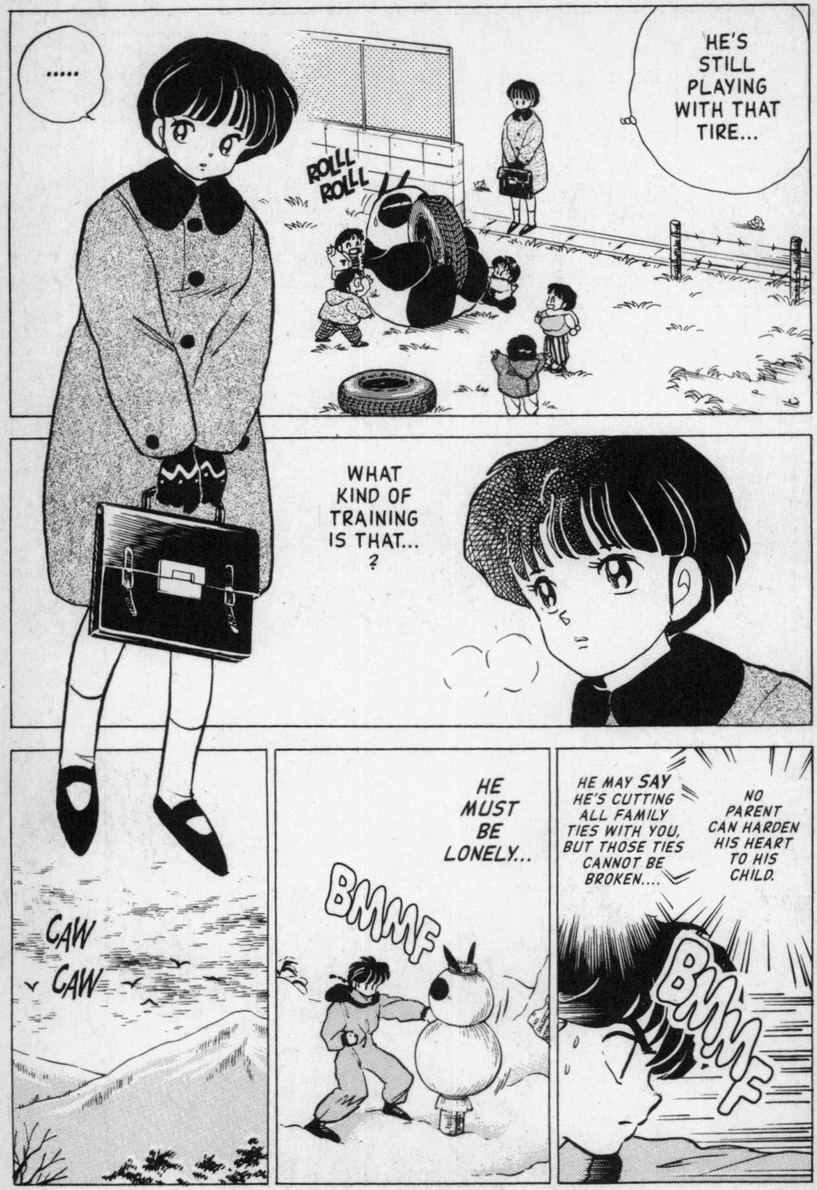

.....
ROLLL ROLLL
HE'S STILL PLAYING WITH THAT TIRE...
WHAT KIND OF TRAINING IS THAT... ?
CAW CAW
HE MUST BE LONELY...
BMMF
HE MAY SAY HE'S CUTTING ALL FAMILY TIES WITH YOU, BUT THOSE TIES CANNOT BE BROKEN....
NO PARENT CAN HARDEN HIS HEART TO HIS CHILD.
BMMF

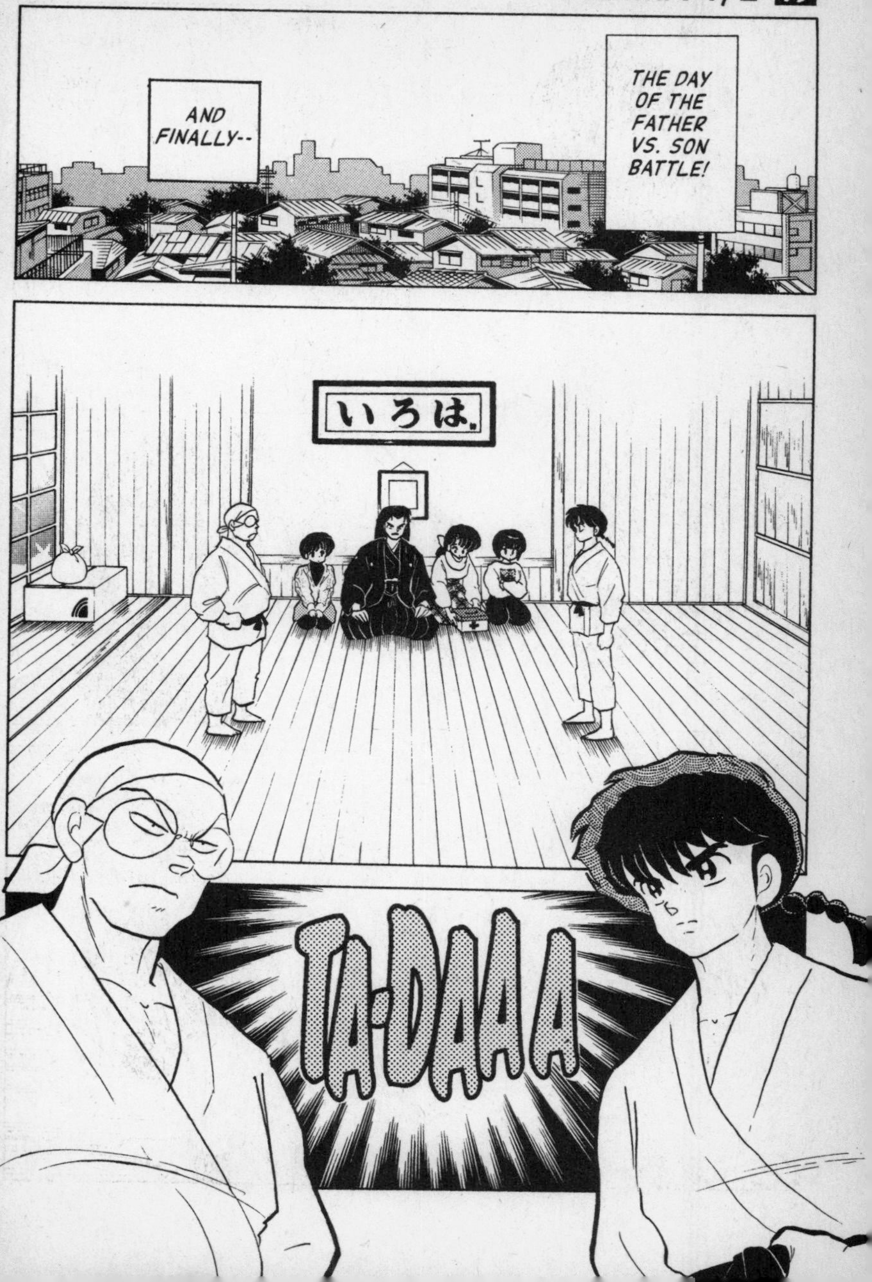
AND FINALLY--
THE DAY OF THE FATHER VS. SON BATTLE!
いろは
TA-DAAA

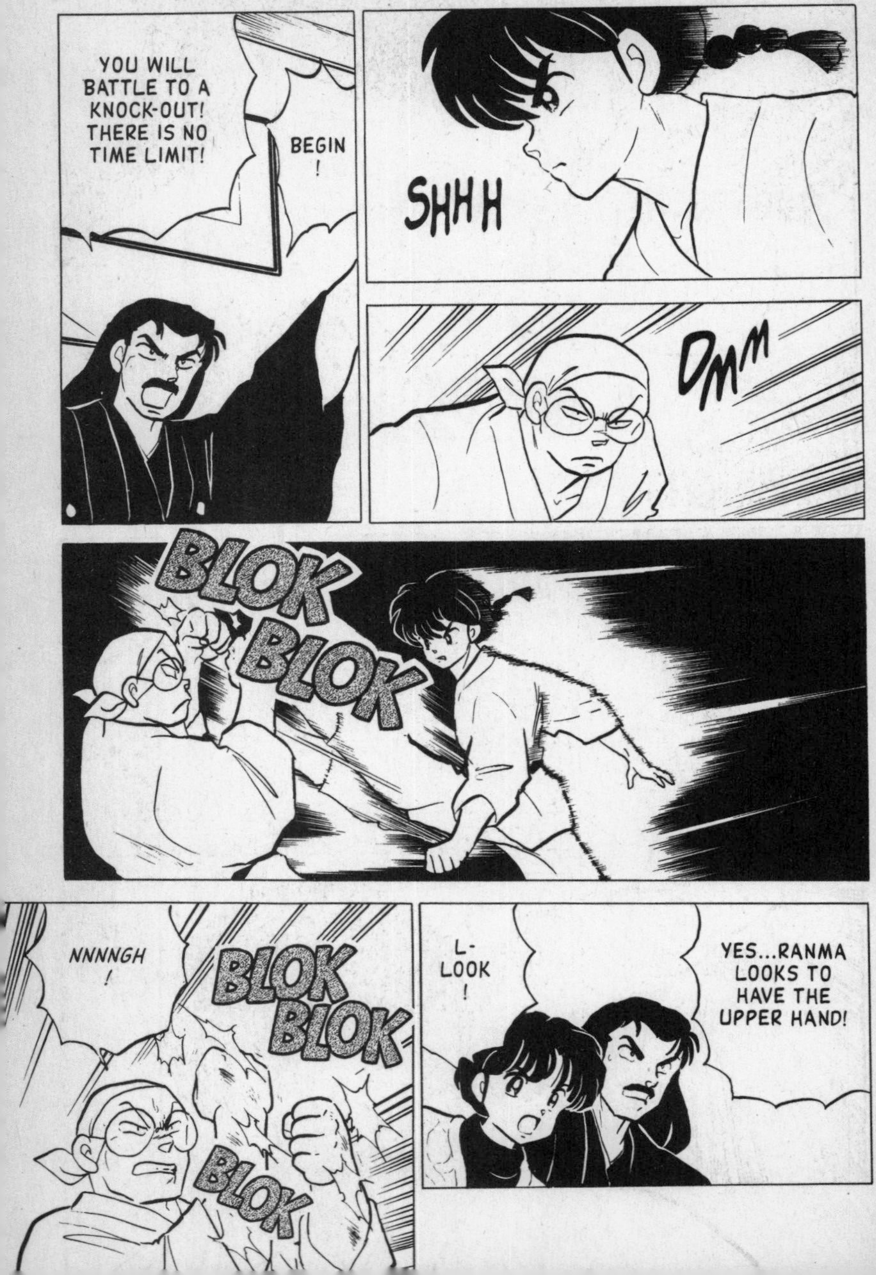
YOU WILL BATTLE TO A KNOCK-OUT! THERE IS NO TIME LIMIT!
BEGIN!
SHHH
DMM
BLOK
BLOK
NNNNGH!
BLOK
BLOK
BLOK
L-LOOK!
YES...RANMA LOOKS TO HAVE THE UPPER HAND!

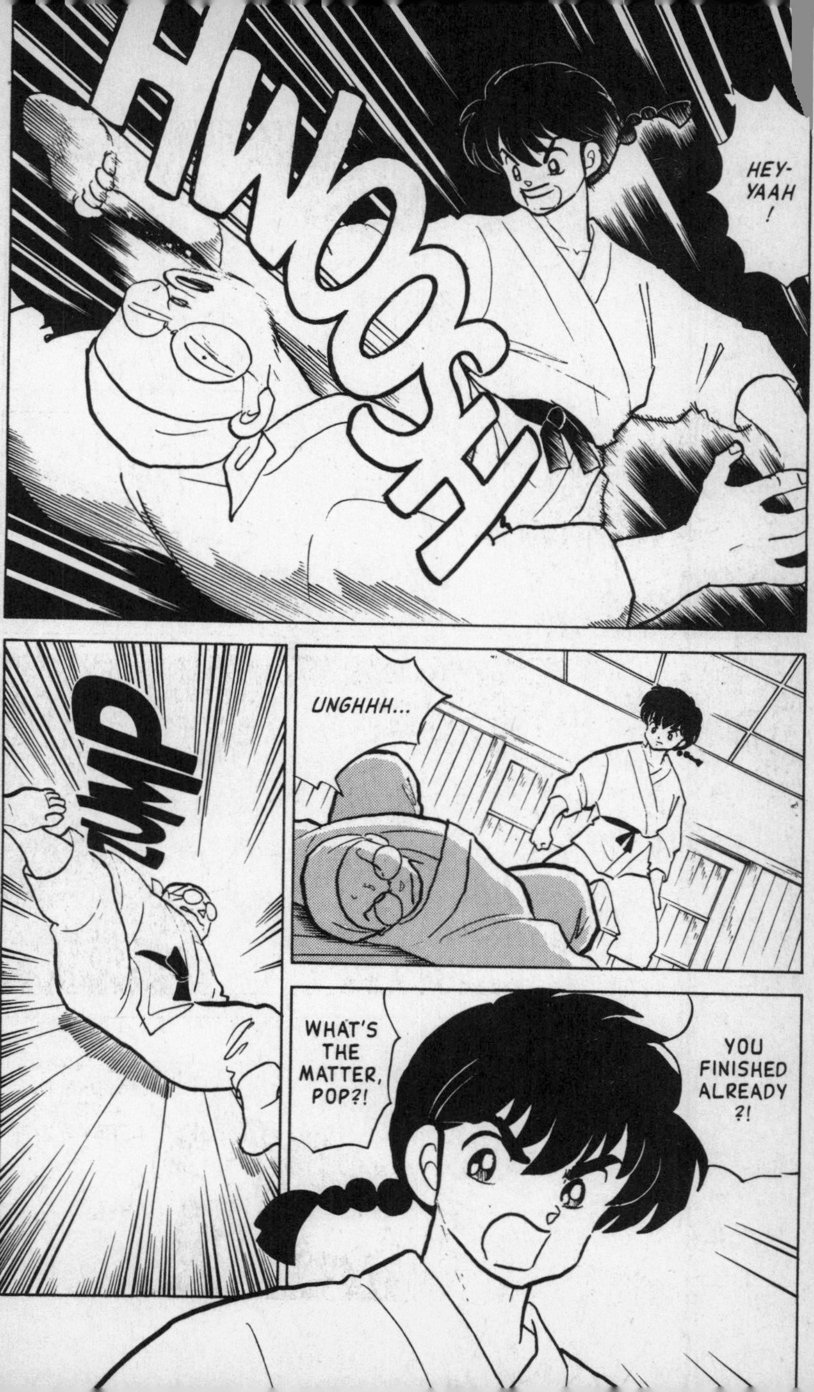
HWOOSH
HEY-YAAH!
THUMP
UNGHHH...
WHAT'S THE MATTER, POP?!
YOU FINISHED ALREADY?!

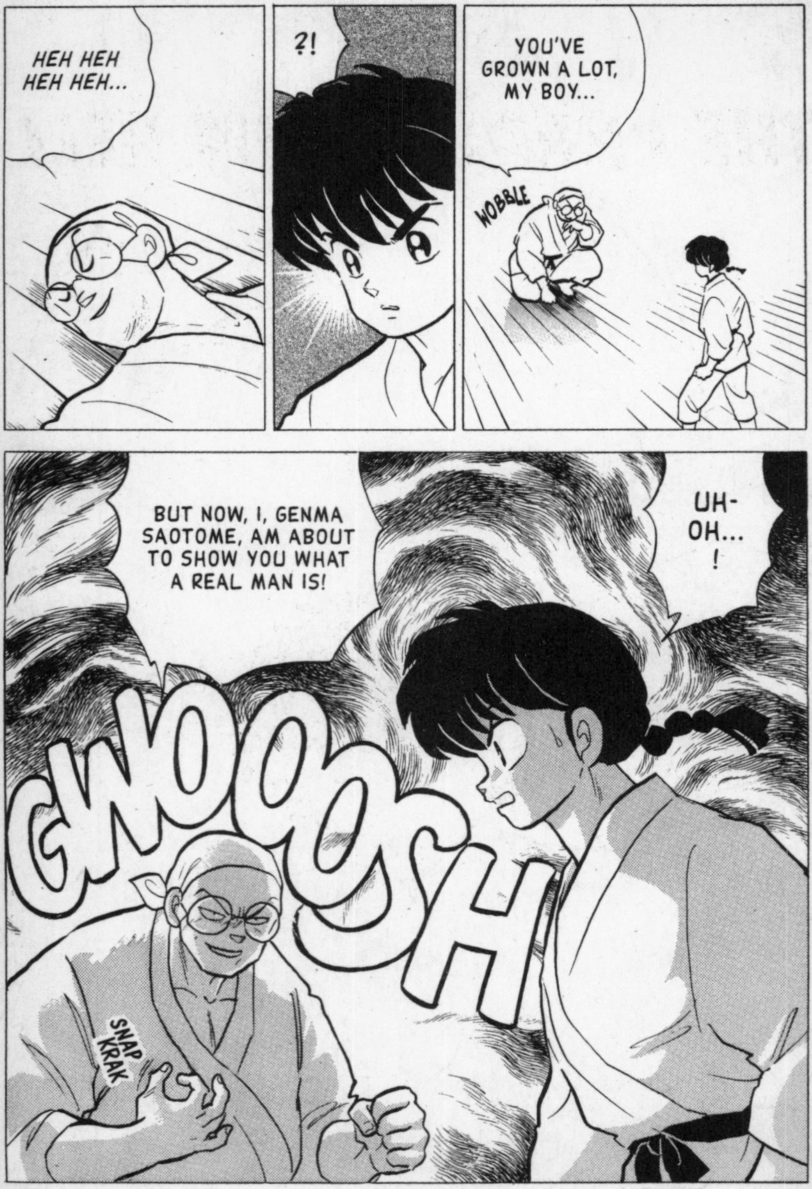
HEH HEH
HEH HEH...
?!
YOU'VE
GROWN A LOT,
MY BOY...
WOBBLE
BUT NOW, I, GENMA
SAOTOME, AM ABOUT
TO SHOW YOU WHAT
A REAL MAN IS!
UH-
OH...
!
GWOOOSH
SNAP
KRAK

Part 3

THE CRADLE FROM HELL

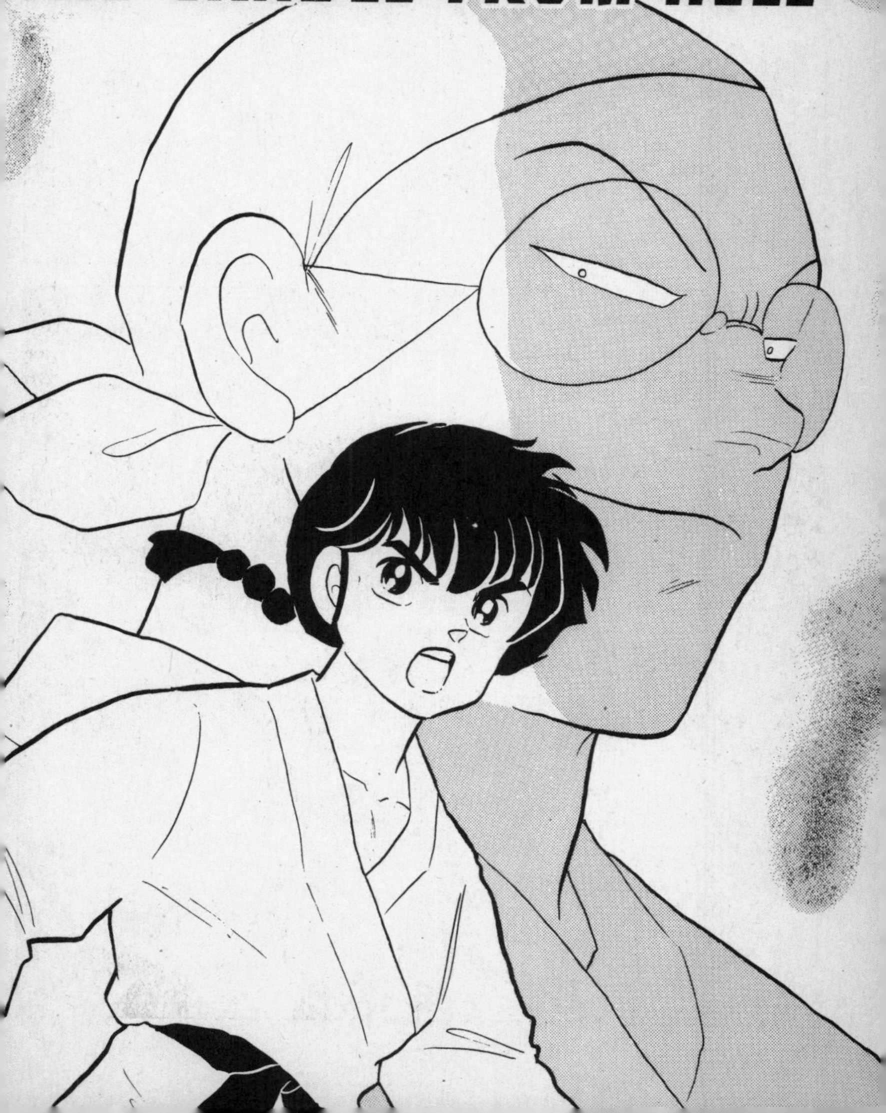

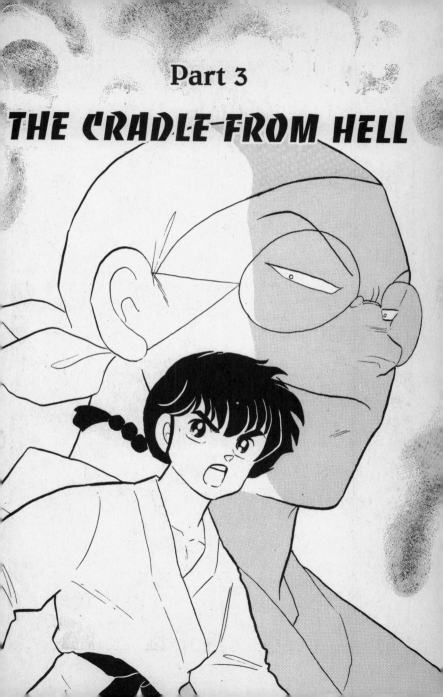

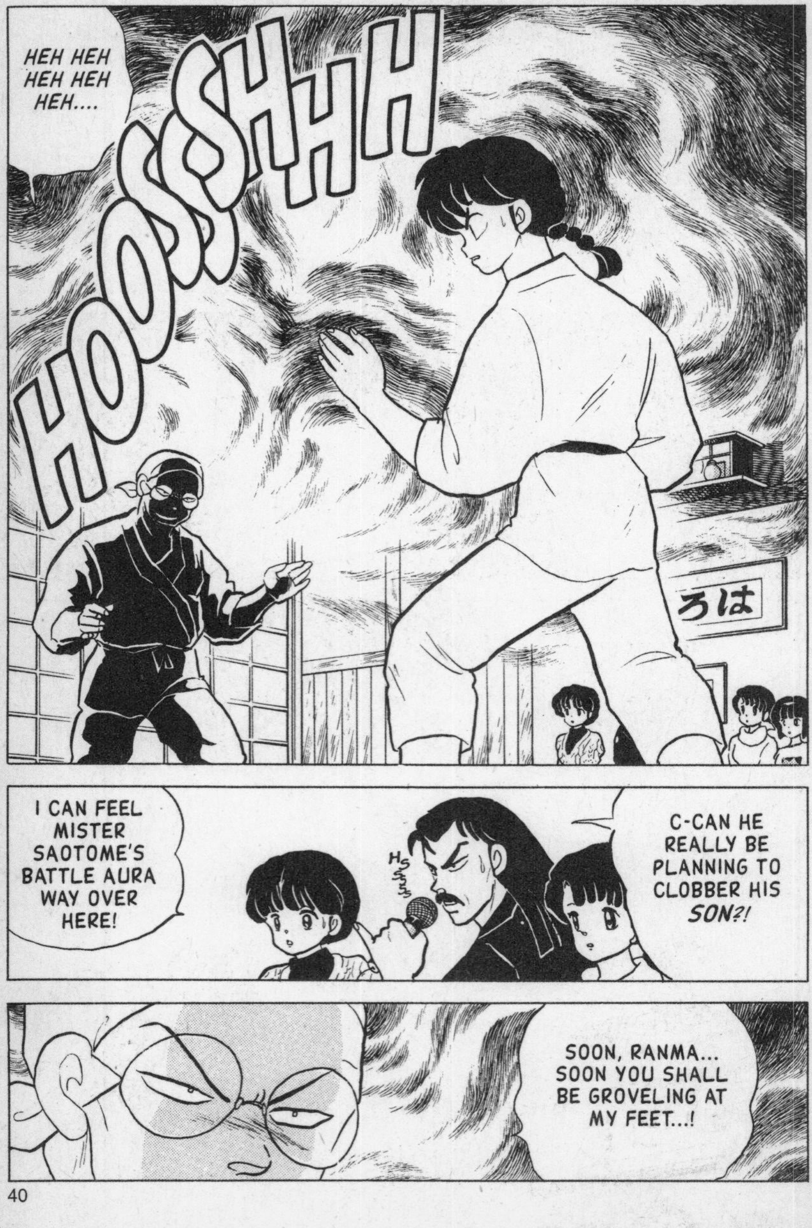
HEH HEH HEH HEH HEH....
HOOSSHHH
ろは
I CAN FEEL MISTER SAOTOME'S BATTLE AURA WAY OVER HERE!
HSSSS
C-CAN HE REALLY BE PLANNING TO CLOBBER HIS *SON*?!
SOON, RANMA... SOON YOU SHALL BE GROVELING AT MY FEET...!

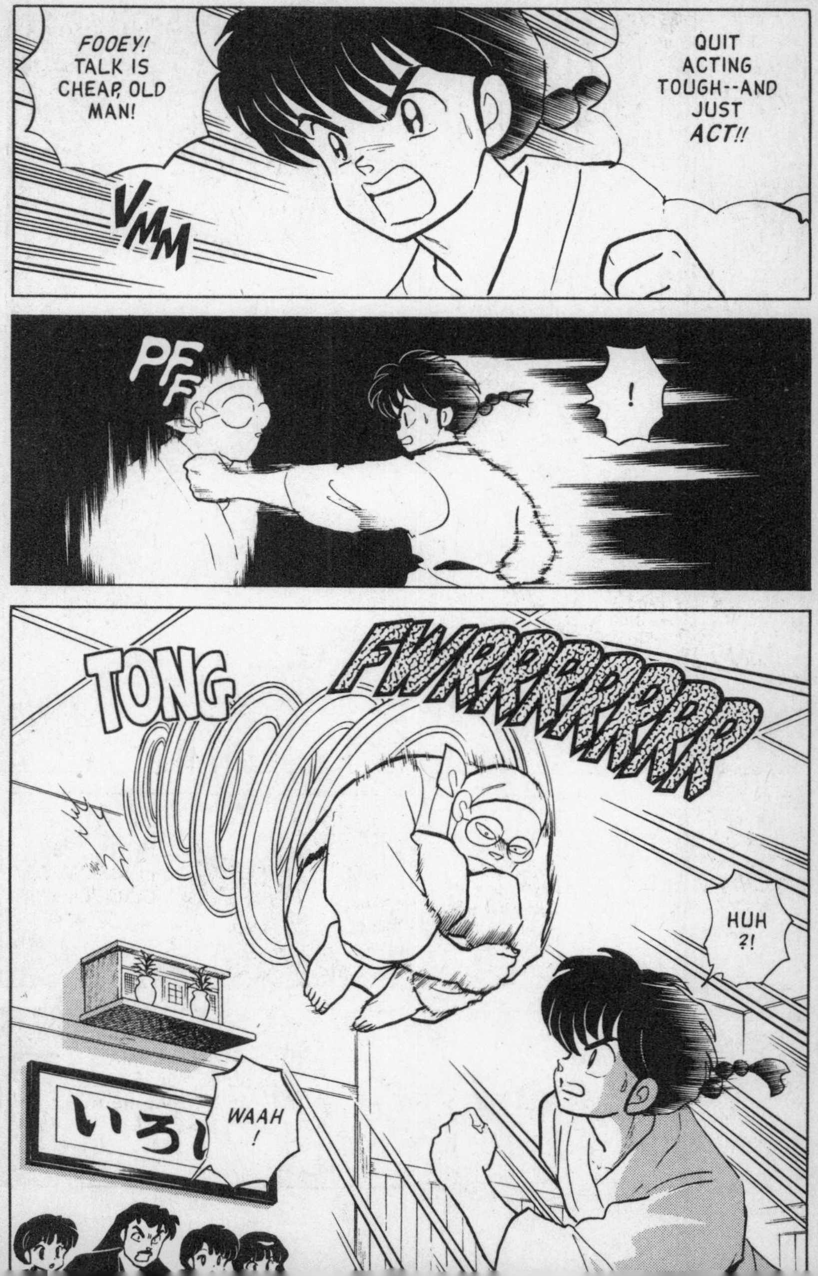
FOOEY! TALK IS CHEAP, OLD MAN!
VMM
QUIT ACTING TOUGH--AND JUST ACT!!
PFF
!
TONG
FWRRRRRRR
HUH ?!
いろ
WAAH !

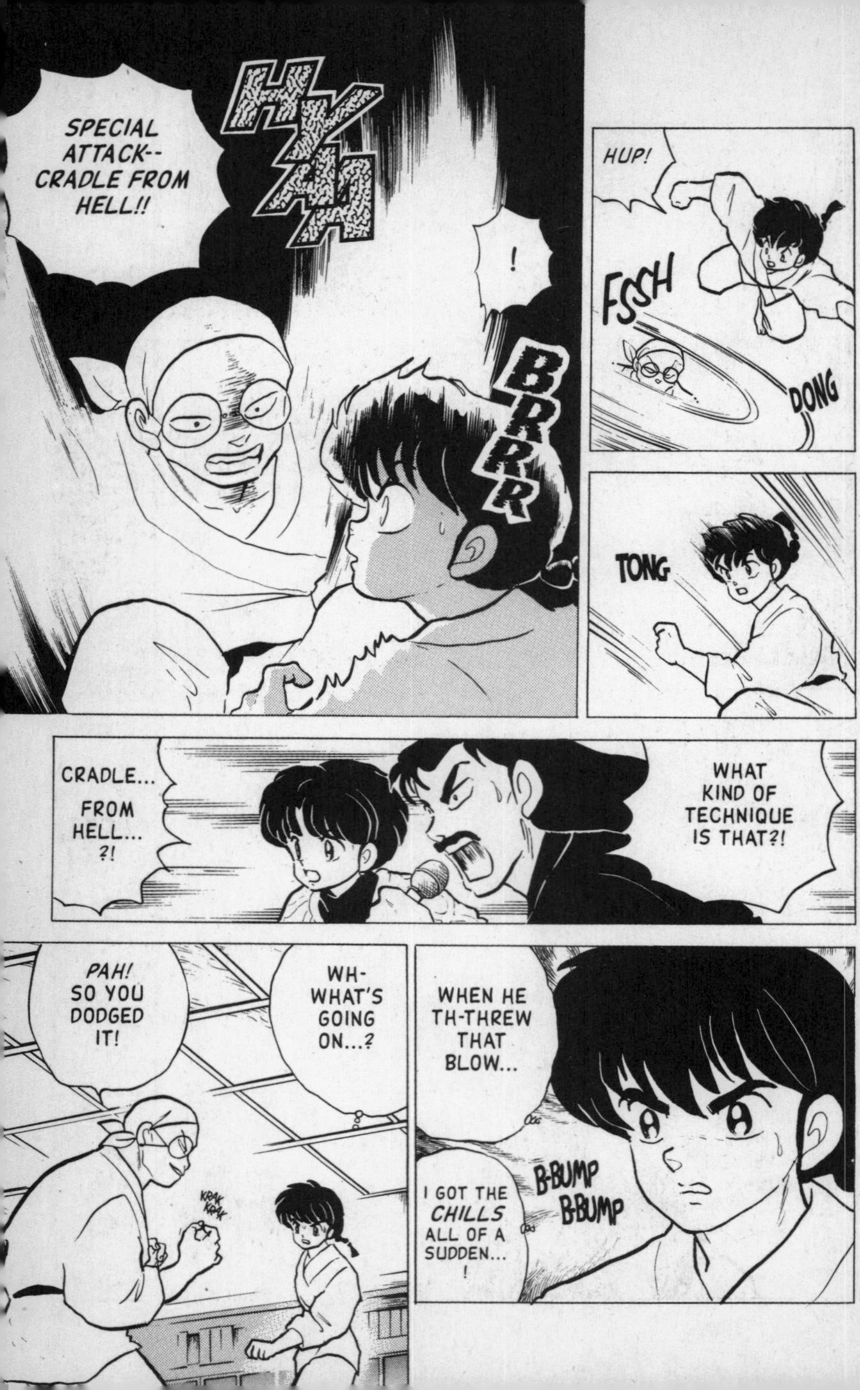
SPECIAL ATTACK-- CRADLE FROM HELL!!
HYAA
!
BRRRR
HUP!
FSSH
DONG
TONG
CRADLE... FROM HELL... ?!
WHAT KIND OF TECHNIQUE IS THAT?!
PAH! SO YOU DODGED IT!
WH-WHAT'S GOING ON...?
KRAK KRAK
WHEN HE TH-THREW THAT BLOW...
B-BUMP B-BUMP
I GOT THE CHILLS ALL OF A SUDDEN... !

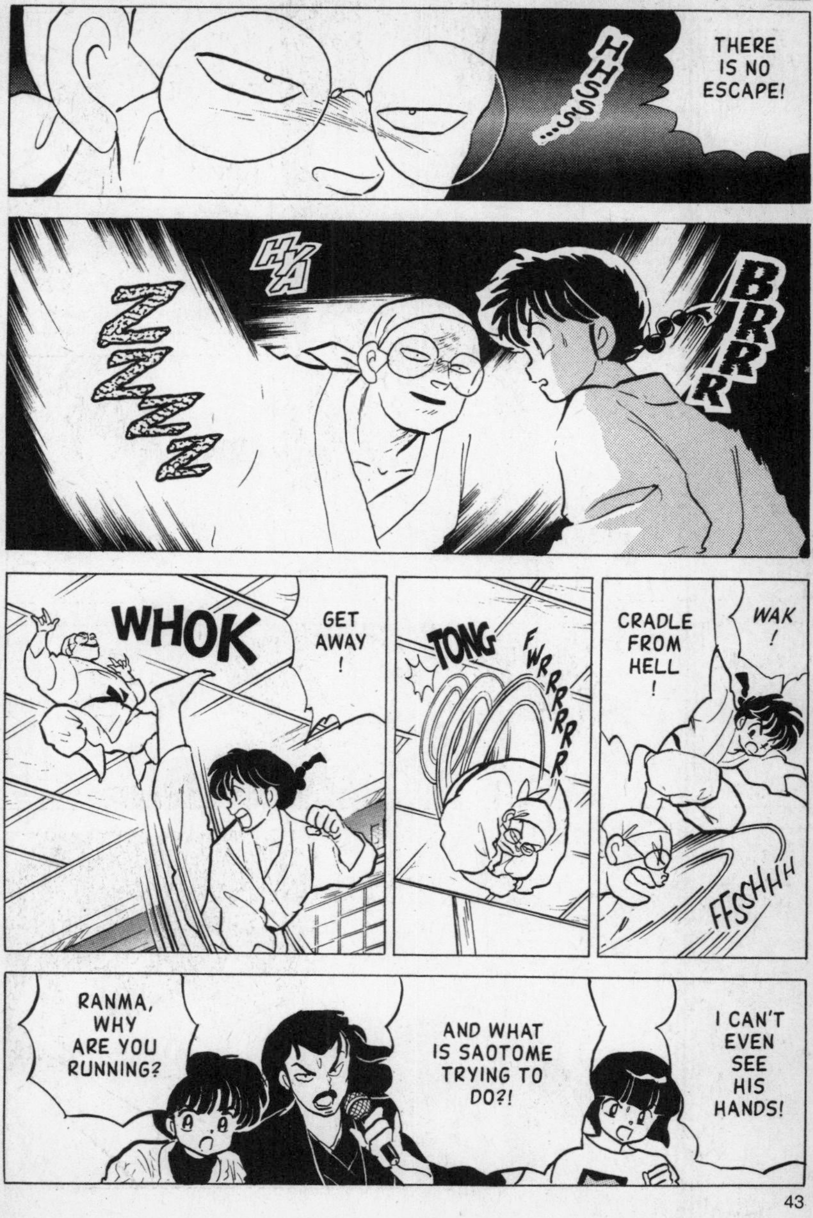
HHSSS...
THERE IS NO ESCAPE!
HYA
ZNNNN
BRRRR
WHOK
GET AWAY!
TONG
FWRRRRRR
CRADLE FROM HELL!
WAK!
FFSSHHH
RANMA, WHY ARE YOU RUNNING?
AND WHAT IS SAOTOME TRYING TO DO?!
I CAN'T EVEN SEE HIS HANDS!

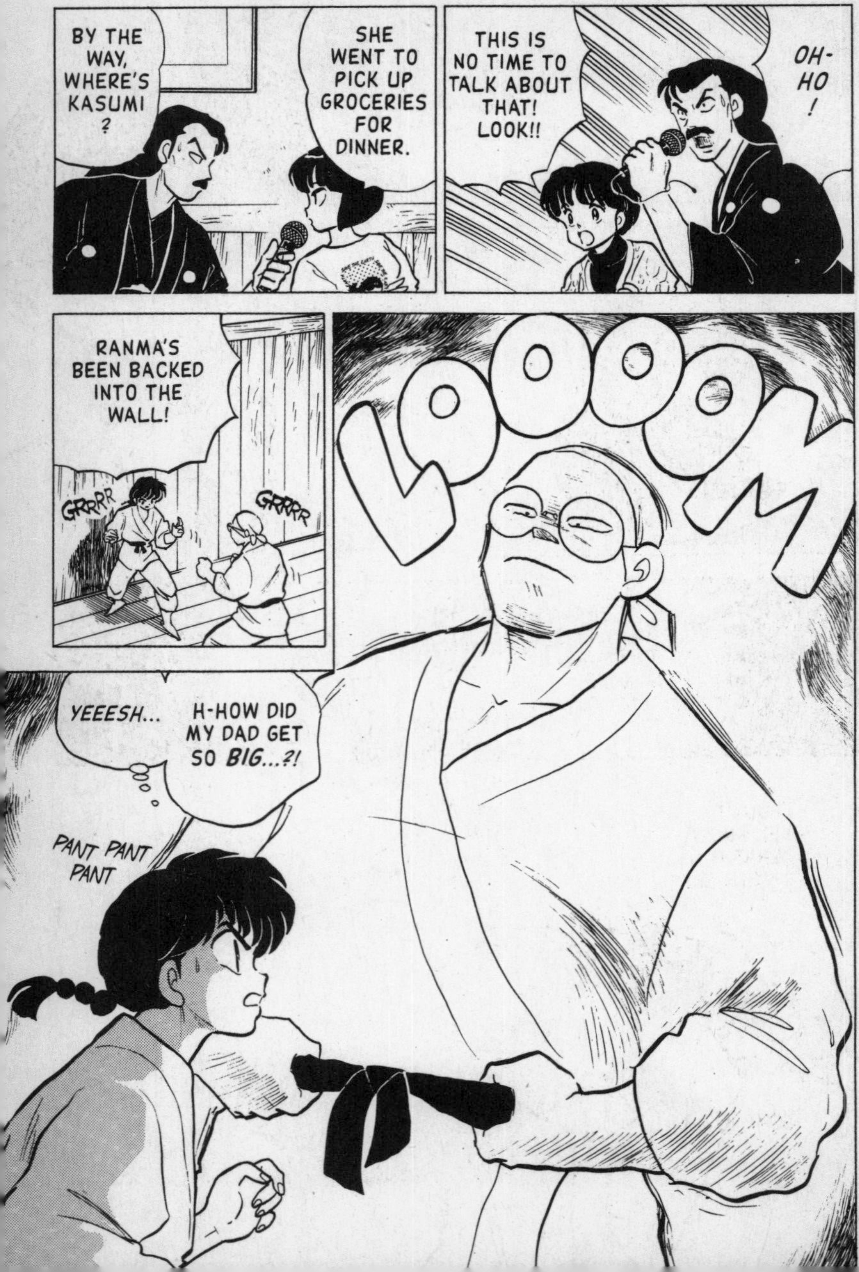
BY THE WAY, WHERE'S KASUMI?
SHE WENT TO PICK UP GROCERIES FOR DINNER.
THIS IS NO TIME TO TALK ABOUT THAT! LOOK!!
OH-HO!
RANMA'S BEEN BACKED INTO THE WALL!
GRRRR
GRRRR
LOOOOM
YEEESH...
H-HOW DID MY DAD GET SO BIG...?!
PANT PANT PANT

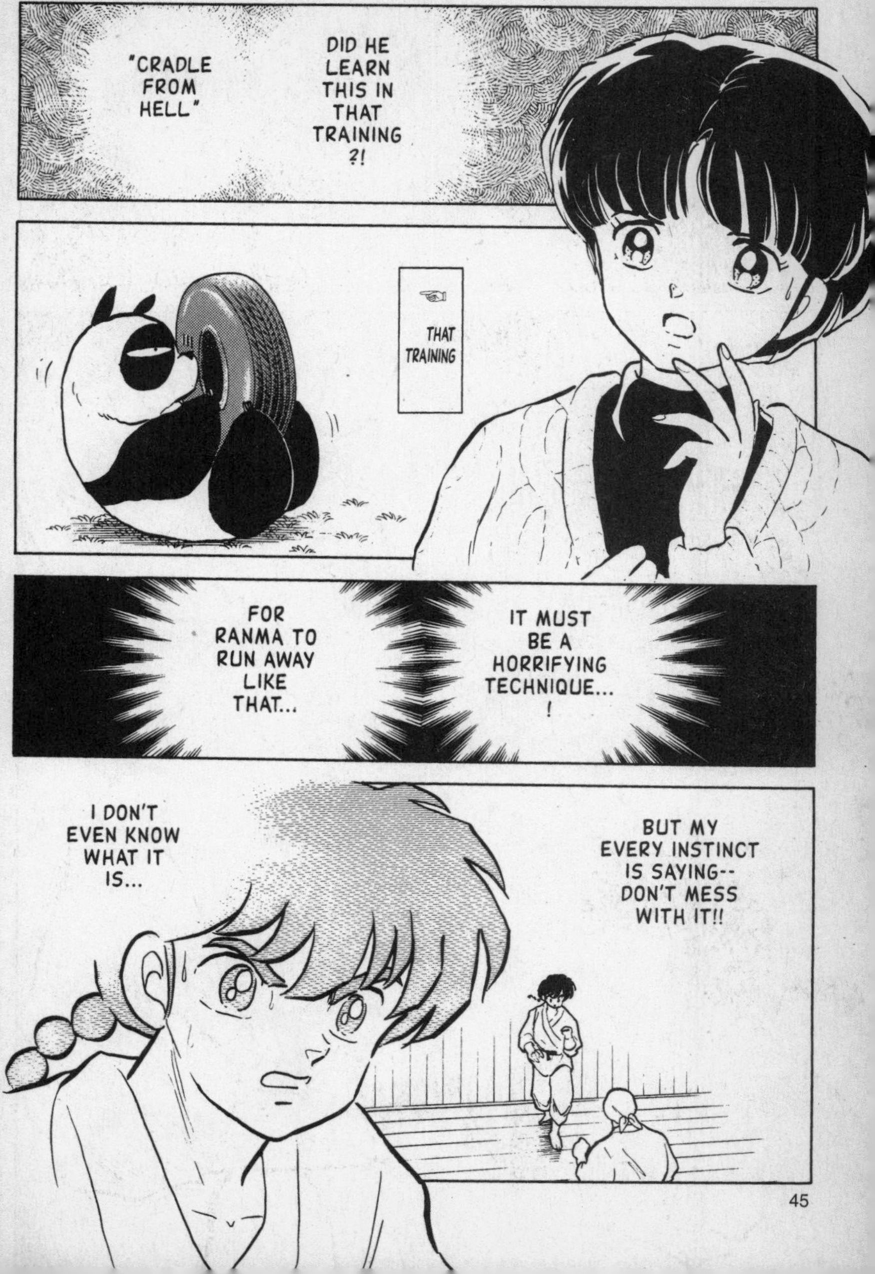
"CRADLE FROM HELL"
DID HE LEARN THIS IN THAT TRAINING ?!
THAT TRAINING
FOR RANMA TO RUN AWAY LIKE THAT...
IT MUST BE A HORRIFYING TECHNIQUE... !
I DON'T EVEN KNOW WHAT IT IS...
BUT MY EVERY INSTINCT IS SAYING-- DON'T MESS WITH IT!!

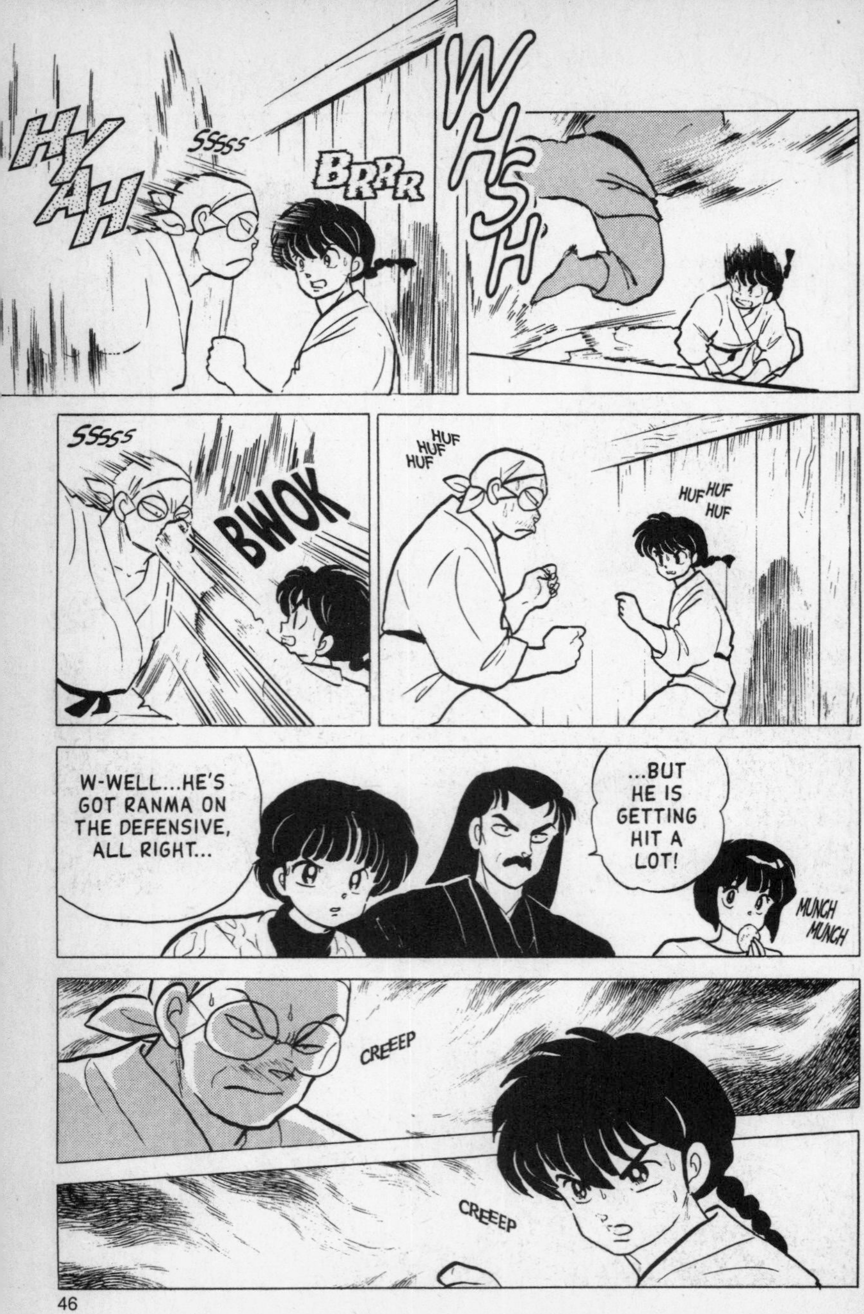
HYAH
SSSSS
BRRRR
WHSH
SSSSS
BWOK
HUF HUF HUF
HUF HUF HUF
W-WELL...HE'S GOT RANMA ON THE DEFENSIVE, ALL RIGHT...
...BUT HE IS GETTING HIT A LOT!
MUNCH MUNCH
CREEEP
CREEEP

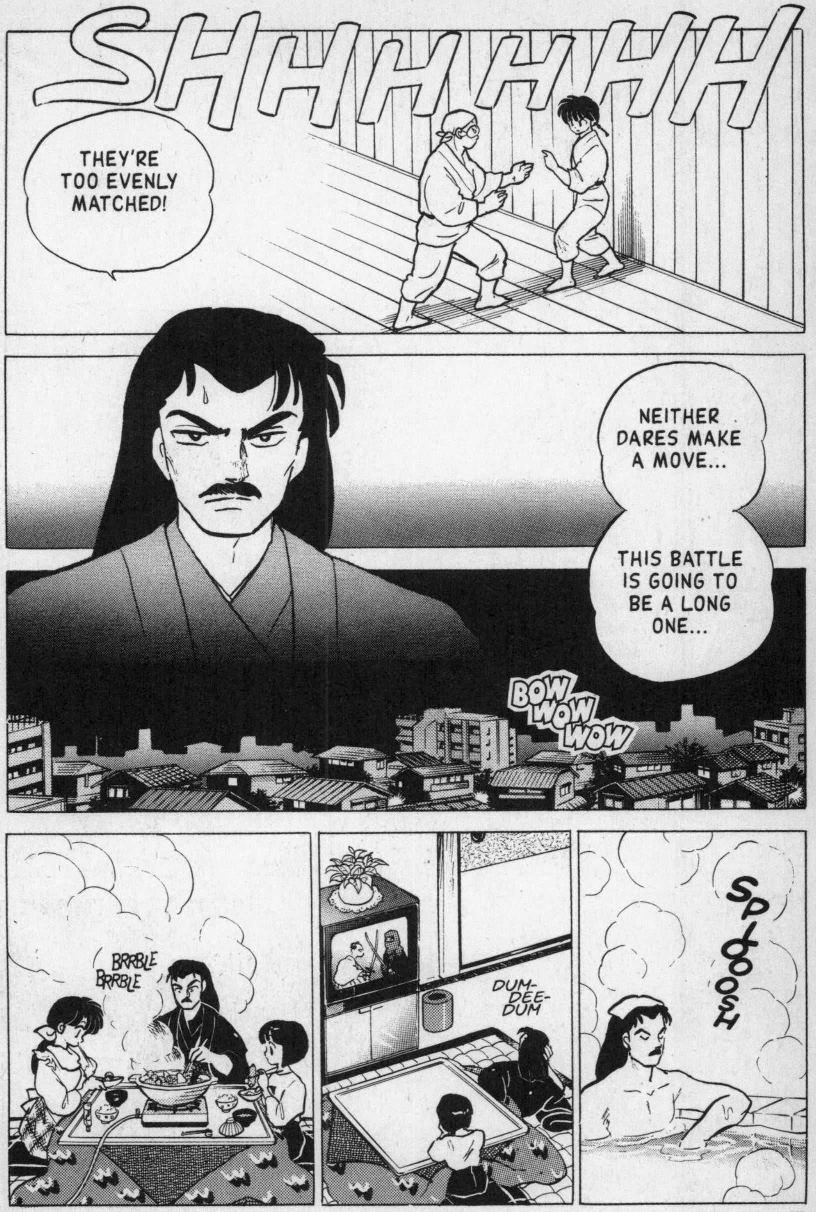
SHHHHHHH
THEY'RE TOO EVENLY MATCHED!
NEITHER DARES MAKE A MOVE...
THIS BATTLE IS GOING TO BE A LONG ONE...
BOW WOW WOW
BRRBLE BRRBLE
DUM-DEE-DUM
SPLOOOSH

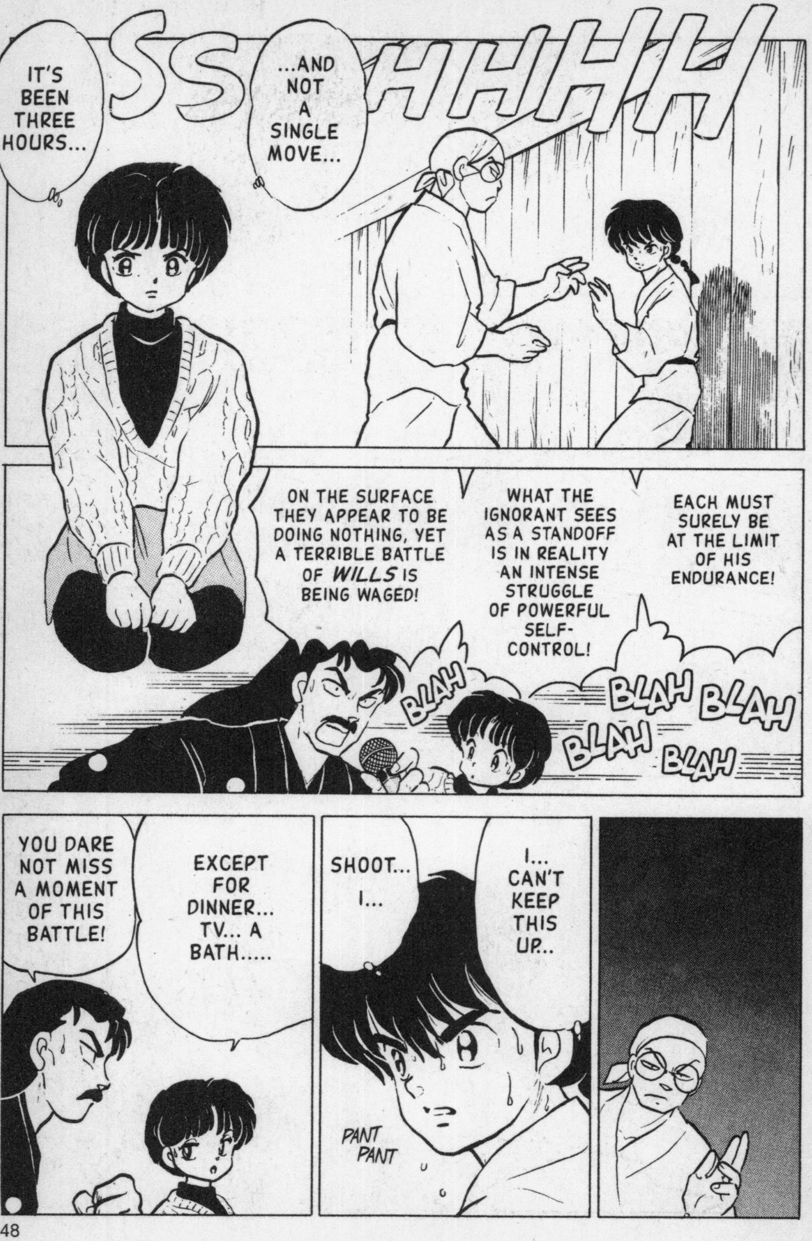
IT'S BEEN THREE HOURS...
SSHHHHHH
...AND NOT A SINGLE MOVE...
ON THE SURFACE THEY APPEAR TO BE DOING NOTHING, YET A TERRIBLE BATTLE OF WILLS IS BEING WAGED!
WHAT THE IGNORANT SEES AS A STANDOFF IS IN REALITY AN INTENSE STRUGGLE OF POWERFUL SELF-CONTROL!
EACH MUST SURELY BE AT THE LIMIT OF HIS ENDURANCE!
BLAH
BLAH BLAH
BLAH
BLAH
YOU DARE NOT MISS A MOMENT OF THIS BATTLE!
EXCEPT FOR DINNER... TV... A BATH.....
SHOOT... I...
I... CAN'T KEEP THIS UP...
PANT PANT

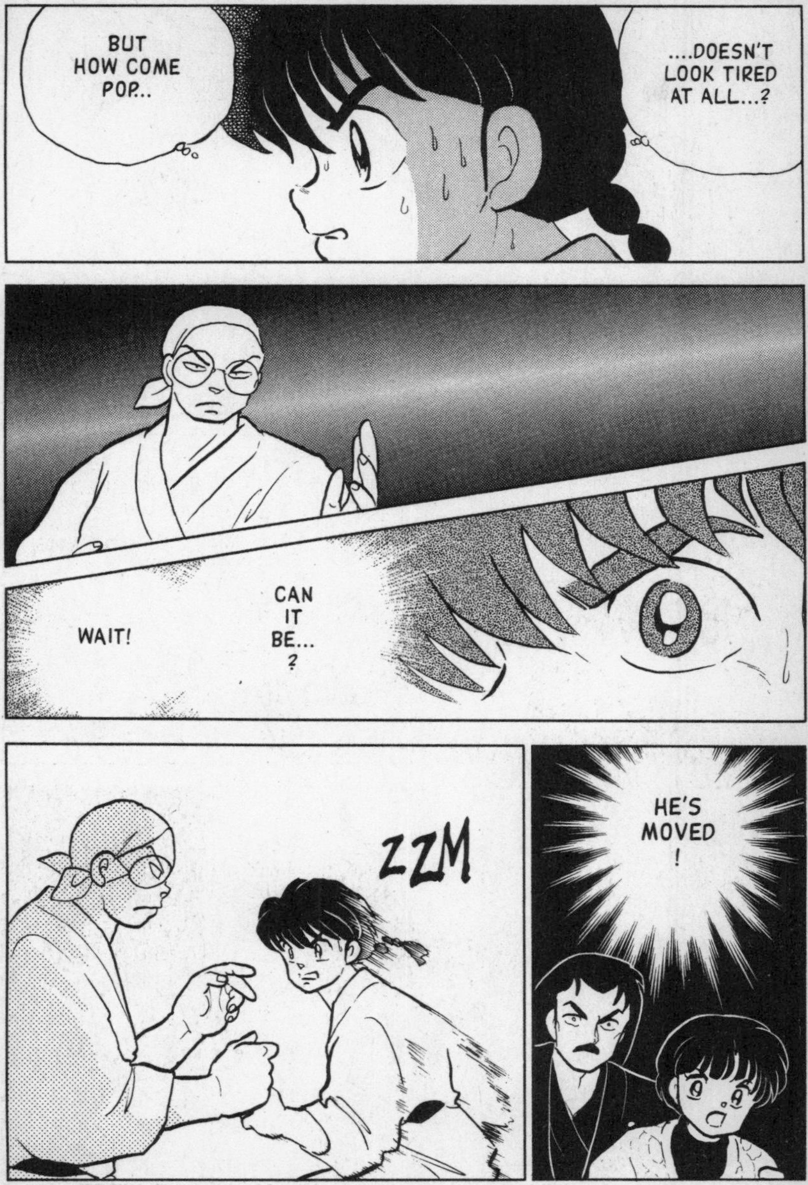
BUT HOW COME POP...
....DOESN'T LOOK TIRED AT ALL...?
WAIT!
CAN IT BE...?
ZZM
HE'S MOVED!

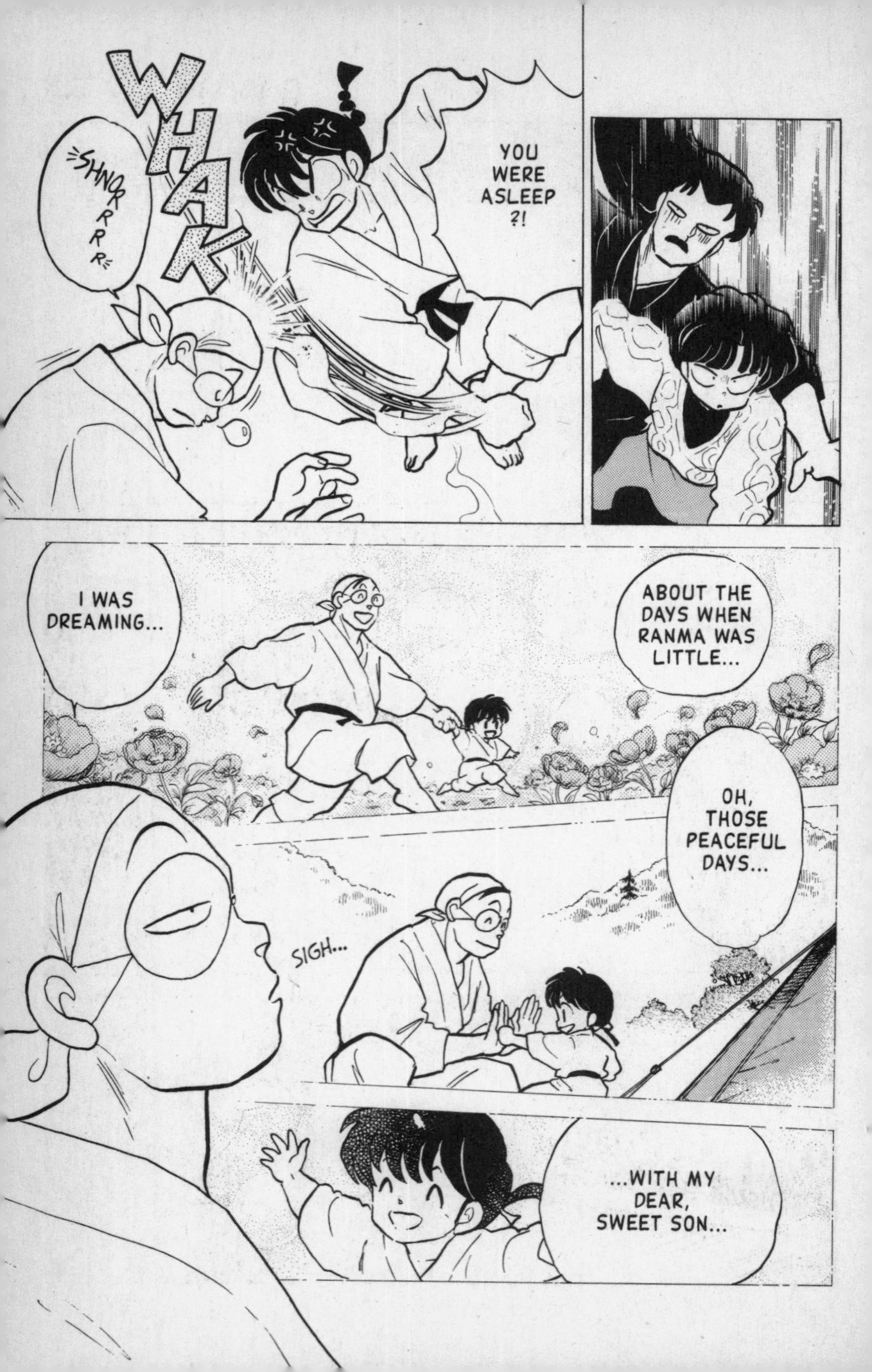
SHNORRRRR
WHAK
YOU WERE ASLEEP ?!
I WAS DREAMING...
ABOUT THE DAYS WHEN RANMA WAS LITTLE...
OH, THOSE PEACEFUL DAYS...
SIGH...
...WITH MY DEAR, SWEET SON...

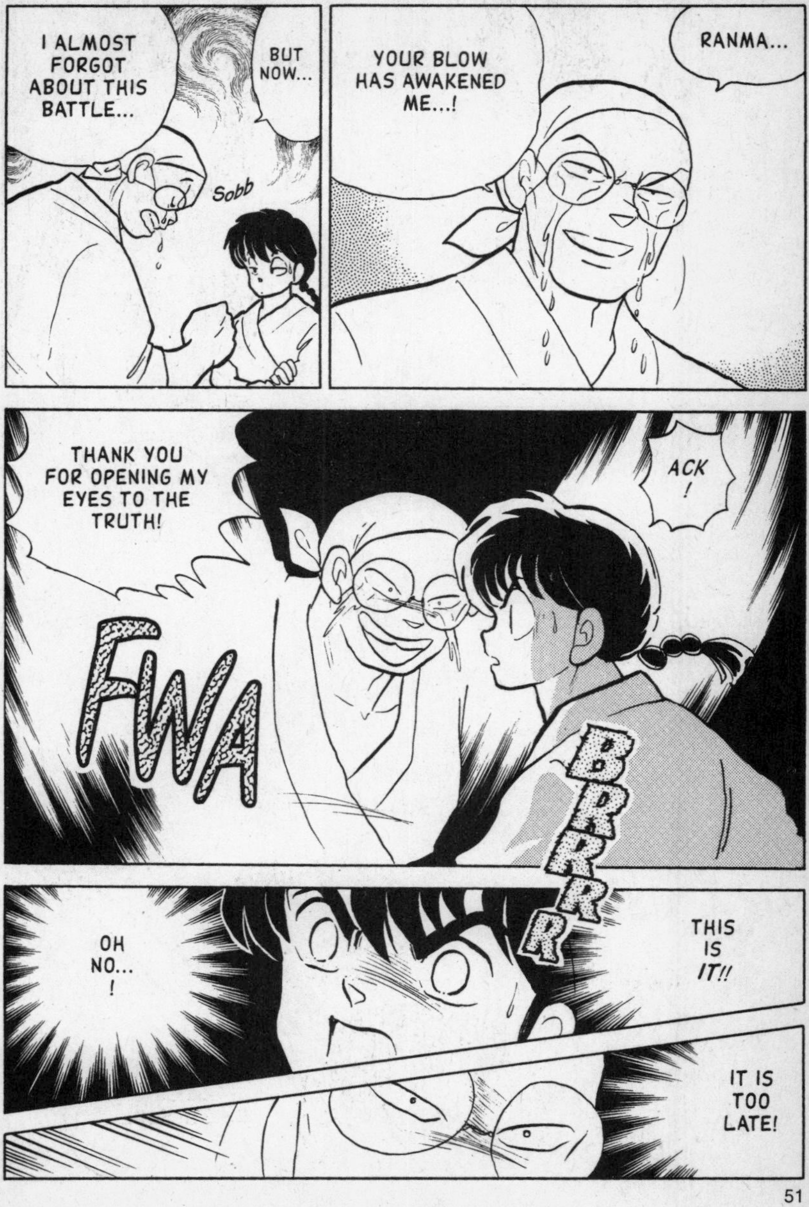
I ALMOST FORGOT ABOUT THIS BATTLE...
BUT NOW...
Sobb
YOUR BLOW HAS AWAKENED ME...!
RANMA...
THANK YOU FOR OPENING MY EYES TO THE TRUTH!
ACK!
FWA
BRRRRR
OH NO...!
THIS IS IT!!
IT IS TOO LATE!

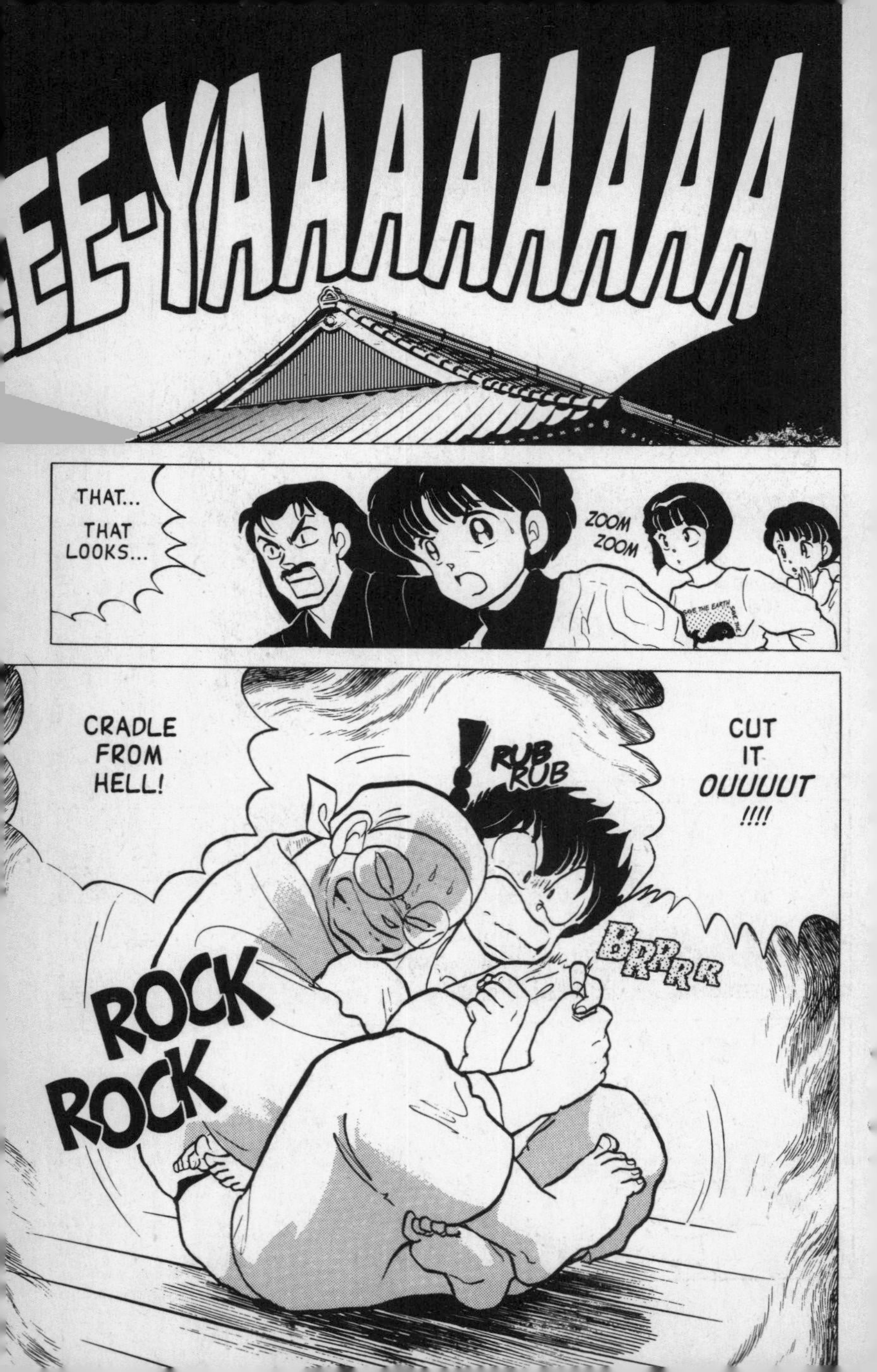
EE-YAAAAAAAA
THAT... THAT LOOKS...
ZOOM ZOOM
SAVE THE EARTH
CRADLE FROM HELL!
RUB RUB
CUT IT OUUUUT !!!!
BRRRRR
ROCK ROCK

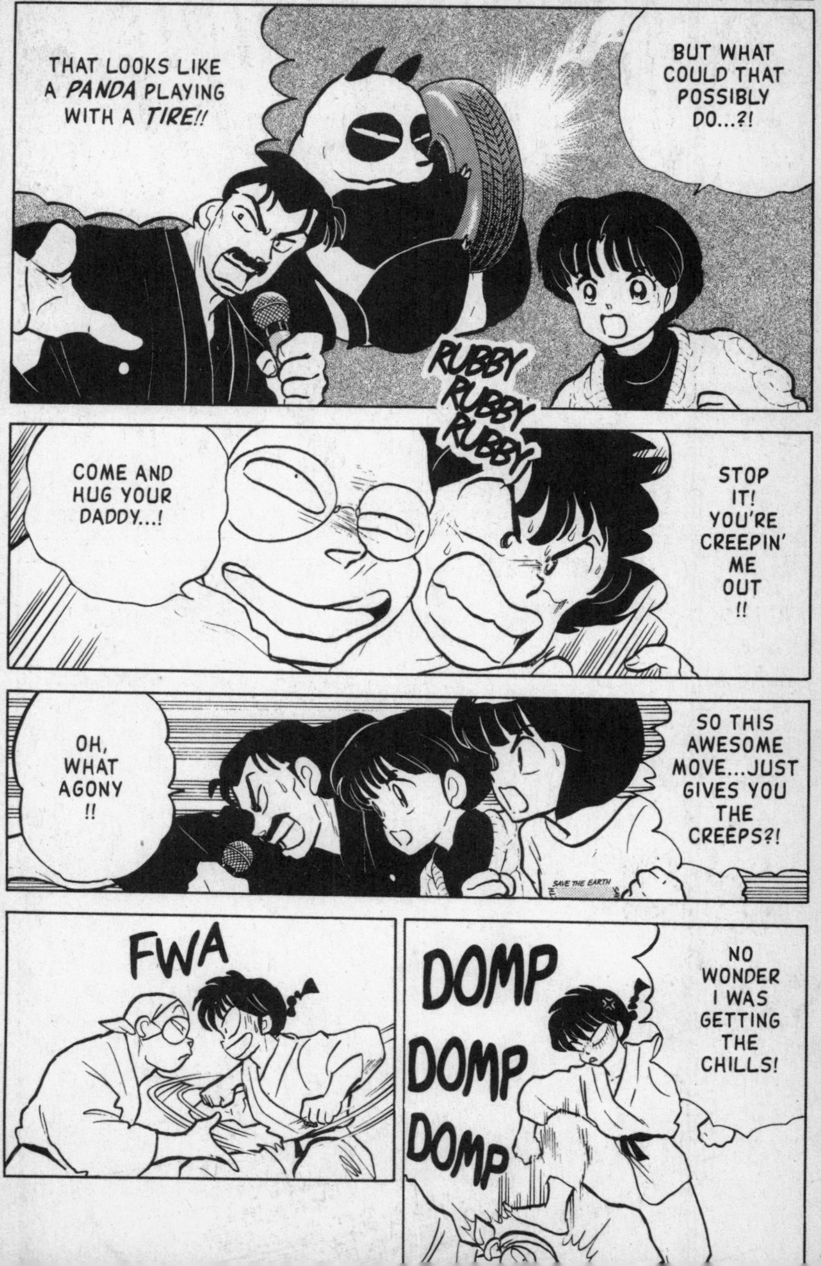
THAT LOOKS LIKE A *PANDA* PLAYING WITH A *TIRE!!*
BUT WHAT COULD THAT POSSIBLY DO...?!
RUBBY RUBBY RUBBY
COME AND HUG YOUR DADDY...!
STOP IT! YOU'RE CREEPIN' ME OUT !!
OH, WHAT AGONY !!
SO THIS AWESOME MOVE...JUST GIVES YOU THE CREEPS?!
SAVE THE EARTH
FWA
DOMP DOMP DOMP
NO WONDER I WAS GETTING THE CHILLS!

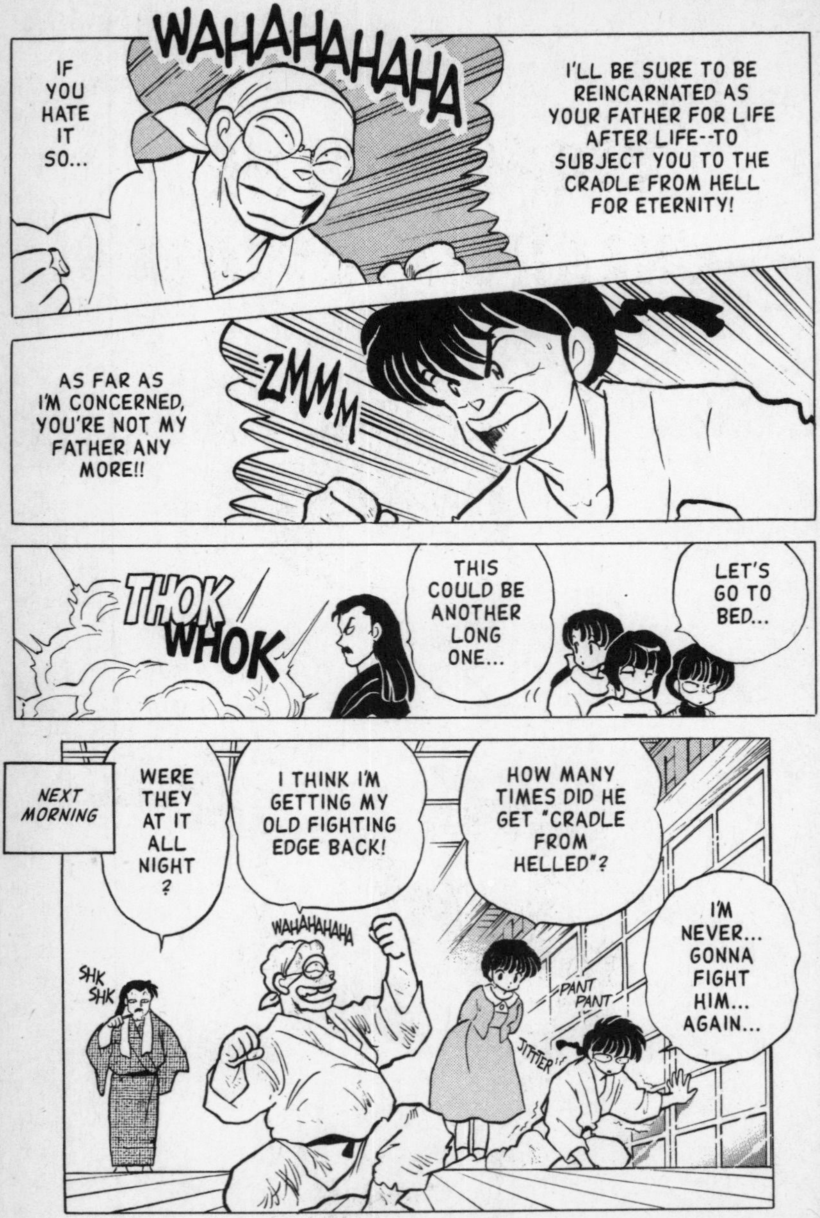
IF YOU HATE IT SO...
WAHAHAHAHAHA
I'LL BE SURE TO BE REINCARNATED AS YOUR FATHER FOR LIFE AFTER LIFE--TO SUBJECT YOU TO THE CRADLE FROM HELL FOR ETERNITY!
AS FAR AS I'M CONCERNED, YOU'RE NOT MY FATHER ANY MORE!!
ZMMM
THOK WHOK
THIS COULD BE ANOTHER LONG ONE...
LET'S GO TO BED...
NEXT MORNING
WERE THEY AT IT ALL NIGHT ?
I THINK I'M GETTING MY OLD FIGHTING EDGE BACK!
HOW MANY TIMES DID HE GET "CRADLE FROM HELLED"?
I'M NEVER... GONNA FIGHT HIM... AGAIN...
WAHAHAHAHA
SHK SHK
PANT PANT
JITTER

Part 4

MARK OF THE CHERRY BLOSSOM

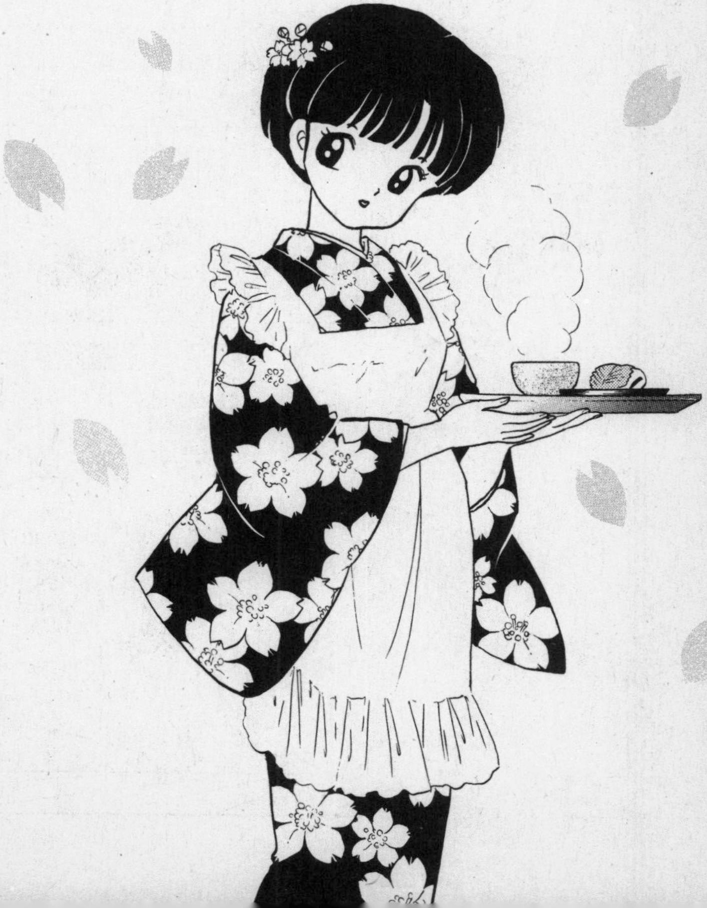

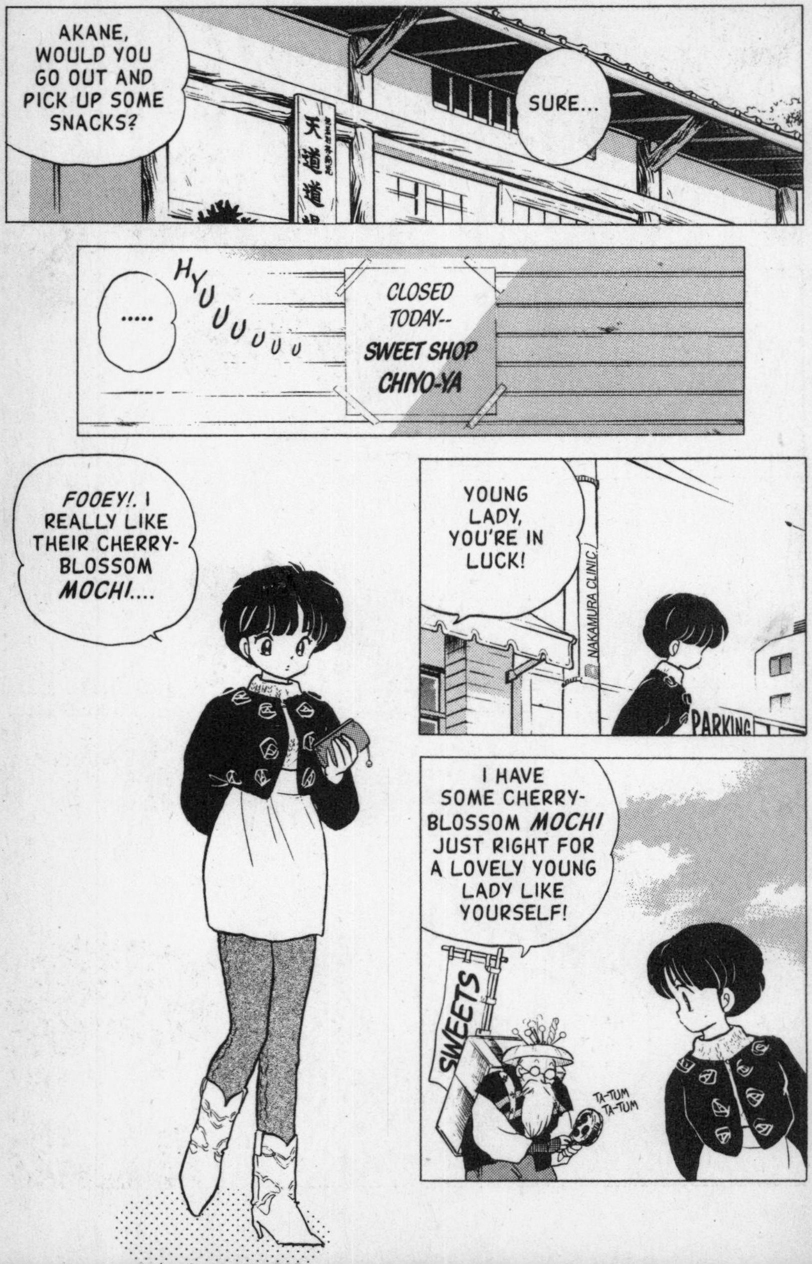
AKANE, WOULD YOU GO OUT AND PICK UP SOME SNACKS?
天道道
SURE...
.....
HYUUUUUUU
CLOSED TODAY-- SWEET SHOP CHIYO-YA
FOOEY!. I REALLY LIKE THEIR CHERRY-BLOSSOM MOCHI....
YOUNG LADY, YOU'RE IN LUCK!
NAKAMURA CLINIC
PARKING
I HAVE SOME CHERRY-BLOSSOM MOCHI JUST RIGHT FOR A LOVELY YOUNG LADY LIKE YOURSELF!
SWEETS
TA-TUM TA-TUM

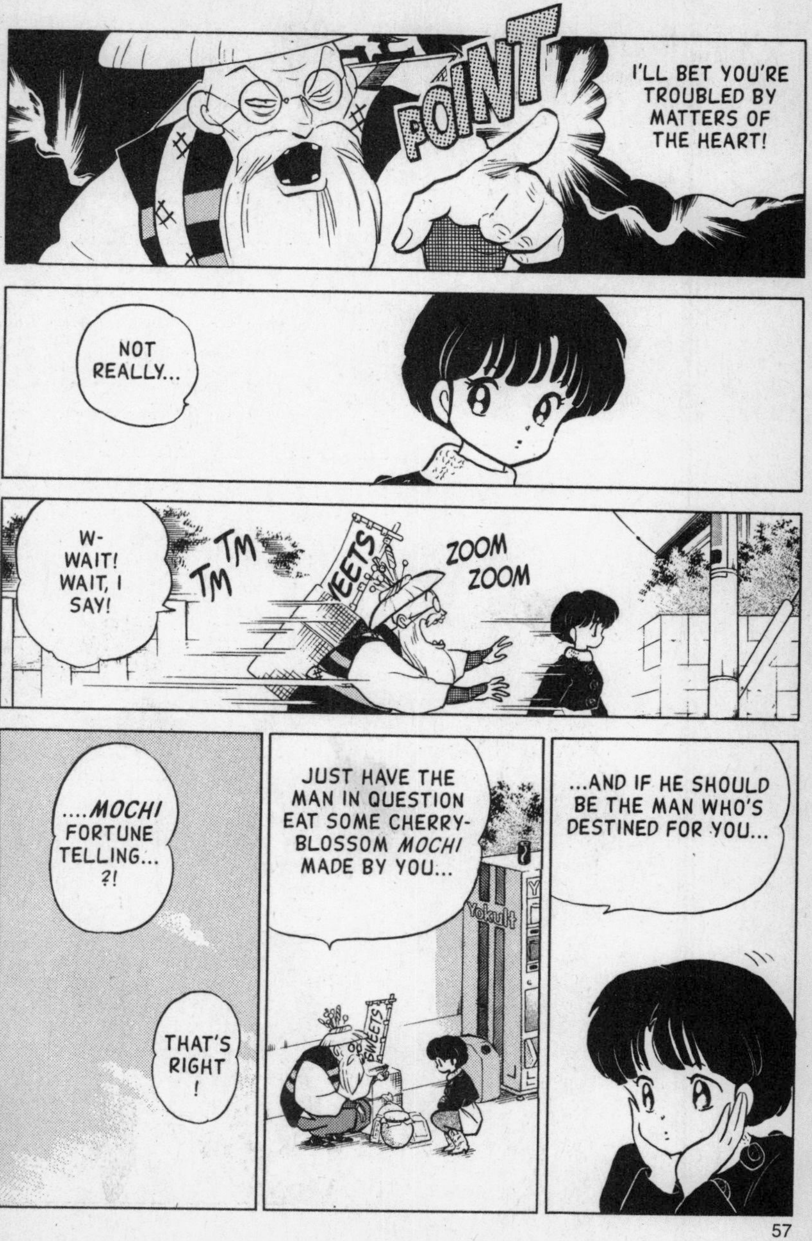
POINT
I'LL BET YOU'RE TROUBLED BY MATTERS OF THE HEART!
NOT REALLY...
W- WAIT! WAIT, I SAY!
TM TM
ZOOM ZOOM
....*MOCHI* FORTUNE TELLING... ?!
THAT'S RIGHT !
JUST HAVE THE MAN IN QUESTION EAT SOME CHERRY-BLOSSOM *MOCHI* MADE BY YOU...
Yokult
SWEETS
...AND IF HE SHOULD BE THE MAN WHO'S DESTINED FOR YOU...

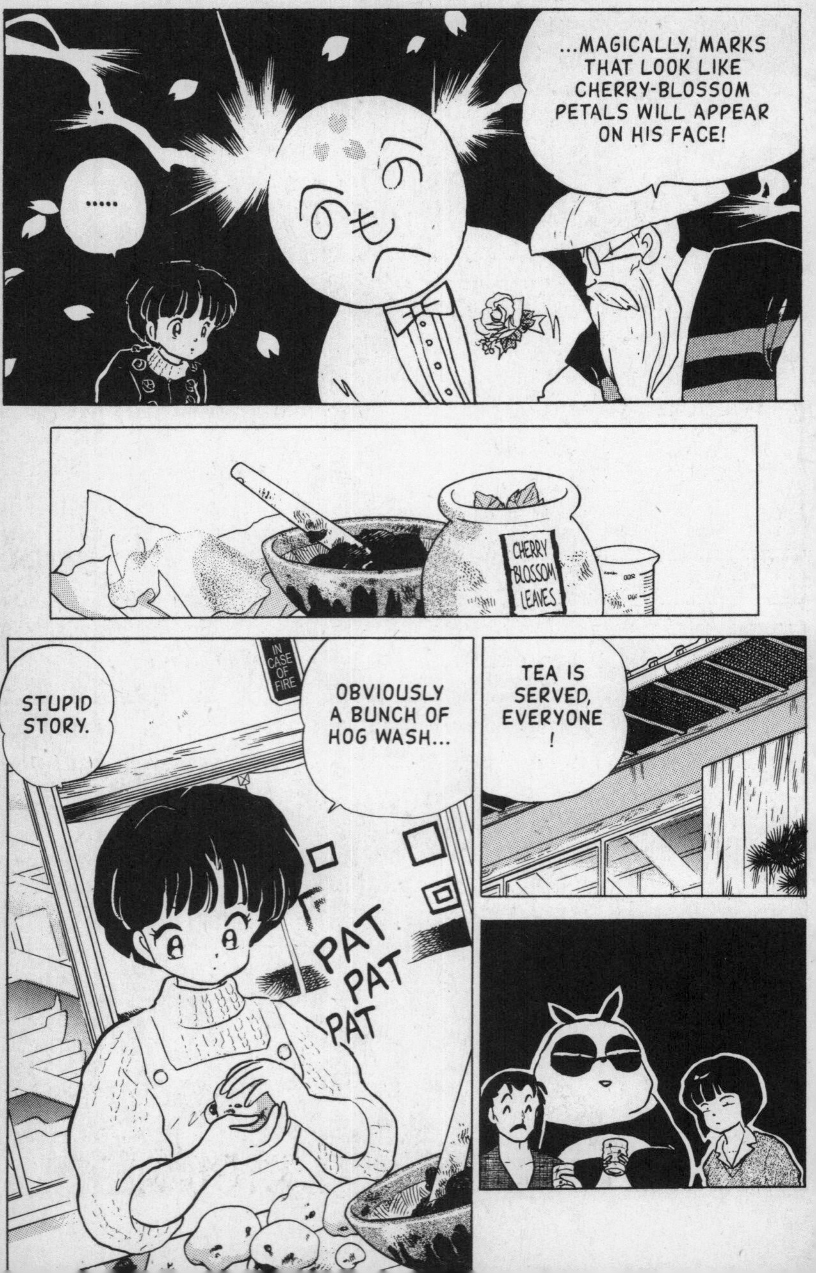
......
...MAGICALLY, MARKS THAT LOOK LIKE CHERRY-BLOSSOM PETALS WILL APPEAR ON HIS FACE!
CHERRY BLOSSOM LEAVES
IN CASE OF FIRE
STUPID STORY.
OBVIOUSLY A BUNCH OF HOG WASH...
PAT PAT PAT
TEA IS SERVED, EVERYONE !

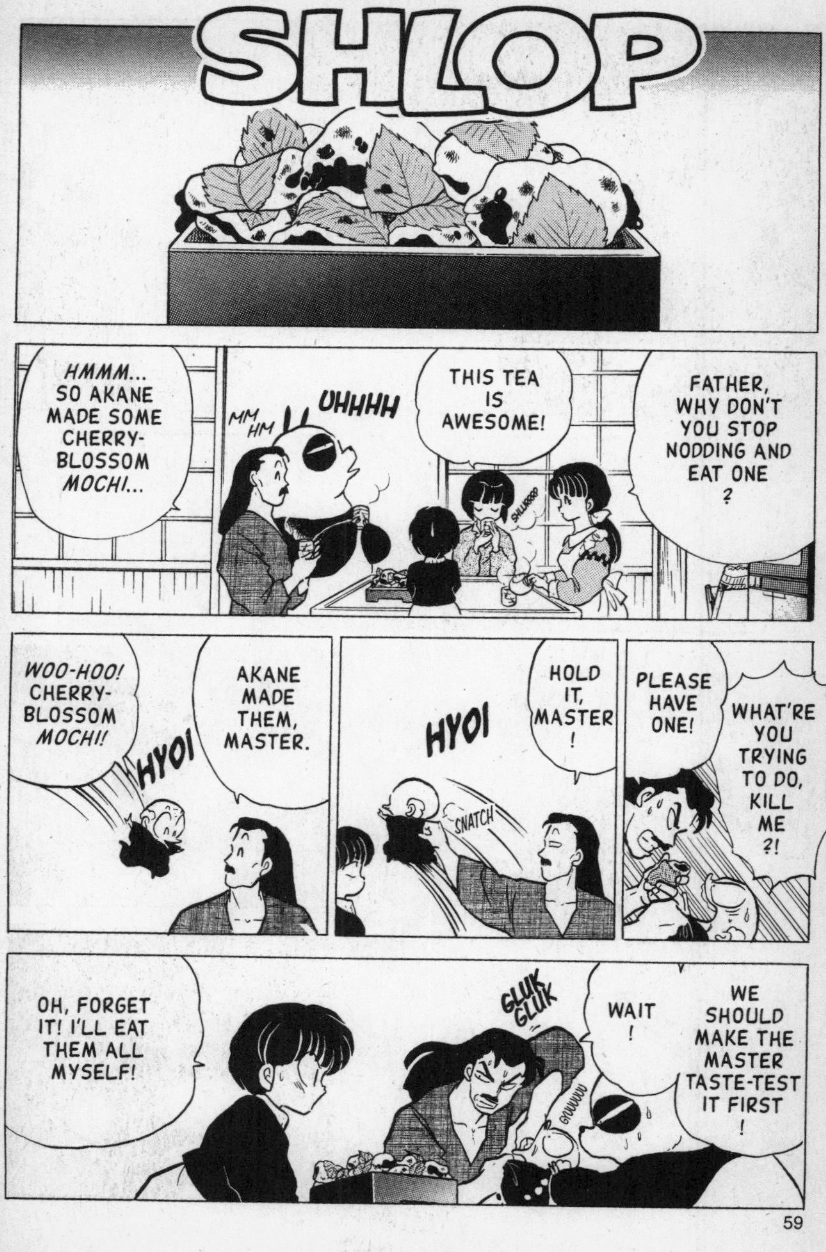
SHLOP
HMMM... SO AKANE MADE SOME CHERRY-BLOSSOM MOCHI...
MM HM
UHHHH
THIS TEA IS AWESOME!
SHLURRRP
FATHER, WHY DON'T YOU STOP NODDING AND EAT ONE ?
WOO-HOO! CHERRY-BLOSSOM MOCHI!
HYOI
AKANE MADE THEM, MASTER.
HYOI
HOLD IT, MASTER !
SNATCH
PLEASE HAVE ONE!
WHAT'RE YOU TRYING TO DO, KILL ME ?!
OH, FORGET IT! I'LL EAT THEM ALL MYSELF!
GLUK GLUK
WAIT !
WE SHOULD MAKE THE MASTER TASTE-TEST IT FIRST !

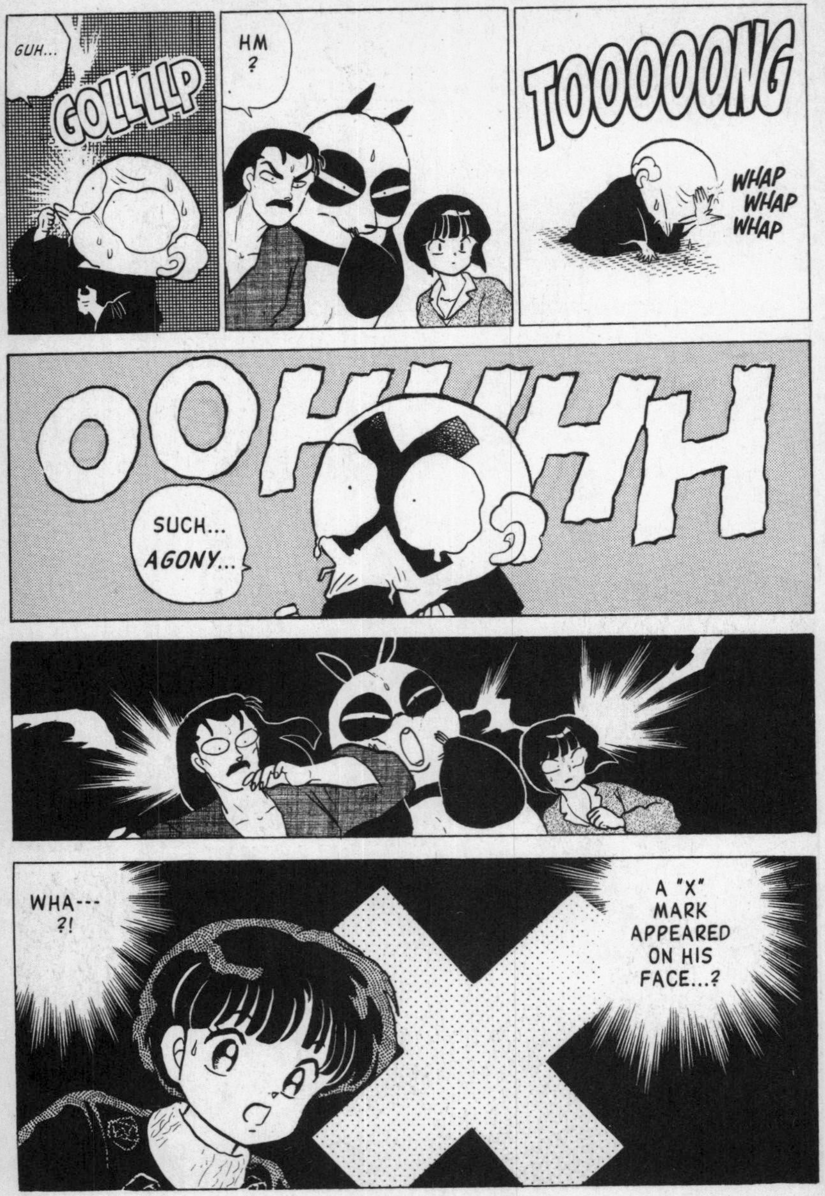
GUH...
GOLLLLP
HM ?
TOOOOONG
WHAP WHAP WHAP
OOHHHH
SUCH... AGONY...
WHA--- ?!
A "X" MARK APPEARED ON HIS FACE...?

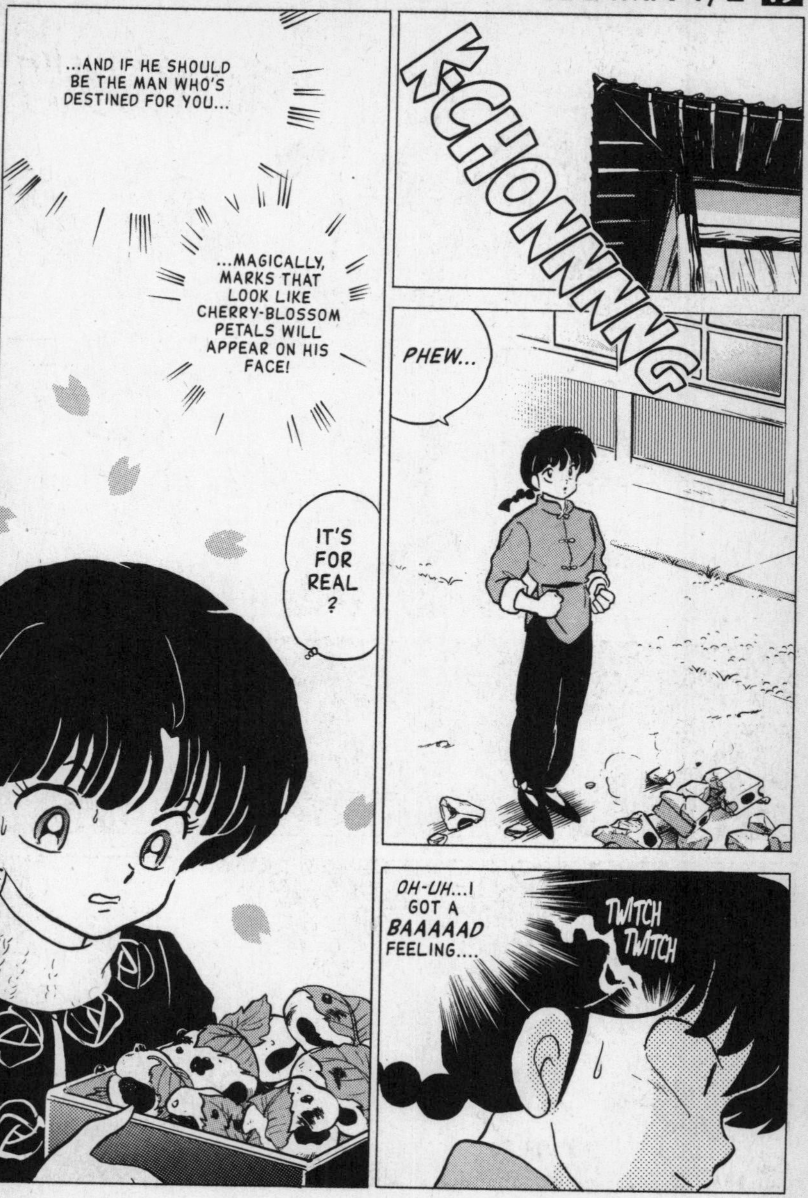
...AND IF HE SHOULD BE THE MAN WHO'S DESTINED FOR YOU...
...MAGICALLY, MARKS THAT LOOK LIKE CHERRY-BLOSSOM PETALS WILL APPEAR ON HIS FACE!
IT'S FOR REAL?
K-CHONNNNG
PHEW...
OH-UH...I GOT A BAAAAAD FEELING....
TWITCH TWITCH

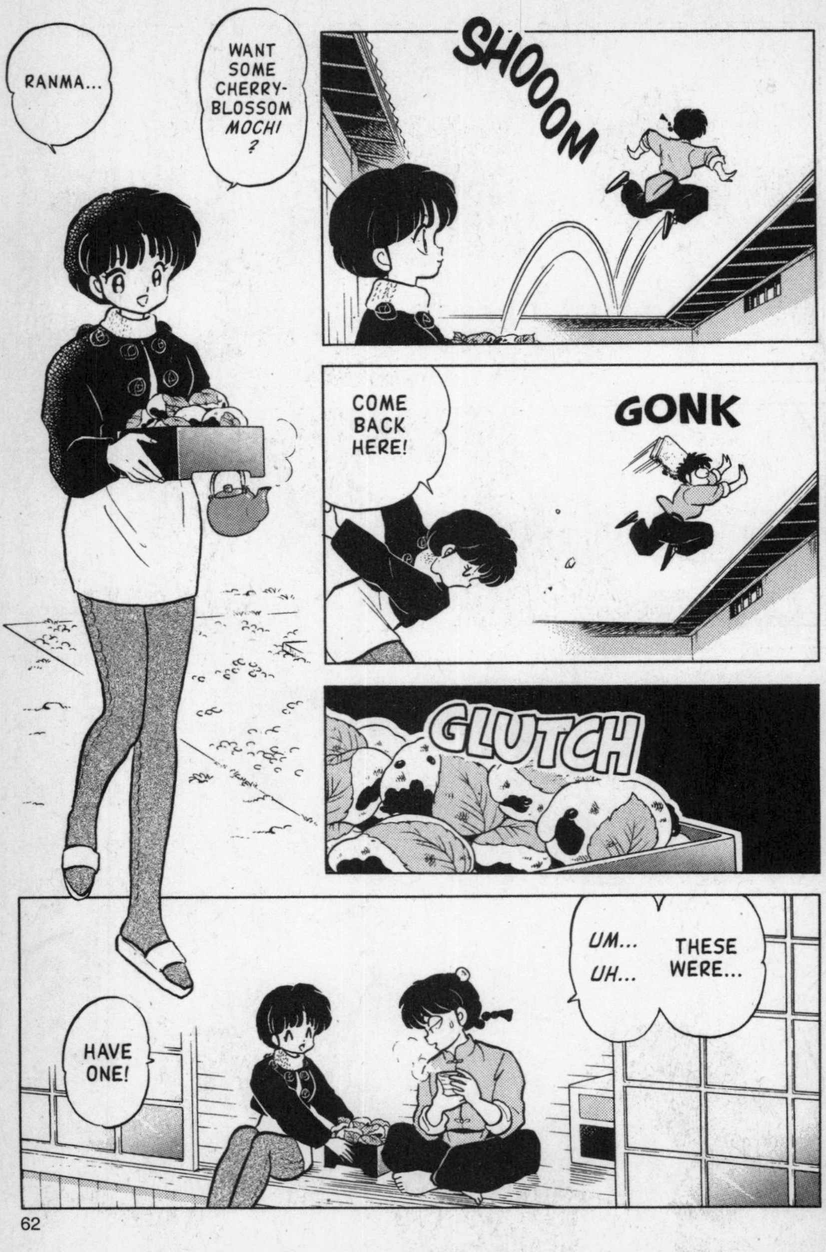
RANMA...
WANT SOME CHERRY-BLOSSOM *MOCHI* ?
SHOOOM
COME BACK HERE!
GONK
GLUTCH
HAVE ONE!
UM... UH...
THESE WERE...

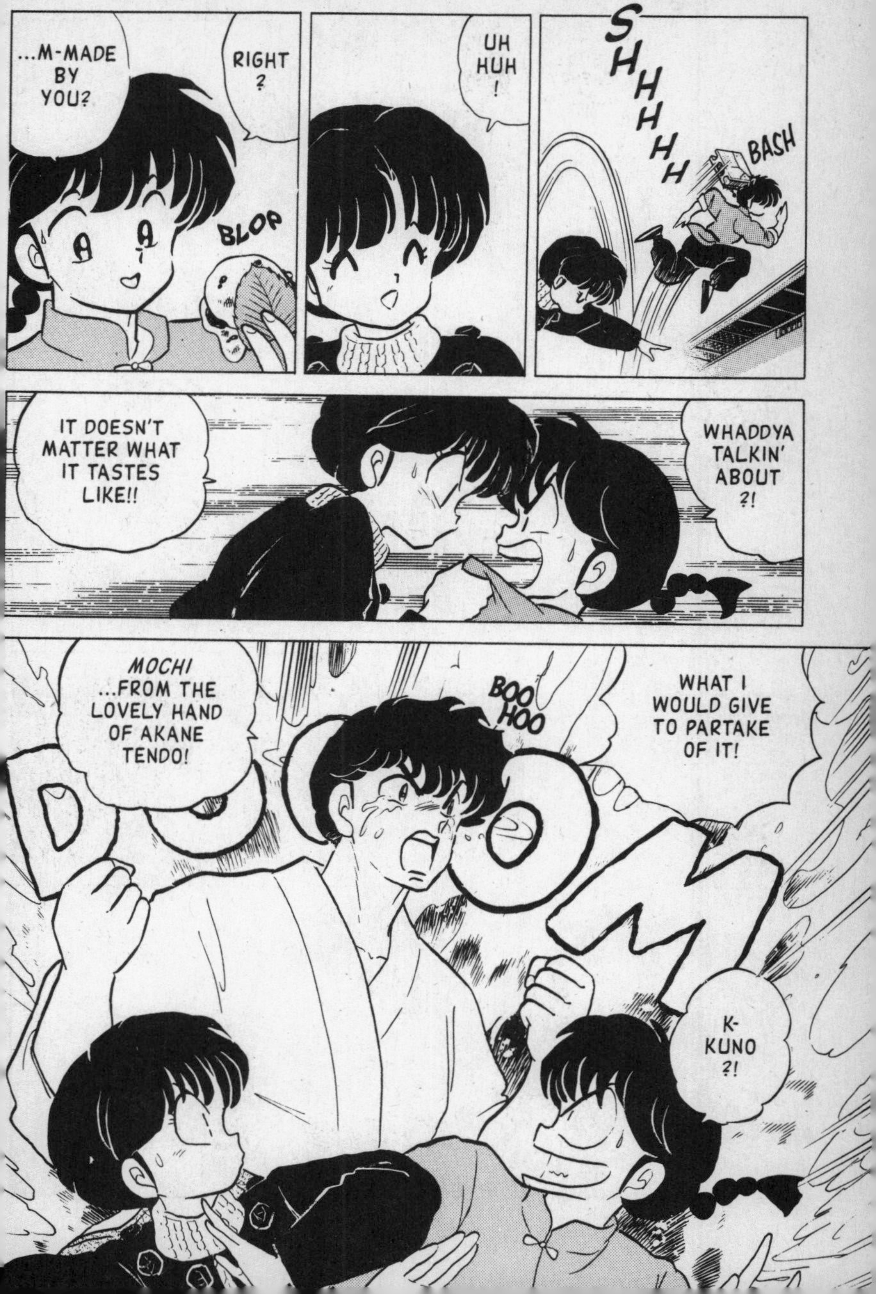
...M-MADE BY YOU?
RIGHT?
BLOP
UH HUH!
SHHHHH
BASH
IT DOESN'T MATTER WHAT IT TASTES LIKE!!
WHADDYA TALKIN' ABOUT?!
MOCHI ...FROM THE LOVELY HAND OF AKANE TENDO!
BOO HOO
WHAT I WOULD GIVE TO PARTAKE OF IT!
DOOM
K-KUNO?!

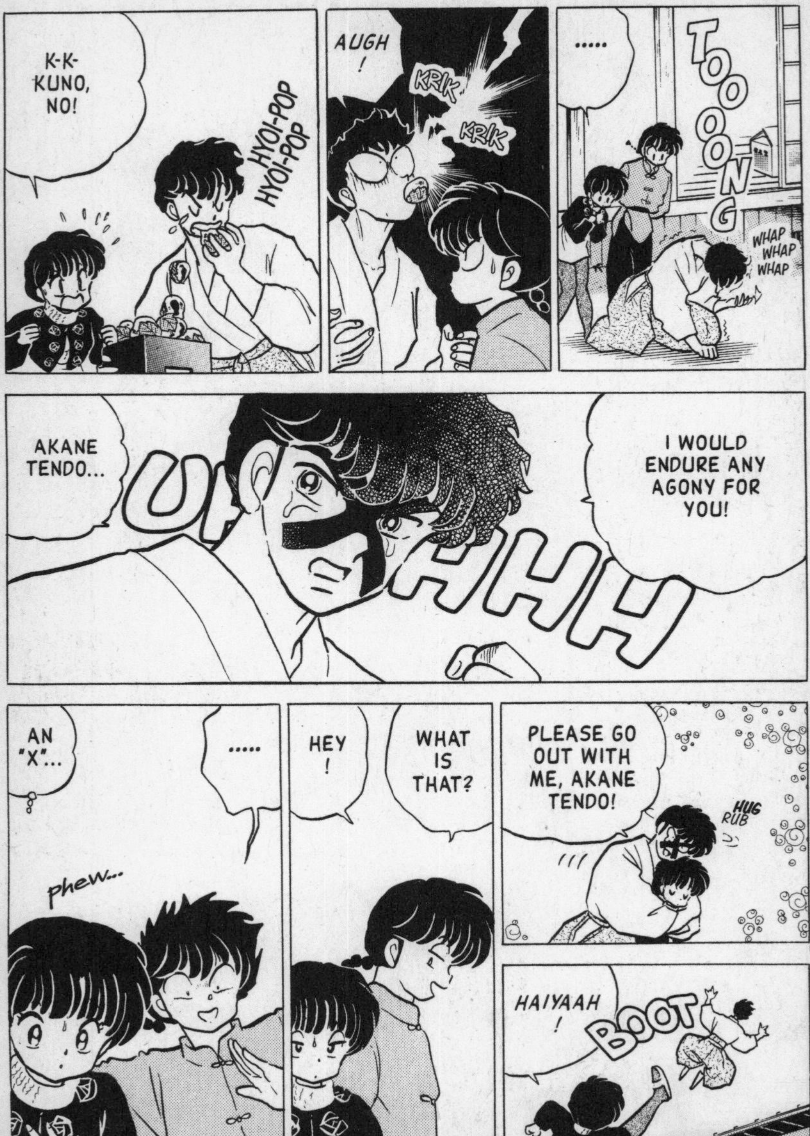
K-K-KUNO, NO!
HYOI-POP HYOI-POP
AUGH!
KRIK
KRIK
.....
TOOOOONG
WHAP WHAP WHAP
AKANE TENDO...
UHHHH
I WOULD ENDURE ANY AGONY FOR YOU!
AN "X"...
.....
phew...
HEY!
WHAT IS THAT?
PLEASE GO OUT WITH ME, AKANE TENDO!
HUG RUB
HAIYAAH!
BOOT

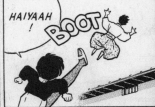

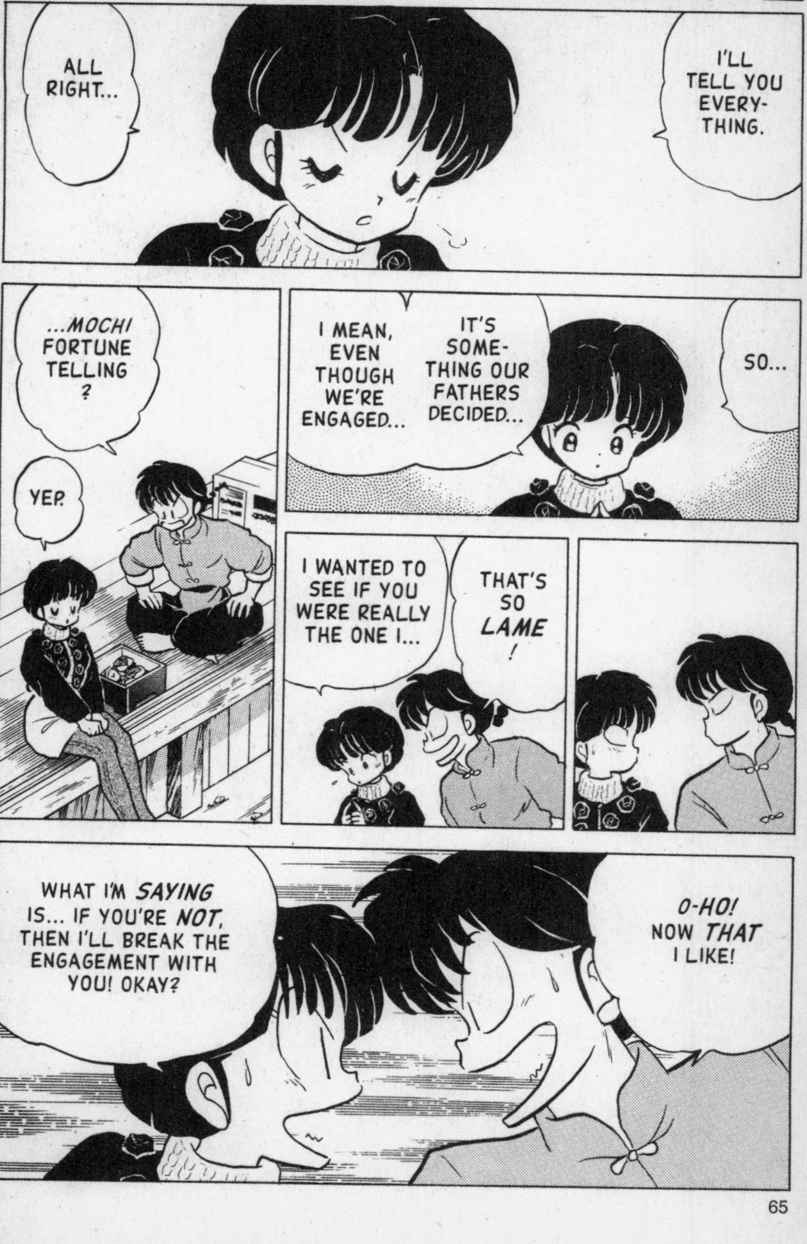
ALL RIGHT...
I'LL TELL YOU EVERY-THING.
...MOCHI FORTUNE TELLING?
YEP.
I MEAN, EVEN THOUGH WE'RE ENGAGED...
IT'S SOME-THING OUR FATHERS DECIDED...
SO...
I WANTED TO SEE IF YOU WERE REALLY THE ONE I...
THAT'S SO LAME!
WHAT I'M SAYING IS... IF YOU'RE NOT, THEN I'LL BREAK THE ENGAGEMENT WITH YOU! OKAY?
O-HO! NOW THAT I LIKE!

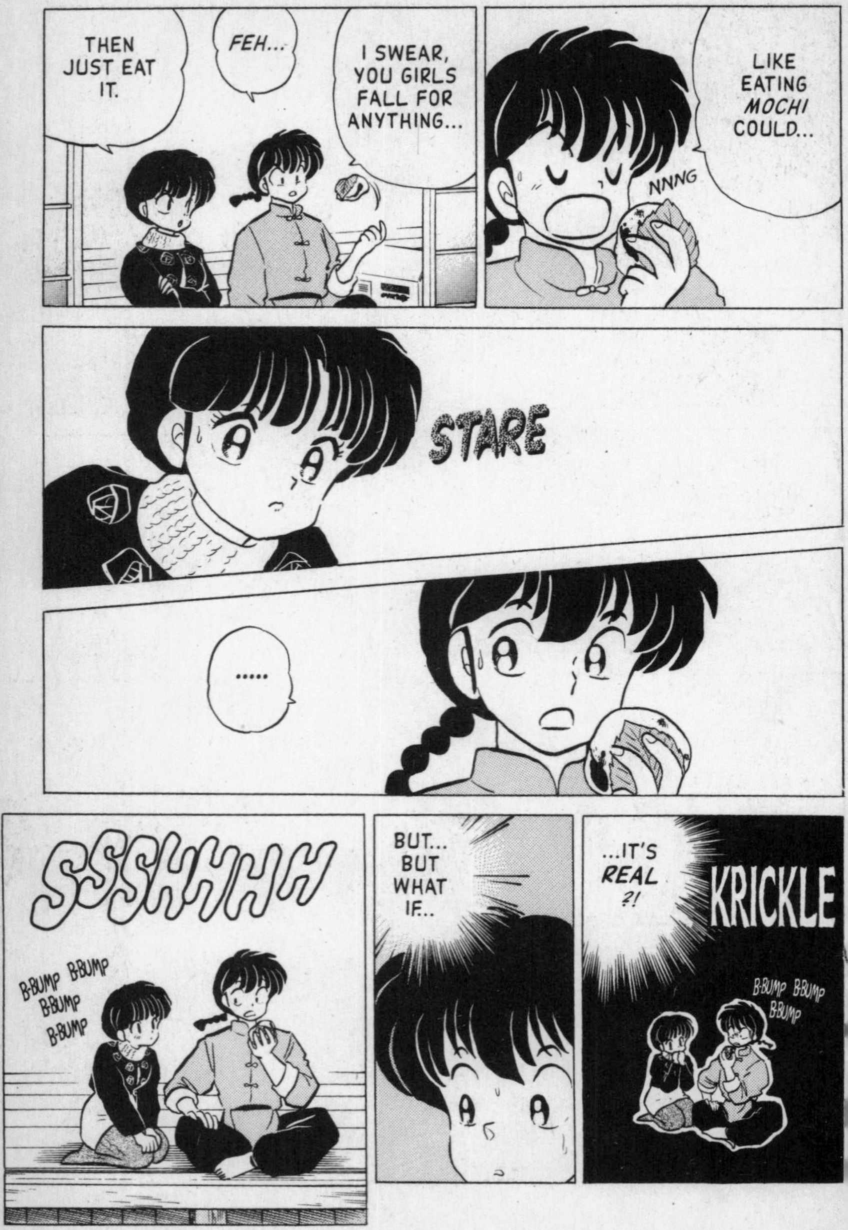
THEN JUST EAT IT.
FEH...
I SWEAR, YOU GIRLS FALL FOR ANYTHING...
LIKE EATING MOCHI COULD...
NNNG
STARE
......
SSSHHHH
B-BUMP B-BUMP B-BUMP B-BUMP
BUT... BUT WHAT IF...
...IT'S REAL ?!
KRICKLE
B-BUMP B-BUMP B-BUMP

NO !

NO WAY !

NOW WHAT ?

WELL, I'M SCARED...

...BUT NOT OF A *SNACK* SEALING MY FATE...

...WHAT I'M REALLY TERRIFIED OF..

BRRR BRRR BRRR

...IS EATING FOOD MADE BY *YOU*!!

CHHHOOOM

HYUUUUUU

RANMA! YOU WAIT UP!

GWIP

GET BACK HERE, YOU!

NEVER !

CHHHOOOM

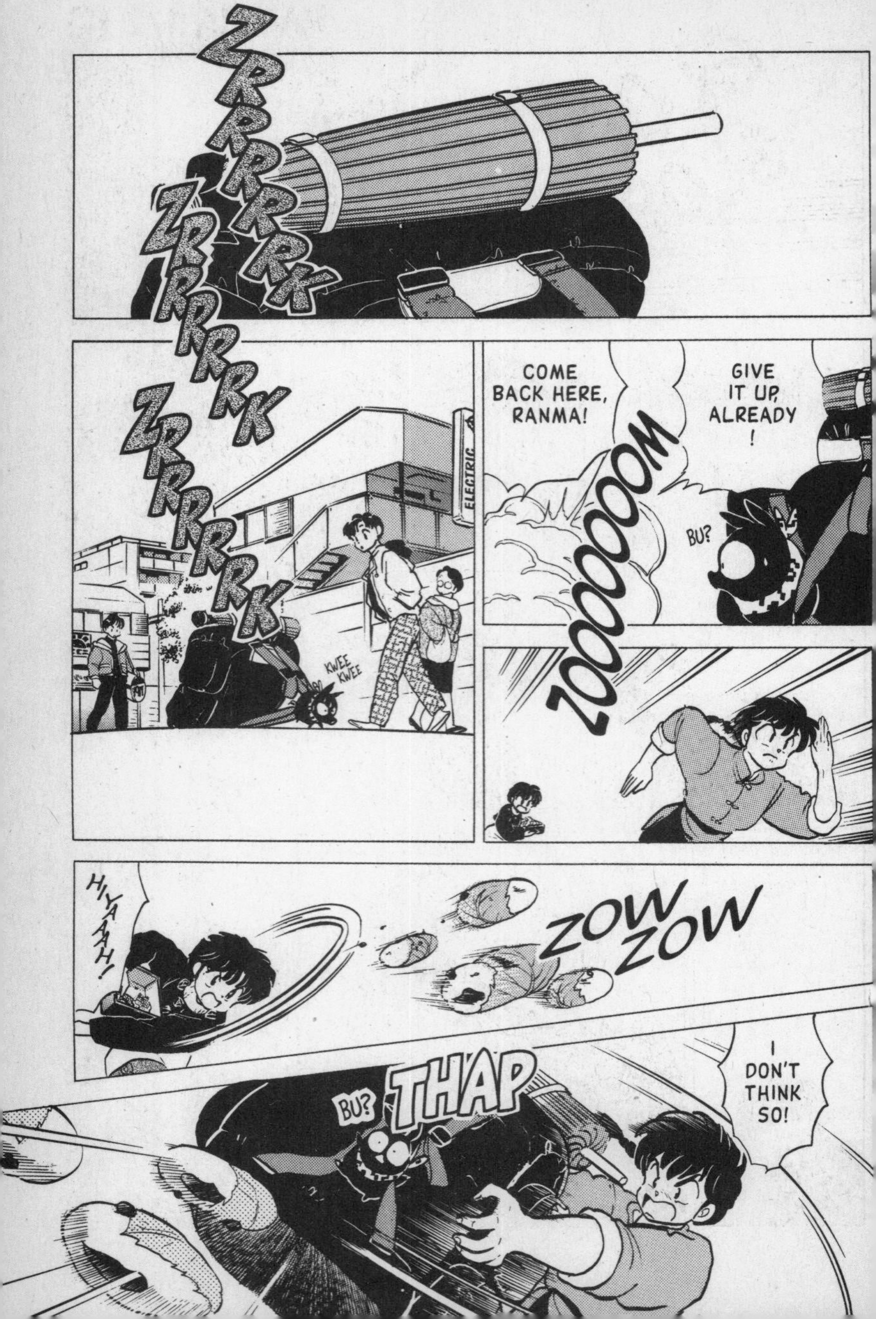
ZRRRRK
ZRRRRRK
ZRRRRRRK
ELECTRIC
KWEE KWEE
COME BACK HERE, RANMA!
GIVE IT UP, ALREADY!
ZOOOOOOM
BU?
HIYAAAH!
ZOW ZOW
BU?
THAP
I DON'T THINK SO!

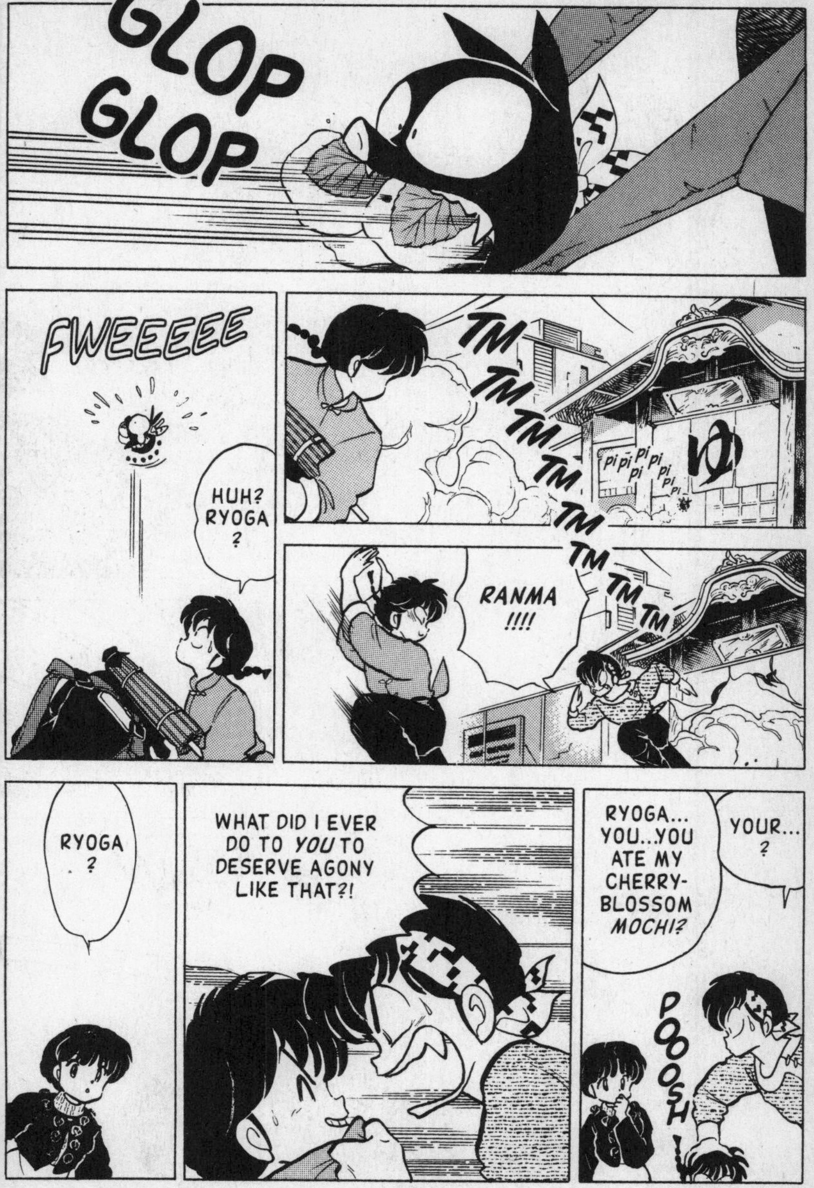
GLOP GLOP
FWEEEEE
HUH? RYOGA ?
TM TM TM TM TM
pi pi pi pi pi pi pi
RANMA !!!!
TM TM TM
RYOGA ?
WHAT DID I EVER DO TO *YOU* TO DESERVE AGONY LIKE THAT?!
RYOGA... YOU...YOU ATE MY CHERRY-BLOSSOM *MOCHI*?
YOUR... ?
POOOSH

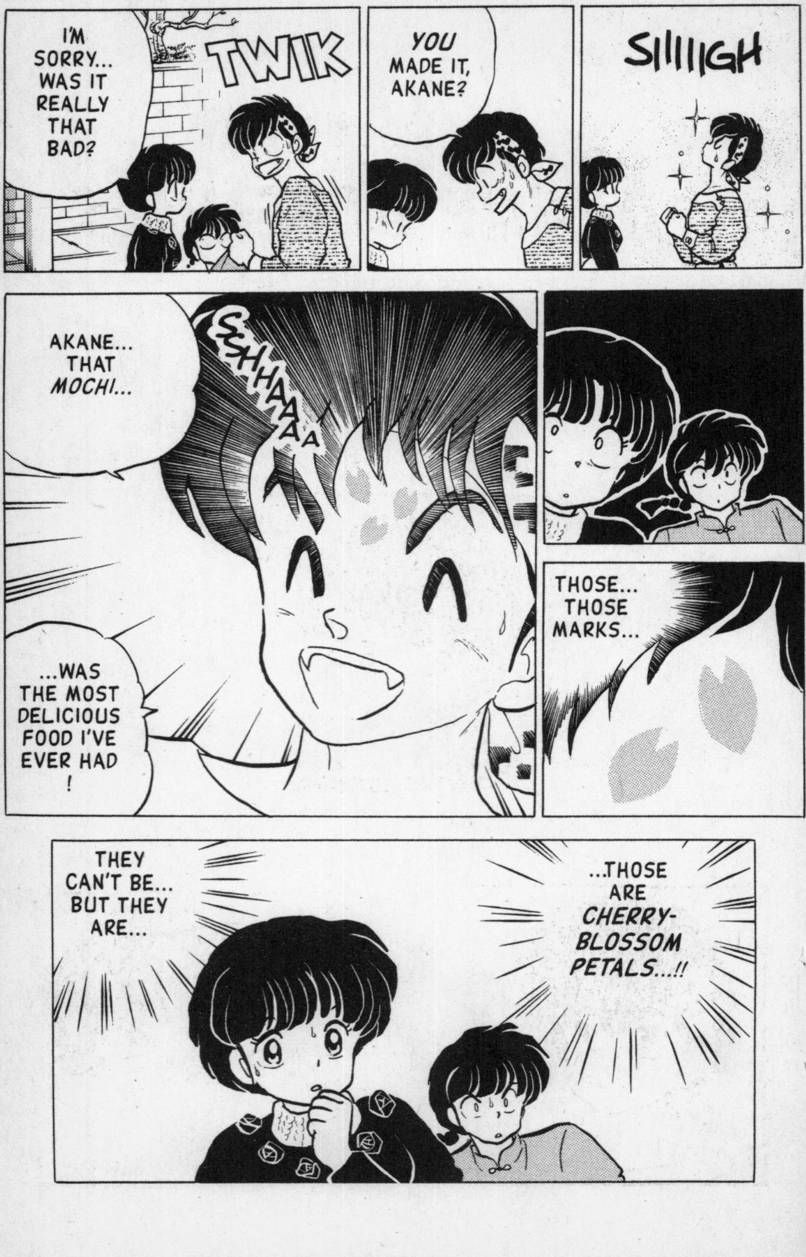
I'M SORRY... WAS IT REALLY THAT BAD?
TWIK
YOU MADE IT, AKANE?
SIIIIGH
AKANE... THAT *MOCHI*...
SSHHAAAAA
...WAS THE MOST DELICIOUS FOOD I'VE EVER HAD!
THOSE... THOSE MARKS...
THEY CAN'T BE... BUT THEY ARE...
...THOSE ARE *CHERRY-BLOSSOM PETALS*...!!

Part 5
AKANE'S FEELINGS

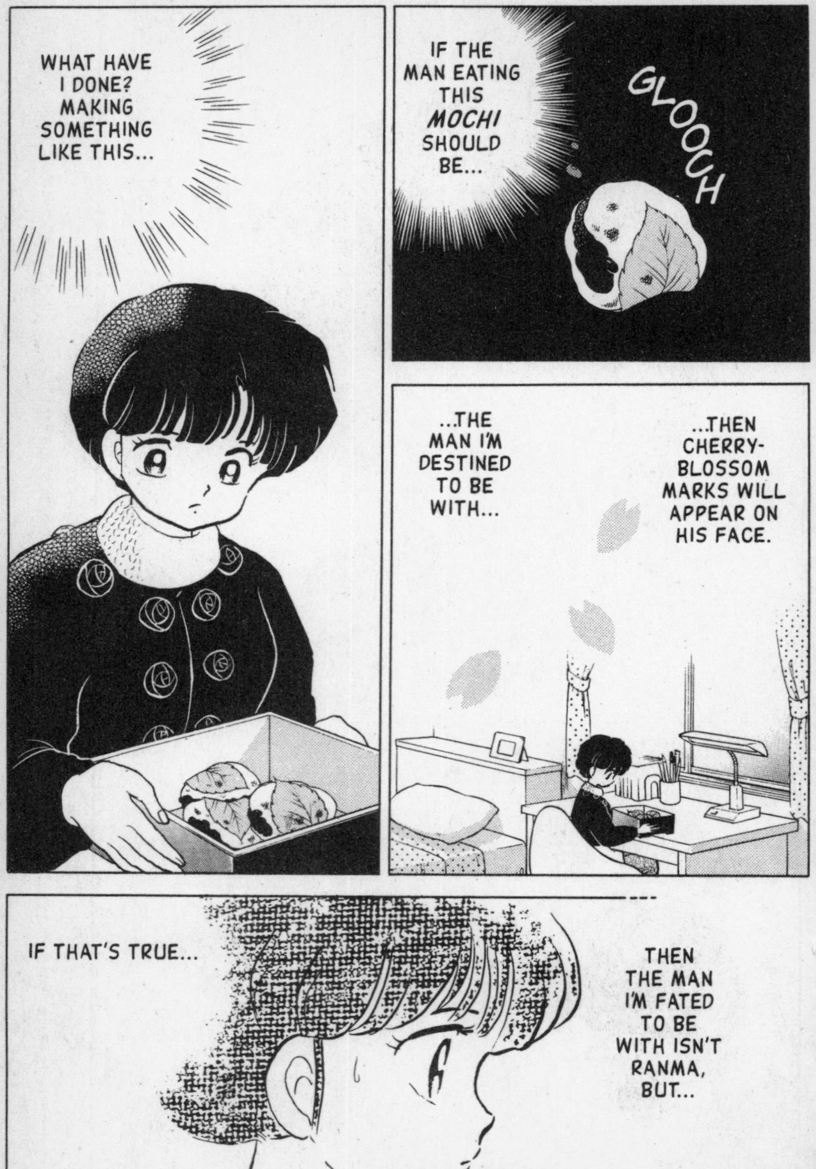
WHAT HAVE I DONE? MAKING SOMETHING LIKE THIS...
IF THE MAN EATING THIS *MOCHI* SHOULD BE...
GLOOCH
...THE MAN I'M DESTINED TO BE WITH...
...THEN CHERRY-BLOSSOM MARKS WILL APPEAR ON HIS FACE.
IF THAT'S TRUE...
THEN THE MAN I'M FATED TO BE WITH ISN'T RANMA, BUT...

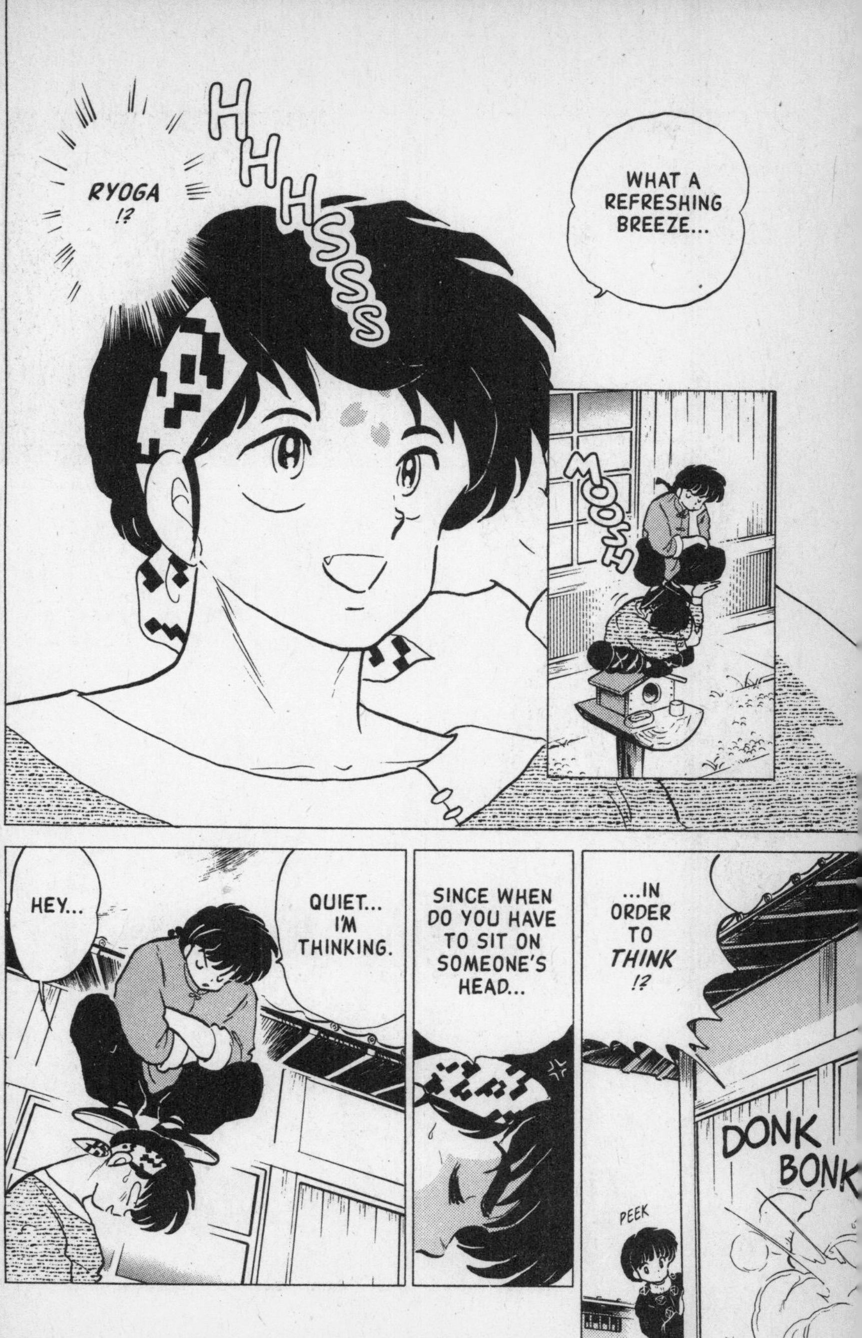
RYOGA !?
HHHSSS
WHAT A REFRESHING BREEZE...
WOOSH
HEY...
QUIET... I'M THINKING.
SINCE WHEN DO YOU HAVE TO SIT ON SOMEONE'S HEAD...
...IN ORDER TO THINK !?
DONK
BONK
PEEK

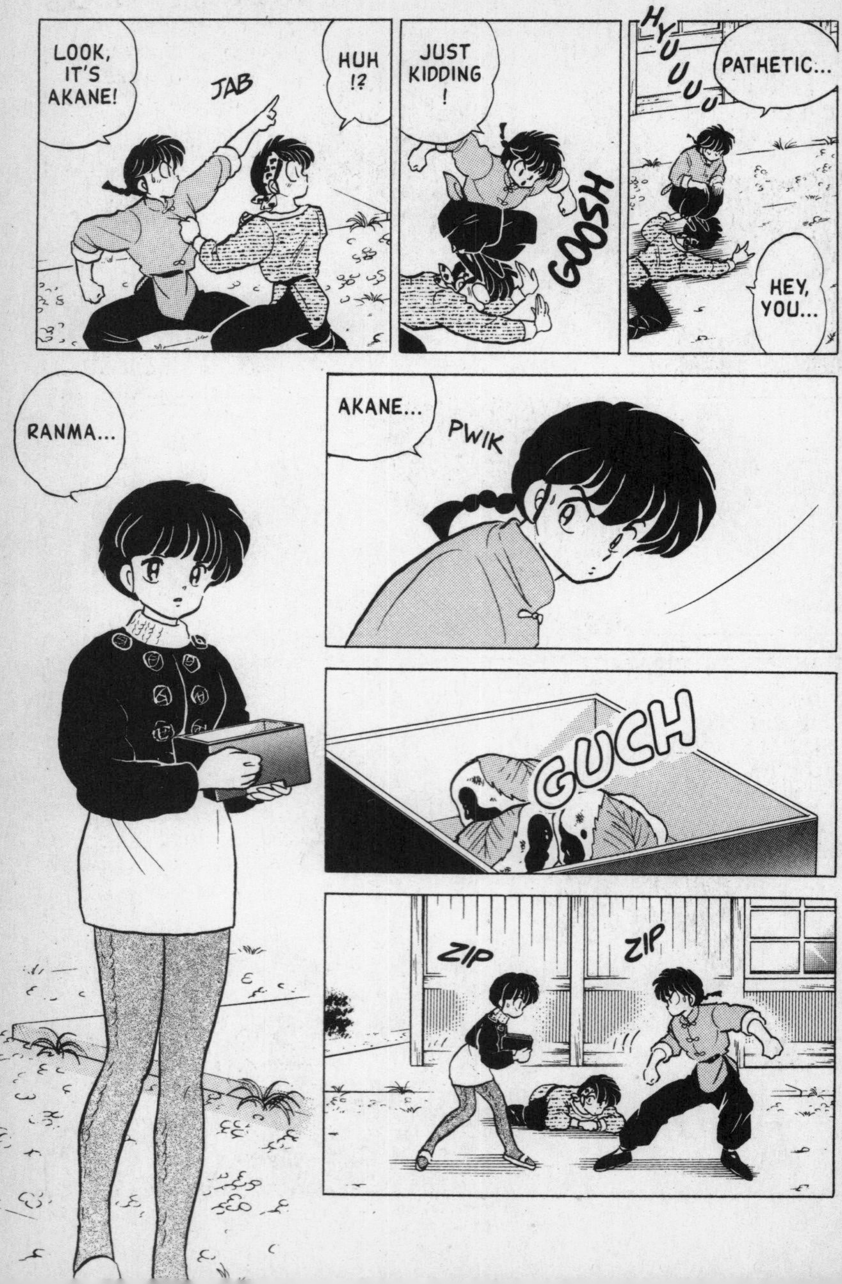
LOOK, IT'S AKANE!
JAB
HUH !?
JUST KIDDING !
GOOSH
HYUUUUU
PATHETIC...
HEY, YOU...
RANMA...
AKANE...
PWIK
GUCH
ZIP
ZIP

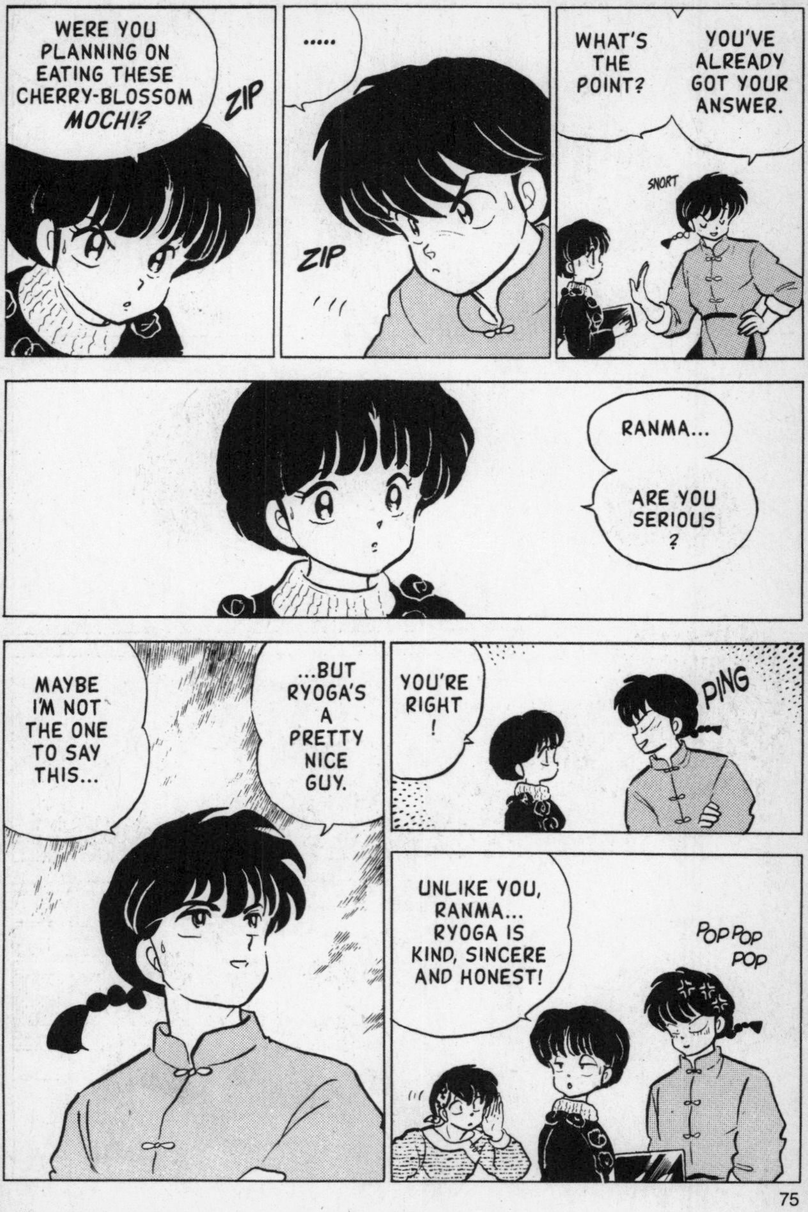
WERE YOU PLANNING ON EATING THESE CHERRY-BLOSSOM *MOCHI?*
ZIP
.....
ZIP
WHAT'S THE POINT?
YOU'VE ALREADY GOT YOUR ANSWER.
SNORT
RANMA...
ARE YOU SERIOUS ?
MAYBE I'M NOT THE ONE TO SAY THIS...
...BUT RYOGA'S A PRETTY NICE GUY.
YOU'RE RIGHT !
PING
UNLIKE YOU, RANMA... RYOGA IS KIND, SINCERE AND HONEST!
POP POP POP

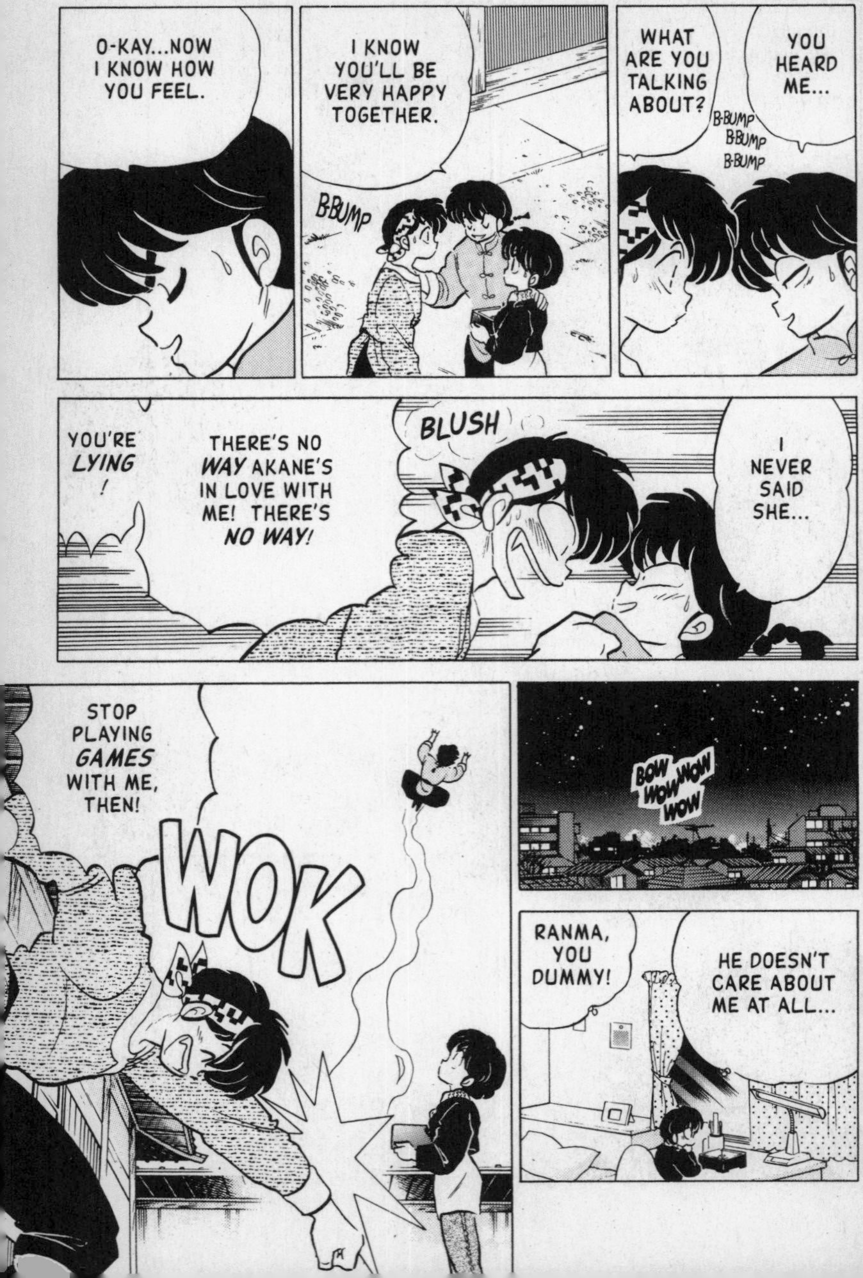
O-KAY...NOW I KNOW HOW YOU FEEL.
I KNOW YOU'LL BE VERY HAPPY TOGETHER.
B-BUMP
WHAT ARE YOU TALKING ABOUT?
B-BUMP B-BUMP B-BUMP
YOU HEARD ME...
YOU'RE *LYING*!
THERE'S NO *WAY* AKANE'S IN LOVE WITH ME! THERE'S *NO WAY!*
BLUSH
I NEVER SAID SHE...
STOP PLAYING *GAMES* WITH ME, THEN!
WOK
BOW WOW WOW WOW
RANMA, YOU DUMMY!
HE DOESN'T CARE ABOUT ME AT ALL...

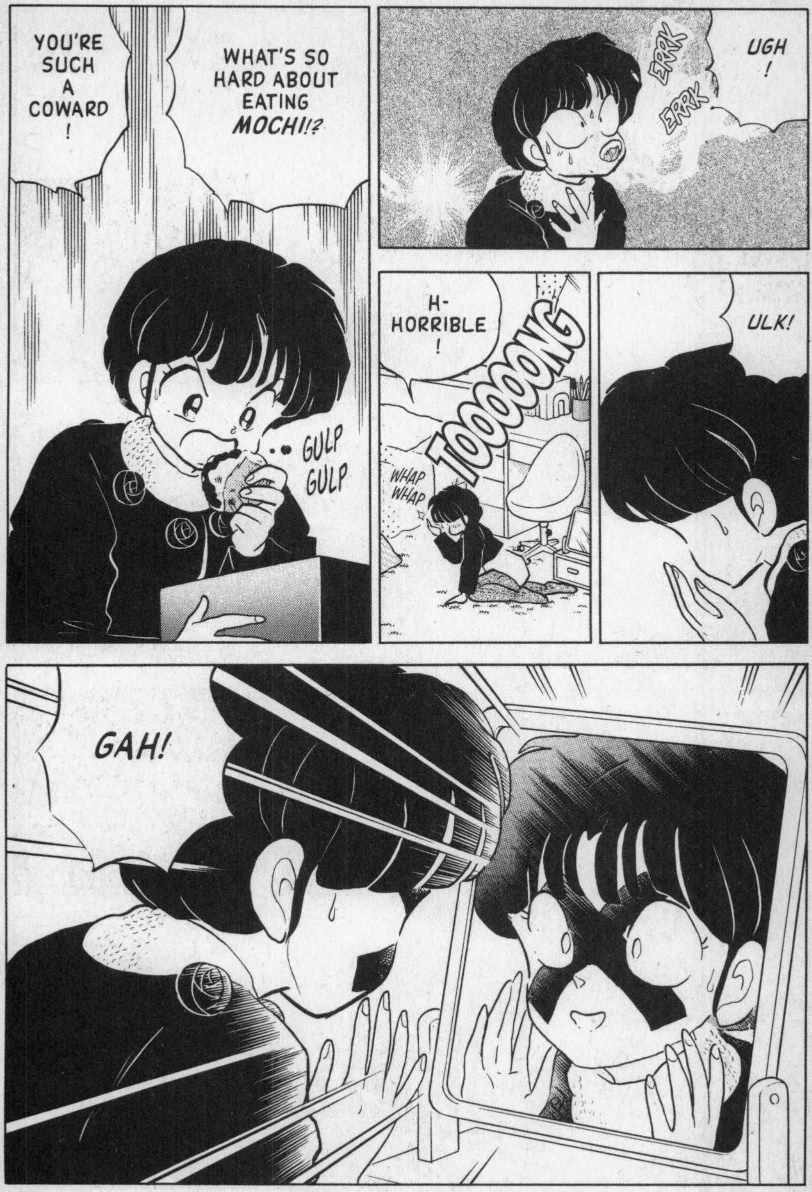
YOU'RE SUCH A COWARD!
WHAT'S SO HARD ABOUT EATING MOCHI!?
GULP GULP
ERRK
ERRK
UGH!
H-HORRIBLE!
TOOOOOONG
WHAP WHAP
ULK!
GAH!

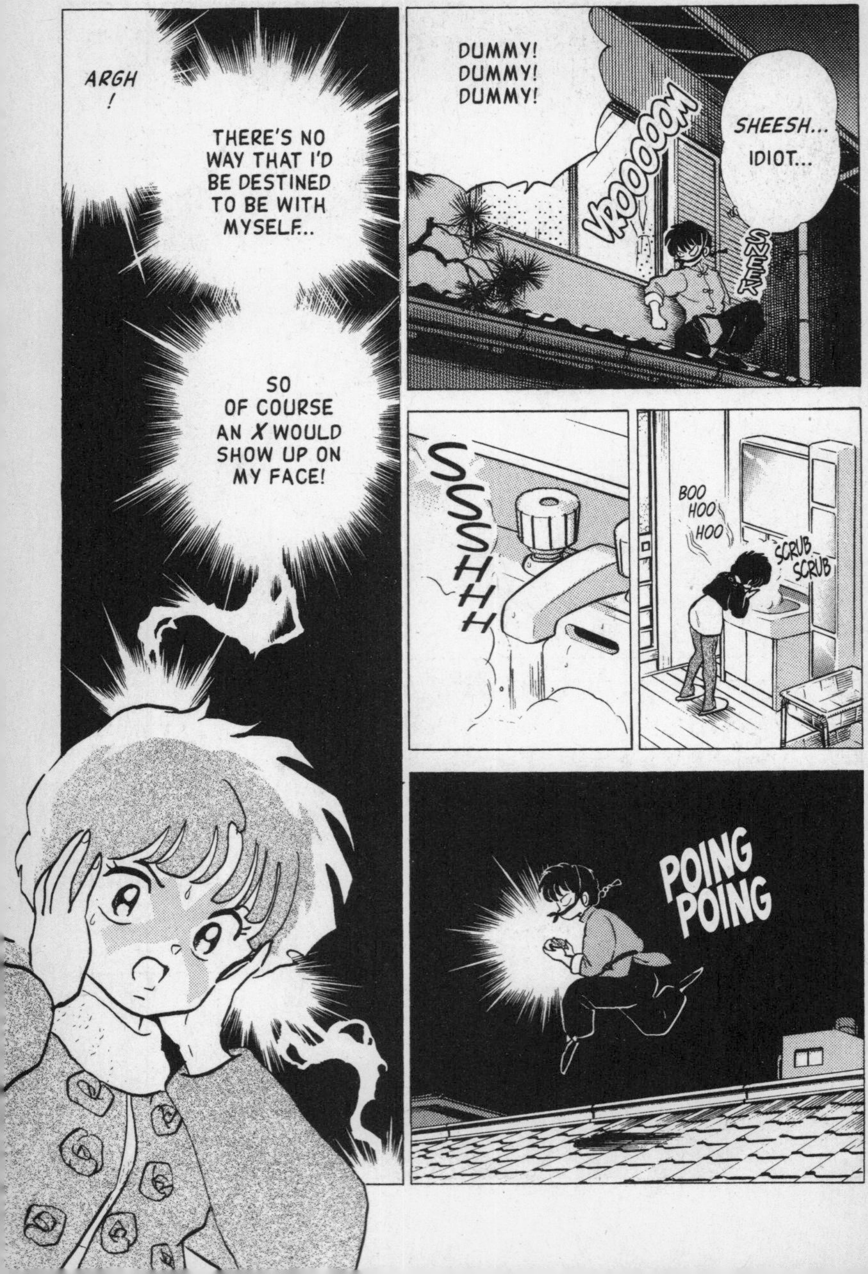
ARGH!
THERE'S NO WAY THAT I'D BE DESTINED TO BE WITH MYSELF...
SO OF COURSE AN X WOULD SHOW UP ON MY FACE!
DUMMY! DUMMY! DUMMY!
VROOOOOM
SHEESH... IDIOT...
SNEEK
SSSHHH
BOO HOO HOO
SCRUB SCRUB
POING POING

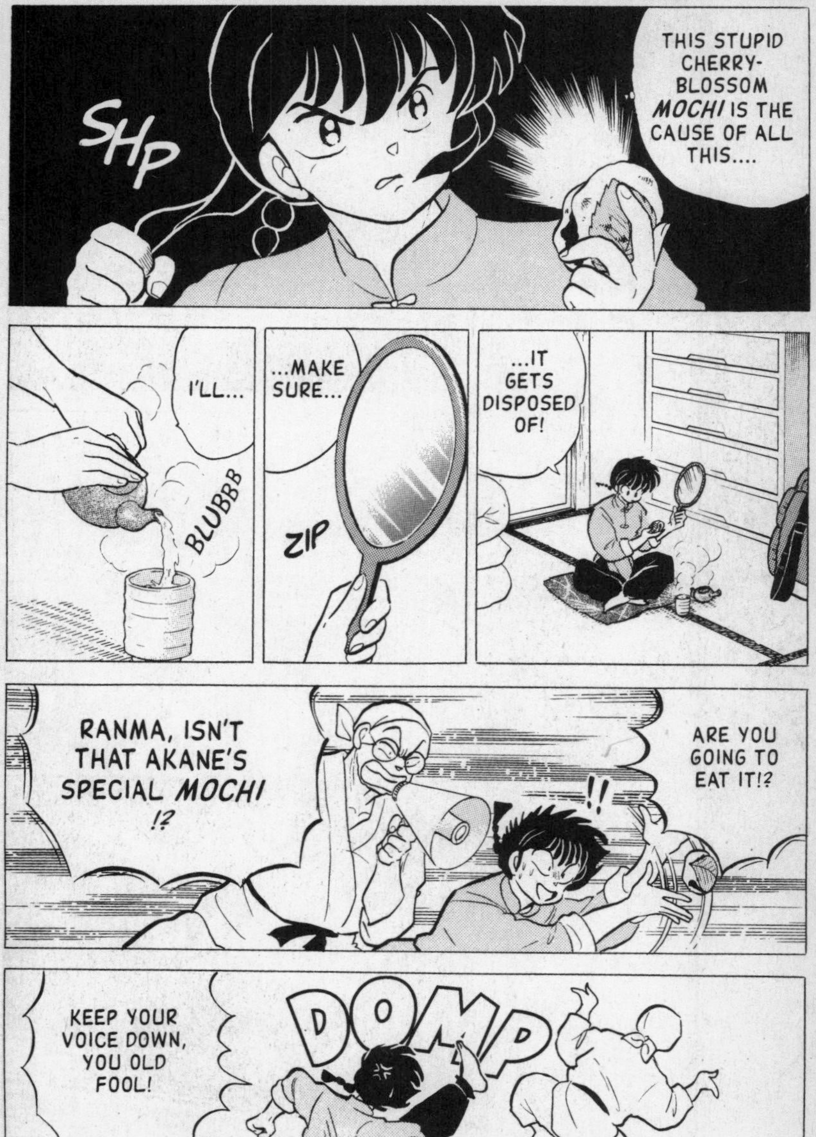
SHP
THIS STUPID CHERRY-BLOSSOM *MOCHI* IS THE CAUSE OF ALL THIS....
I'LL...
BLUBBB
...MAKE SURE...
ZIP
...IT GETS DISPOSED OF!
RANMA, ISN'T THAT AKANE'S SPECIAL *MOCHI* !?
!!
ARE YOU GOING TO EAT IT!?
KEEP YOUR VOICE DOWN, YOU OLD FOOL!
DOMP

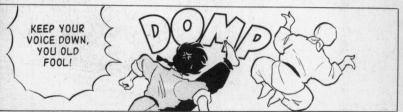

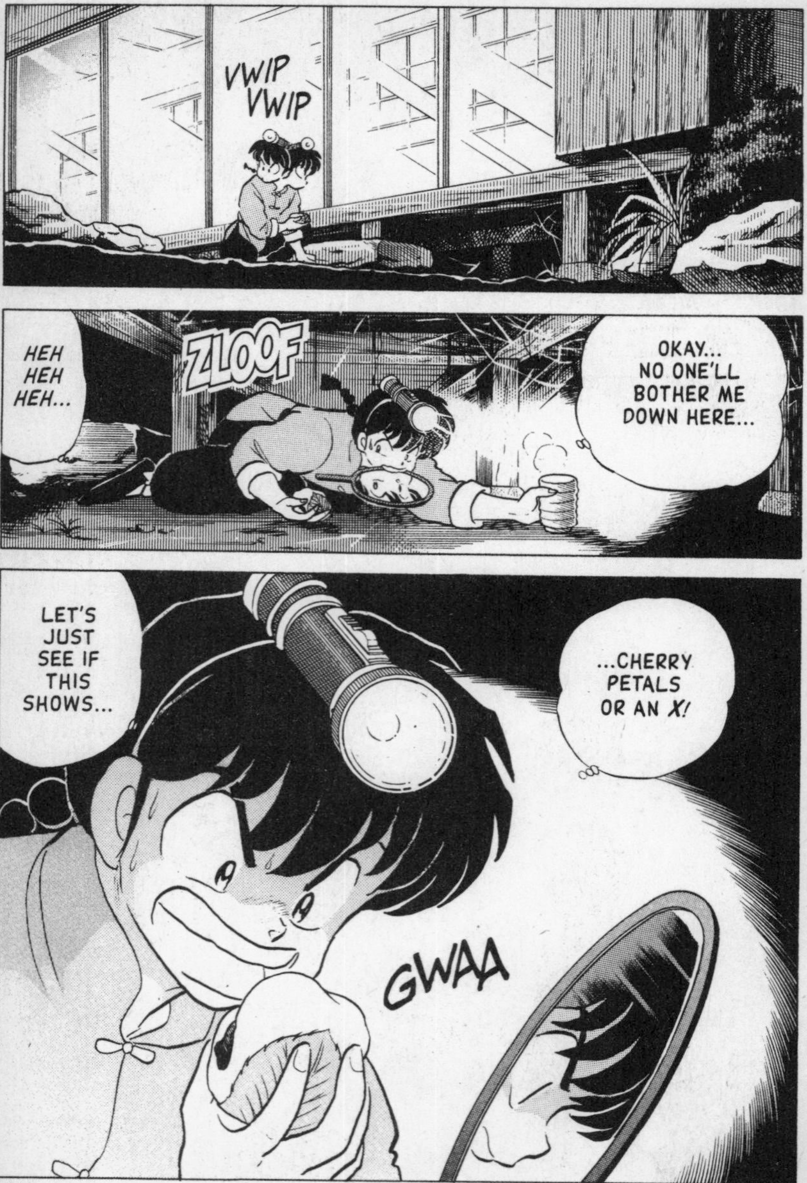
VWIP VWIP
HEH HEH HEH...
ZLOOF
OKAY... NO ONE'LL BOTHER ME DOWN HERE...
LET'S JUST SEE IF THIS SHOWS...
...CHERRY PETALS OR AN X!
GWAA

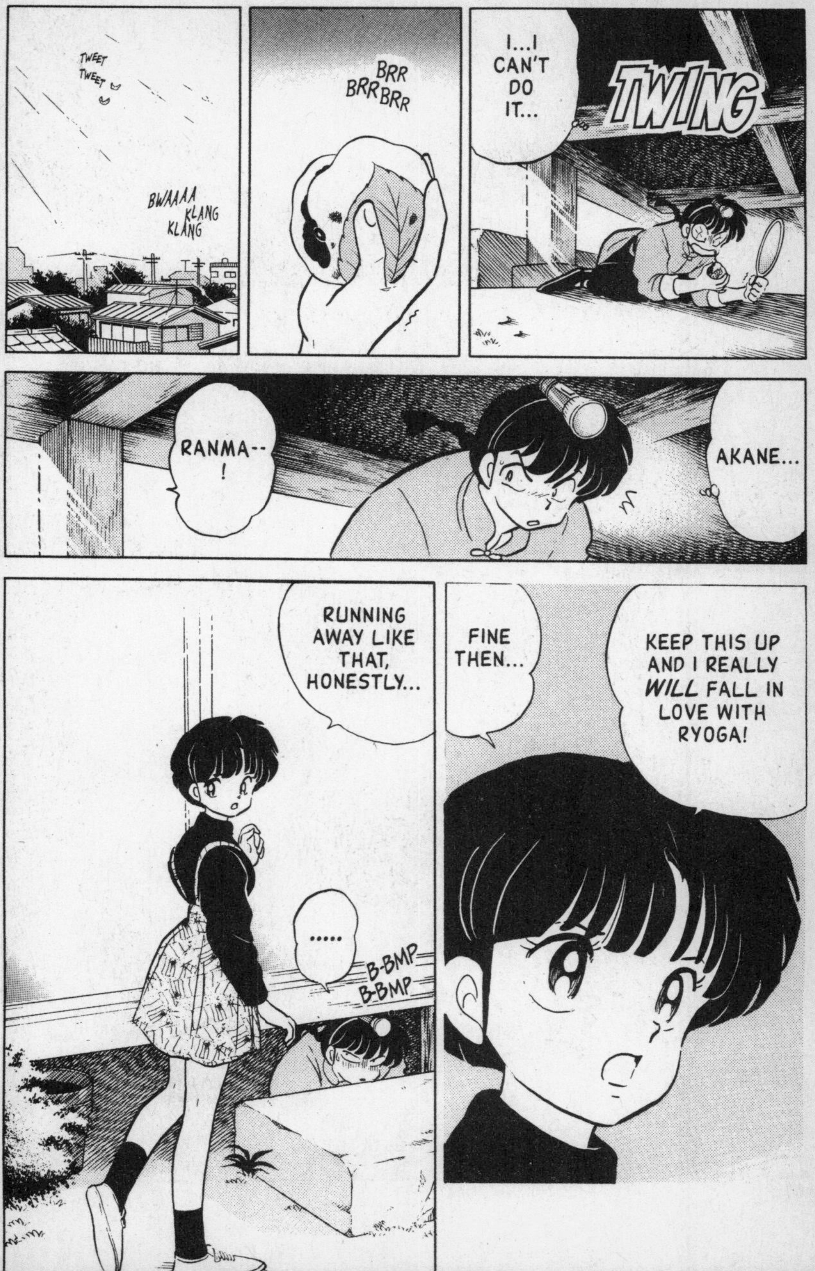
TWEET
TWEET
BWAAAA
KLANG
KLANG
BRR
BRRBRR
I...I CAN'T DO IT...
TWING
RANMA--!
AKANE...
RUNNING AWAY LIKE THAT, HONESTLY...
.....
B-BMP
B-BMP
FINE THEN...
KEEP THIS UP AND I REALLY WILL FALL IN LOVE WITH RYOGA!

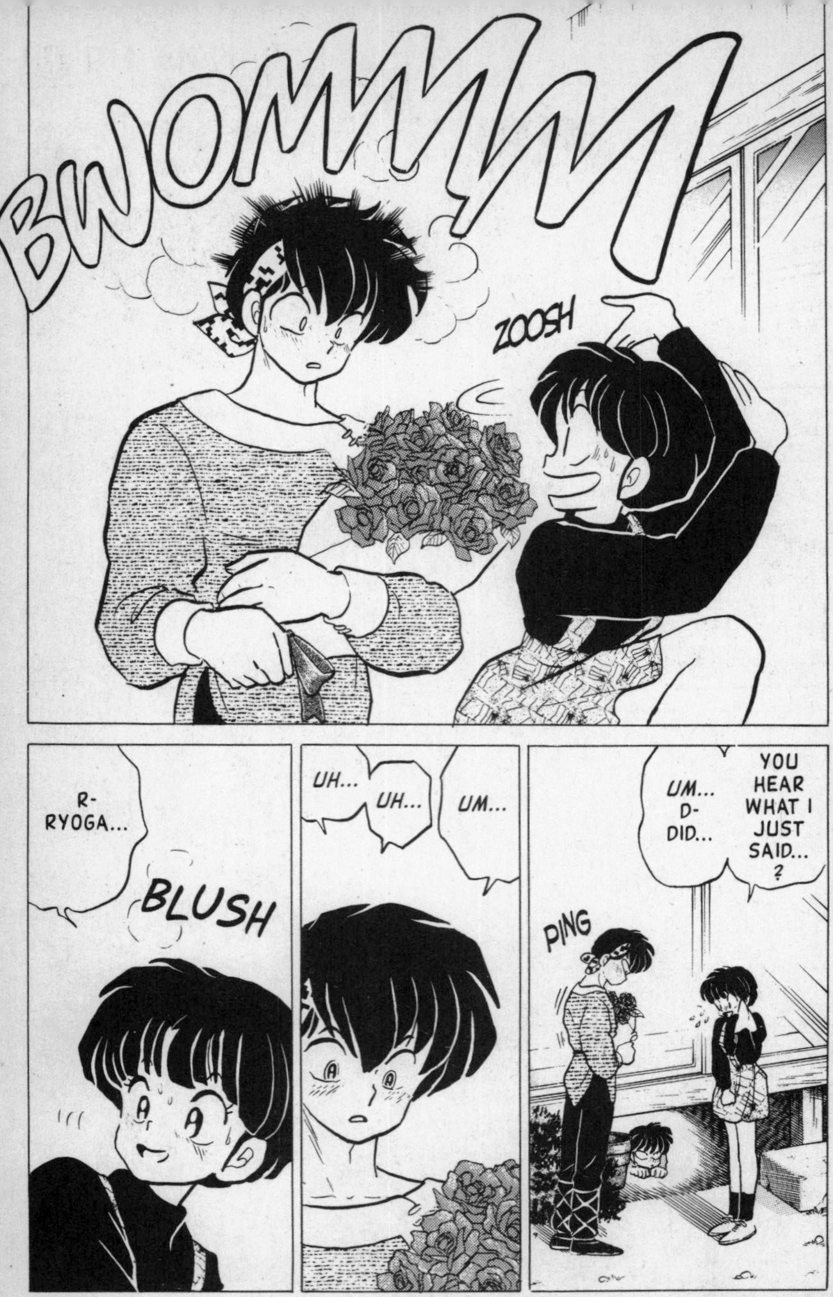
BWOMMM
ZOOSH
R-RYOGA...
BLUSH
UH...
UH...
UM...
UM... D-DID...
YOU HEAR WHAT I JUST SAID...?
PING

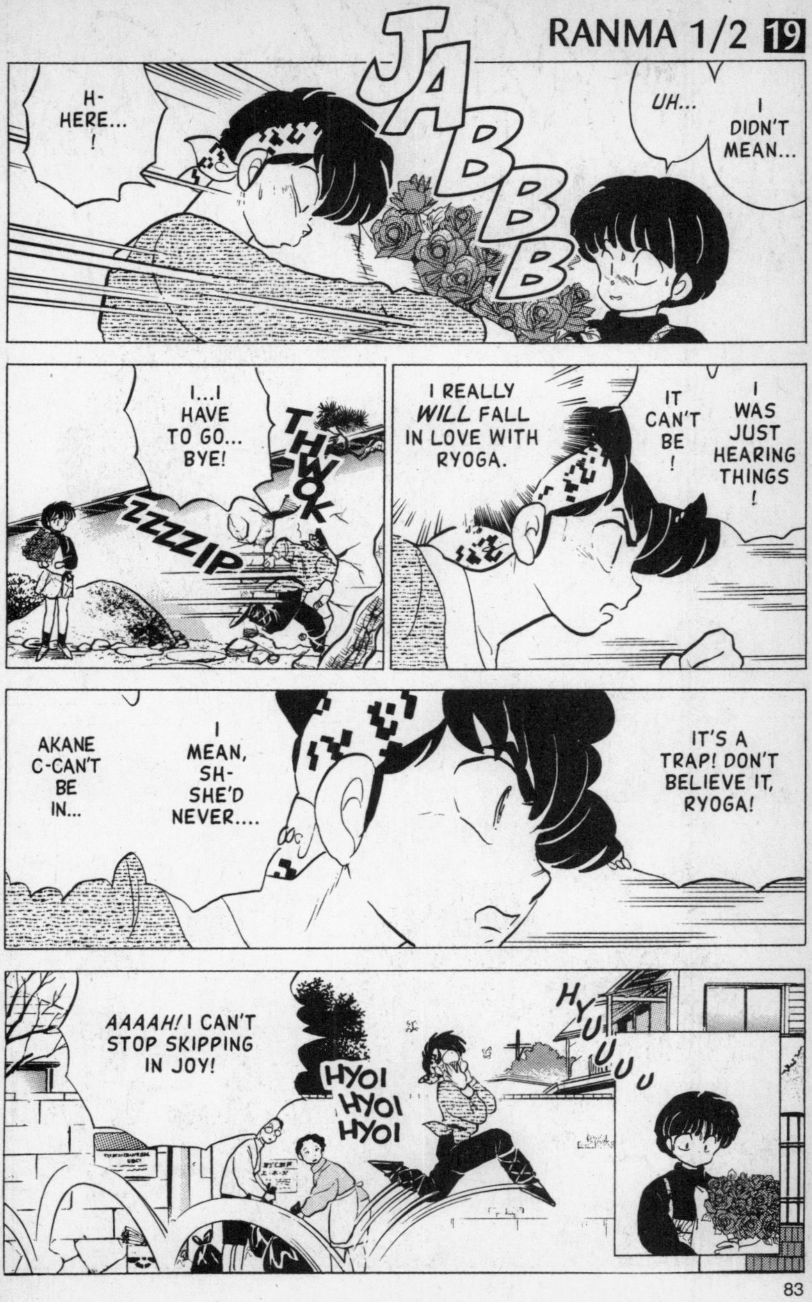
H-HERE...!
JABBB
UH...
I DIDN'T MEAN...
I...I HAVE TO GO... BYE!
THWOK
ZZZZIP
I REALLY *WILL* FALL IN LOVE WITH RYOGA.
IT CAN'T BE!
I WAS JUST HEARING THINGS!
AKANE C-CAN'T BE IN...
I MEAN, SH-SHE'D NEVER....
IT'S A TRAP! DON'T BELIEVE IT, RYOGA!
AAAAH! I CAN'T STOP SKIPPING IN JOY!
HYOI HYOI HYOI
HYUUUUU

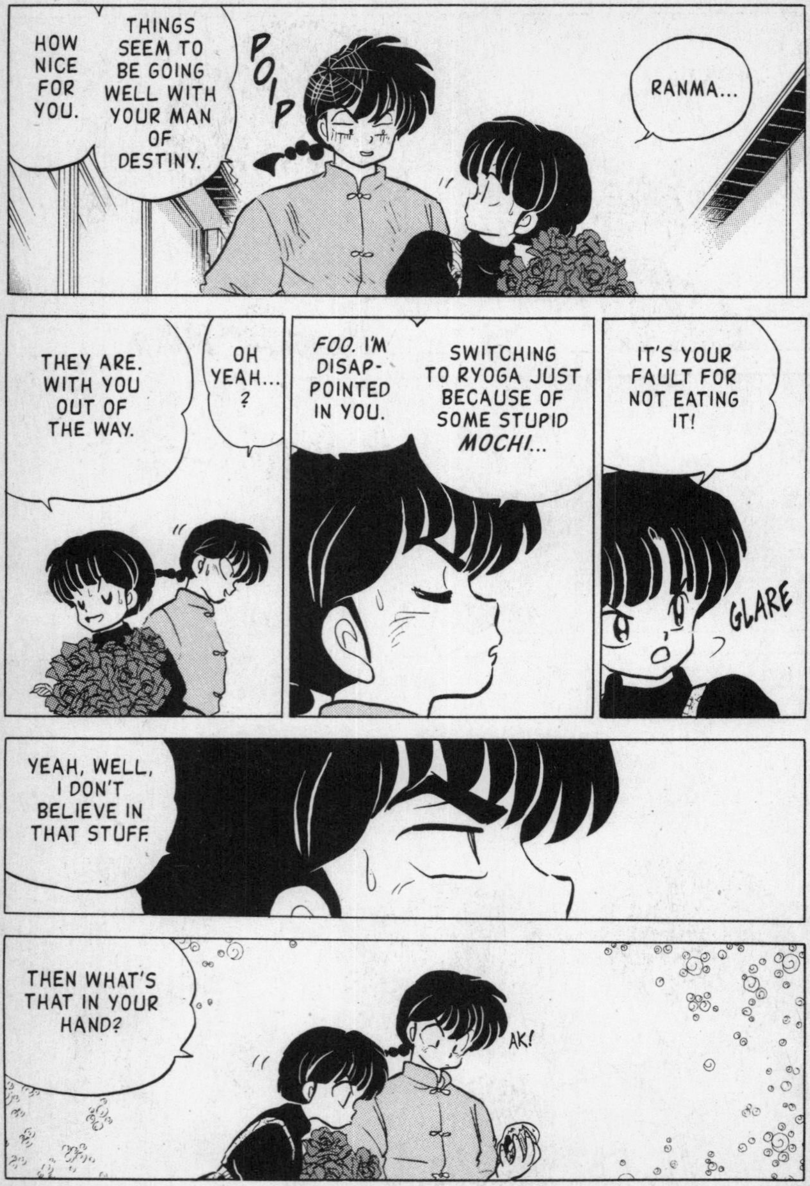
HOW NICE FOR YOU.
THINGS SEEM TO BE GOING WELL WITH YOUR MAN OF DESTINY.
POIP
RANMA...
THEY ARE. WITH YOU OUT OF THE WAY.
OH YEAH...?
FOO. I'M DISAP-POINTED IN YOU.
SWITCHING TO RYOGA JUST BECAUSE OF SOME STUPID MOCHI...
IT'S YOUR FAULT FOR NOT EATING IT!
GLARE
YEAH, WELL, I DON'T BELIEVE IN THAT STUFF.
THEN WHAT'S THAT IN YOUR HAND?
AK!

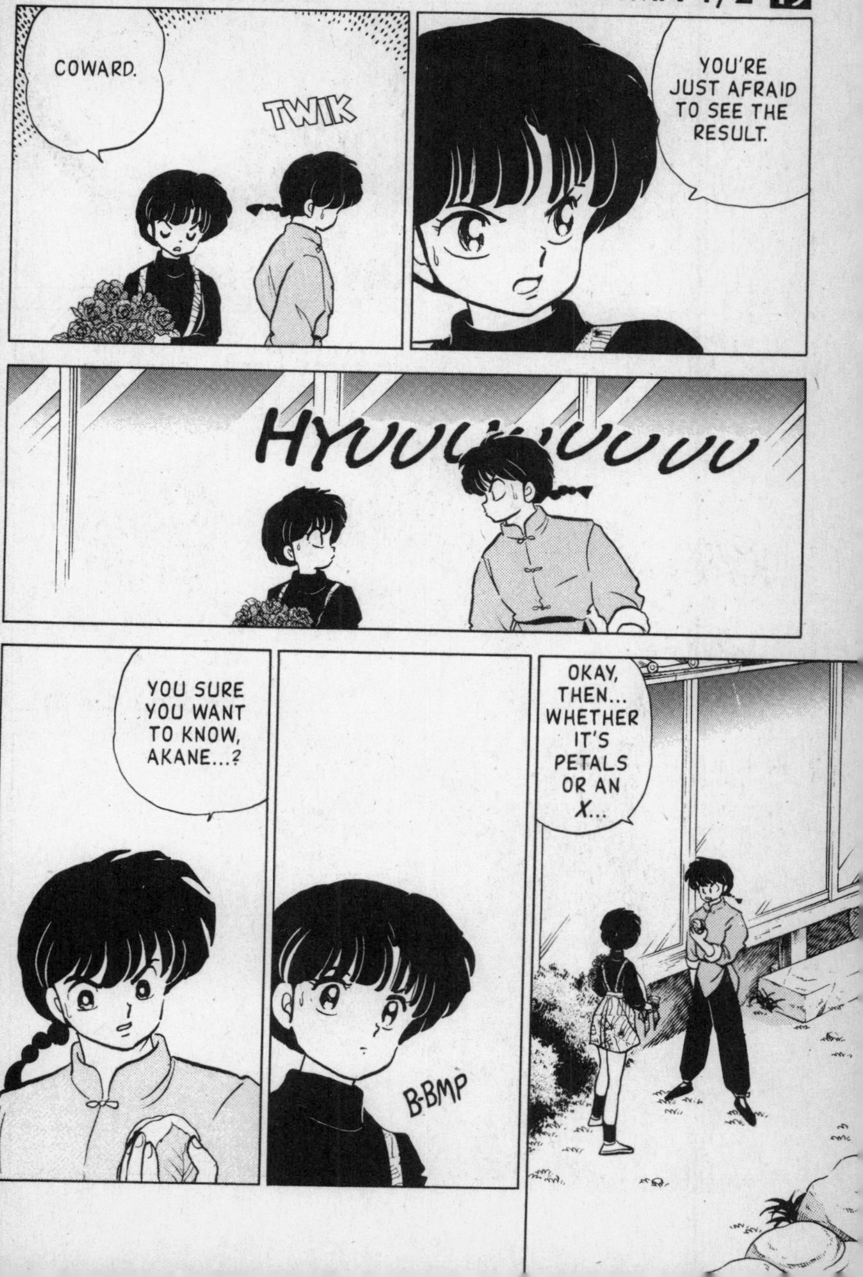
COWARD.
TWIK
YOU'RE JUST AFRAID TO SEE THE RESULT.
HYUUUUUUUUU
YOU SURE YOU WANT TO KNOW, AKANE...?
B-BMP
OKAY, THEN... WHETHER IT'S PETALS OR AN X...

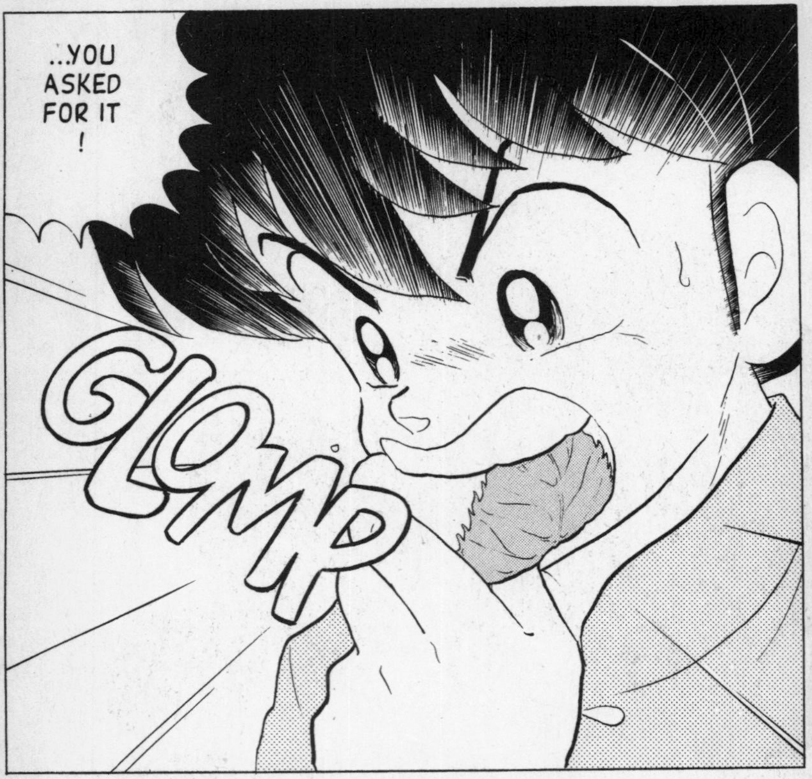
...YOU ASKED FOR IT !
GLOMP
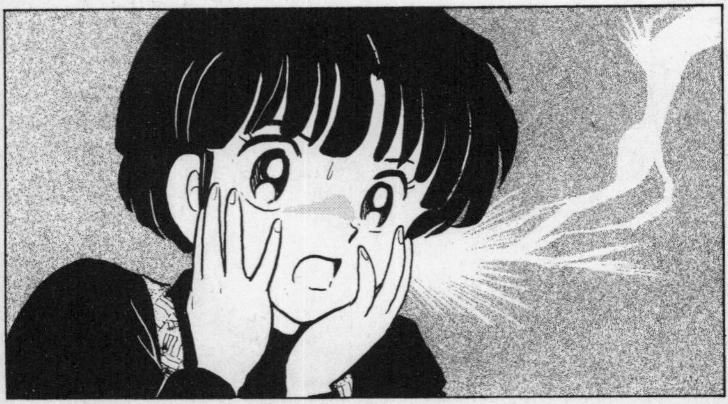

Part 6
STORM OF PETALS

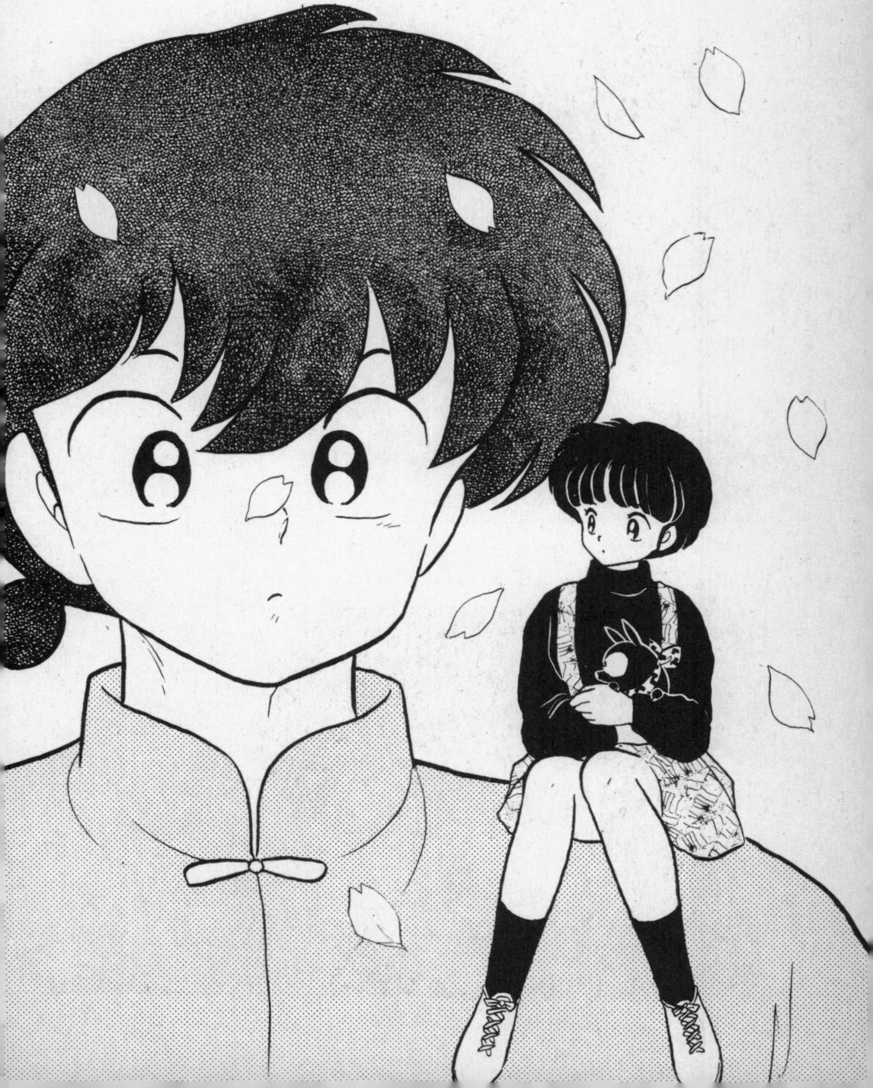

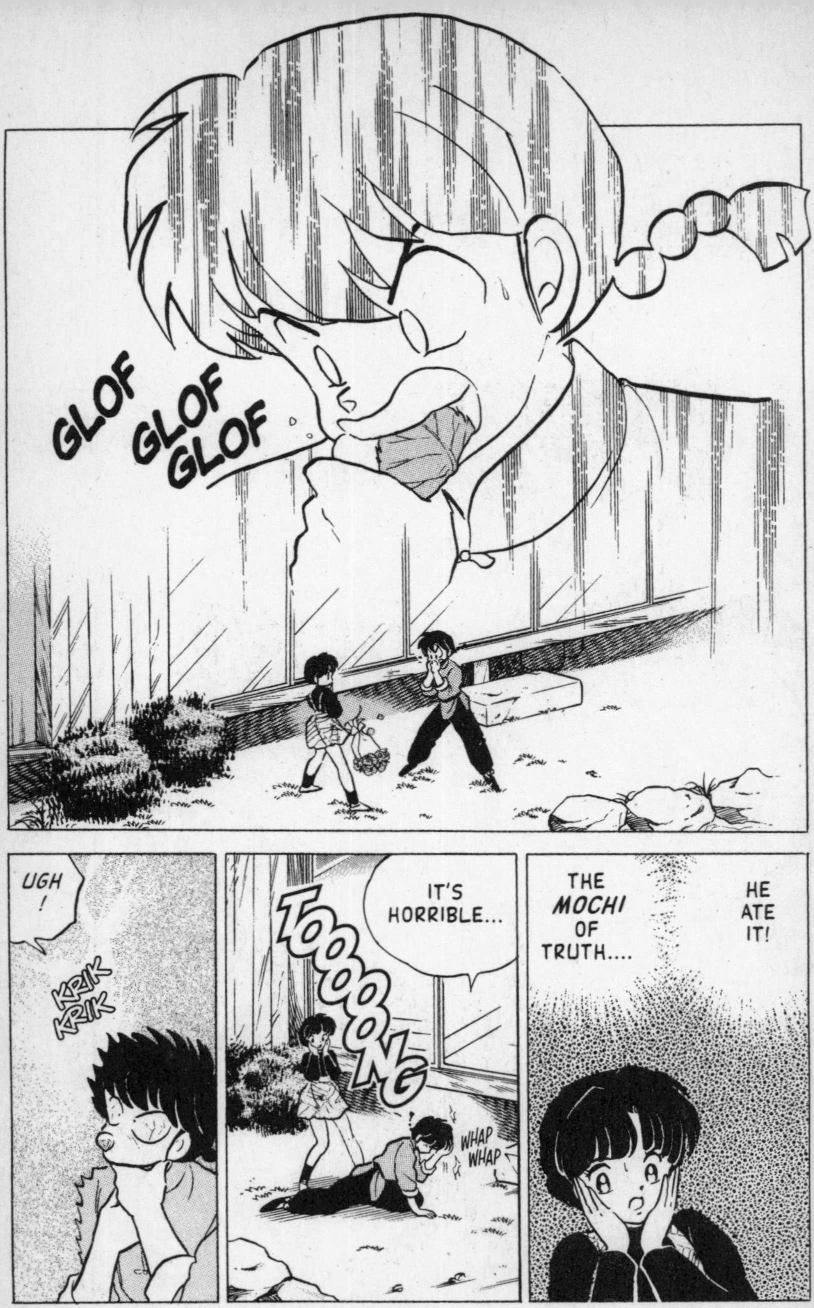
GLOF GLOF GLOF
UGH!
KRIK KRIK
TOOOOONG
IT'S HORRIBLE...
WHAP WHAP
THE MOCHI OF TRUTH....
HE ATE IT!

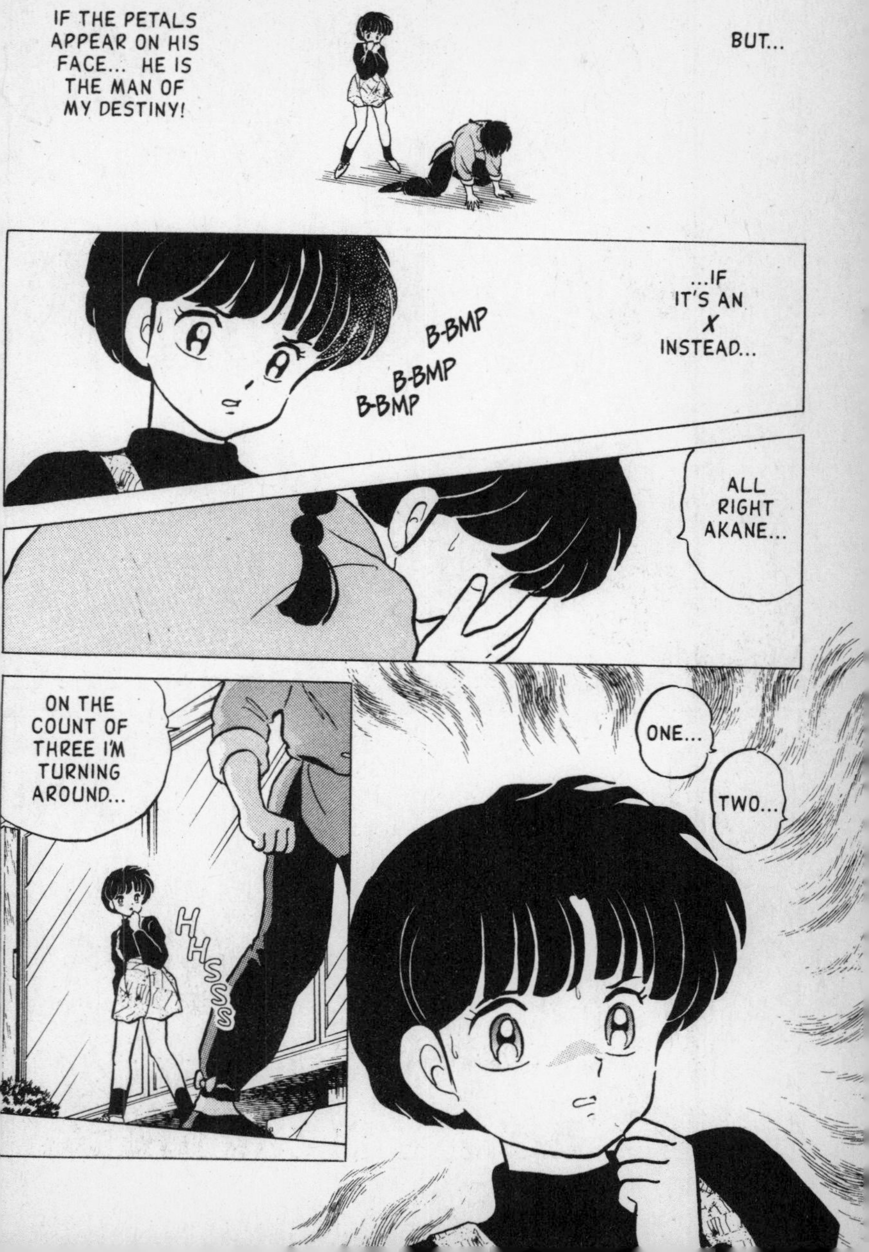
IF THE PETALS APPEAR ON HIS FACE... HE IS THE MAN OF MY DESTINY!
BUT...
...IF IT'S AN X INSTEAD...
B-BMP
B-BMP
B-BMP
ALL RIGHT AKANE...
ON THE COUNT OF THREE I'M TURNING AROUND...
HHSSS
ONE...
TWO...

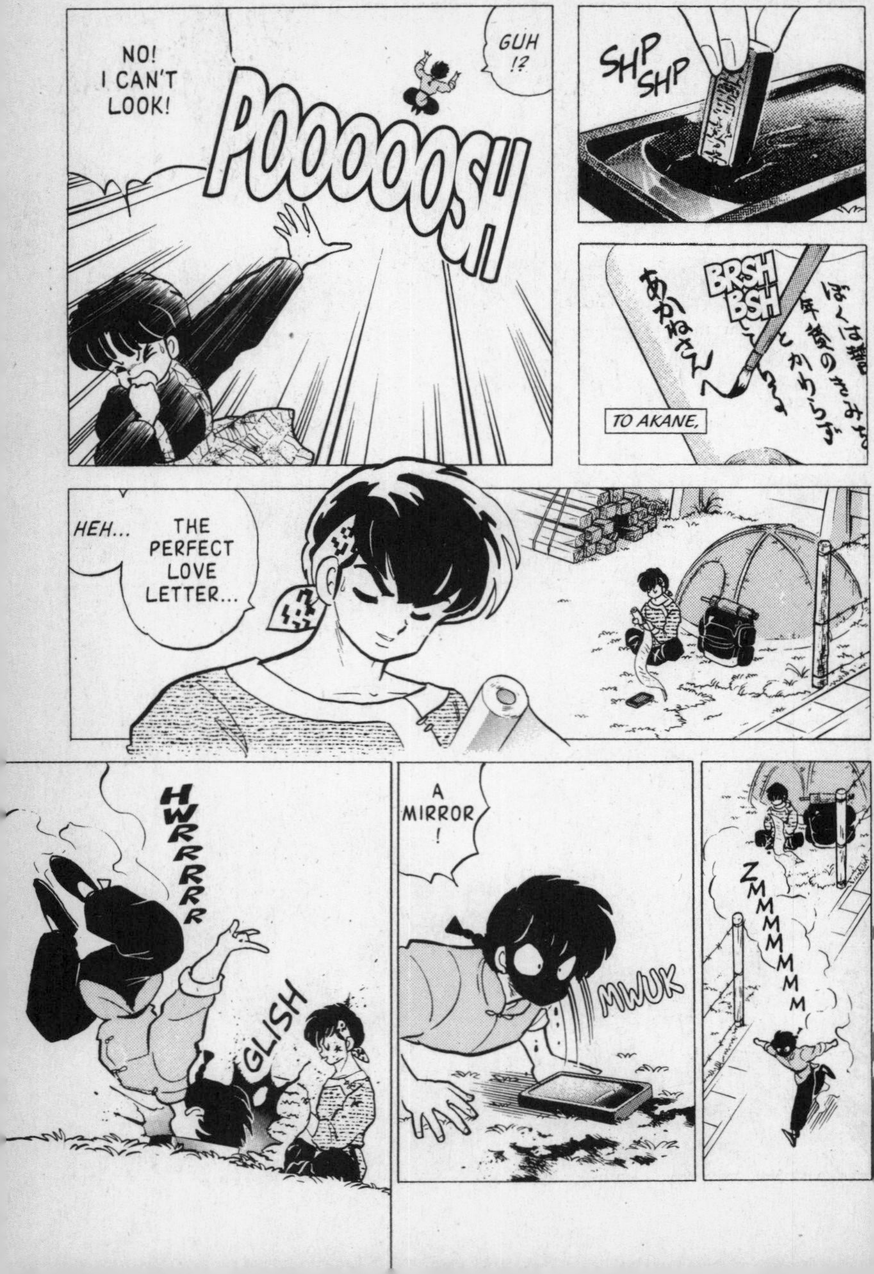
NO! I CAN'T LOOK!
POOOOOOSH
GUH !?
SHP SHP
あかねさんへ
BRSH BSH
TO AKANE,
HEH...
THE PERFECT LOVE LETTER...
HWRRRRR
GLISH
A MIRROR !
MWUK
ZMMMMMMM

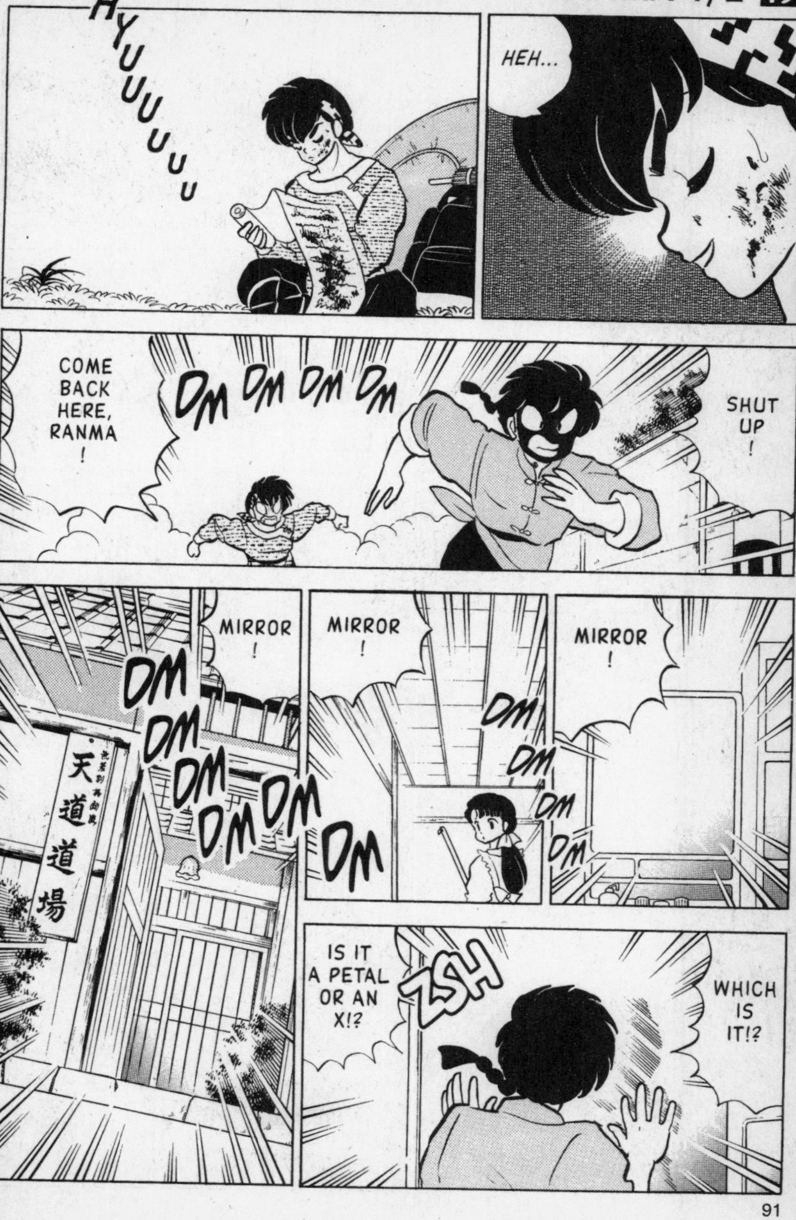
HYUUUUUUU
HEH...
COME BACK HERE, RANMA!
DM DM DM DM
SHUT UP!
MIRROR!
DM DM DM DM DM DM DM
天道道場
MIRROR!
DM DM DM DM
MIRROR!
IS IT A PETAL OR AN X!?
ZSH
WHICH IS IT!?

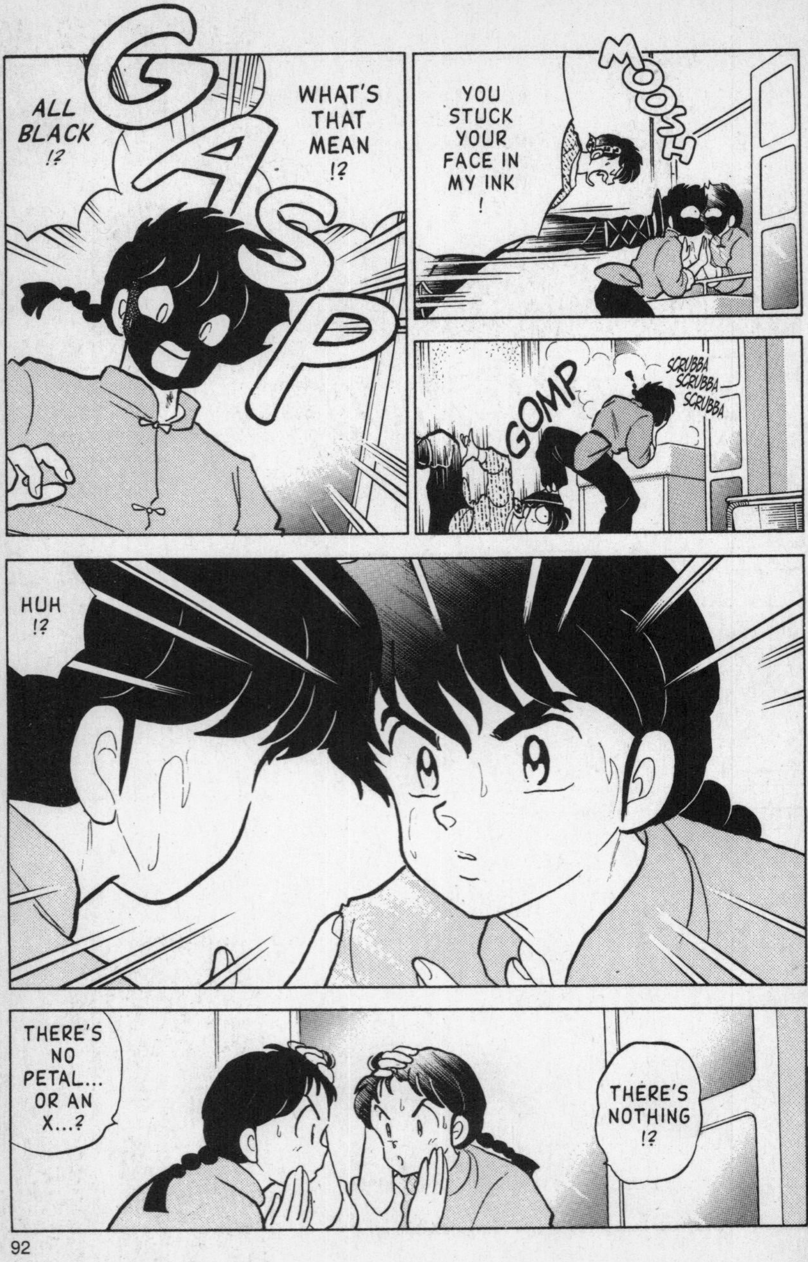
ALL BLACK !?
GASP
WHAT'S THAT MEAN !?
YOU STUCK YOUR FACE IN MY INK !
WOOSH
GOMP
SCRUBBA SCRUBBA SCRUBBA
HUH !?
THERE'S NO PETAL... OR AN X...?
THERE'S NOTHING !?

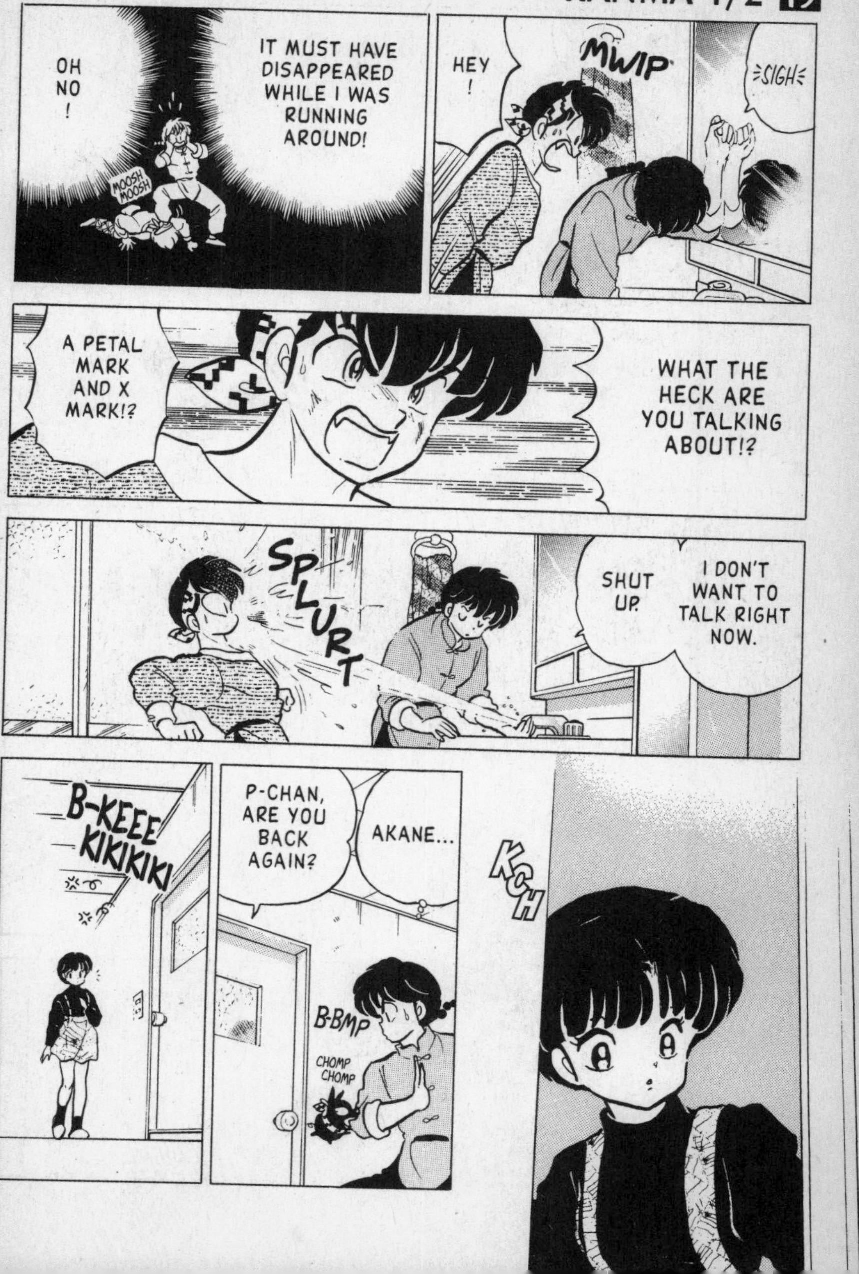
OH NO !
IT MUST HAVE DISAPPEARED WHILE I WAS RUNNING AROUND!
MOOSH MOOSH
HEY !
MWIP
SIGH
A PETAL MARK AND X MARK!?
WHAT THE HECK ARE YOU TALKING ABOUT!?
SPLURT
SHUT UP.
I DON'T WANT TO TALK RIGHT NOW.
B-KEEE KIKIKIKI
P-CHAN, ARE YOU BACK AGAIN?
AKANE...
B-BMP
CHOMP CHOMP
KCH

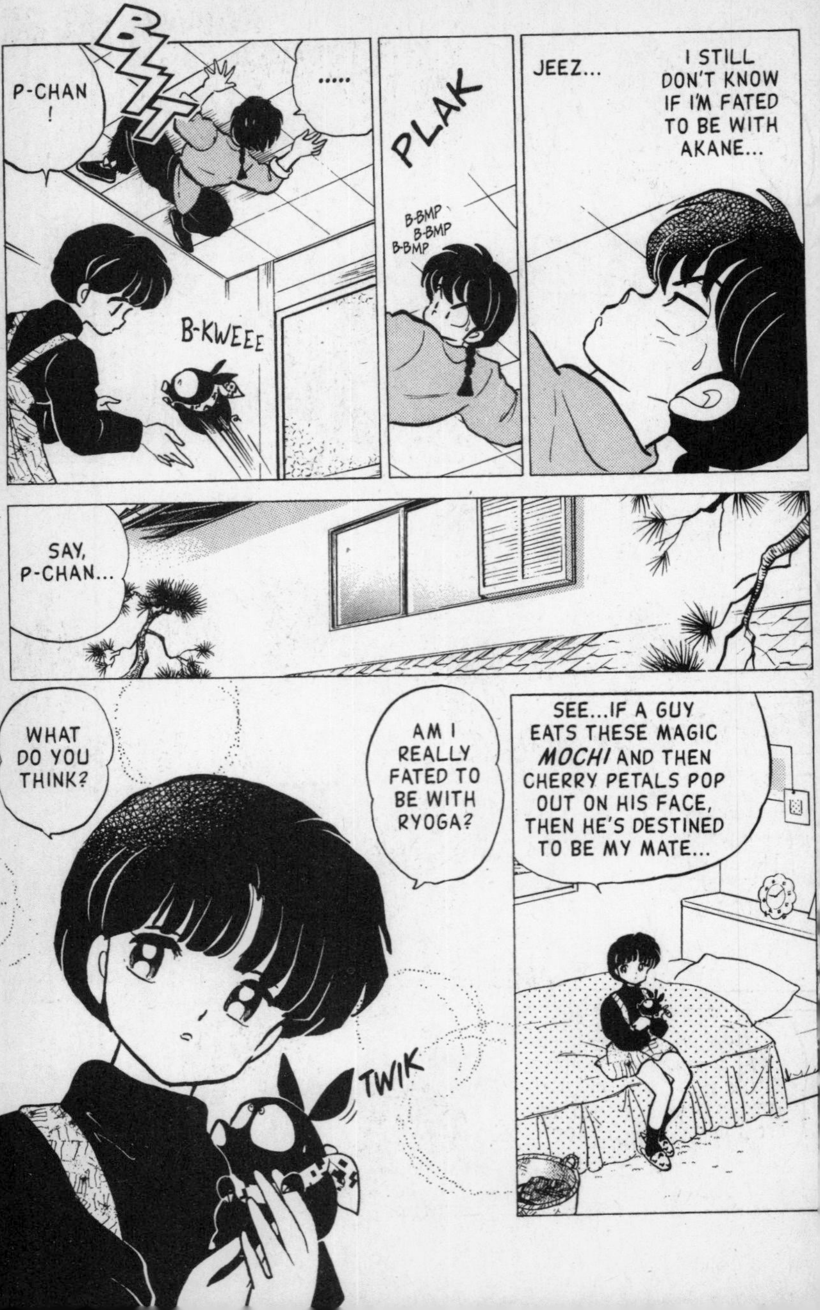
P-CHAN!
BLIT
.....
B-KWEEE
PLAK
B-BMP B-BMP B-BMP
JEEZ...
I STILL DON'T KNOW IF I'M FATED TO BE WITH AKANE...
SAY, P-CHAN...
WHAT DO YOU THINK?
AM I REALLY FATED TO BE WITH RYOGA?
TWIK
SEE...IF A GUY EATS THESE MAGIC *MOCHI* AND THEN CHERRY PETALS POP OUT ON HIS FACE, THEN HE'S DESTINED TO BE MY MATE...

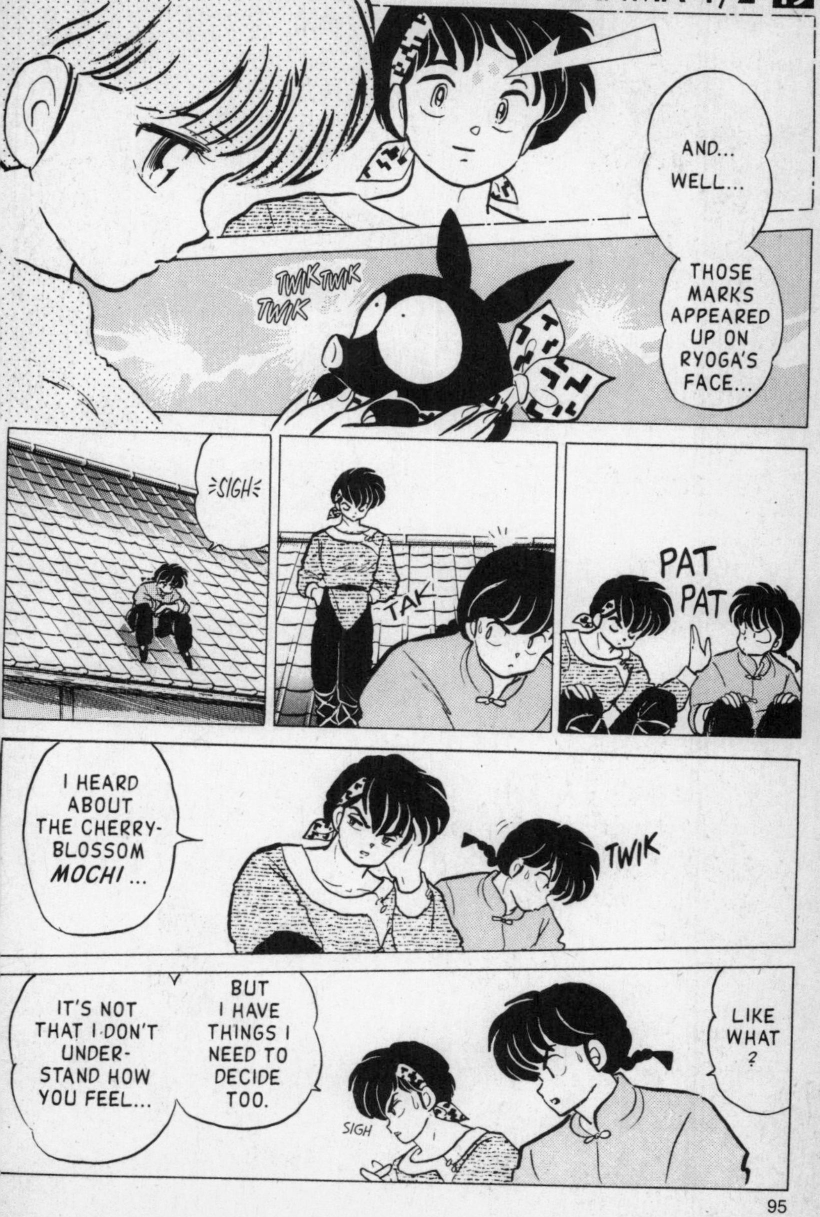
AND... WELL...
TWIK TWIK TWIK
THOSE MARKS APPEARED UP ON RYOGA'S FACE...
SIGH
TAK
PAT PAT
I HEARD ABOUT THE CHERRY-BLOSSOM MOCHI ...
TWIK
IT'S NOT THAT I DON'T UNDER-STAND HOW YOU FEEL...
BUT I HAVE THINGS I NEED TO DECIDE TOO.
SIGH
LIKE WHAT?

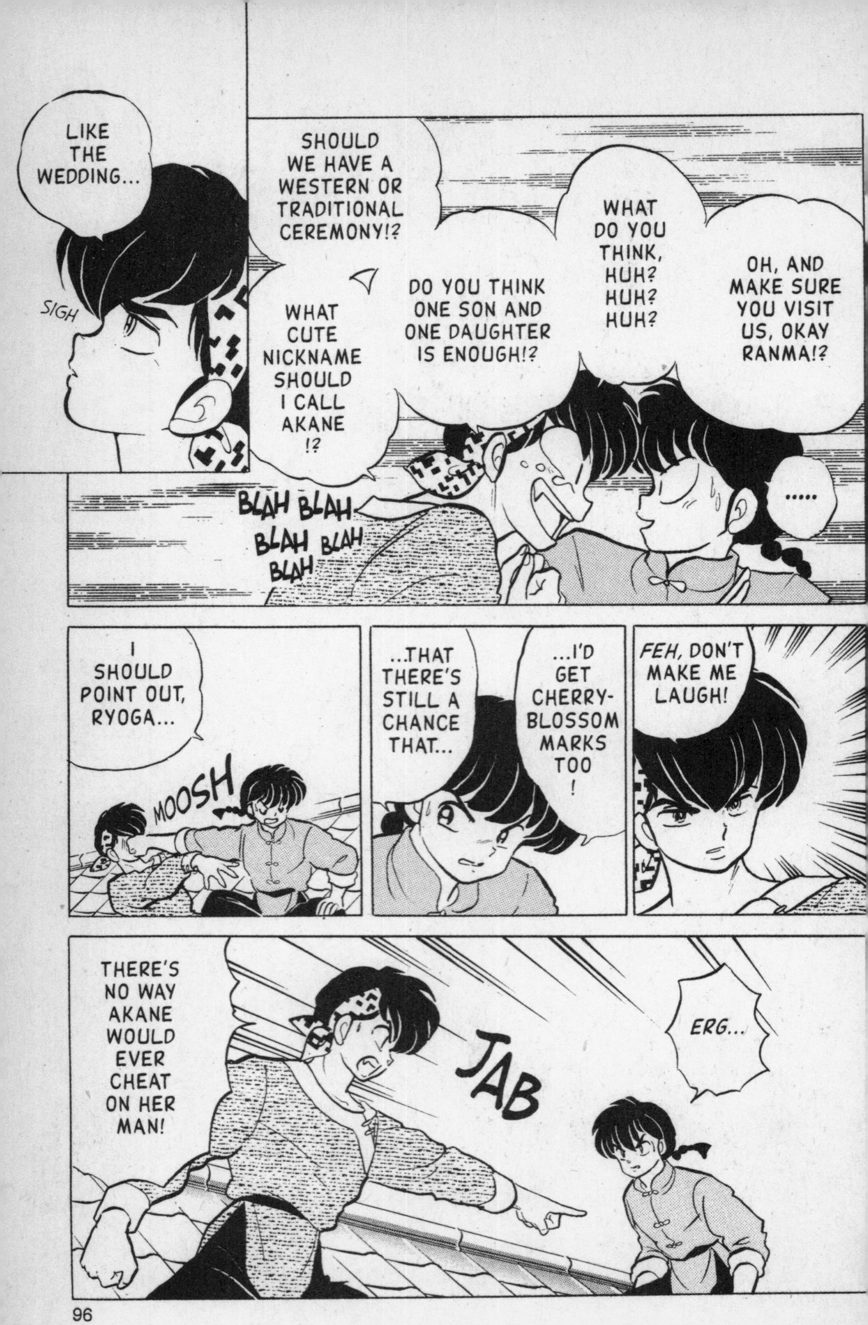
LIKE THE WEDDING...
SIGH
SHOULD WE HAVE A WESTERN OR TRADITIONAL CEREMONY!?
WHAT CUTE NICKNAME SHOULD I CALL AKANE !?
DO YOU THINK ONE SON AND ONE DAUGHTER IS ENOUGH!?
WHAT DO YOU THINK, HUH? HUH? HUH?
OH, AND MAKE SURE YOU VISIT US, OKAY RANMA!?
BLAH BLAH BLAH BLAH BLAH
.....
I SHOULD POINT OUT, RYOGA...
MOOSH
...THAT THERE'S STILL A CHANCE THAT...
...I'D GET CHERRY-BLOSSOM MARKS TOO !
FEH, DON'T MAKE ME LAUGH!
THERE'S NO WAY AKANE WOULD EVER CHEAT ON HER MAN!
JAB
ERG...

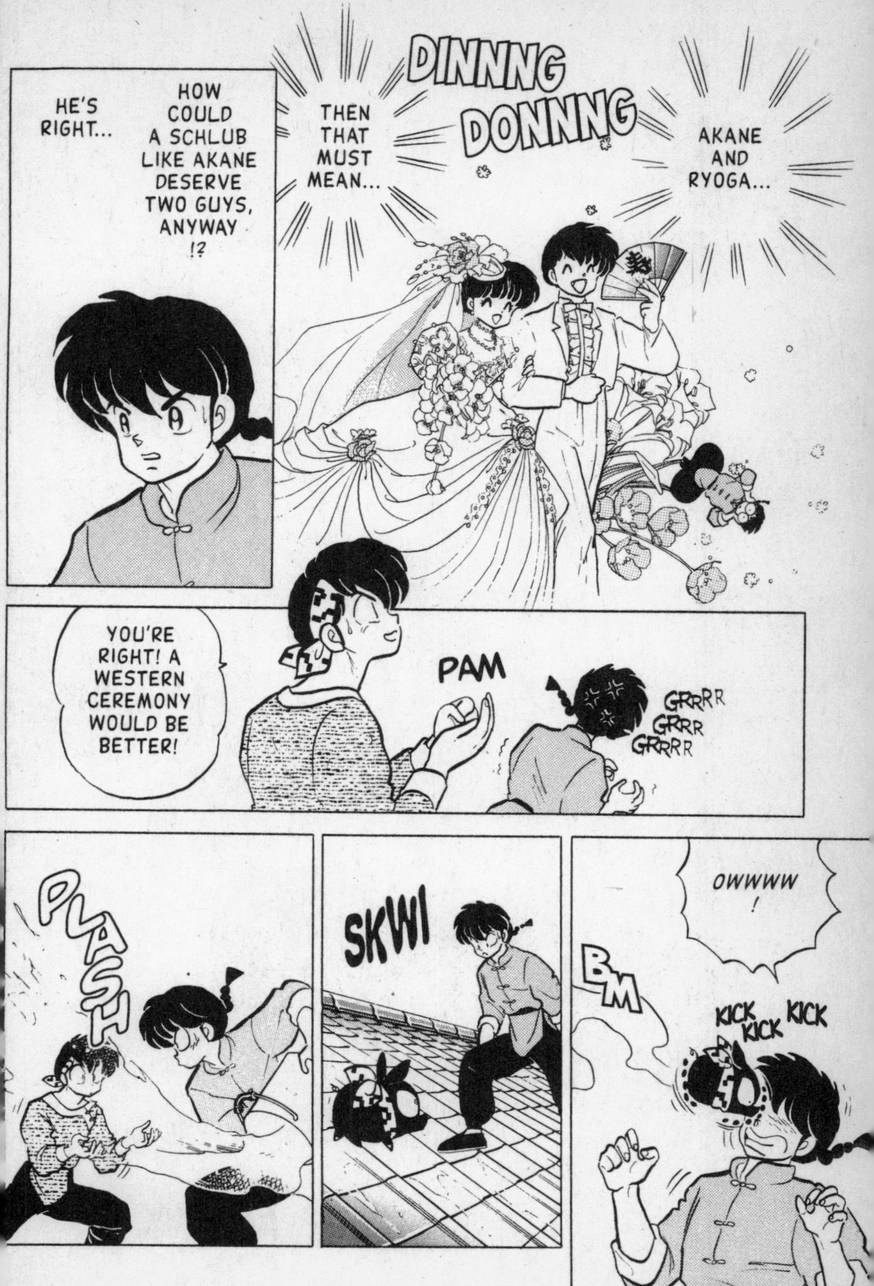
HE'S RIGHT...
HOW COULD A SCHLUB LIKE AKANE DESERVE TWO GUYS, ANYWAY !?
DINNNG DONNNG
THEN THAT MUST MEAN...
AKANE AND RYOGA...
YOU'RE RIGHT! A WESTERN CEREMONY WOULD BE BETTER!
PAM
GRRRR
GRRR
GRRRR
PLASH
SKWI
BM
OWWWW !
KICK
KICK
KICK

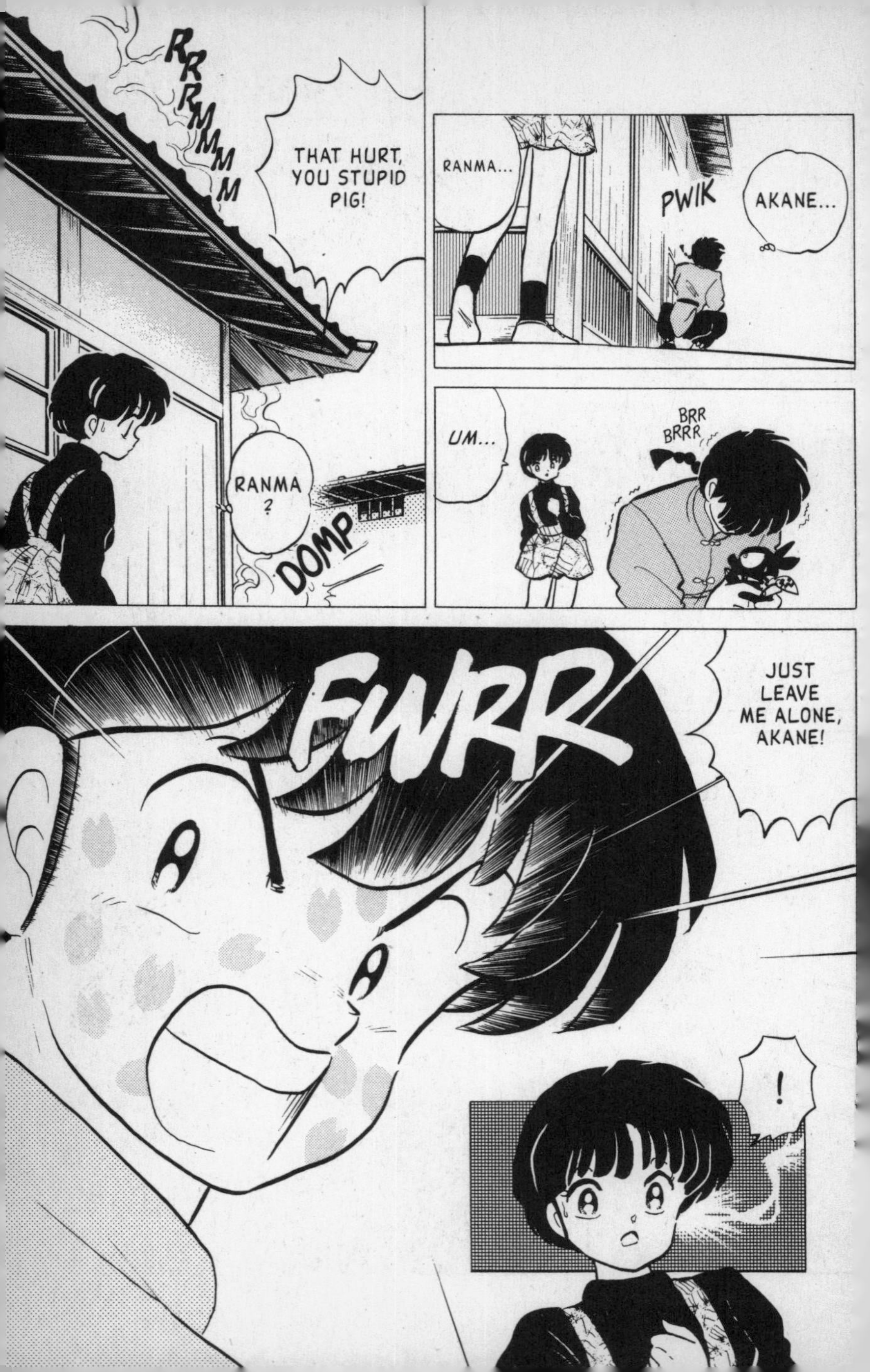
RRRMMMM
THAT HURT, YOU STUPID PIG!
RANMA ?
DOMP
RANMA...
PWIK
AKANE...
UM...
BRR BRRR
FURR
JUST LEAVE ME ALONE, AKANE!
!

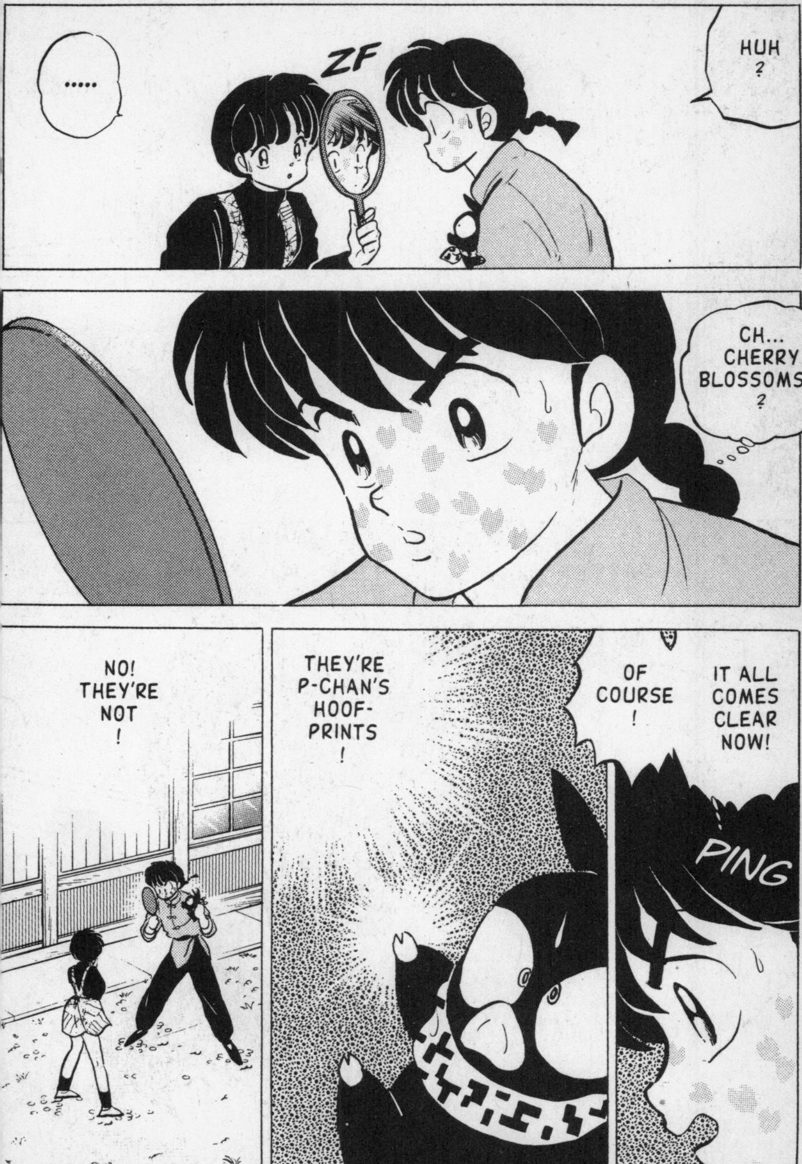
......
ZF
HUH ?
CH... CHERRY BLOSSOMS... ?
NO! THEY'RE NOT !
THEY'RE P-CHAN'S HOOF-PRINTS !
OF COURSE !
IT ALL COMES CLEAR NOW!
PING

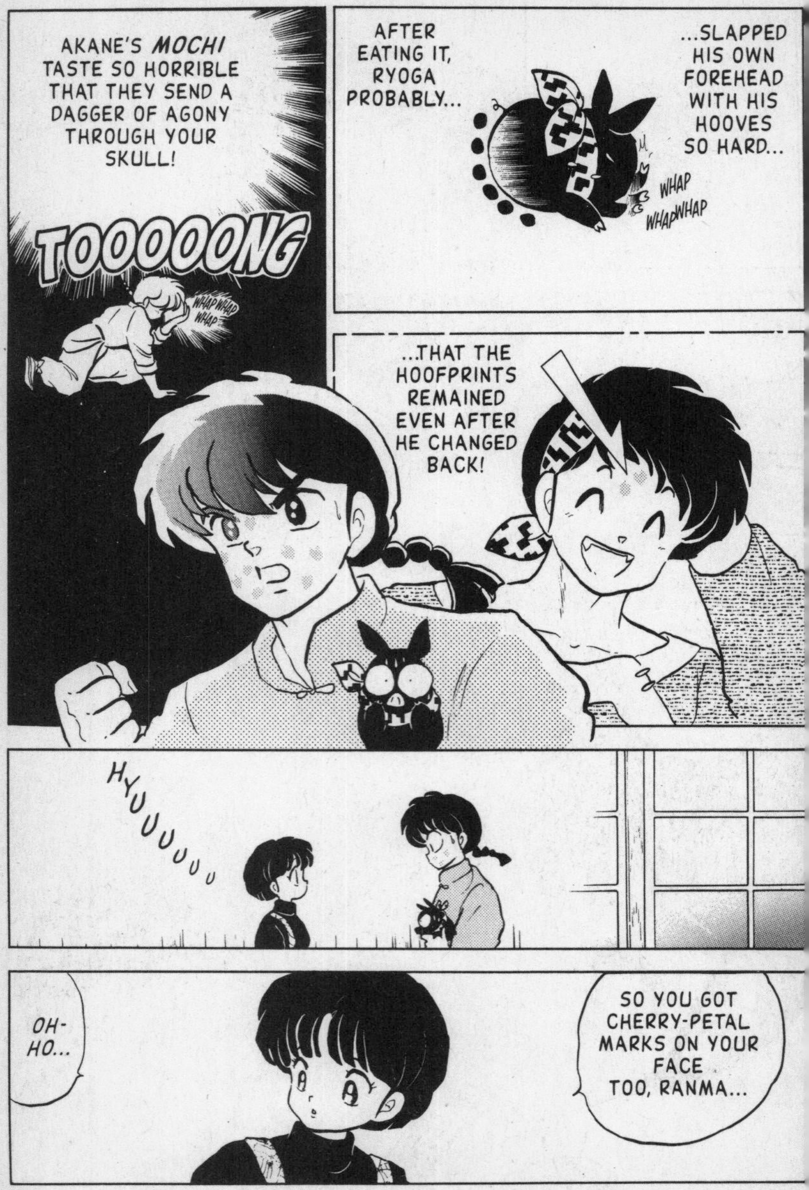
AKANE'S *MOCHI* TASTE SO HORRIBLE THAT THEY SEND A DAGGER OF AGONY THROUGH YOUR SKULL!
TOOOOONG
WHAP WHAP WHAP
AFTER EATING IT, RYOGA PROBABLY...
...SLAPPED HIS OWN FOREHEAD WITH HIS HOOVES SO HARD...
WHAP
WHAPWHAP
...THAT THE HOOFPRINTS REMAINED EVEN AFTER HE CHANGED BACK!
HYUUUUUUU
OH-HO...
SO YOU GOT CHERRY-PETAL MARKS ON YOUR FACE TOO, RANMA...

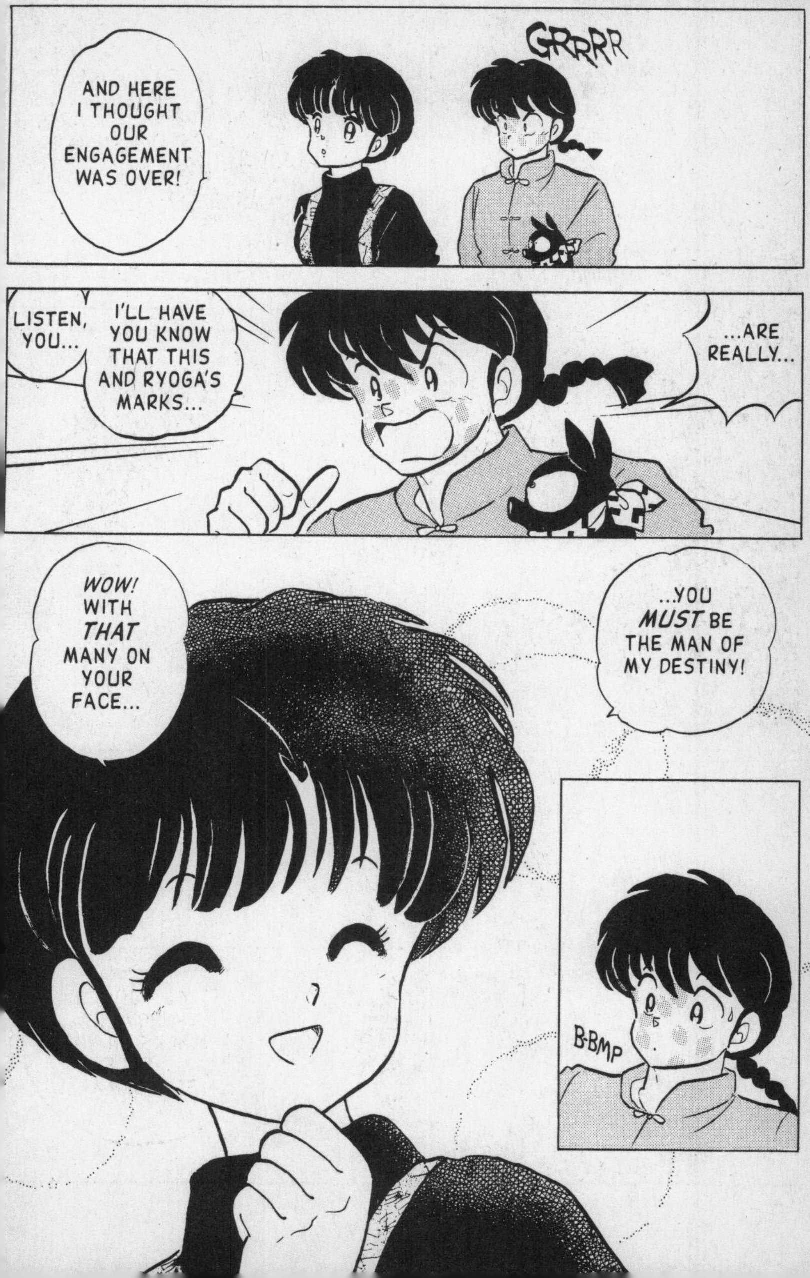
AND HERE I THOUGHT OUR ENGAGEMENT WAS OVER!
GRRRR
LISTEN, YOU...
I'LL HAVE YOU KNOW THAT THIS AND RYOGA'S MARKS...
...ARE REALLY...
WOW! WITH *THAT* MANY ON YOUR FACE...
...YOU *MUST* BE THE MAN OF MY DESTINY!
B-BMP

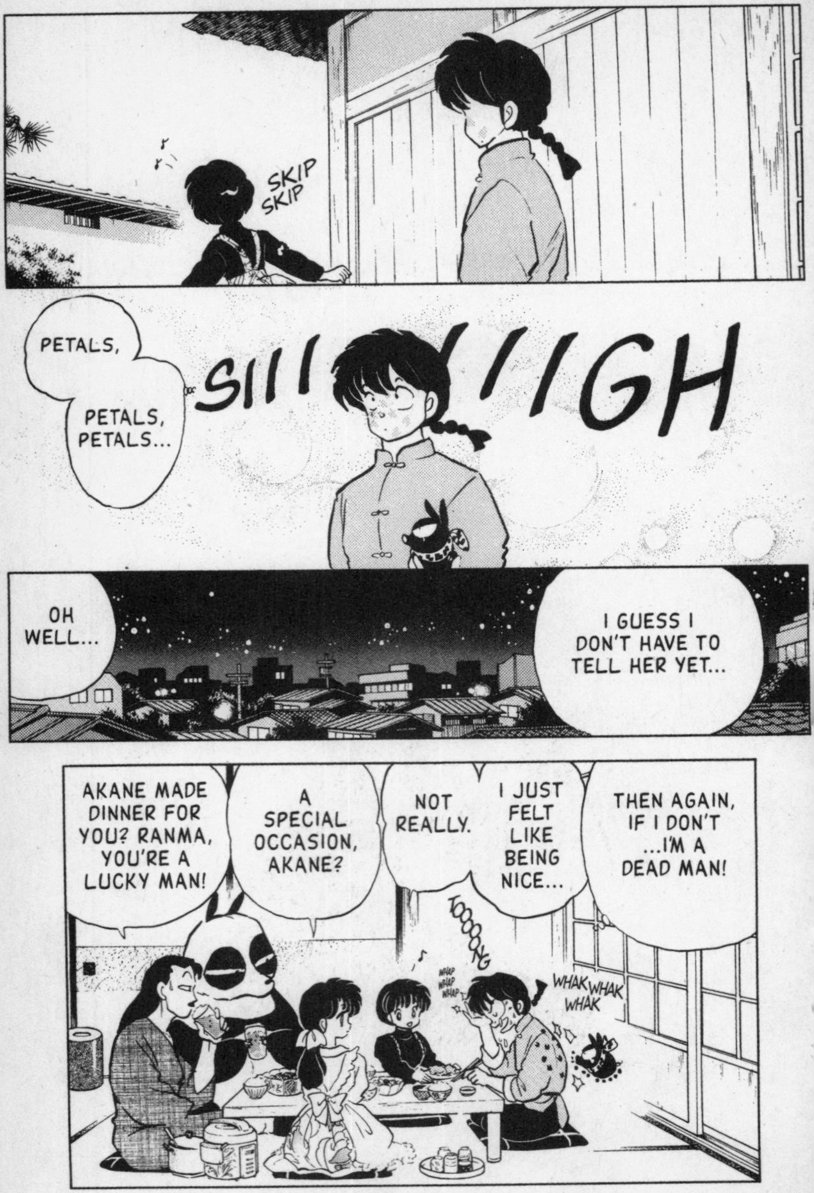
SKIP
SKIP
PETALS,
PETALS, PETALS...
SIII
IIGH
OH WELL...
I GUESS I DON'T HAVE TO TELL HER YET...
AKANE MADE DINNER FOR YOU? RANMA, YOU'RE A LUCKY MAN!
A SPECIAL OCCASION, AKANE?
NOT REALLY.
I JUST FELT LIKE BEING NICE...
TOOOOONG
WHAP WHAP WHAP
WHAK WHAK WHAK
THEN AGAIN, IF I DON'T ...I'M A DEAD MAN!

Part 7

L! O! V! E!

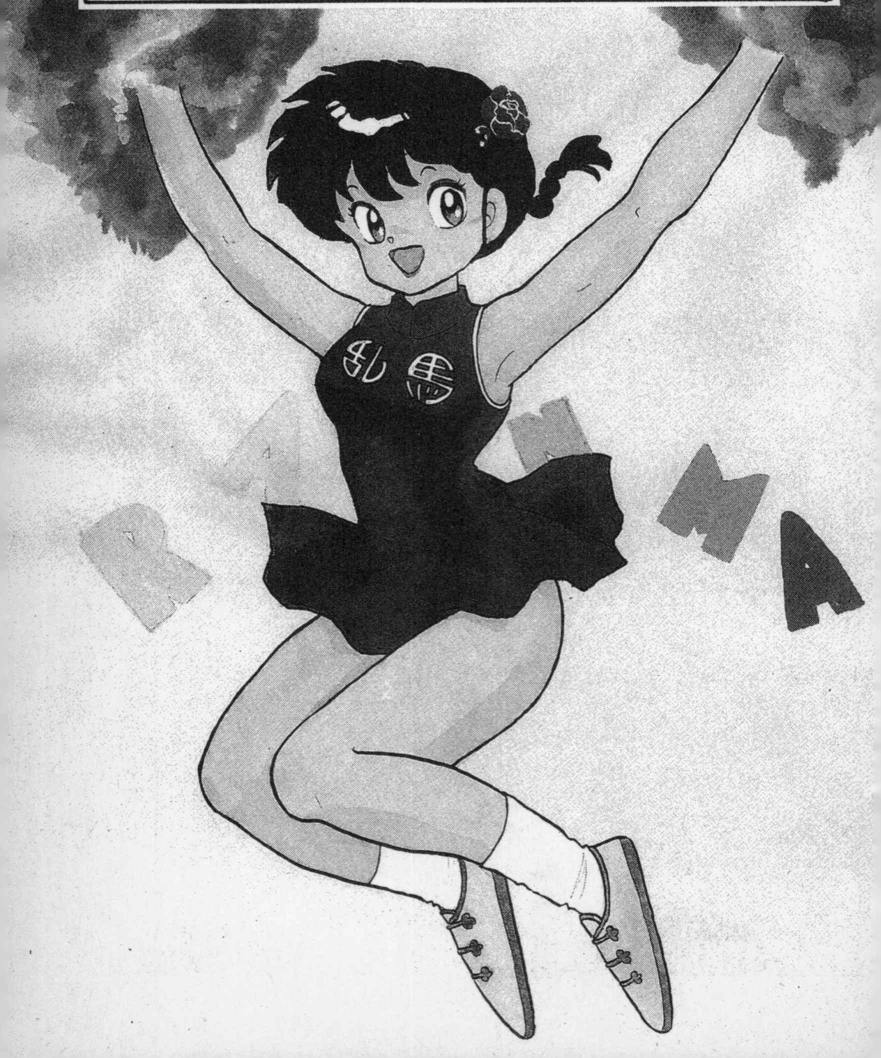
RANMA

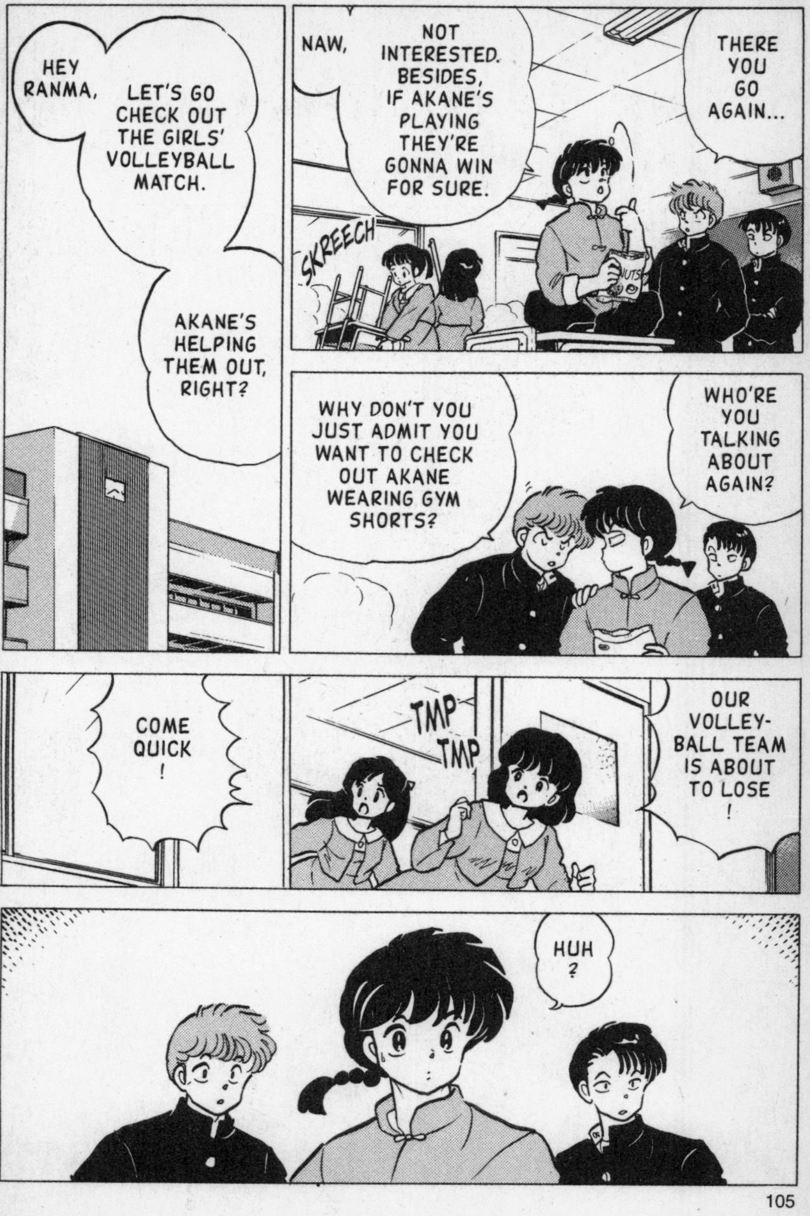
HEY RANMA,
LET'S GO CHECK OUT THE GIRLS' VOLLEYBALL MATCH.
AKANE'S HELPING THEM OUT, RIGHT?
NAW,
NOT INTERESTED. BESIDES, IF AKANE'S PLAYING THEY'RE GONNA WIN FOR SURE.
THERE YOU GO AGAIN...
SKREECH
NUTS
WHY DON'T YOU JUST ADMIT YOU WANT TO CHECK OUT AKANE WEARING GYM SHORTS?
WHO'RE YOU TALKING ABOUT AGAIN?
COME QUICK!
TMP TMP
OUR VOLLEY-BALL TEAM IS ABOUT TO LOSE!
HUH?

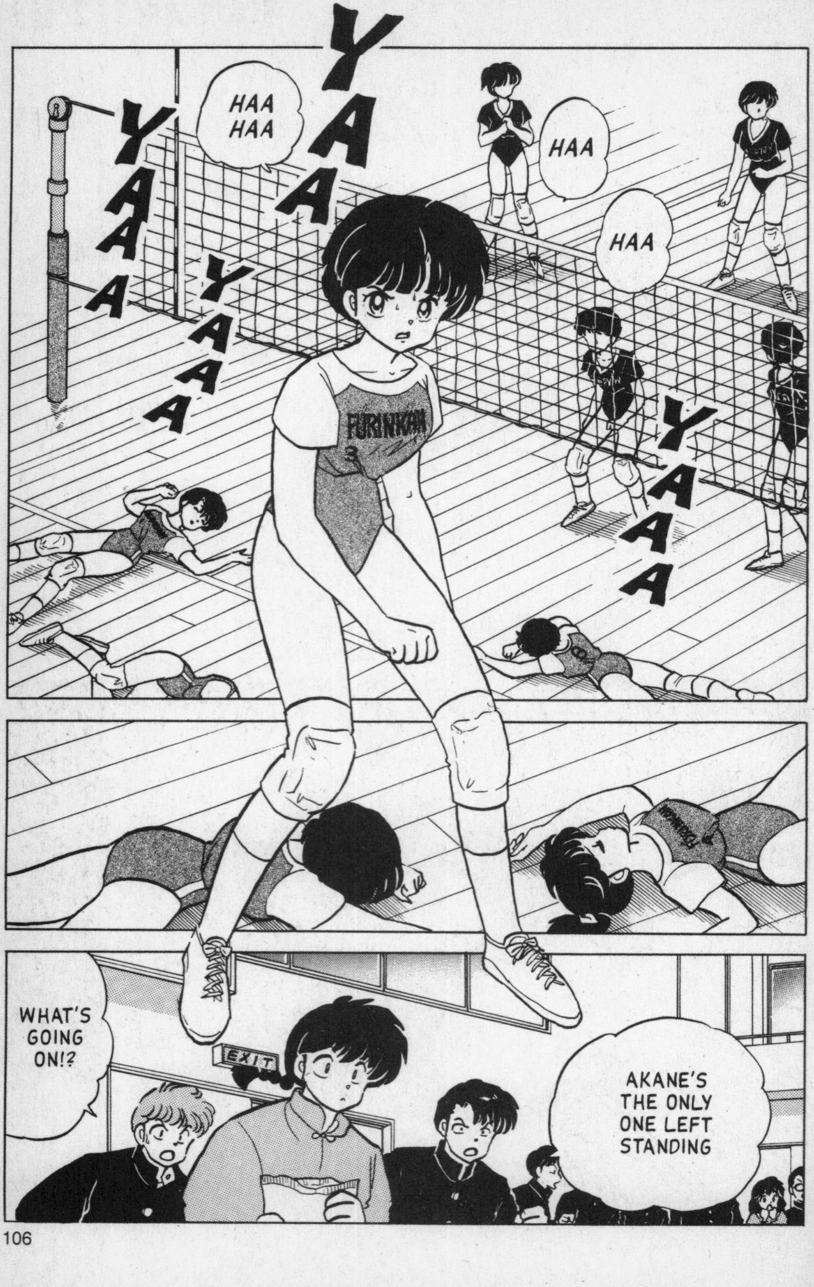
HAA HAA
YAAAA
YAAA
YAAAA
HAA
HAA
FURINKAN
YAAAA
WHAT'S GOING ON!?
EXIT
AKANE'S THE ONLY ONE LEFT STANDING

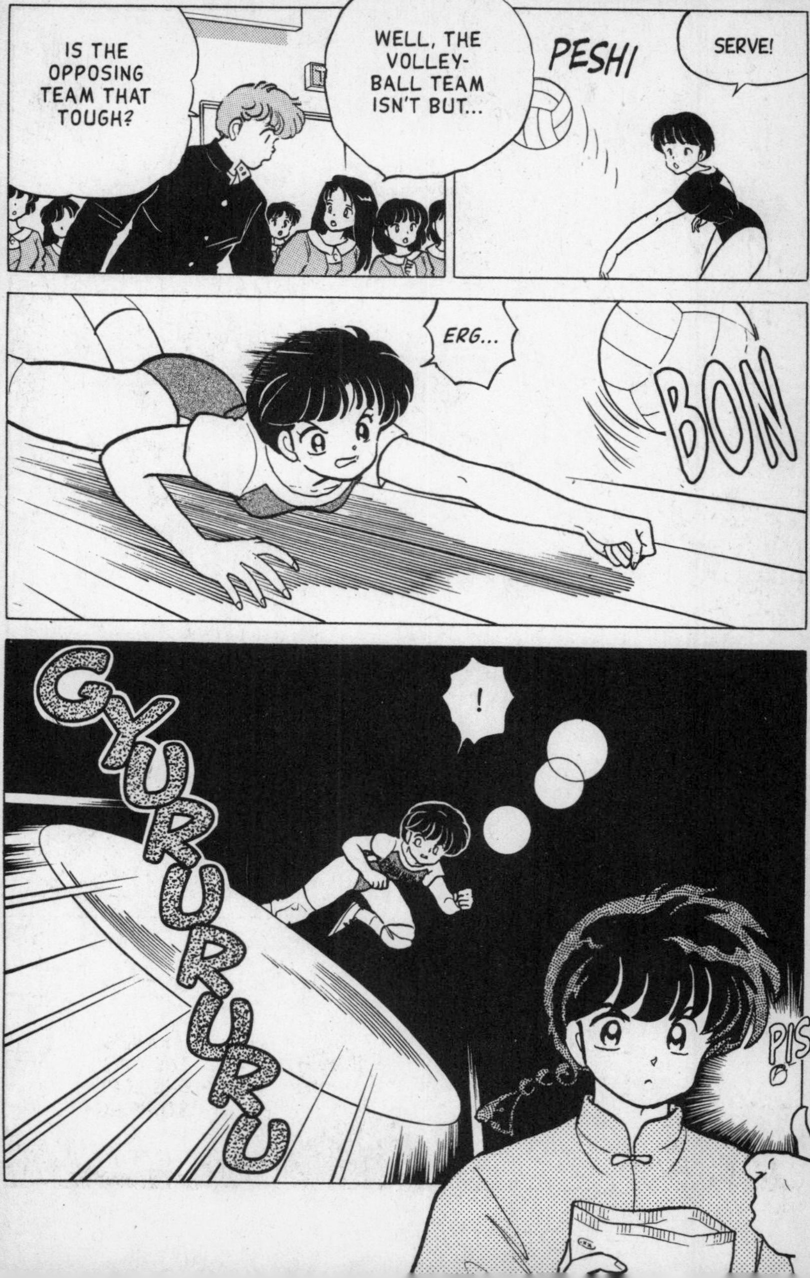
IS THE OPPOSING TEAM THAT TOUGH?
WELL, THE VOLLEY-BALL TEAM ISN'T BUT...
PESHI
SERVE!
ERG...
BON
GYURURURURU
!
PISHI

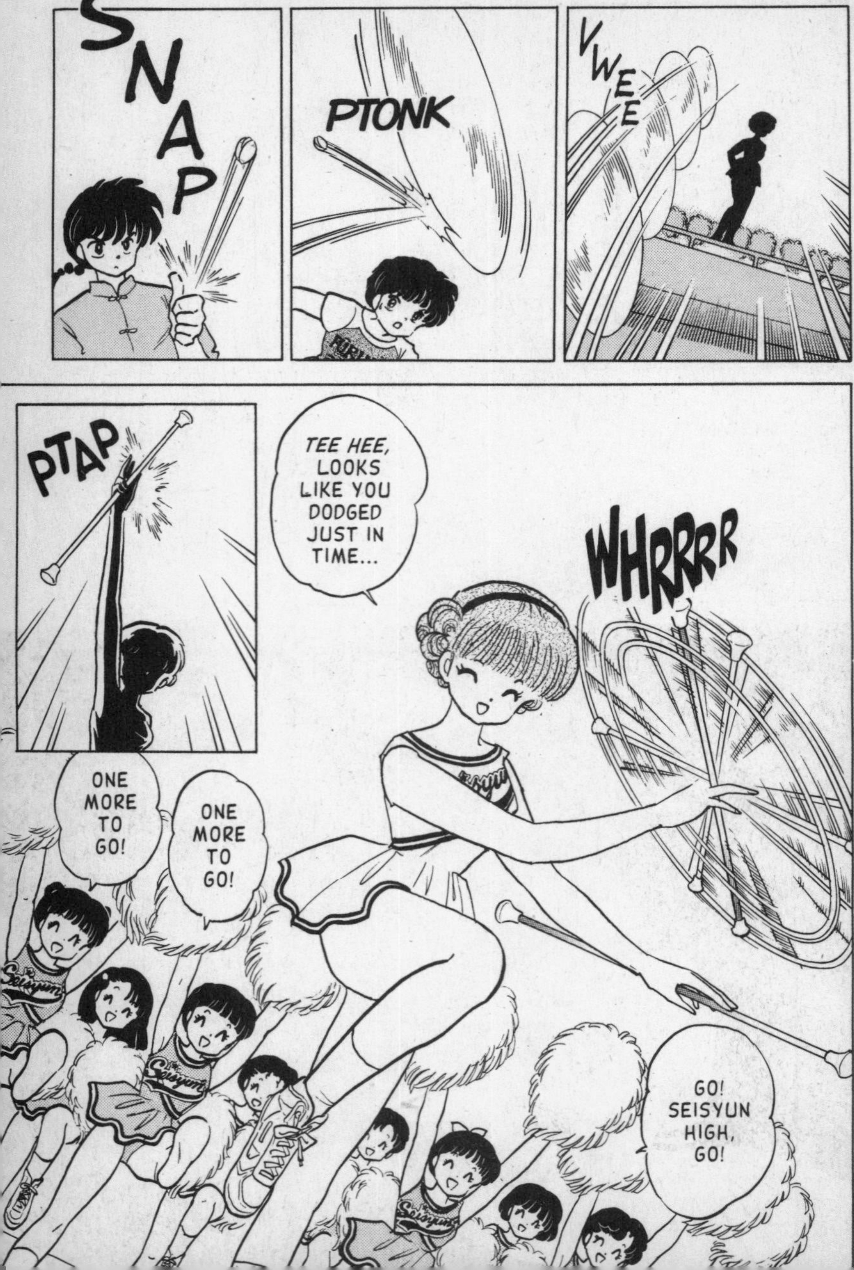
SNAP
PTONK
VWEE
PTAP
TEE HEE, LOOKS LIKE YOU DODGED JUST IN TIME...
WHRRRR
ONE MORE TO GO!
ONE MORE TO GO!
GO! SEISYUN HIGH, GO!

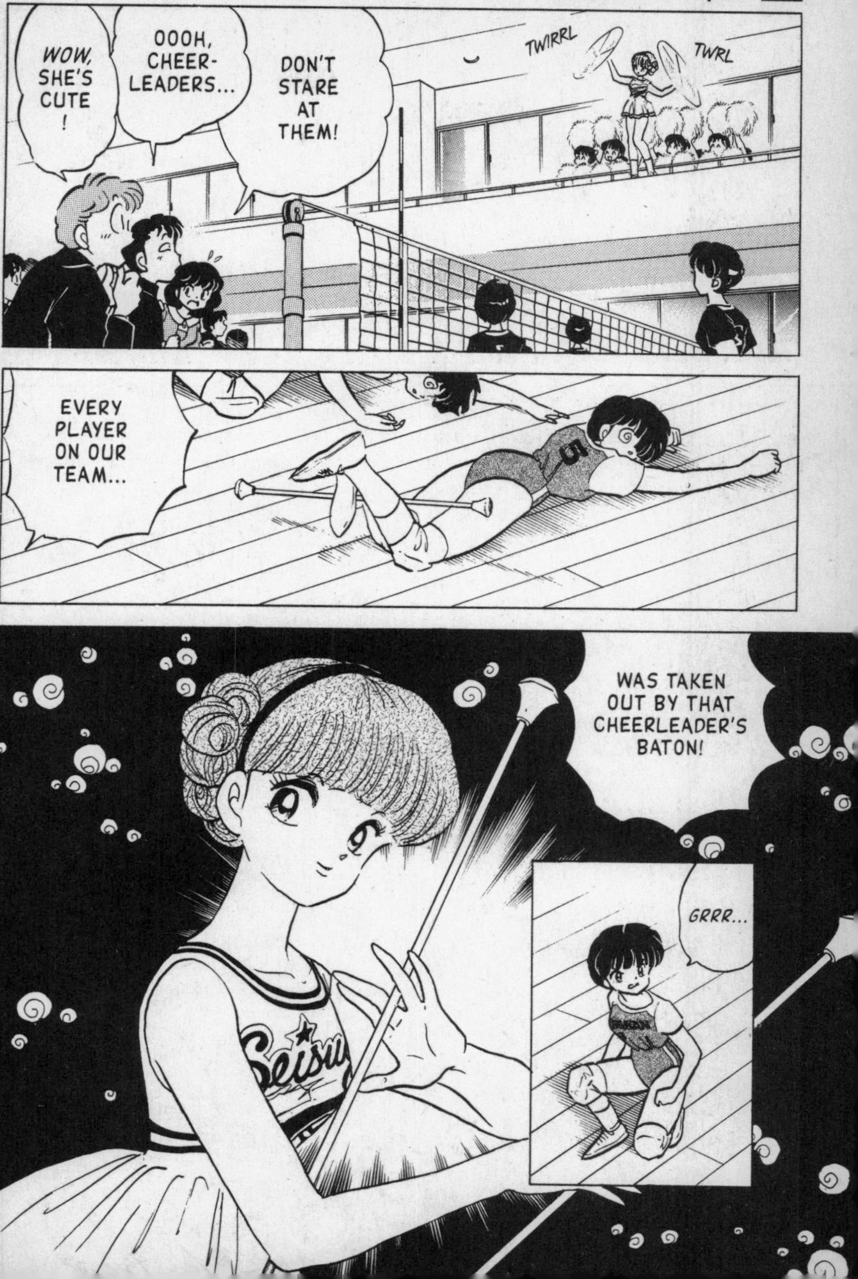
WOW, SHE'S CUTE !
OOOH, CHEER-LEADERS...
DON'T STARE AT THEM!
TWIRRL
TWRL
EVERY PLAYER ON OUR TEAM...
WAS TAKEN OUT BY THAT CHEERLEADER'S BATON!
GRRR...

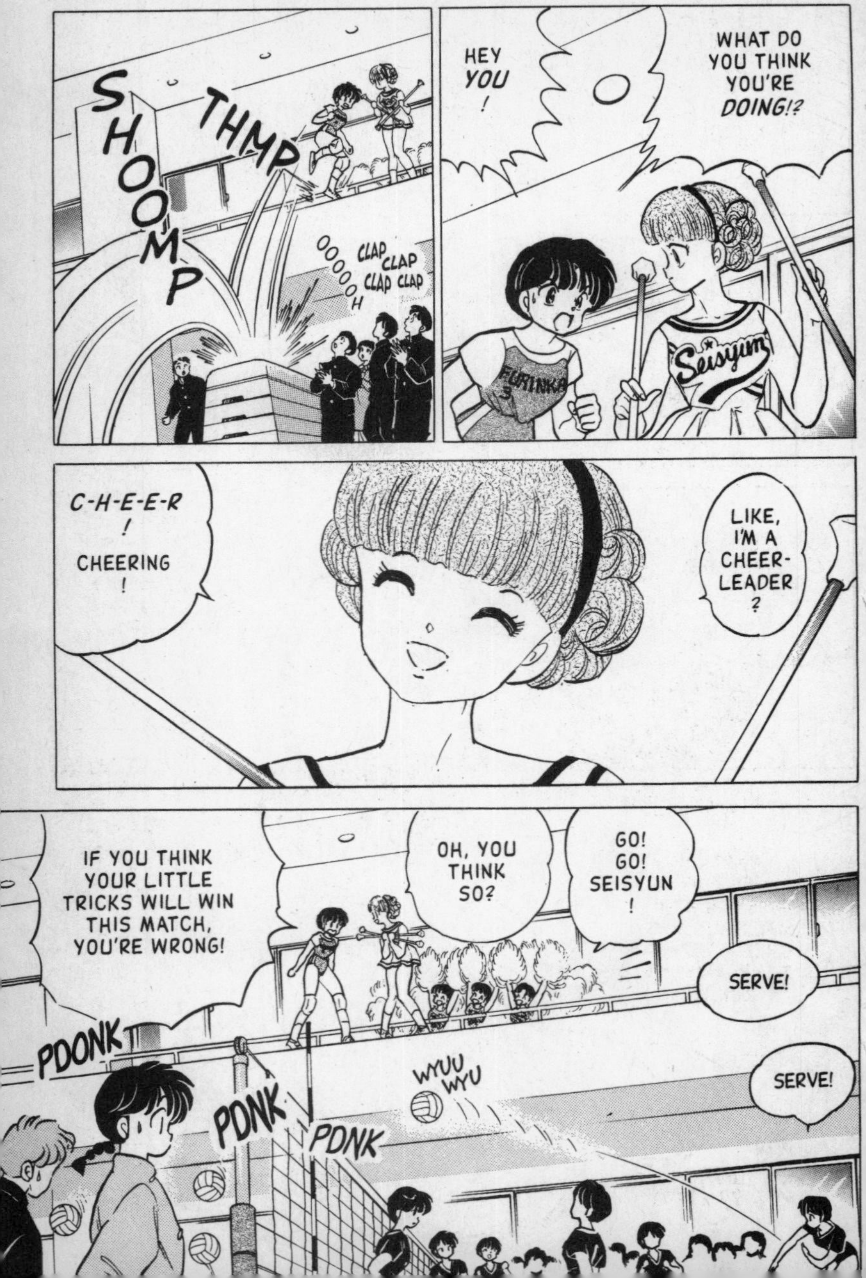
SHOOMP
THMP
OOOOOOH
CLAP CLAP CLAP CLAP
HEY YOU!
WHAT DO YOU THINK YOU'RE DOING!?
C-H-E-E-R! CHEERING!
LIKE, I'M A CHEER-LEADER?
IF YOU THINK YOUR LITTLE TRICKS WILL WIN THIS MATCH, YOU'RE WRONG!
OH, YOU THINK SO?
GO! GO! SEISYUN!
SERVE!
PDONK
PDNK
PDNK
WYUU WYU
SERVE!

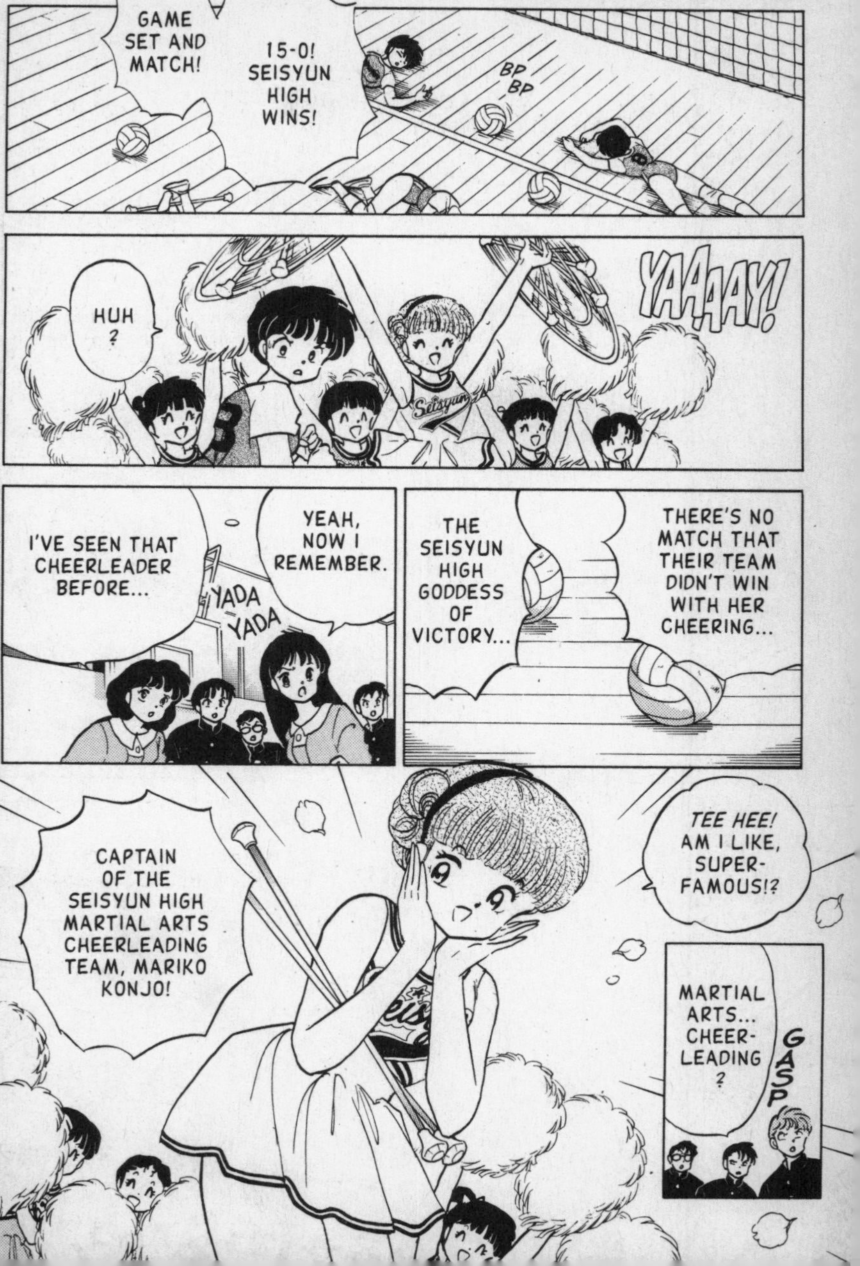
GAME SET AND MATCH!
15-0! SEISYUN HIGH WINS!
BP BP
HUH ?
YAAAAY!
I'VE SEEN THAT CHEERLEADER BEFORE...
YADA YADA
YEAH, NOW I REMEMBER.
THE SEISYUN HIGH GODDESS OF VICTORY...
THERE'S NO MATCH THAT THEIR TEAM DIDN'T WIN WITH HER CHEERING...
CAPTAIN OF THE SEISYUN HIGH MARTIAL ARTS CHEERLEADING TEAM, MARIKO KONJO!
TEE HEE! AM I LIKE, SUPER-FAMOUS!?
MARTIAL ARTS... CHEER-LEADING ?
GASP

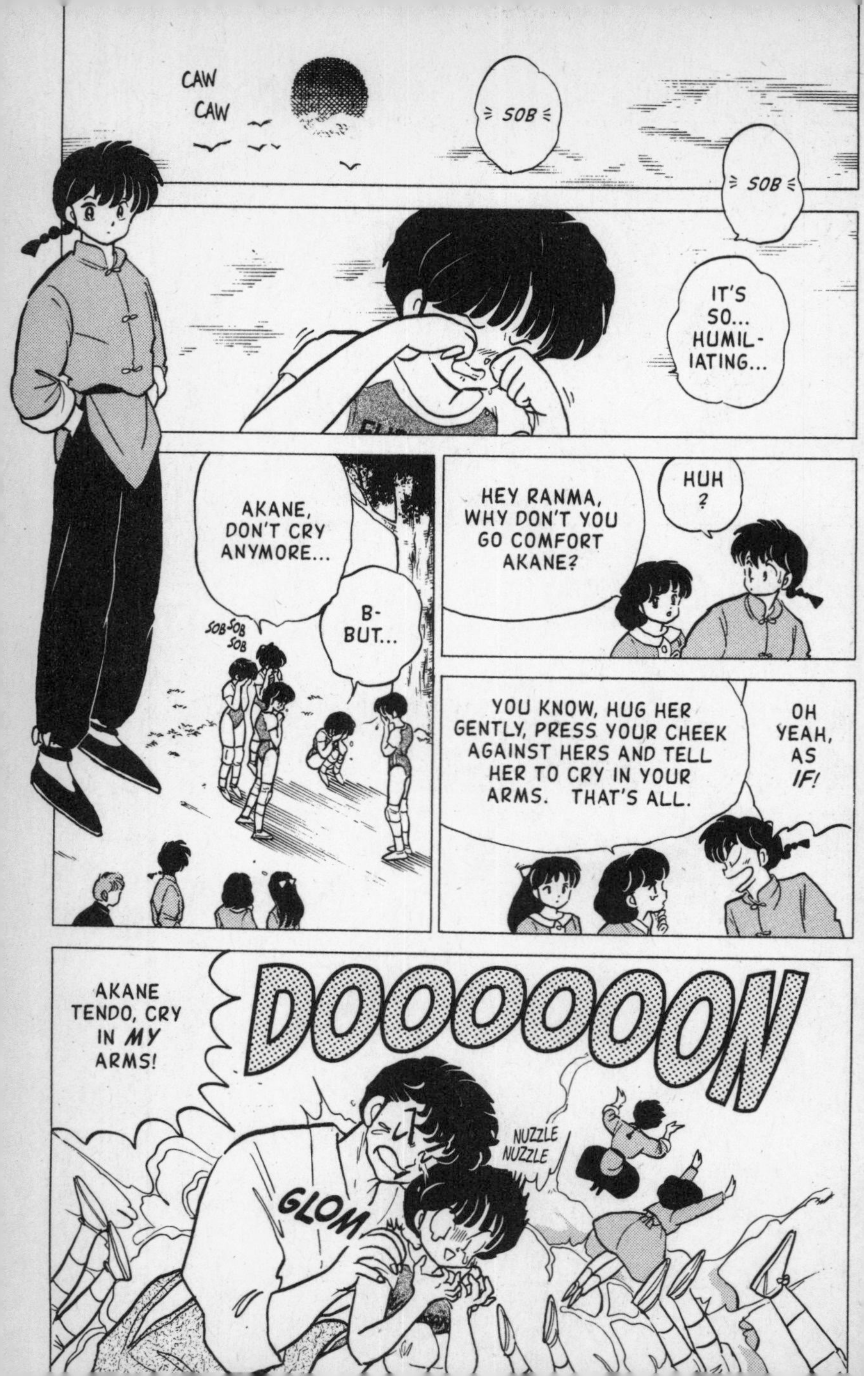

CAW
CAW
SOB
SOB
IT'S SO... HUMIL-IATING...
AKANE, DON'T CRY ANYMORE...
SOB-SOB SOB
B-BUT...
HEY RANMA, WHY DON'T YOU GO COMFORT AKANE?
HUH ?
YOU KNOW, HUG HER GENTLY, PRESS YOUR CHEEK AGAINST HERS AND TELL HER TO CRY IN YOUR ARMS. THAT'S ALL.
OH YEAH, AS IF!
AKANE TENDO, CRY IN MY ARMS!
DOOOOOOON
NUZZLE NUZZLE
GLOM

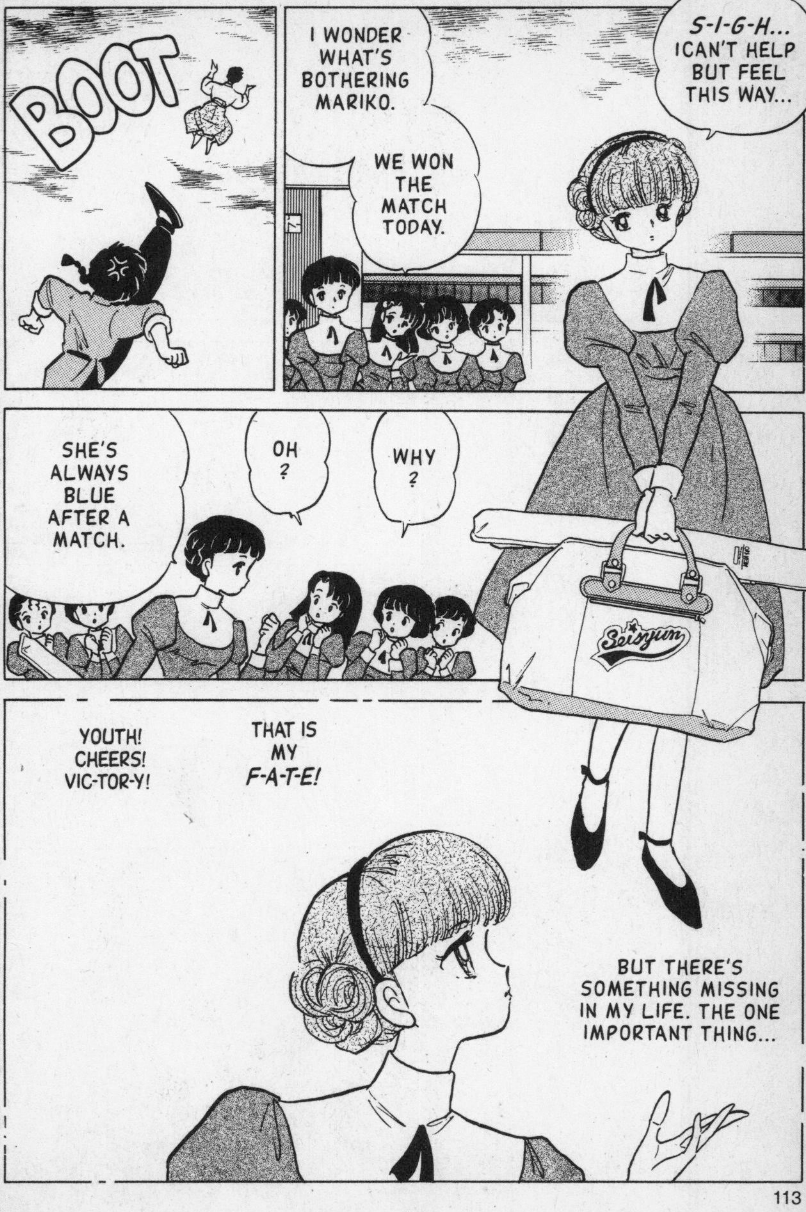

BOOT
I WONDER WHAT'S BOTHERING MARIKO.
WE WON THE MATCH TODAY.
S-I-G-H... I CAN'T HELP BUT FEEL THIS WAY...
SHE'S ALWAYS BLUE AFTER A MATCH.
OH?
WHY?
Seisyun
YOUTH! CHEERS! VIC-TOR-Y!
THAT IS MY F-A-T-E!
BUT THERE'S SOMETHING MISSING IN MY LIFE. THE ONE IMPORTANT THING...

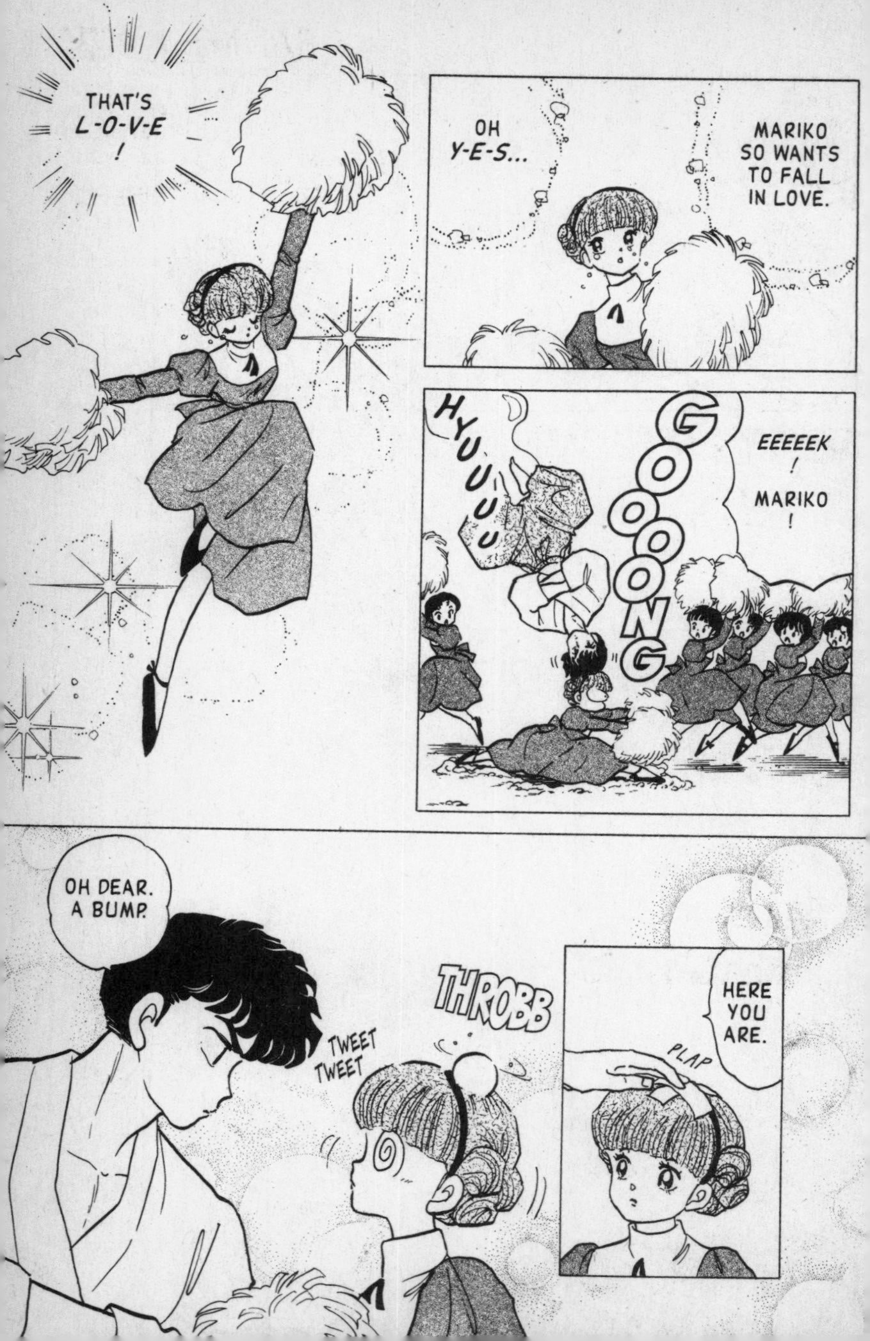
THAT'S L-O-V-E !
OH Y-E-S...
MARIKO SO WANTS TO FALL IN LOVE.
HYUUUUU
GOOOOONG
EEEEEK ! MARIKO !
OH DEAR. A BUMP.
TWEET TWEET
THROBB
PLAP
HERE YOU ARE.

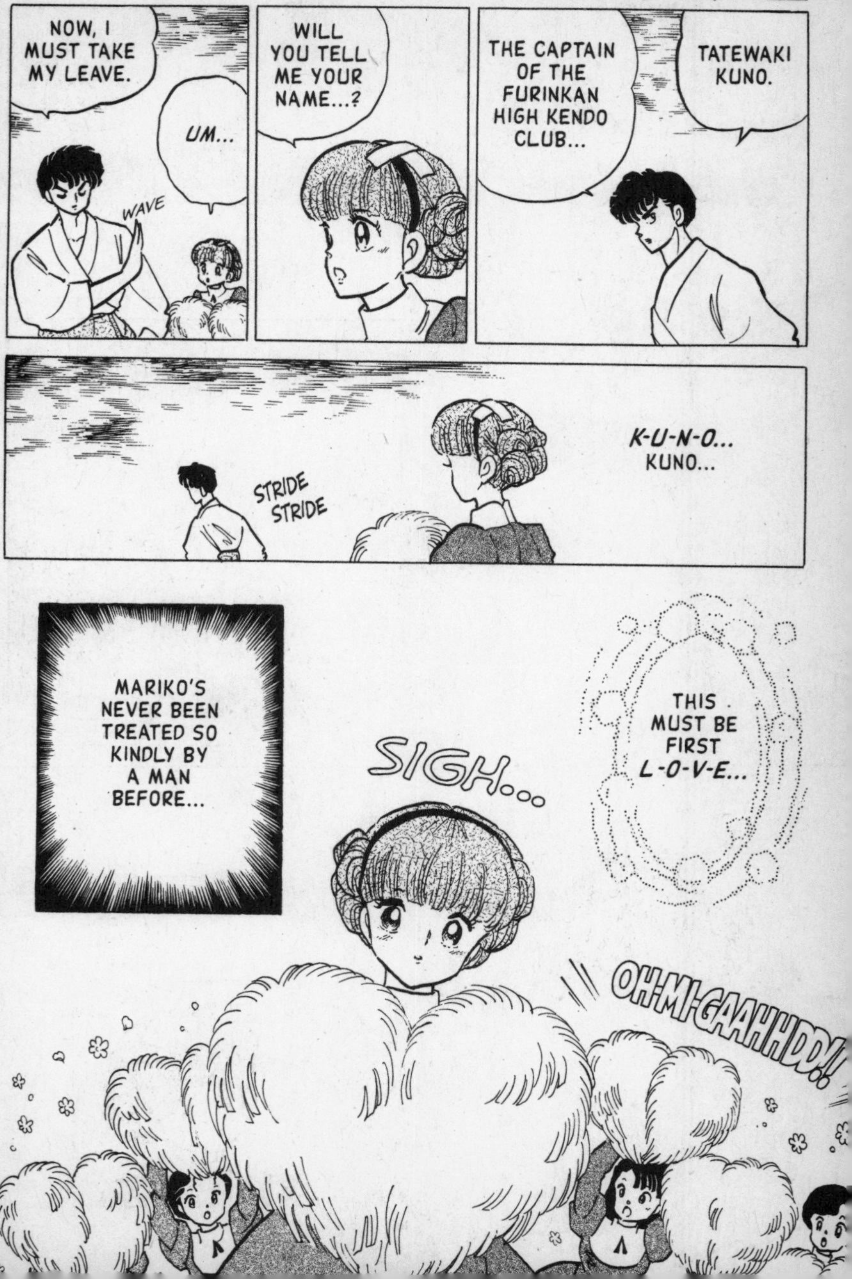
NOW, I MUST TAKE MY LEAVE.
UM...
WAVE
WILL YOU TELL ME YOUR NAME...?
THE CAPTAIN OF THE FURINKAN HIGH KENDO CLUB...
TATEWAKI KUNO.
STRIDE STRIDE
K-U-N-O... KUNO...
MARIKO'S NEVER BEEN TREATED SO KINDLY BY A MAN BEFORE...
SIGH...
THIS MUST BE FIRST L-O-V-E...
OH-MI-GAAHHDD!!

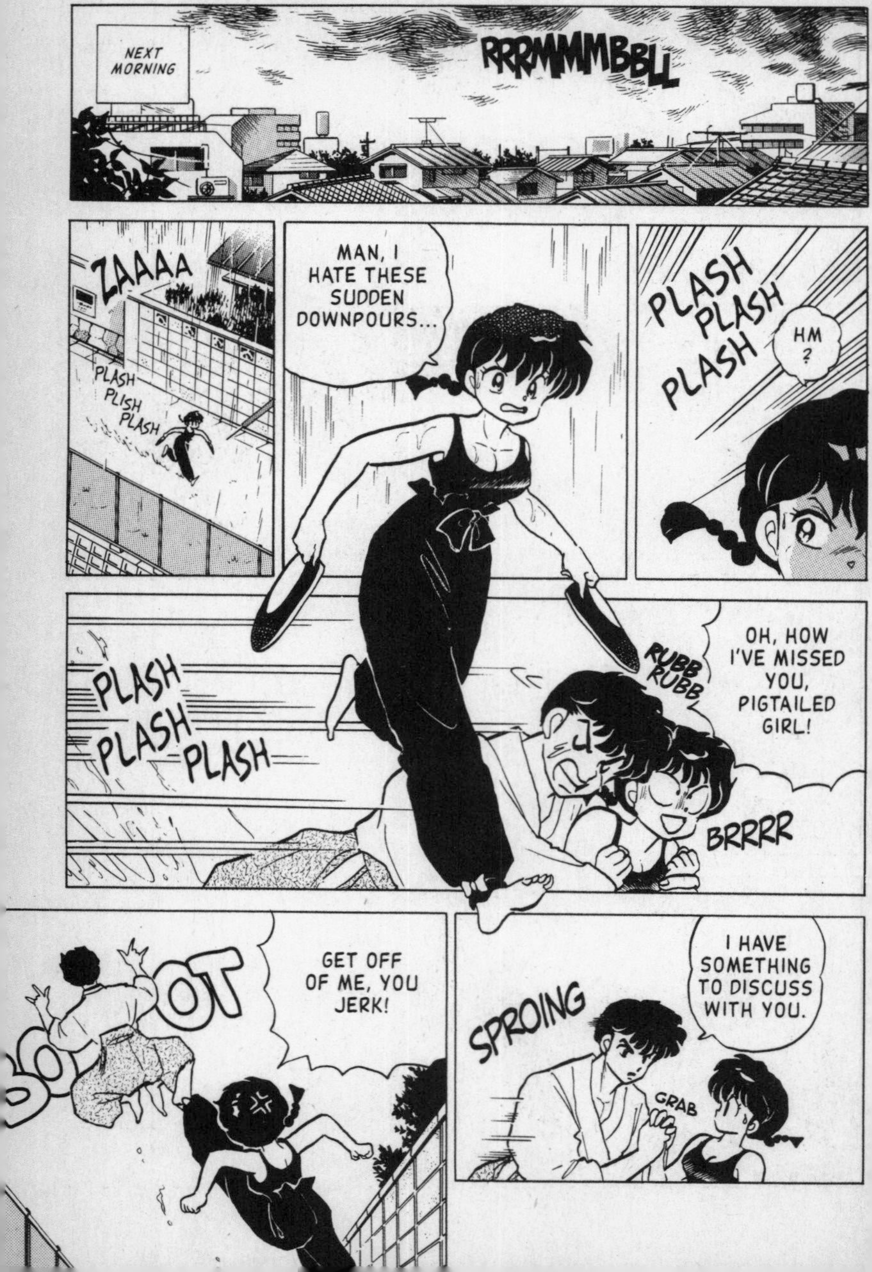
NEXT MORNING
RRRMMMMBBLL
ZAAAA
PLASH PLISH PLASH
MAN, I HATE THESE SUDDEN DOWNPOURS...
PLASH PLASH PLASH
HM ?
PLASH PLASH PLASH
RUBB RUBB
OH, HOW I'VE MISSED YOU, PIGTAILED GIRL!
BRRRR
BOOT
GET OFF OF ME, YOU JERK!
SPROING
I HAVE SOMETHING TO DISCUSS WITH YOU.
GRAB

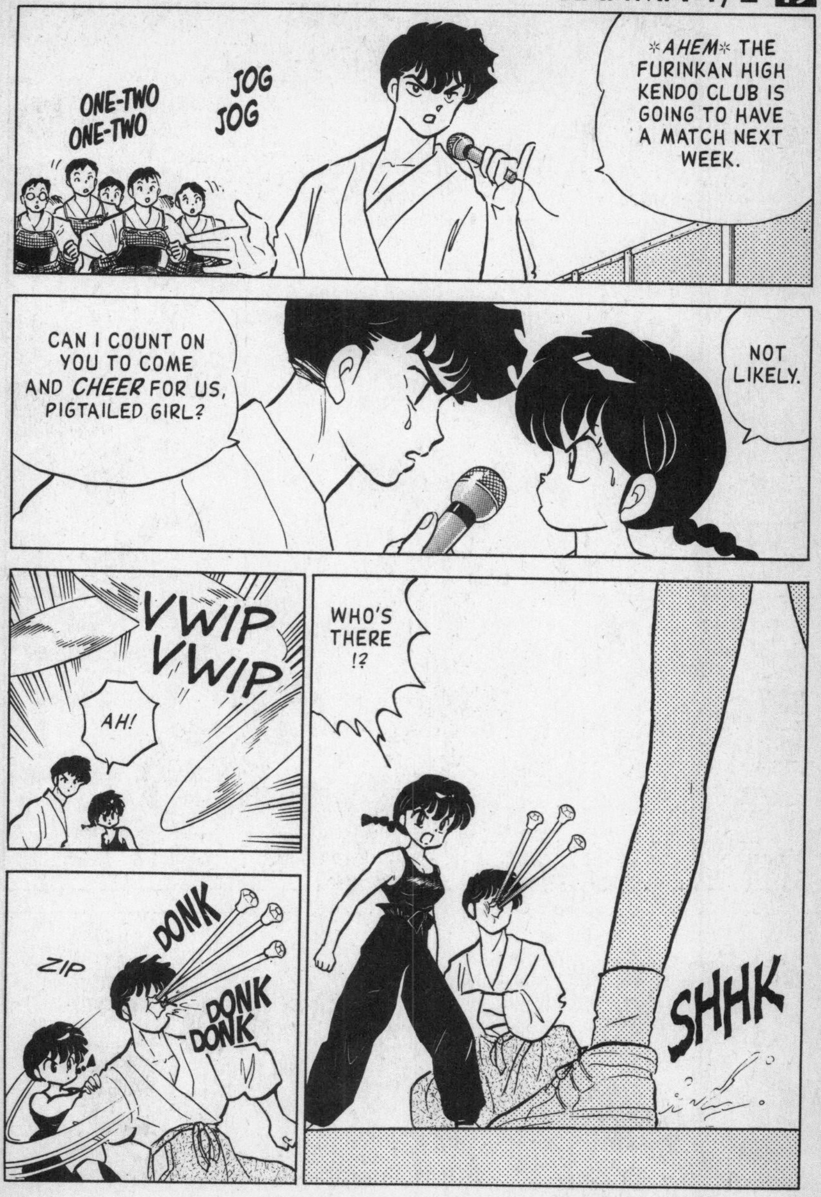
ONE-TWO ONE-TWO
JOG JOG
AHEM THE FURINKAN HIGH KENDO CLUB IS GOING TO HAVE A MATCH NEXT WEEK.
CAN I COUNT ON YOU TO COME AND *CHEER* FOR US, PIGTAILED GIRL?
NOT LIKELY.
VWIP VWIP
AH!
ZIP
DONK
DONK DONK
WHO'S THERE !?
SHHK

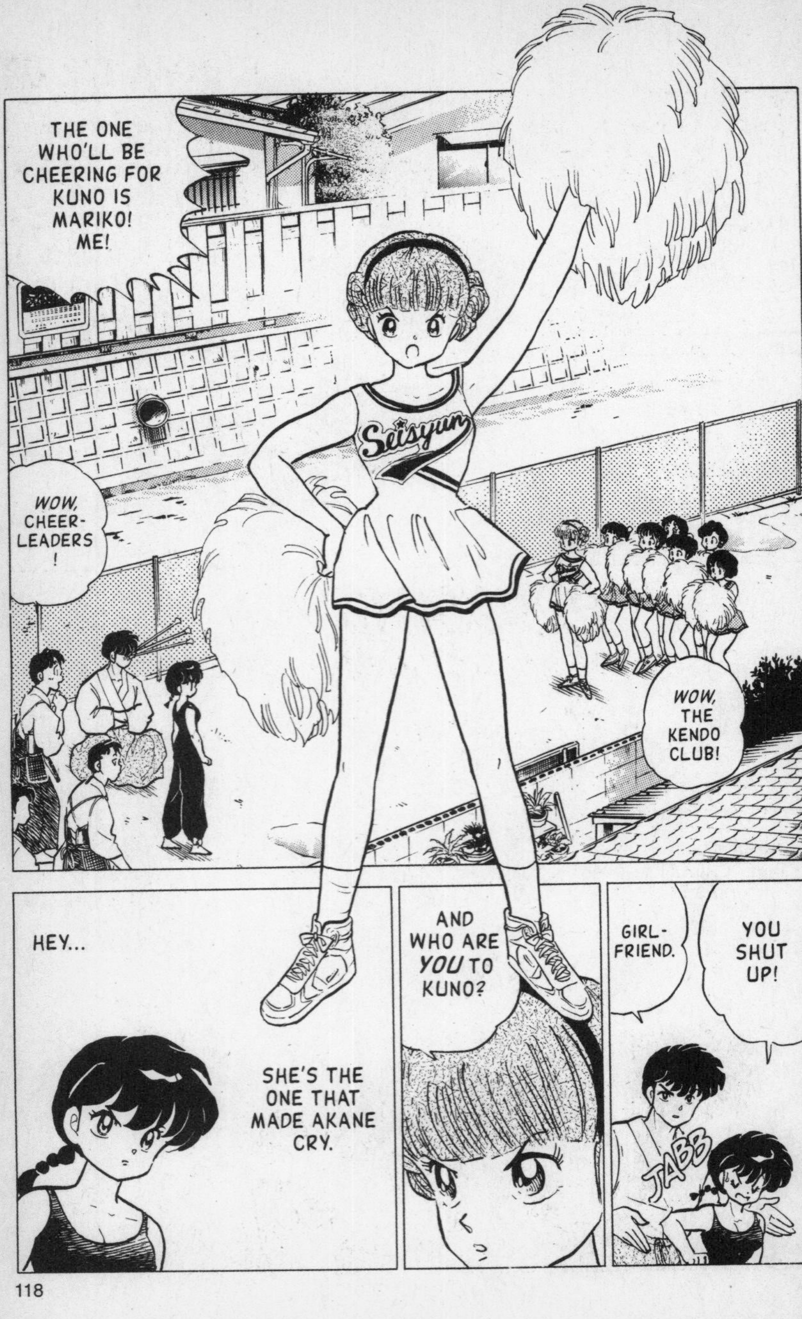
THE ONE WHO'LL BE CHEERING FOR KUNO IS MARIKO! ME!
WOW, CHEER-LEADERS!
WOW, THE KENDO CLUB!
HEY...
SHE'S THE ONE THAT MADE AKANE CRY.
AND WHO ARE *YOU* TO KUNO?
GIRL-FRIEND.
YOU SHUT UP!
JABB

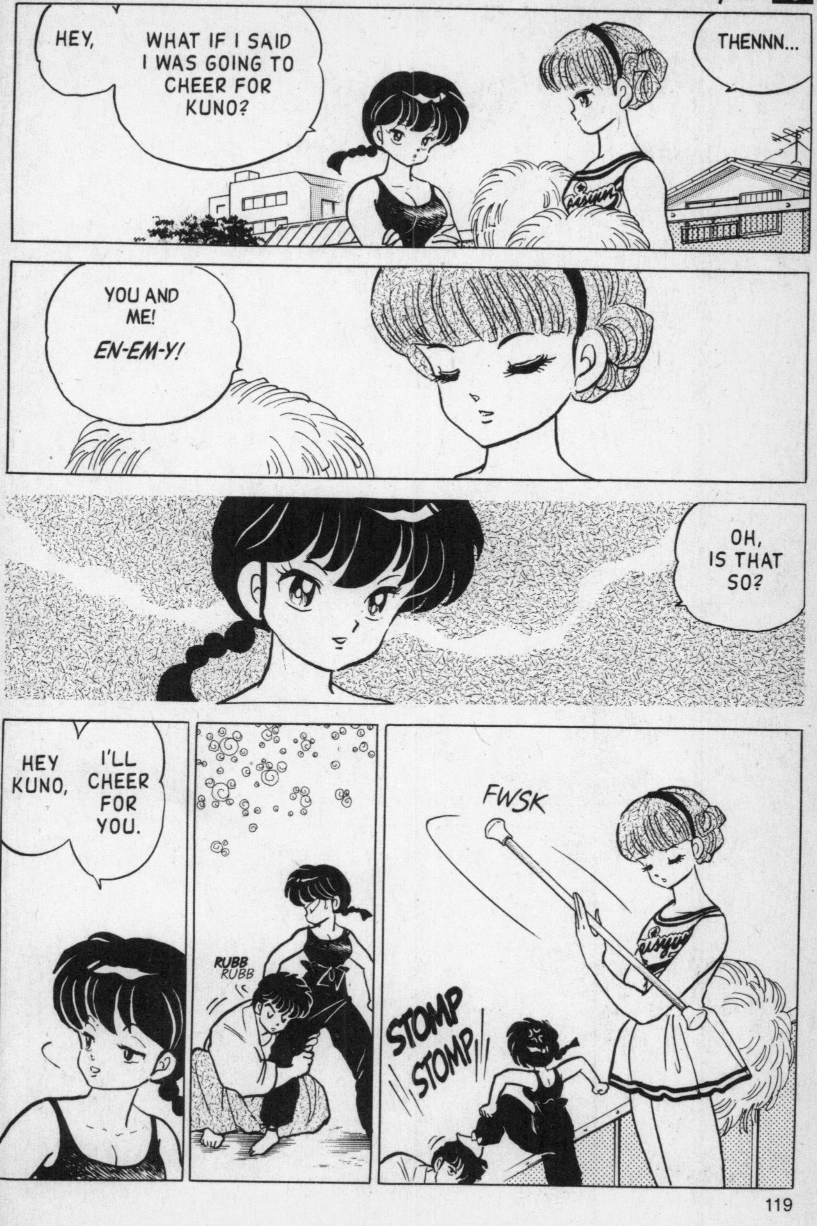
HEY, WHAT IF I SAID I WAS GOING TO CHEER FOR KUNO?
THENNN...
YOU AND ME! EN-EM-Y!
OH, IS THAT SO?
HEY KUNO, I'LL CHEER FOR YOU.
RUBB RUBB
FWSK
STOMP STOMP

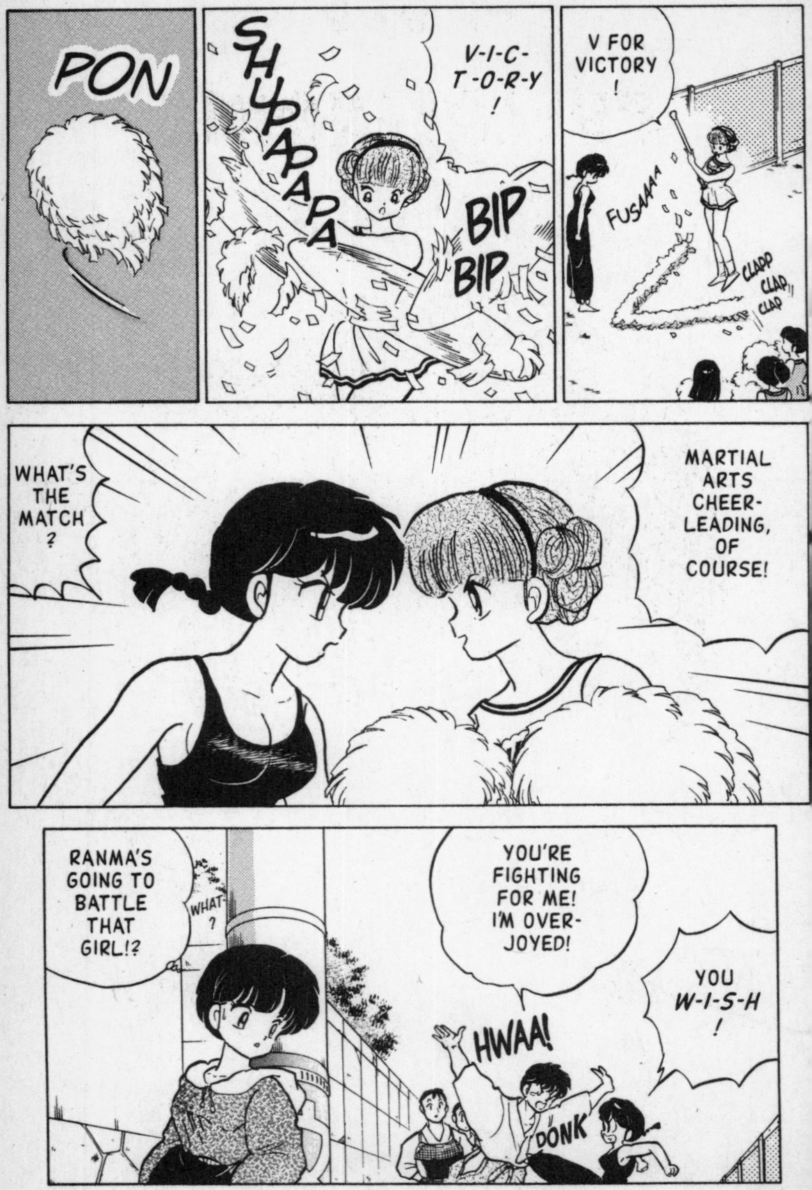
PON
SHUPAPAPA
V-I-C-T-O-R-Y!
BIP BIP
V FOR VICTORY!
FUSAAAA
CLAPP CLAP!! CLAP
WHAT'S THE MATCH?
MARTIAL ARTS CHEER-LEADING, OF COURSE!
RANMA'S GOING TO BATTLE THAT GIRL!?
WHAT?
YOU'RE FIGHTING FOR ME! I'M OVER-JOYED!
YOU W-I-S-H!
HWAA!
DONK

Part 8

CHEERLEADING FOR LOVE

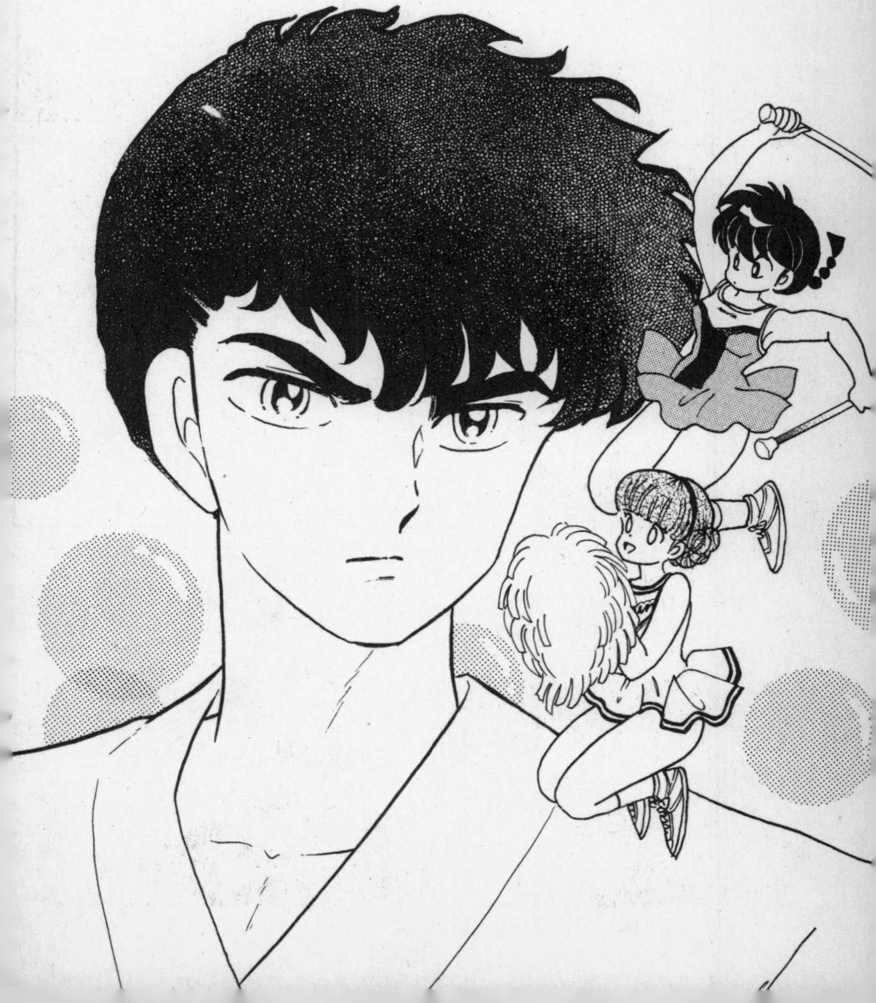

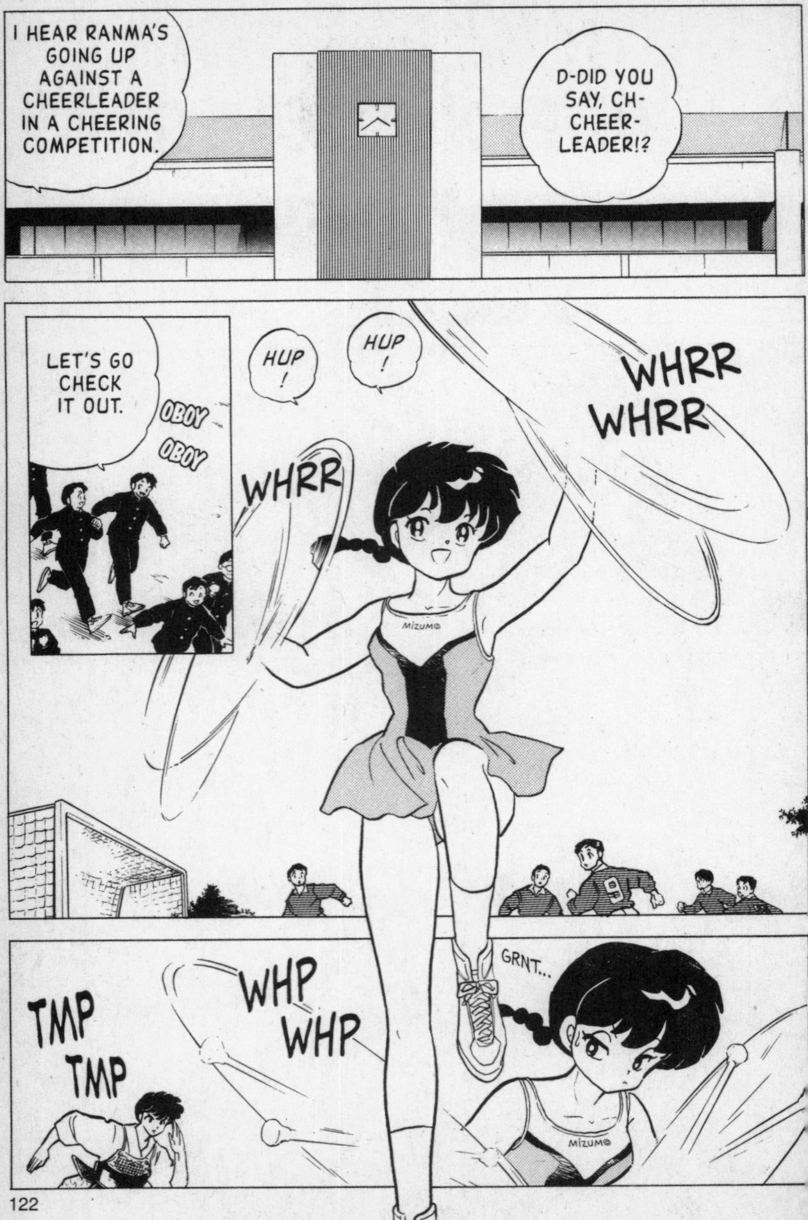
I HEAR RANMA'S GOING UP AGAINST A CHEERLEADER IN A CHEERING COMPETITION.
D-DID YOU SAY, CH-CHEER-LEADER!?
LET'S GO CHECK IT OUT.
OBOY
OBOY
HUP!
HUP!
WHRR
WHRR
WHRR
MIZUMO
TMP
TMP
WHP
WHP
GRNT...
MIZUMO

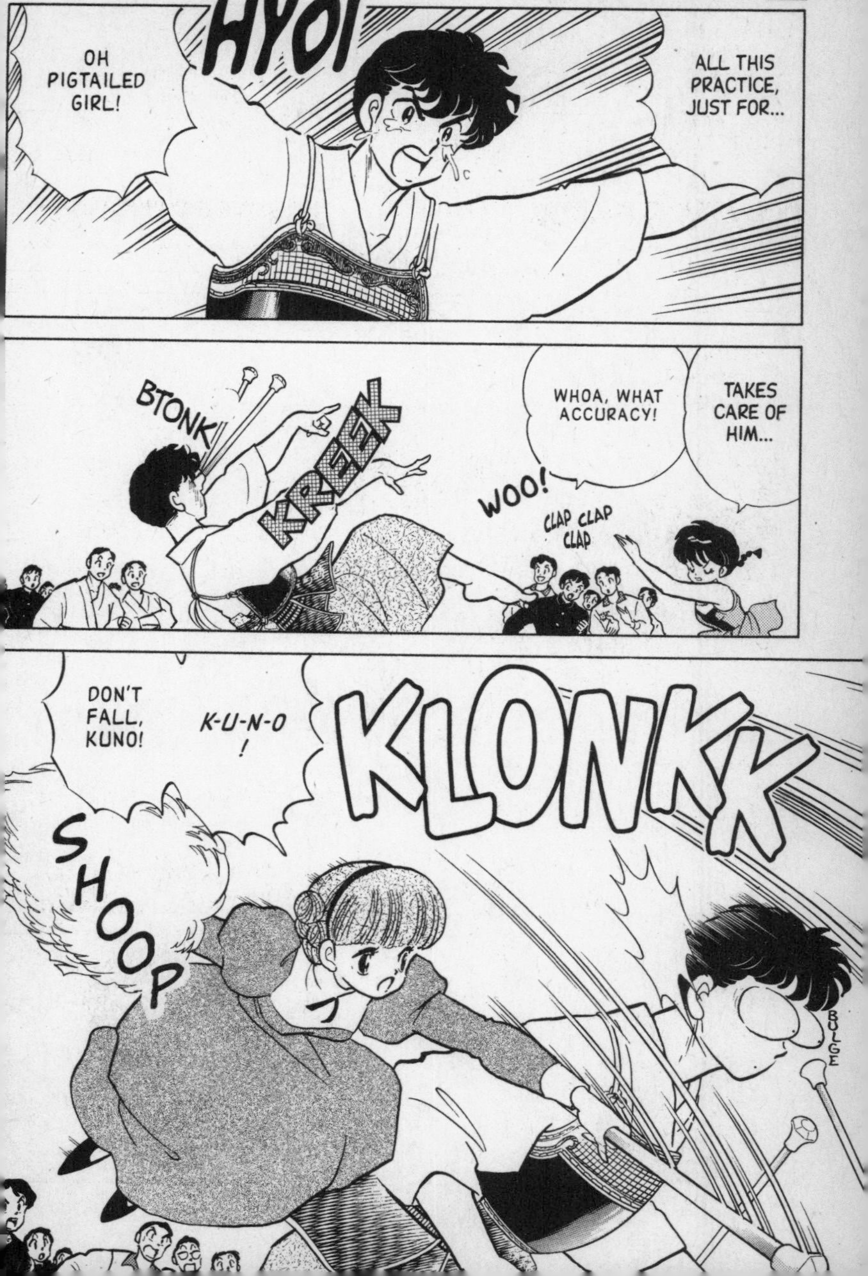
OH PIGTAILED GIRL!
HYOI
ALL THIS PRACTICE, JUST FOR...
BTONK
KREEK
WOO!
WHOA, WHAT ACCURACY!
TAKES CARE OF HIM...
CLAP CLAP CLAP
DON'T FALL, KUNO!
K-U-N-O !
KLONKK
SHOOP
BULGE

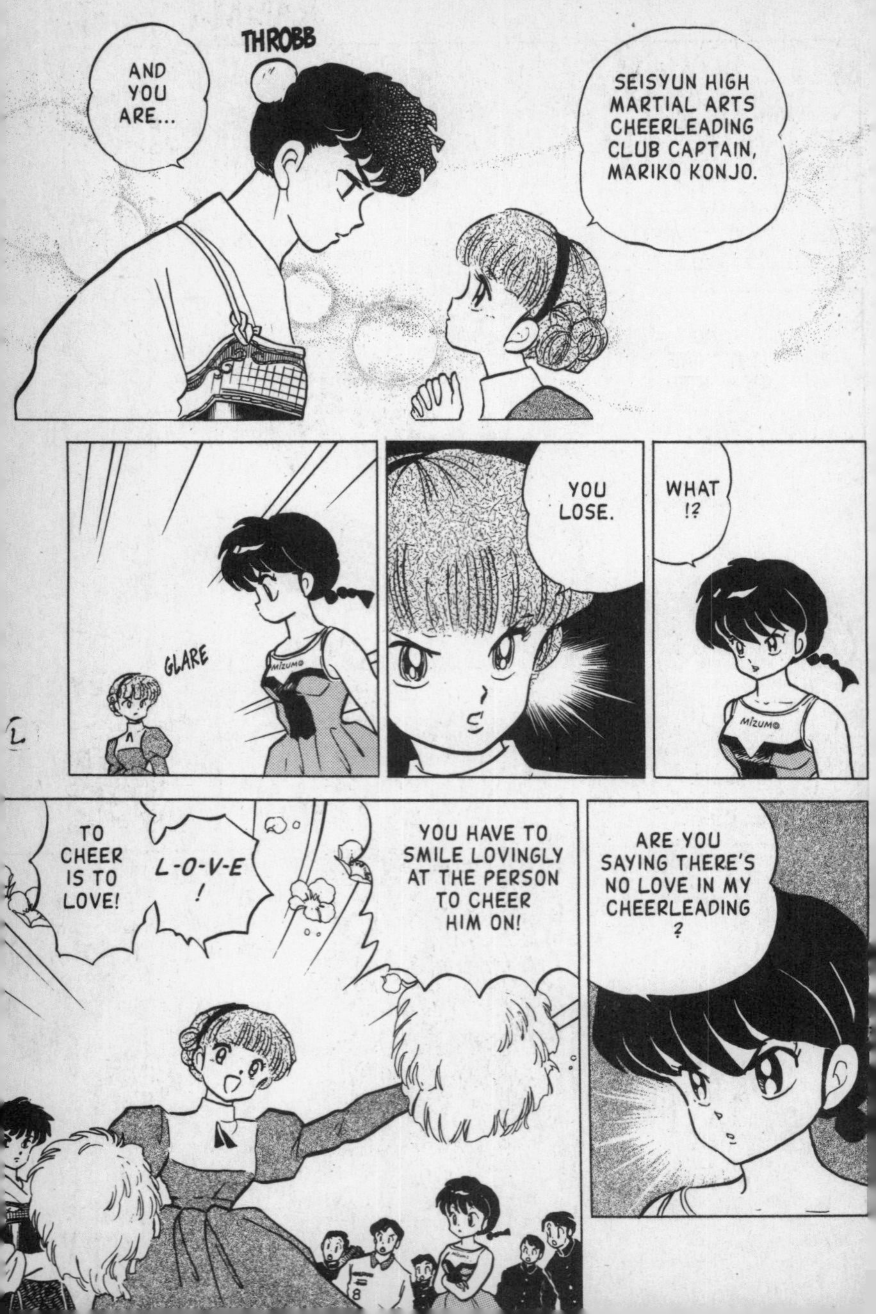
AND YOU ARE...
THROBB
SEISYUN HIGH MARTIAL ARTS CHEERLEADING CLUB CAPTAIN, MARIKO KONJO.
GLARE
YOU LOSE.
WHAT !?
TO CHEER IS TO LOVE!
L-O-V-E !
YOU HAVE TO SMILE LOVINGLY AT THE PERSON TO CHEER HIM ON!
ARE YOU SAYING THERE'S NO LOVE IN MY CHEERLEADING ?

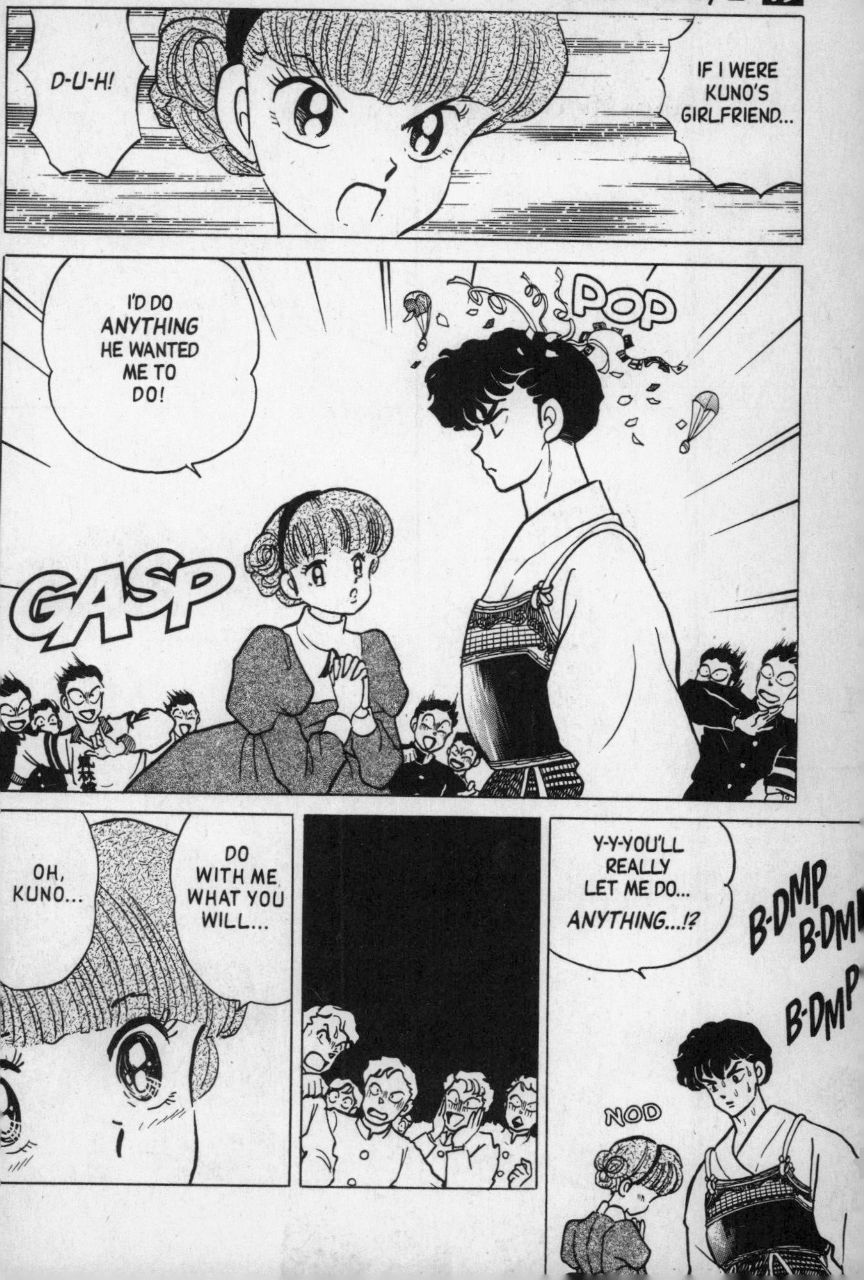
D-U-H!
IF I WERE KUNO'S GIRLFRIEND...
I'D DO ANYTHING HE WANTED ME TO DO!
POP
GASP
OH, KUNO...
DO WITH ME WHAT YOU WILL...
Y-Y-YOU'LL REALLY LET ME DO... ANYTHING...!?
B-DMP
B-DMP
B-DMP
NOD

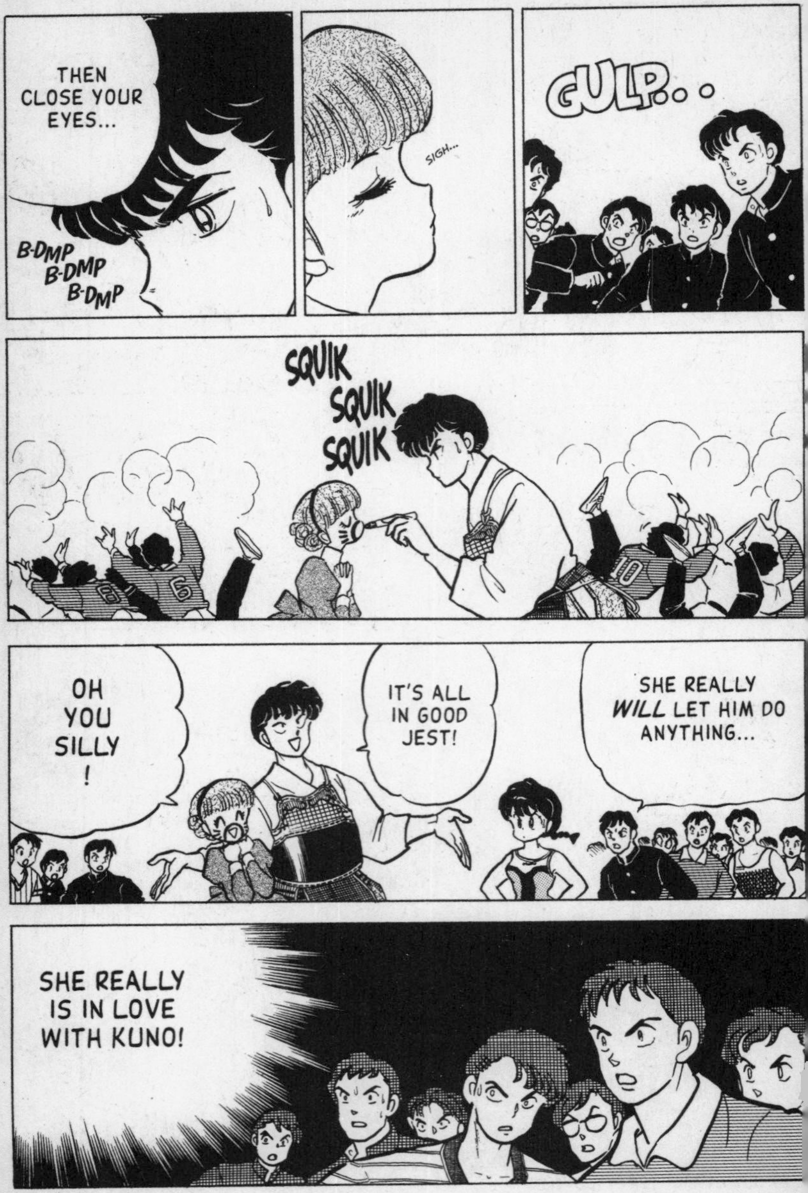
THEN CLOSE YOUR EYES...
B-DMP B-DMP B-DMP
SIGH...
GULP...
SQUIK SQUIK SQUIK
OH YOU SILLY!
IT'S ALL IN GOOD JEST!
SHE REALLY WILL LET HIM DO ANYTHING...
SHE REALLY IS IN LOVE WITH KUNO!

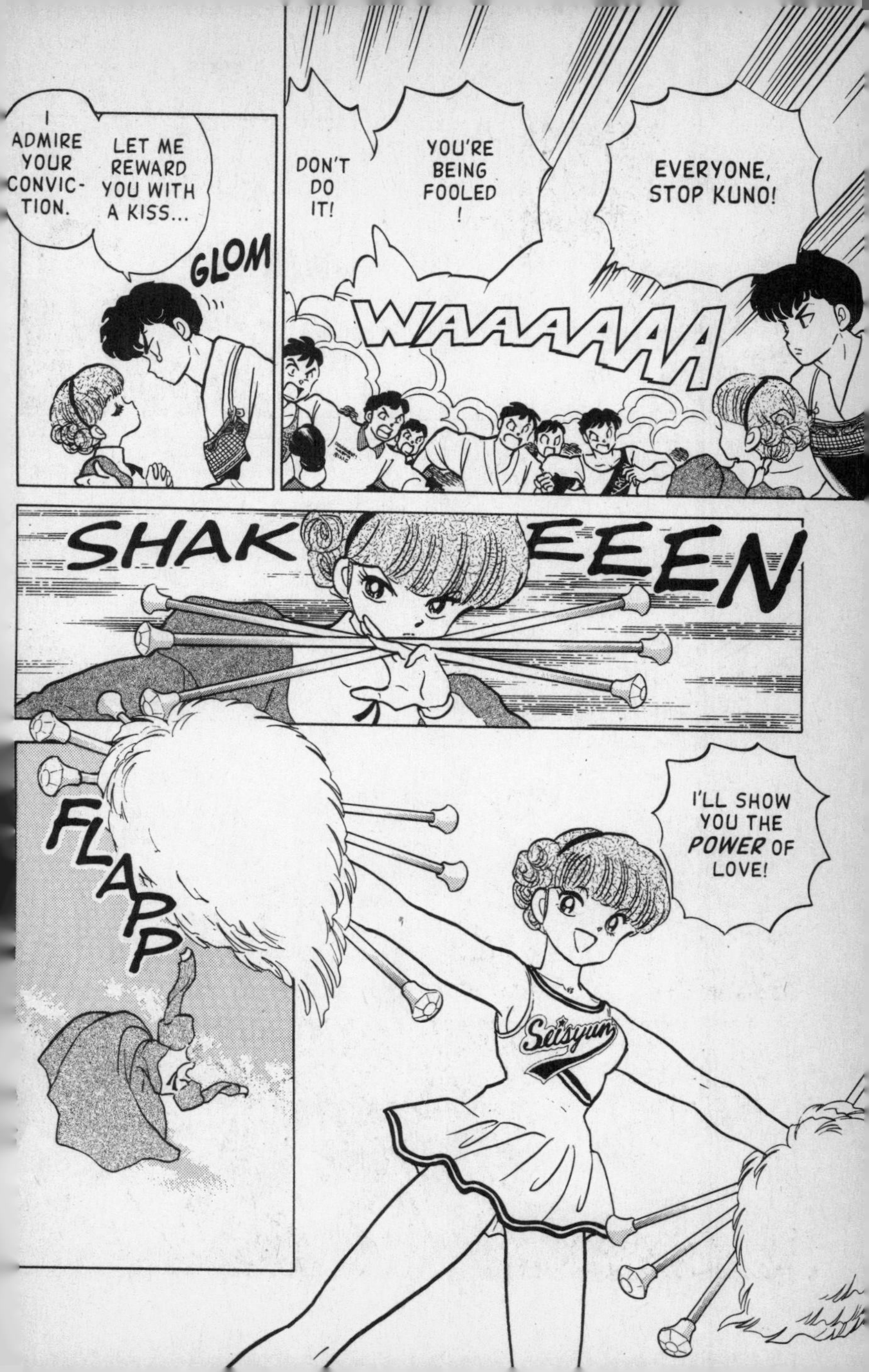
I ADMIRE YOUR CONVICTION.
LET ME REWARD YOU WITH A KISS...
GLOM
DON'T DO IT!
YOU'RE BEING FOOLED!
EVERYONE, STOP KUNO!
WAAAAAAA
SHAK EEEN
FLAPP
I'LL SHOW YOU THE *POWER* OF LOVE!
Seisyun

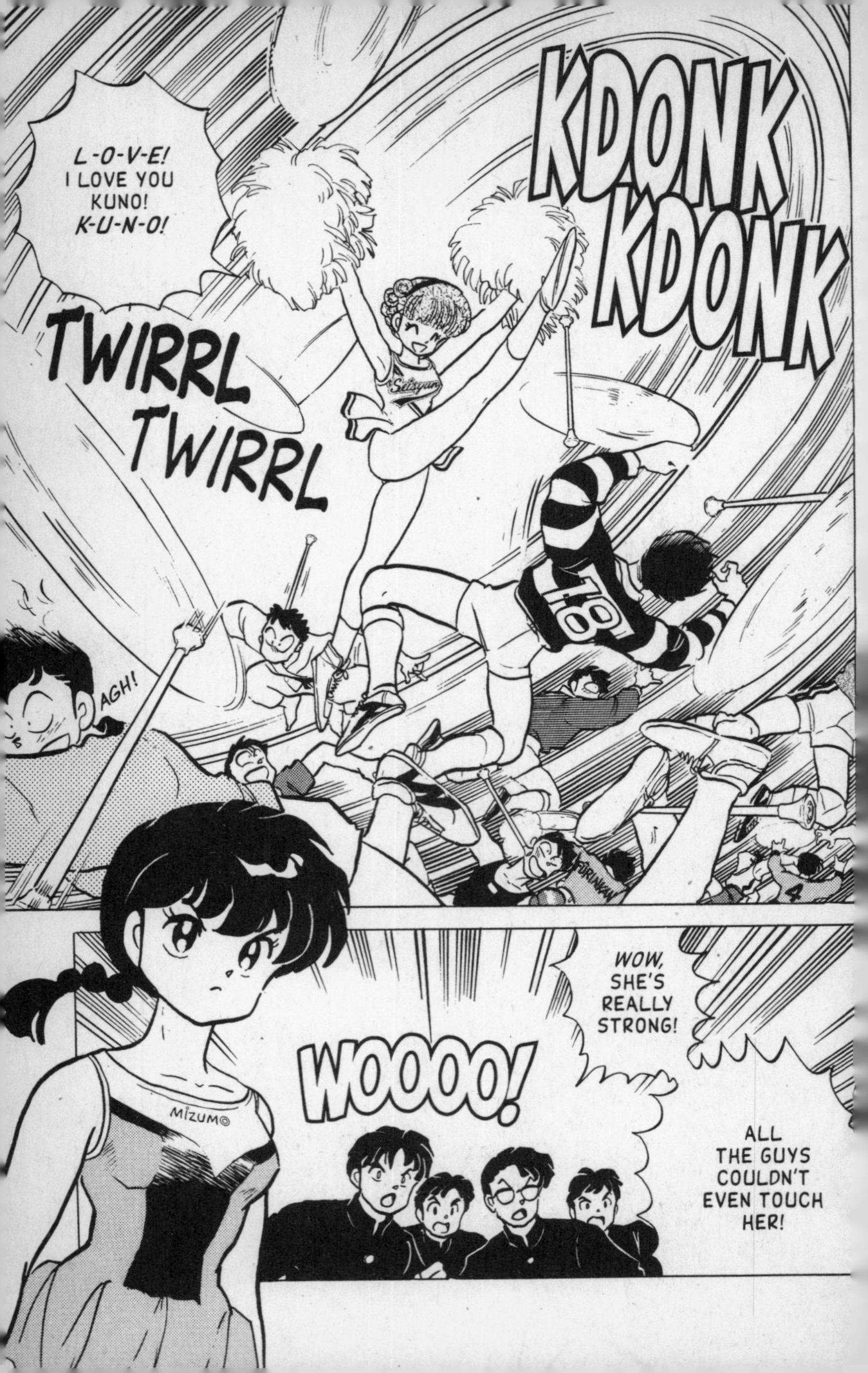
L-O-V-E! I LOVE YOU KUNO! K-U-N-O!
KDONK KDONK
TWIRRL TWIRRL
AGH!
WOW, SHE'S REALLY STRONG!
WOOOO!
ALL THE GUYS COULDN'T EVEN TOUCH HER!

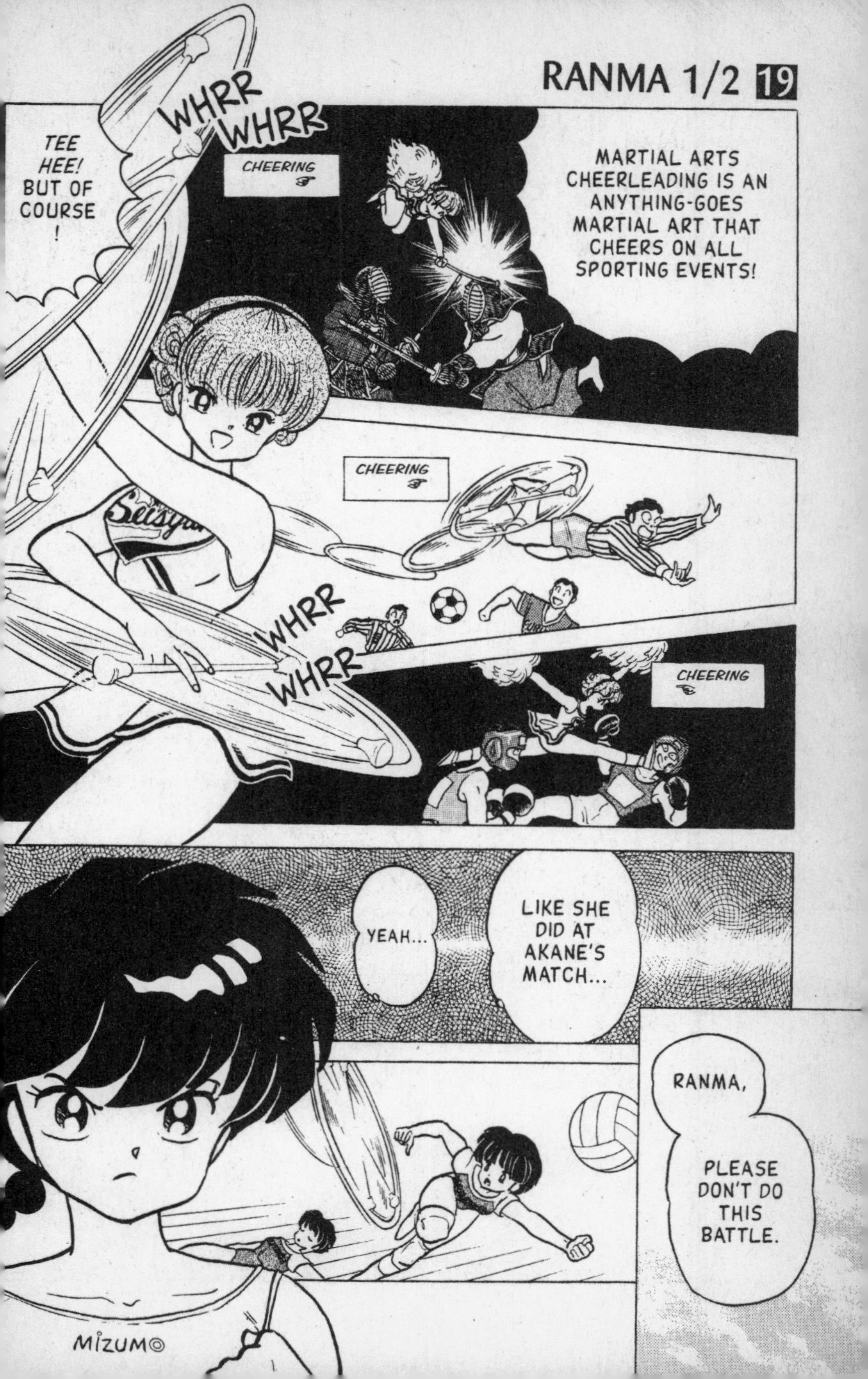
WHRR WHRR
TEE HEE! BUT OF COURSE!
CHEERING
MARTIAL ARTS CHEERLEADING IS AN ANYTHING-GOES MARTIAL ART THAT CHEERS ON ALL SPORTING EVENTS!
CHEERING
WHRR WHRR
CHEERING
YEAH...
LIKE SHE DID AT AKANE'S MATCH...
RANMA,
PLEASE DON'T DO THIS BATTLE.
MIZUMO

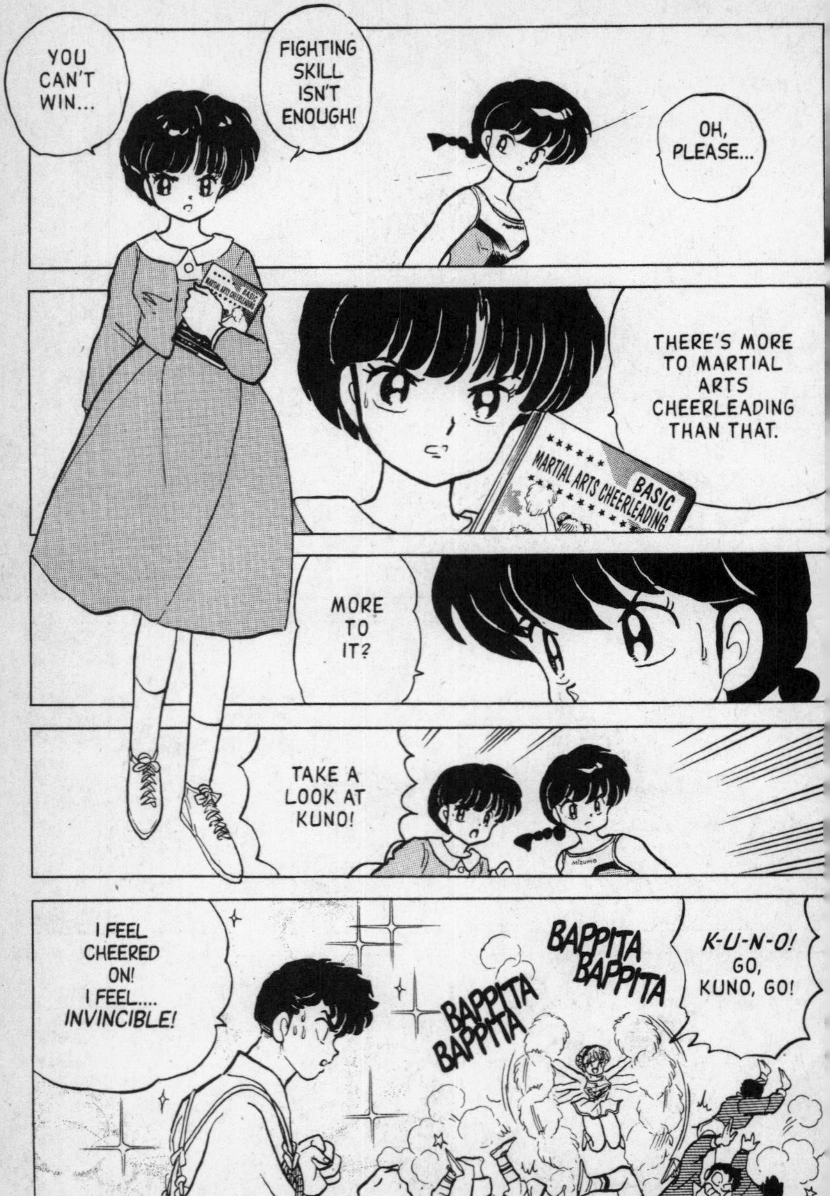
YOU CAN'T WIN...
FIGHTING SKILL ISN'T ENOUGH!
OH, PLEASE...
BASIC MARTIAL ARTS CHEERLEADING
THERE'S MORE TO MARTIAL ARTS CHEERLEADING THAN THAT.
MORE TO IT?
TAKE A LOOK AT KUNO!
MIZUNO
I FEEL CHEERED ON! I FEEL.... *INVINCIBLE!*
BAPPITA BAPPITA
BAPPITA BAPPITA
K-U-N-O! GO, KUNO, GO!

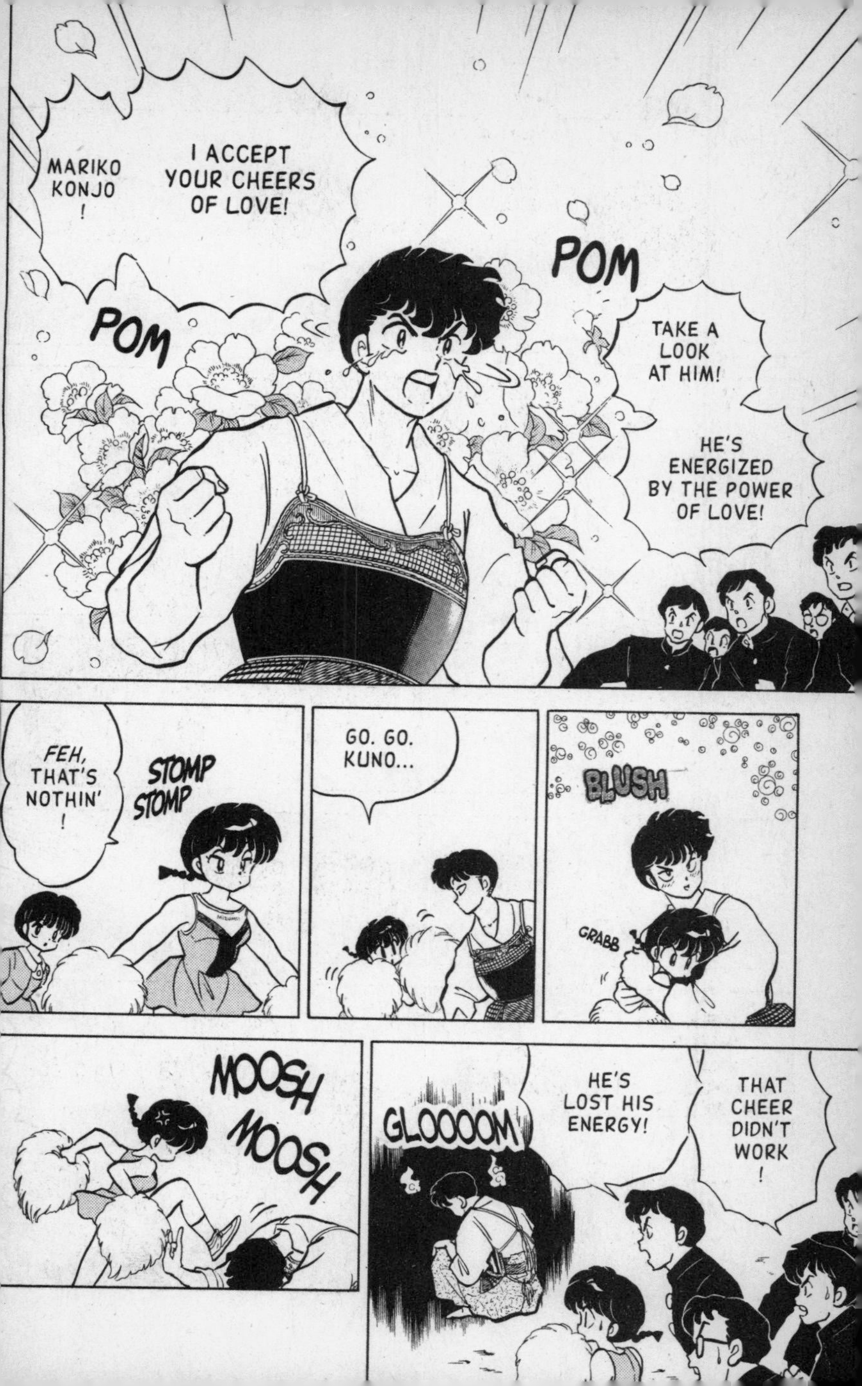
MARIKO KONJO !
I ACCEPT YOUR CHEERS OF LOVE!
POM
POM
TAKE A LOOK AT HIM!
HE'S ENERGIZED BY THE POWER OF LOVE!
FEH, THAT'S NOTHIN' !
STOMP STOMP
GO. GO. KUNO...
BLUSH
GRABB
MOOSH MOOSH
GLOOOOM
HE'S LOST HIS ENERGY!
THAT CHEER DIDN'T WORK !

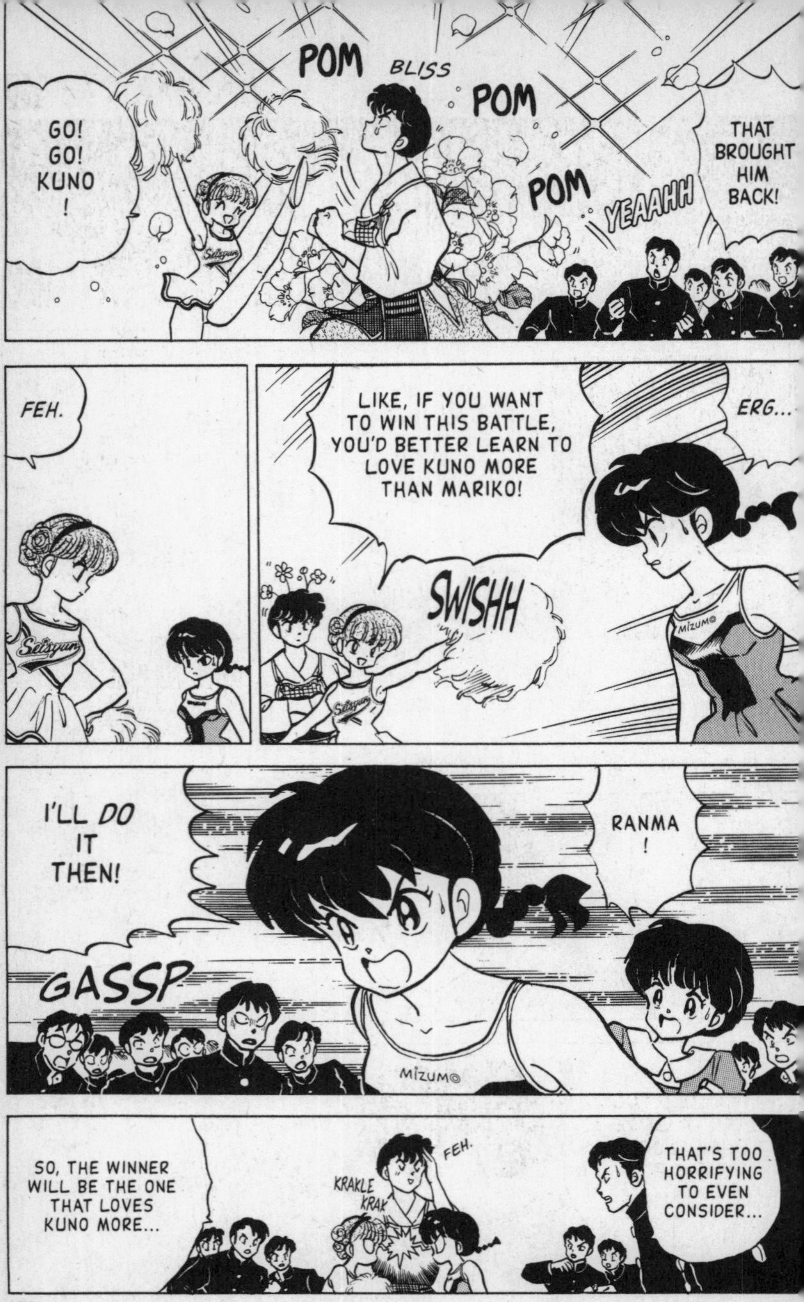
GO! GO! KUNO !
POM
BLISS
POM
POM
YEAAHH
THAT BROUGHT HIM BACK!
FEH.
LIKE, IF YOU WANT TO WIN THIS BATTLE, YOU'D BETTER LEARN TO LOVE KUNO MORE THAN MARIKO!
SWISHH
ERG...
I'LL *DO* IT THEN!
GASSP
RANMA !
SO, THE WINNER WILL BE THE ONE THAT LOVES KUNO MORE...
KRAKLE KRAK
FEH.
THAT'S TOO HORRIFYING TO EVEN CONSIDER...

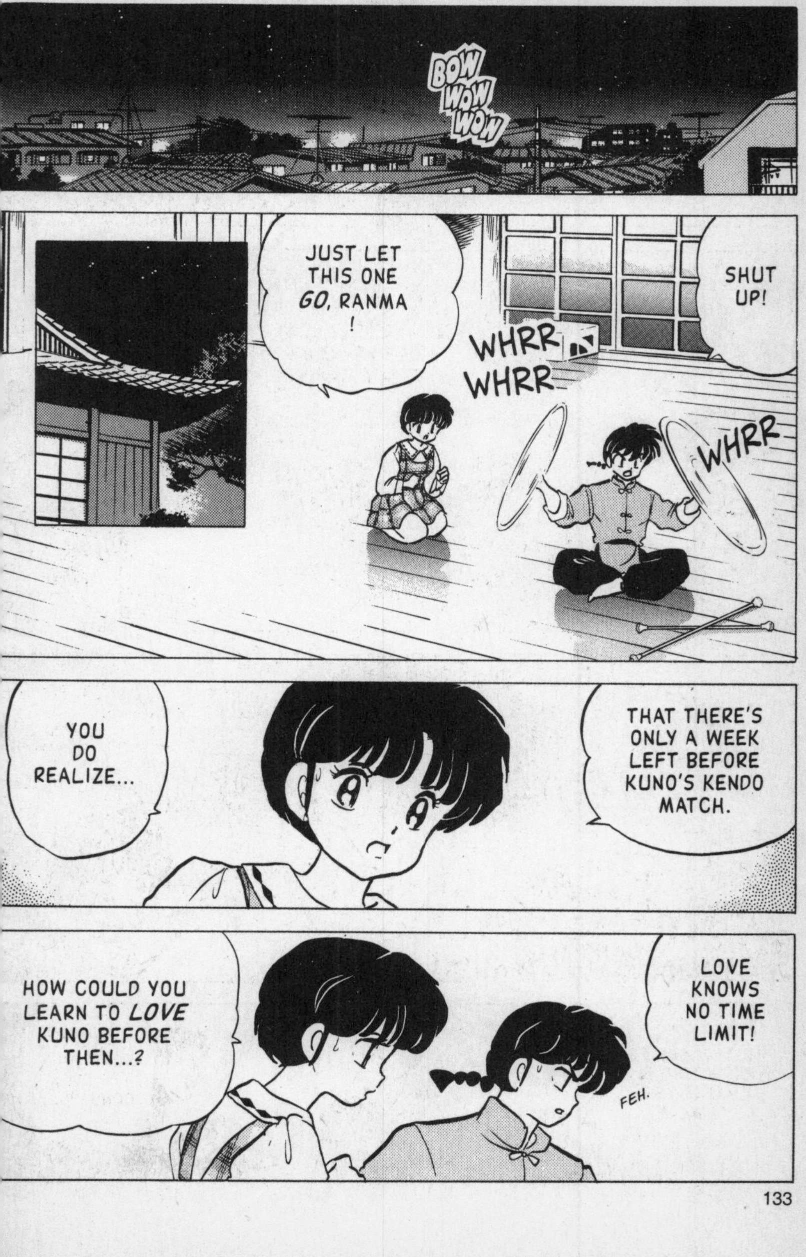
BOW WOW WOW
JUST LET THIS ONE GO, RANMA!
WHRR WHRR
SHUT UP!
WHRR
YOU DO REALIZE...
THAT THERE'S ONLY A WEEK LEFT BEFORE KUNO'S KENDO MATCH.
HOW COULD YOU LEARN TO LOVE KUNO BEFORE THEN...?
FEH.
LOVE KNOWS NO TIME LIMIT!

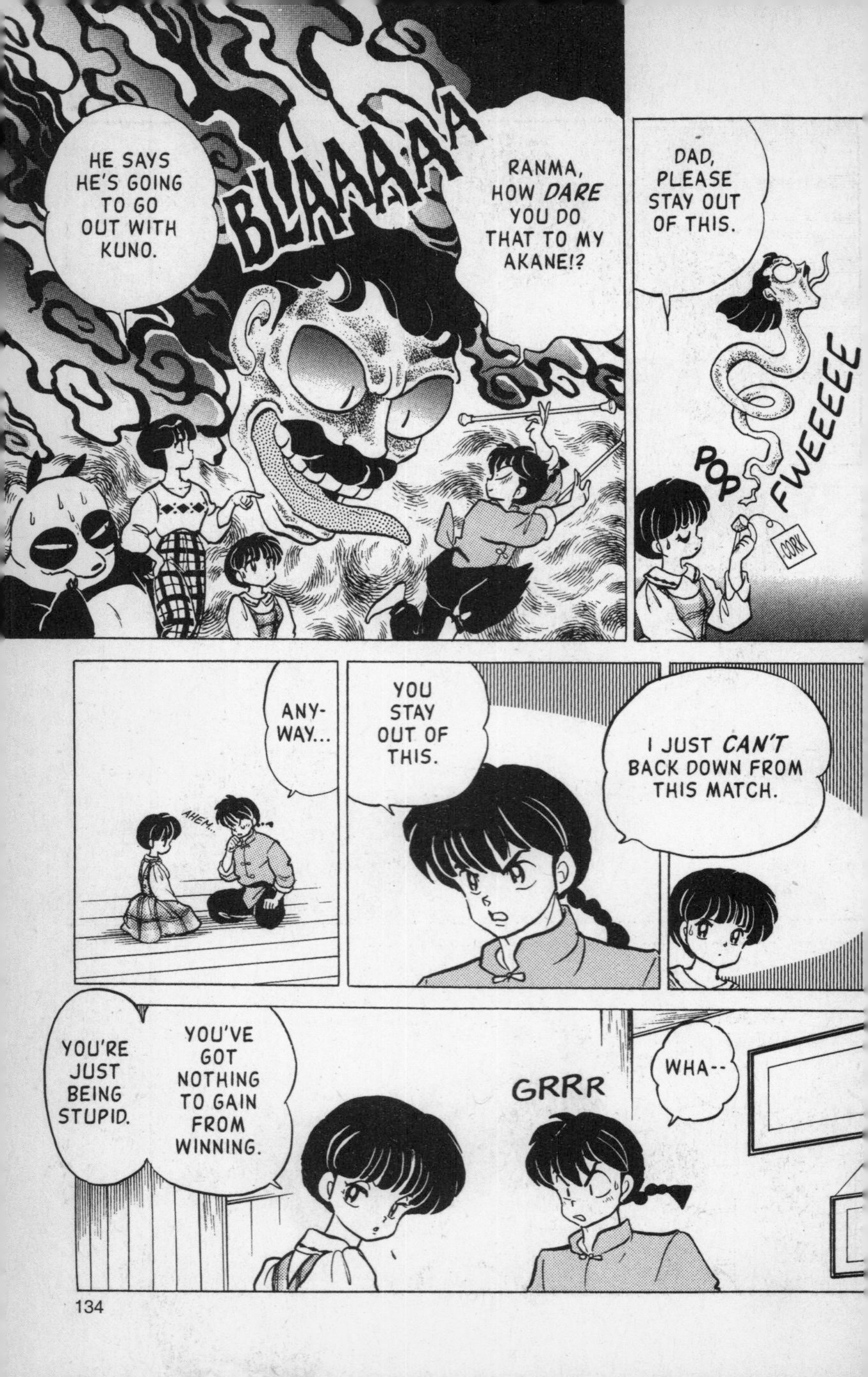
HE SAYS HE'S GOING TO GO OUT WITH KUNO.
BLAAAAAA
RANMA, HOW *DARE* YOU DO THAT TO MY AKANE!?
DAD, PLEASE STAY OUT OF THIS.
POP
FWEEEEE
CORK
ANY-WAY...
AHEM...
YOU STAY OUT OF THIS.
I JUST *CAN'T* BACK DOWN FROM THIS MATCH.
YOU'RE JUST BEING STUPID.
YOU'VE GOT NOTHING TO GAIN FROM WINNING.
GRRR
WHA--

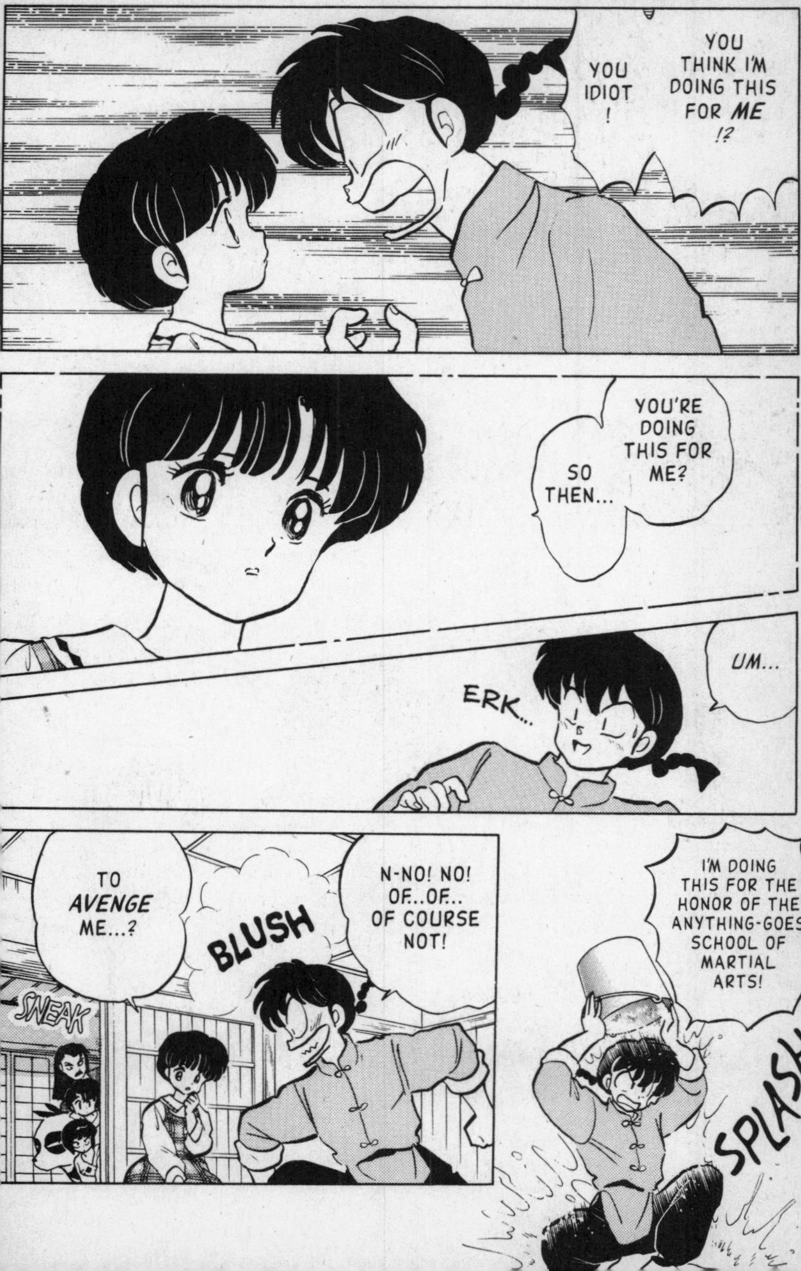
YOU IDIOT !
YOU THINK I'M DOING THIS FOR *ME* !?
SO THEN...
YOU'RE DOING THIS FOR ME?
ERK...
UM...
TO *AVENGE* ME...?
SNEAK
BLUSH
N-NO! NO! OF...OF... OF COURSE NOT!
I'M DOING THIS FOR THE HONOR OF THE ANYTHING-GOES SCHOOL OF MARTIAL ARTS!
SPLASH

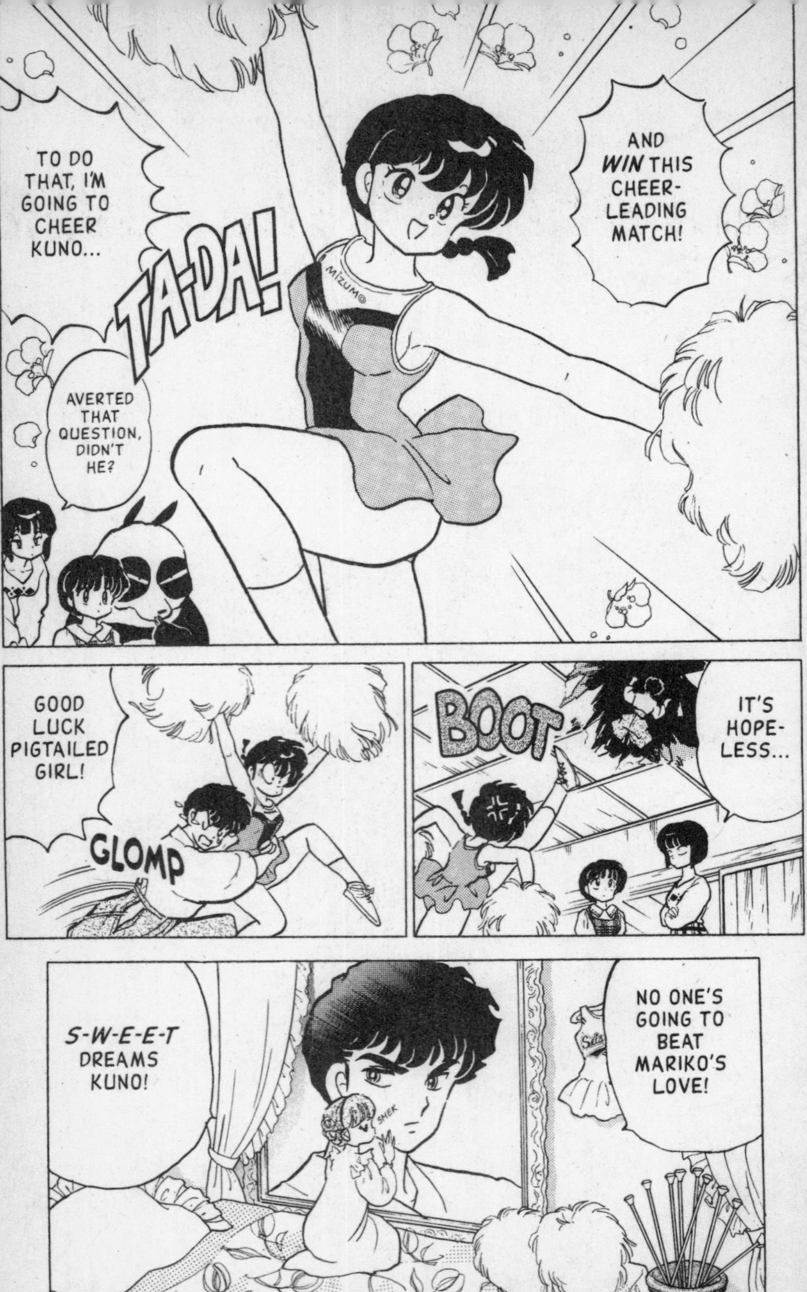
TO DO THAT, I'M GOING TO CHEER KUNO...
TA-DA!
AND WIN THIS CHEER-LEADING MATCH!
MIZUMO
AVERTED THAT QUESTION, DIDN'T HE?
GOOD LUCK PIGTAILED GIRL!
GLOMP
BOOT
IT'S HOPE-LESS...
S-W-E-E-T DREAMS KUNO!
SHEK
NO ONE'S GOING TO BEAT MARIKO'S LOVE!

Part 9

WIN ONE FOR THE LOVER

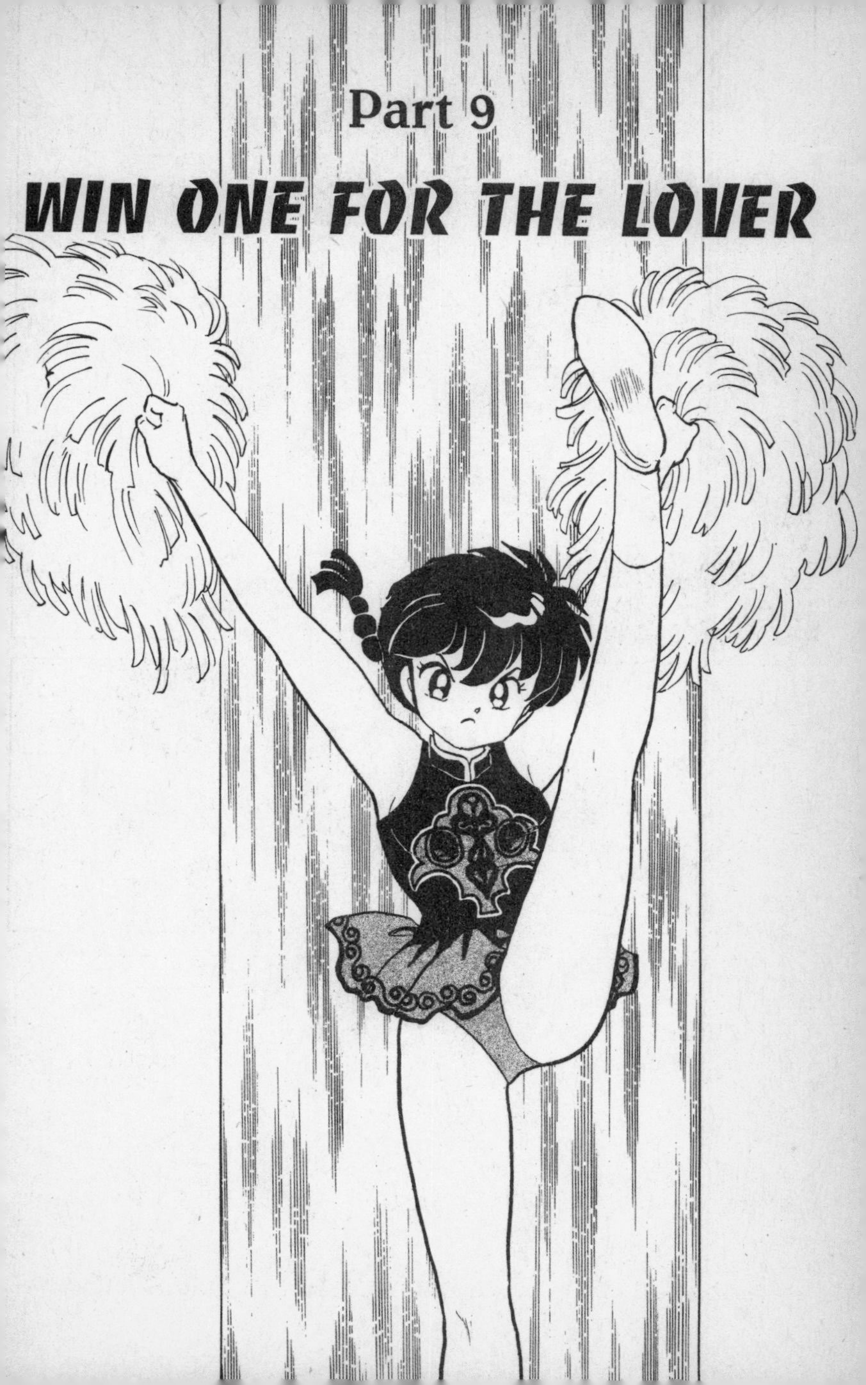

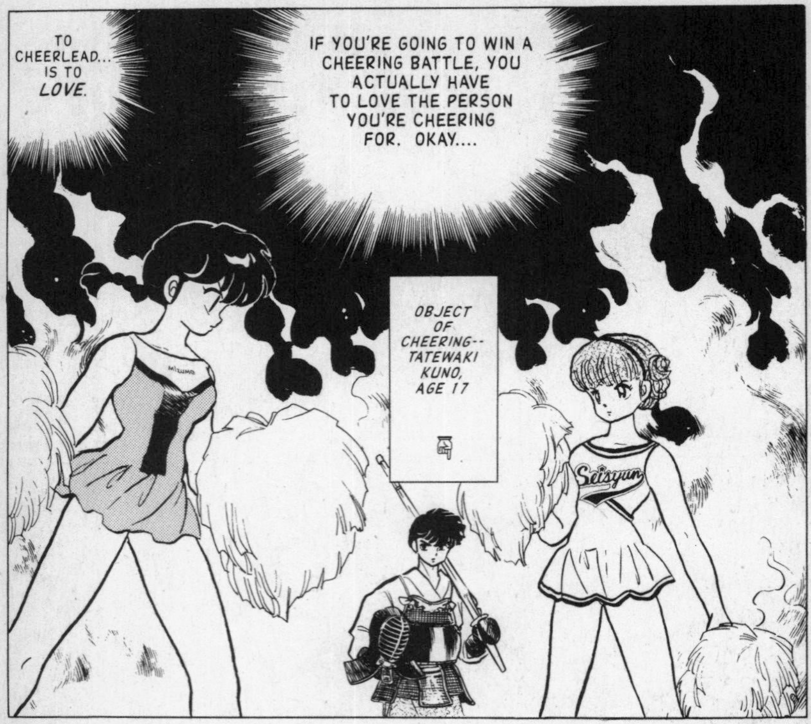
TO CHEERLEAD... IS TO *LOVE*.
IF YOU'RE GOING TO WIN A CHEERING BATTLE, YOU ACTUALLY HAVE TO LOVE THE PERSON YOU'RE CHEERING FOR. OKAY....
OBJECT OF CHEERING--TATEWAKI KUNO, AGE 17
Seisyun

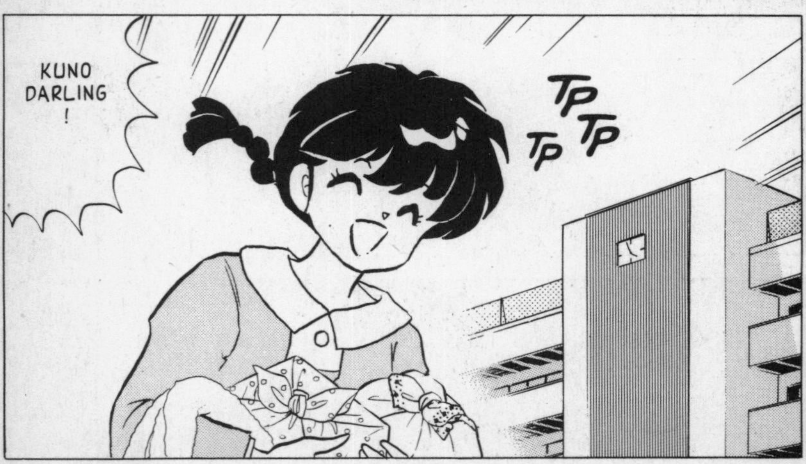
KUNO DARLING!
TP TP TP TP

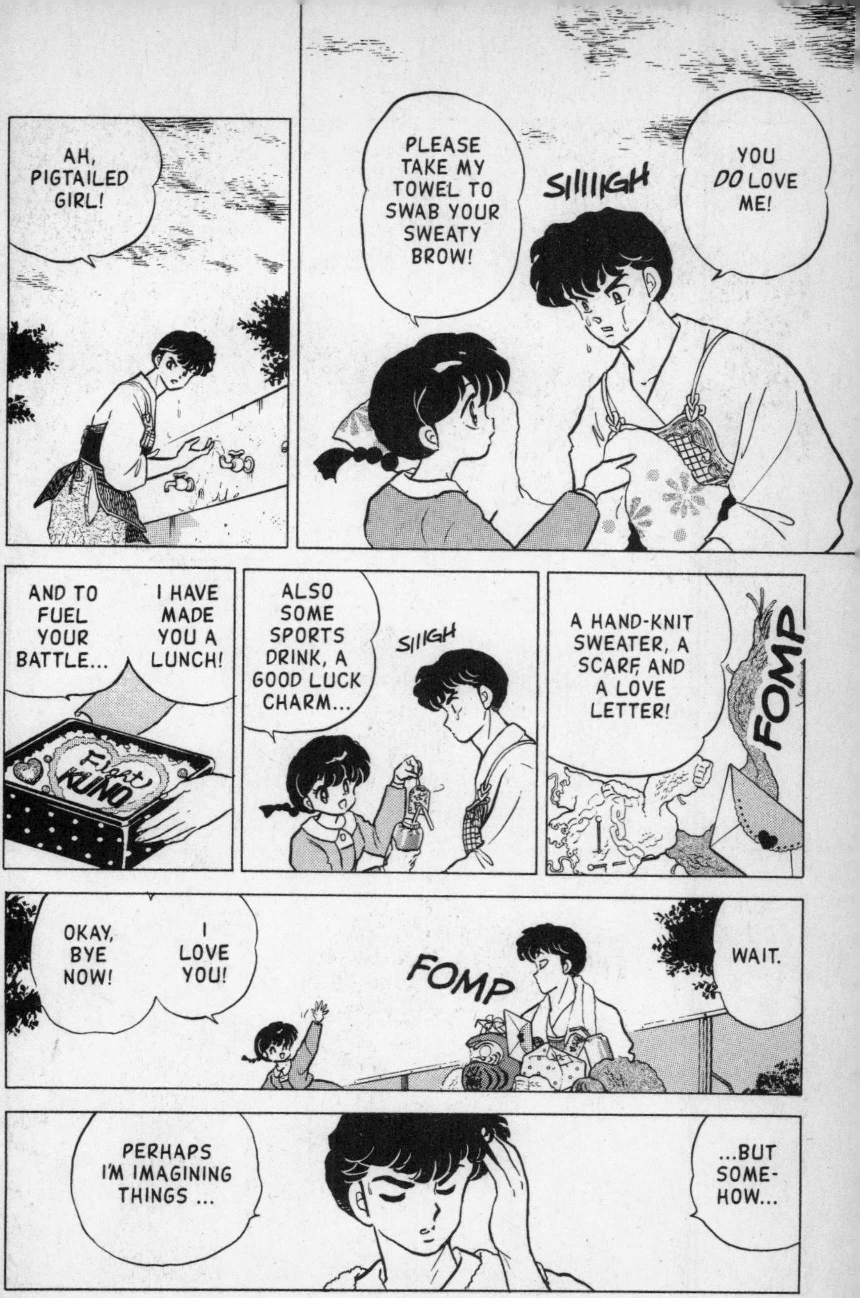
AH, PIGTAILED GIRL!
PLEASE TAKE MY TOWEL TO SWAB YOUR SWEATY BROW!
SIIIIGH
YOU DO LOVE ME!
AND TO FUEL YOUR BATTLE...
I HAVE MADE YOU A LUNCH!
Fight KUNO
ALSO SOME SPORTS DRINK, A GOOD LUCK CHARM...
SIIIGH
A HAND-KNIT SWEATER, A SCARF, AND A LOVE LETTER!
FOMP
OKAY, BYE NOW!
I LOVE YOU!
FOMP
WAIT.
PERHAPS I'M IMAGINING THINGS ...
...BUT SOME-HOW...

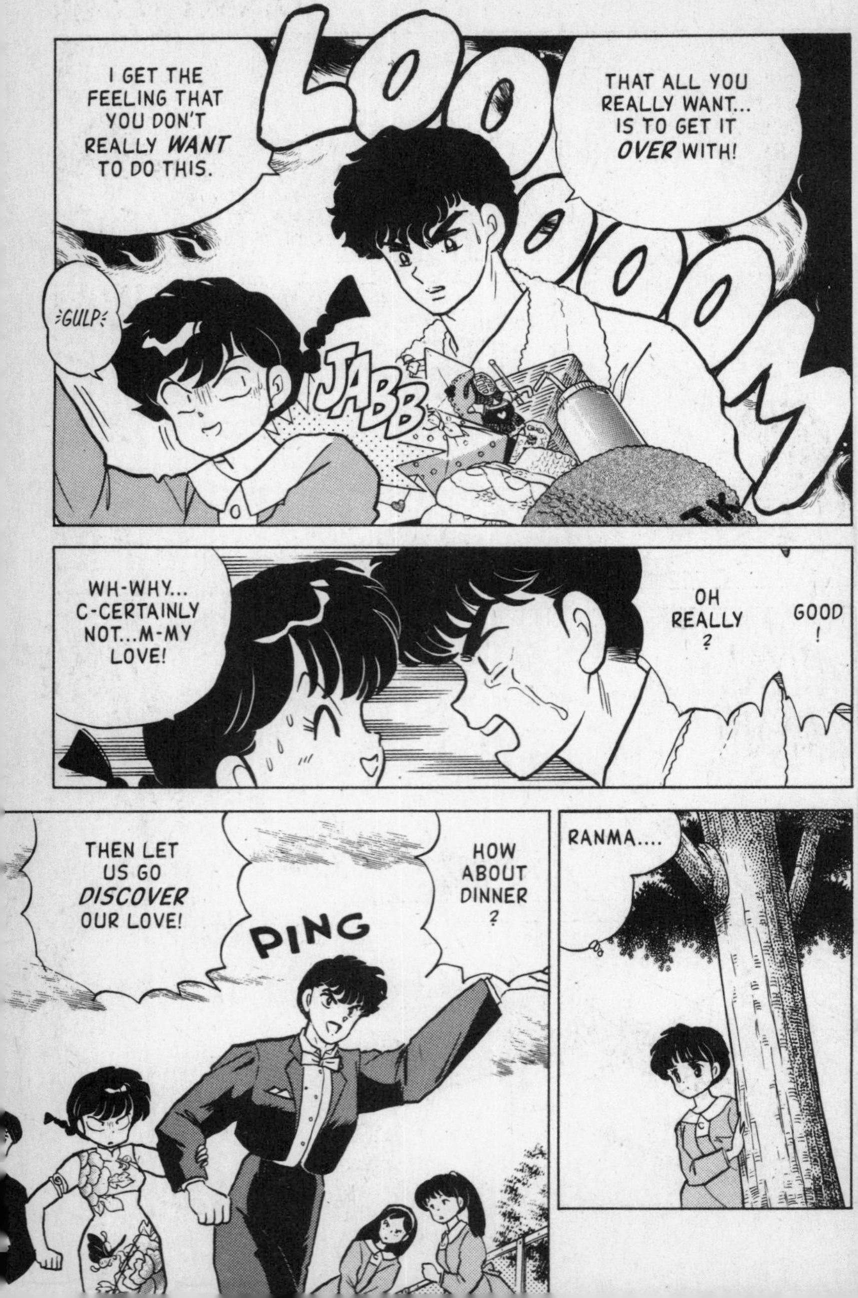
I GET THE FEELING THAT YOU DON'T REALLY *WANT* TO DO THIS.
LOOOOOOOM
THAT ALL YOU REALLY WANT... IS TO GET IT *OVER* WITH!
GULP
JABB
TK
WH-WHY... C-CERTAINLY NOT...M-MY LOVE!
OH REALLY ?
GOOD !
THEN LET US GO *DISCOVER* OUR LOVE!
PING
HOW ABOUT DINNER ?
RANMA....

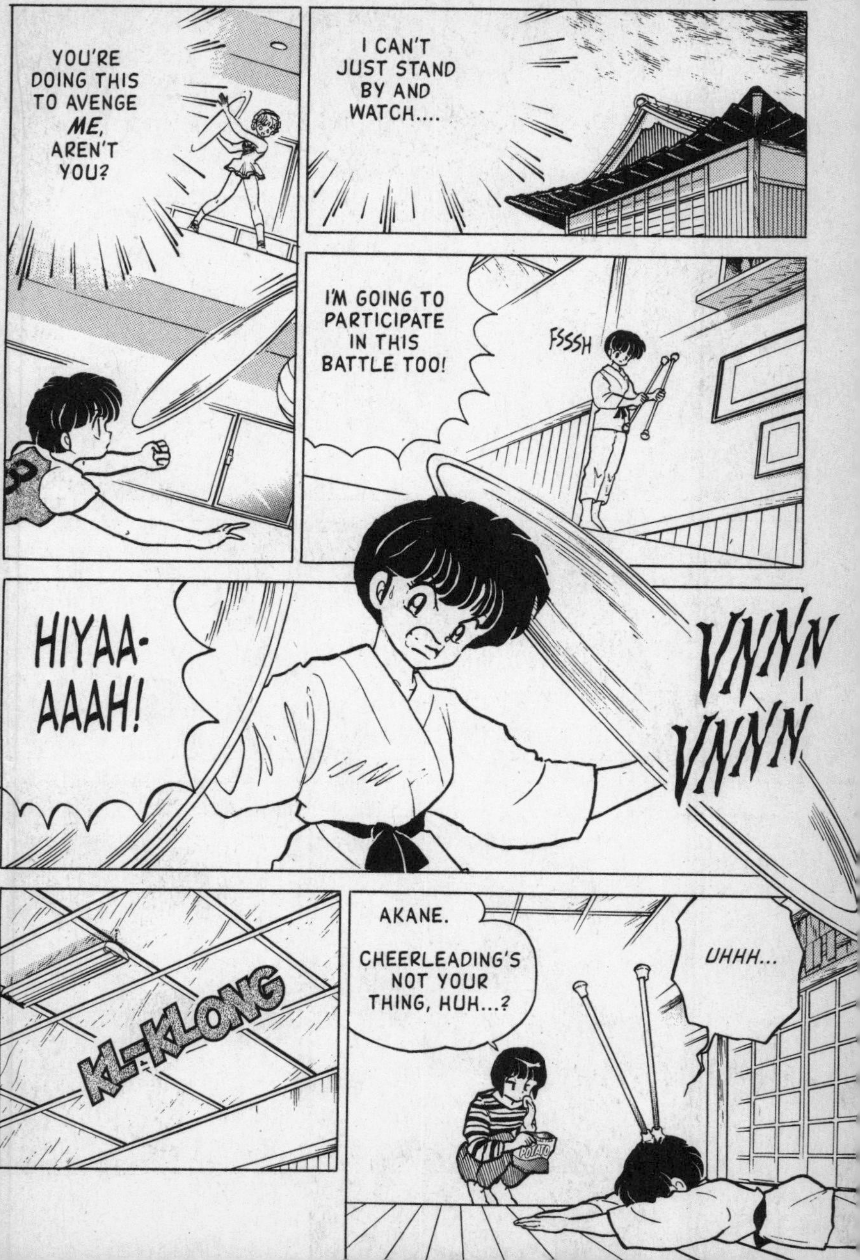
YOU'RE DOING THIS TO AVENGE *ME*, AREN'T YOU?
I CAN'T JUST STAND BY AND WATCH....
I'M GOING TO PARTICIPATE IN THIS BATTLE TOO!
FSSSH
HIYAA-AAAH!
VNNN VNNN
KL-KLONG
AKANE.
CHEERLEADING'S NOT YOUR THING, HUH...?
UHHH...
POTATO

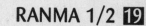

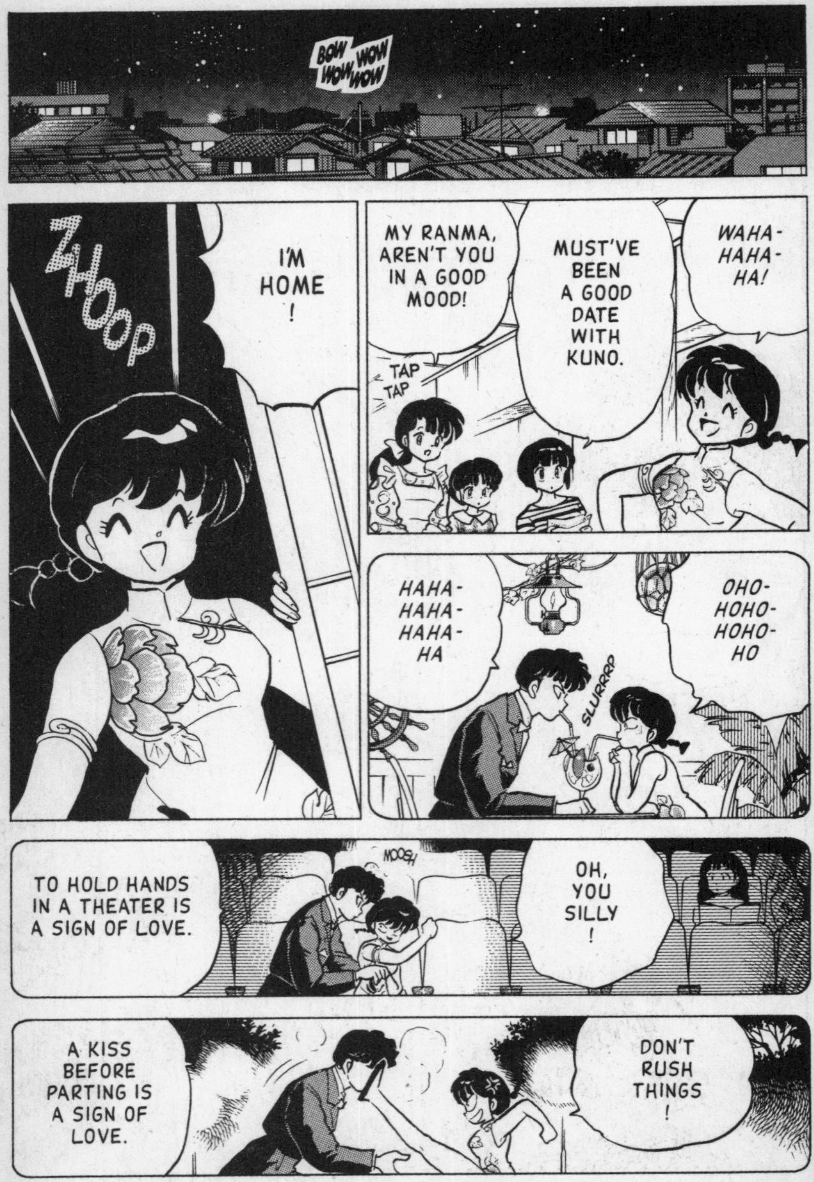
BOW WOW WOW WOW
ZHOOP
I'M HOME!
MY RANMA, AREN'T YOU IN A GOOD MOOD!
TAP TAP
MUST'VE BEEN A GOOD DATE WITH KUNO.
WAHA-HAHA-HA!
HAHA-HAHA-HAHA-HA
SLURRRP
OHO-HOHO-HOHO-HO
TO HOLD HANDS IN A THEATER IS A SIGN OF LOVE.
MOOSH
OH, YOU SILLY!
A KISS BEFORE PARTING IS A SIGN OF LOVE.
DON'T RUSH THINGS!

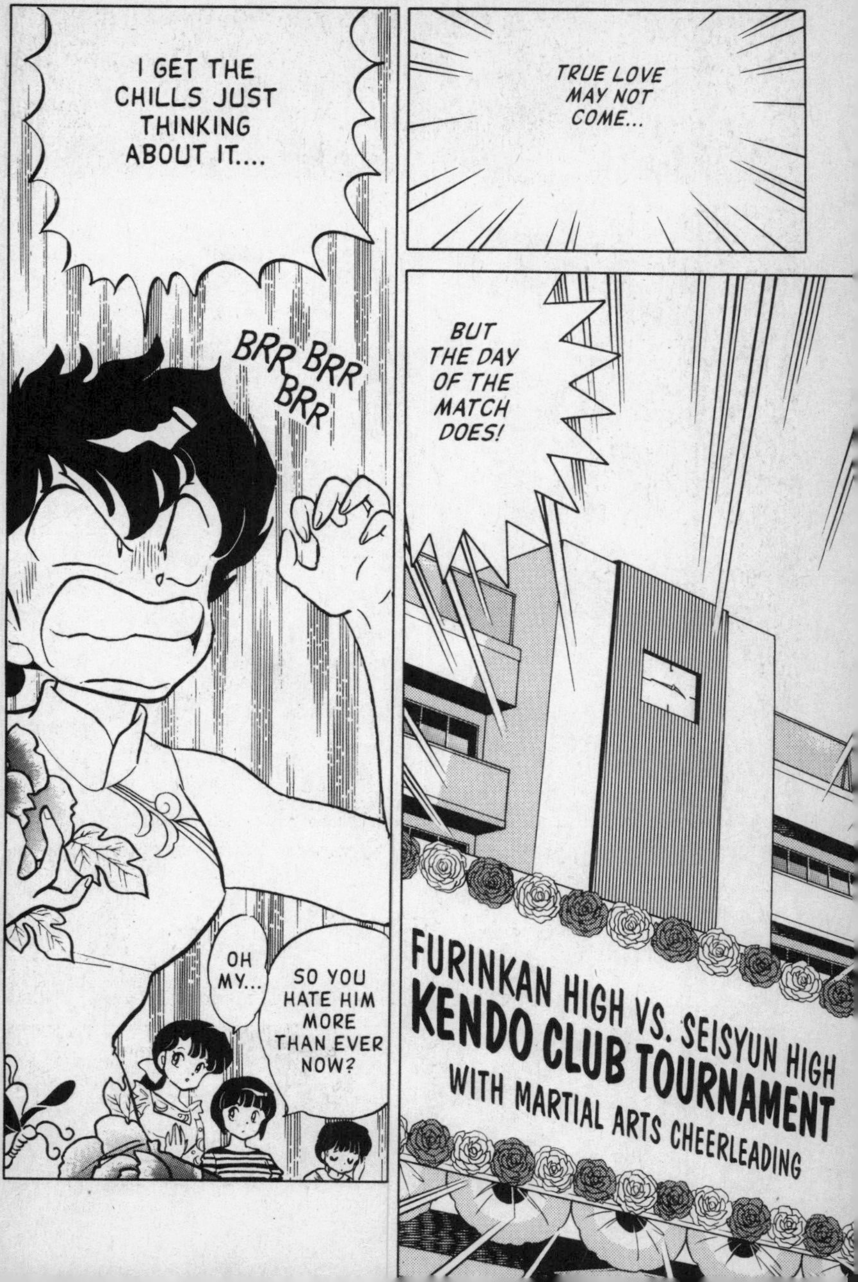
I GET THE CHILLS JUST THINKING ABOUT IT....
BRR BRR BRR
OH MY...
SO YOU HATE HIM MORE THAN EVER NOW?
TRUE LOVE MAY NOT COME...
BUT THE DAY OF THE MATCH DOES!
FURINKAN HIGH VS. SEISYUN HIGH
KENDO CLUB TOURNAMENT
WITH MARTIAL ARTS CHEERLEADING

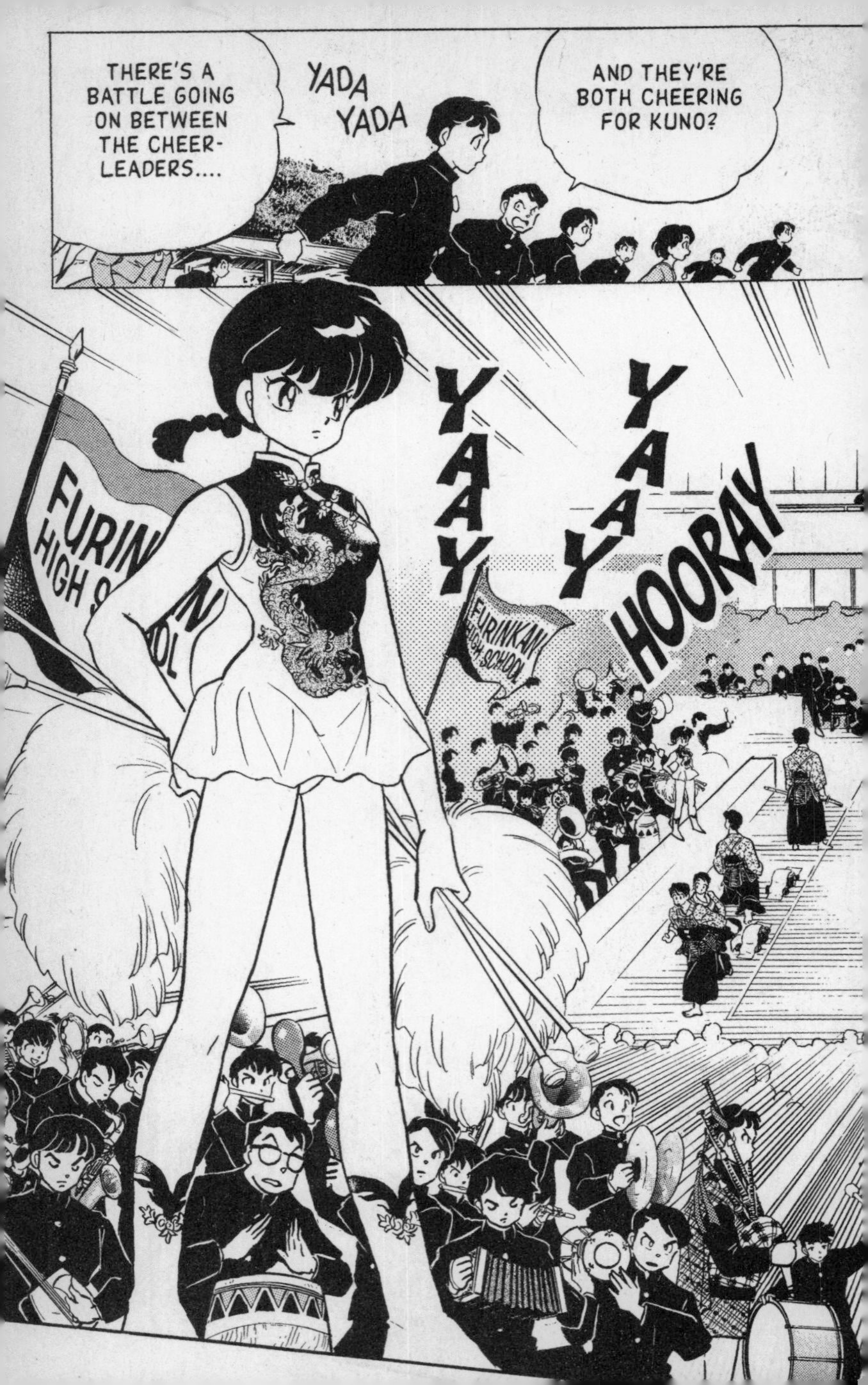
THERE'S A BATTLE GOING ON BETWEEN THE CHEER-LEADERS....
YADA YADA
AND THEY'RE BOTH CHEERING FOR KUNO?
FURINKAN HIGH SCHOOL
YAAY
YAAY
HOORAY
FURINKAN HIGH SCHOOL

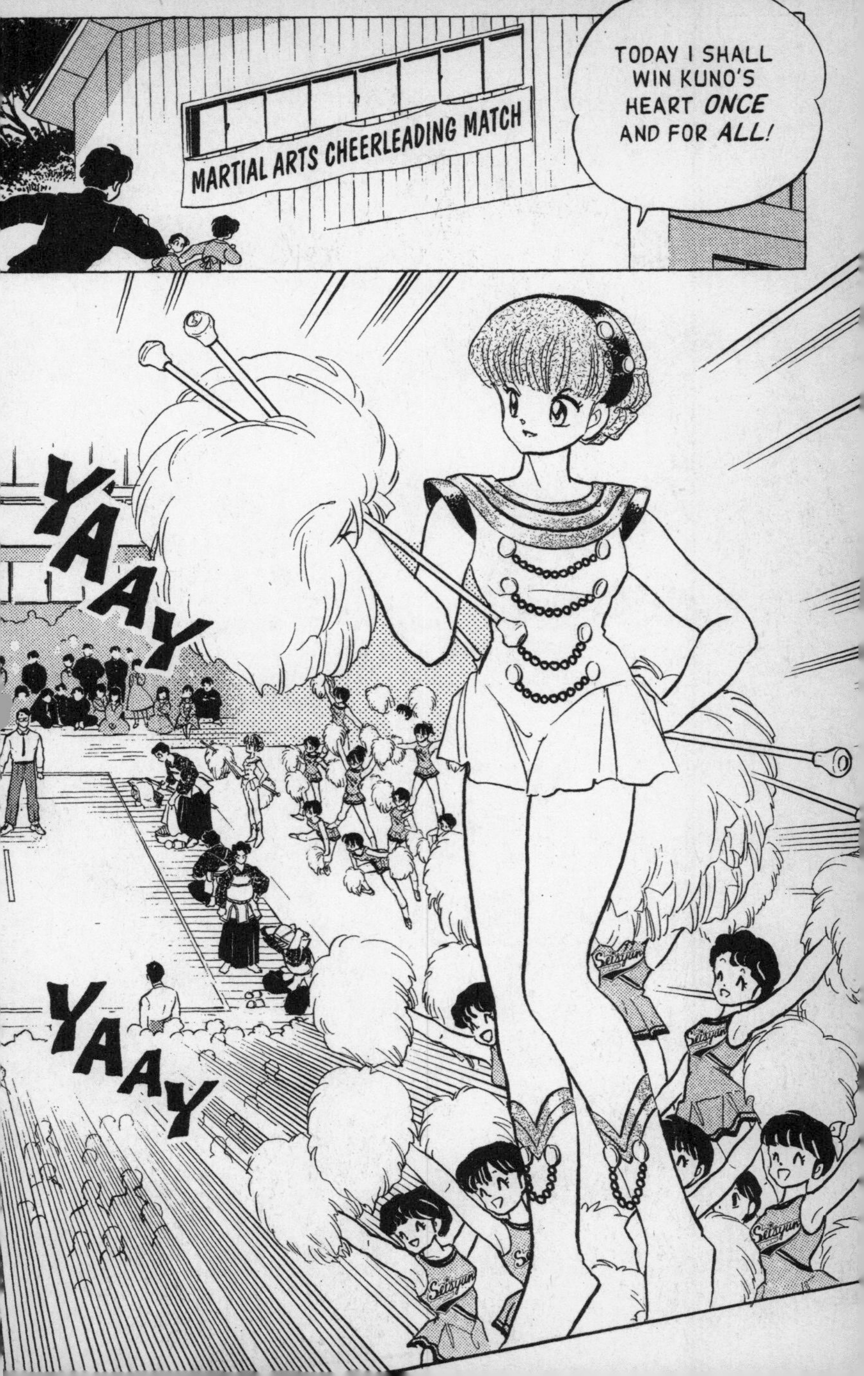
MARTIAL ARTS CHEERLEADING MATCH
TODAY I SHALL WIN KUNO'S HEART *ONCE* AND FOR *ALL*!
YAAY
YAAY

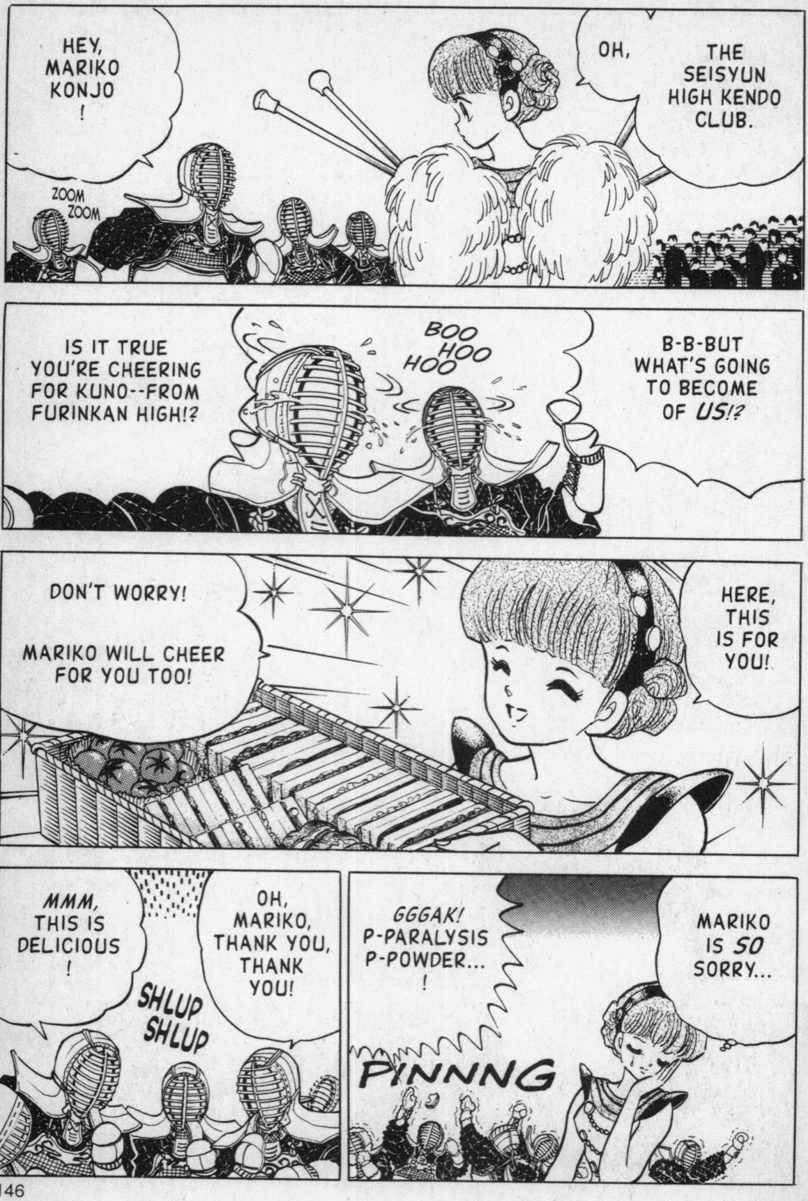
HEY, MARIKO KONJO !
ZOOM ZOOM
OH,
THE SEISYUN HIGH KENDO CLUB.
IS IT TRUE YOU'RE CHEERING FOR KUNO--FROM FURINKAN HIGH!?
BOO HOO HOO
B-B-BUT WHAT'S GOING TO BECOME OF US!?
DON'T WORRY!
MARIKO WILL CHEER FOR YOU TOO!
HERE, THIS IS FOR YOU!
MMM, THIS IS DELICIOUS !
SHLUP SHLUP
OH, MARIKO, THANK YOU, THANK YOU!
GGGAK! P-PARALYSIS P-POWDER... !
PINNNG
MARIKO IS SO SORRY...

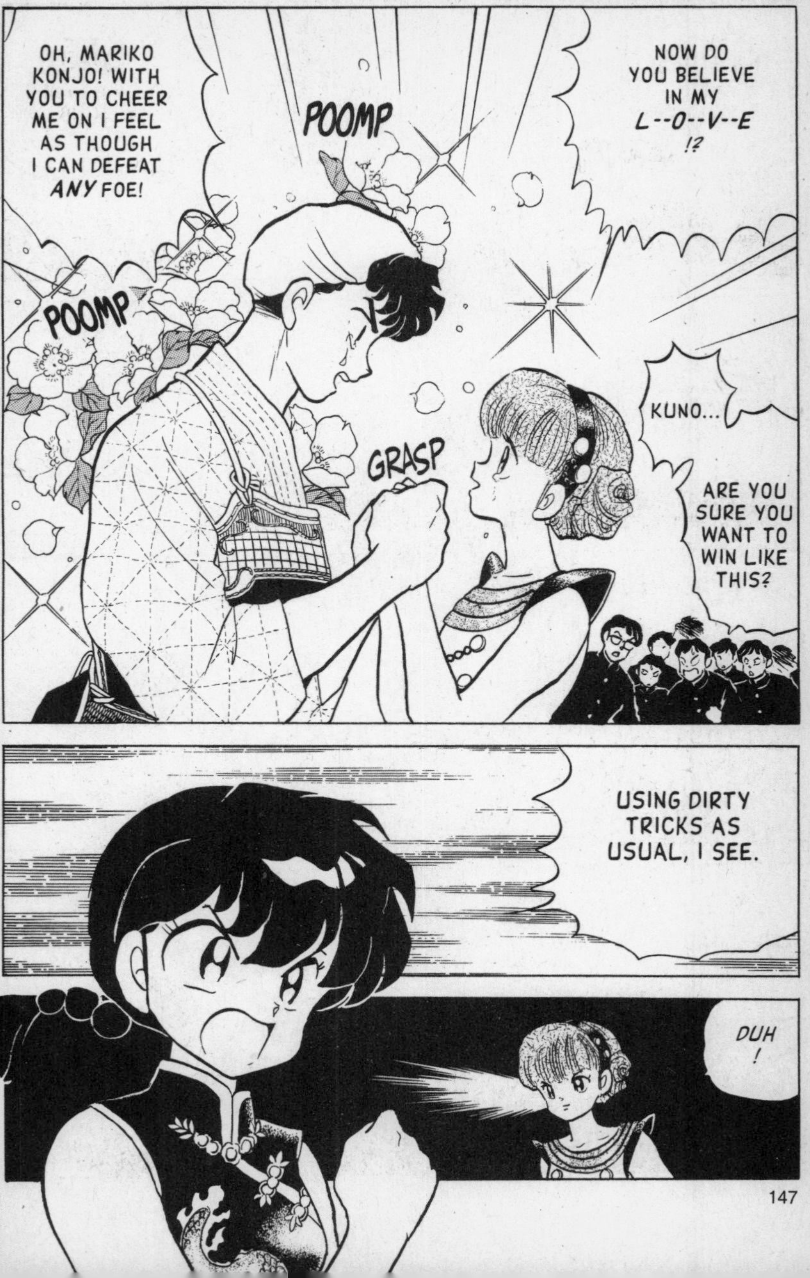
OH, MARIKO KONJO! WITH YOU TO CHEER ME ON I FEEL AS THOUGH I CAN DEFEAT *ANY* FOE!
POOMP
POOMP
NOW DO YOU BELIEVE IN MY *L--O--V--E* !?
KUNO...
GRASP
ARE YOU SURE YOU WANT TO WIN LIKE THIS?
USING DIRTY TRICKS AS USUAL, I SEE.
DUH !

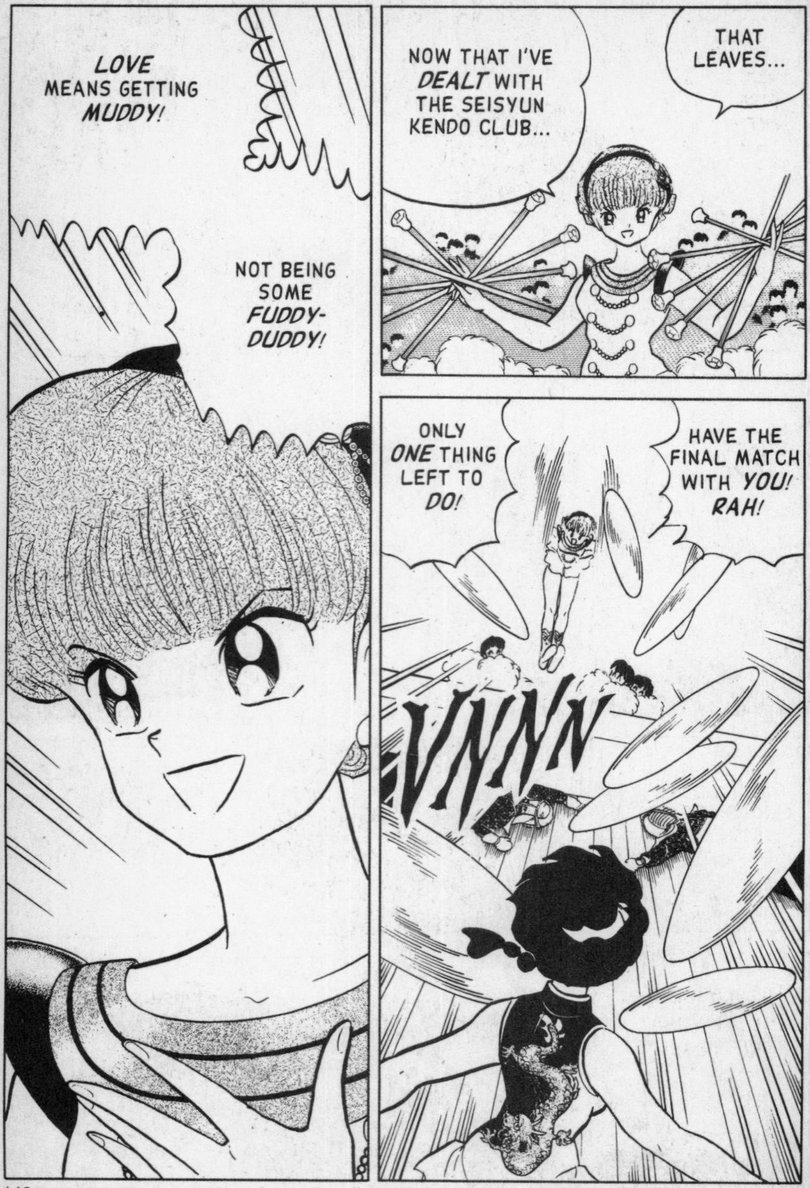
LOVE MEANS GETTING MUDDY!
NOT BEING SOME FUDDY-DUDDY!
NOW THAT I'VE DEALT WITH THE SEISYUN KENDO CLUB...
THAT LEAVES...
ONLY ONE THING LEFT TO DO!
HAVE THE FINAL MATCH WITH YOU! RAH!
VNNN

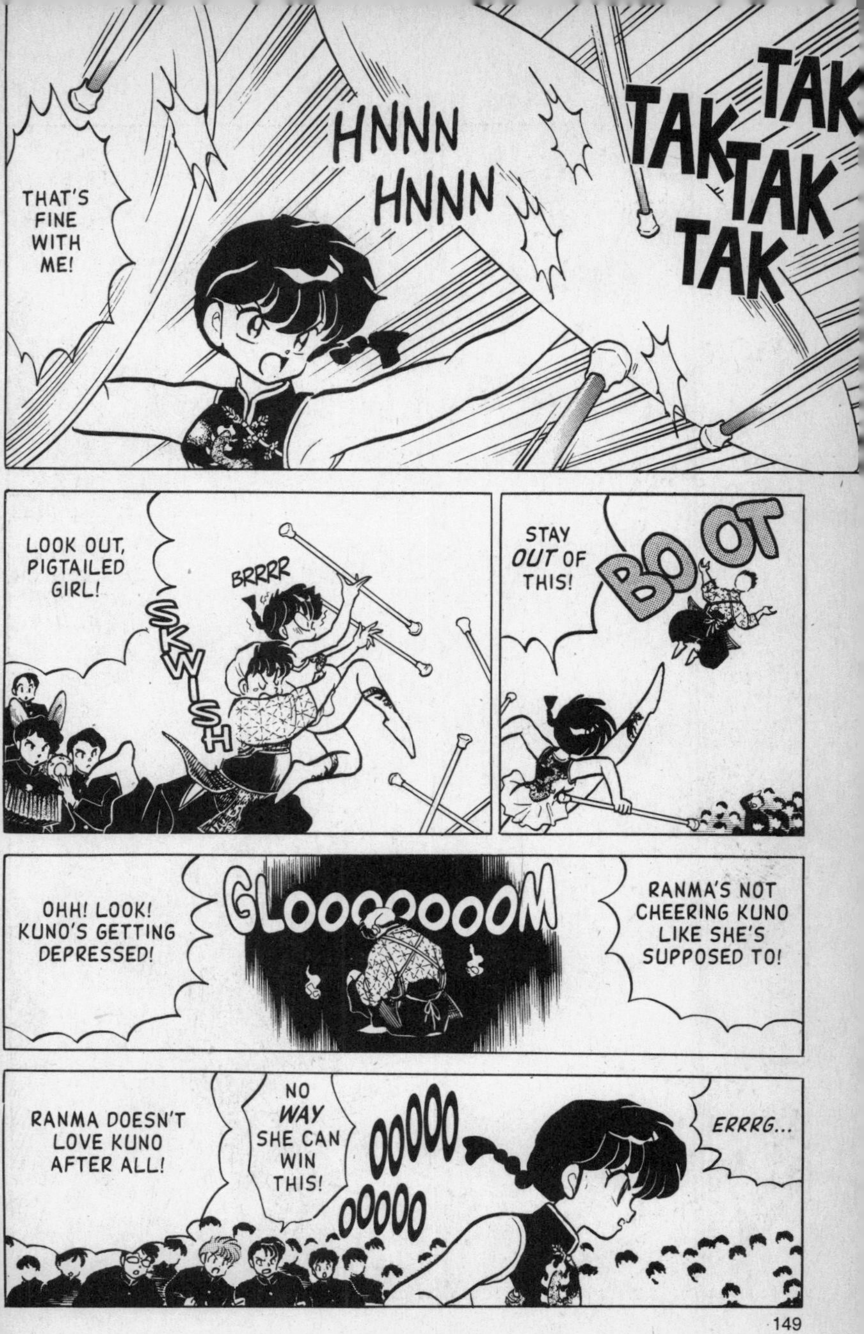
THAT'S FINE WITH ME!
HNNN HNNN
TAK TAK TAK TAK TAK
LOOK OUT, PIGTAILED GIRL!
BRRRR
SKWISH
STAY *OUT* OF THIS!
BOOT
OHH! LOOK! KUNO'S GETTING DEPRESSED!
GLOOOOOOOM
RANMA'S NOT CHEERING KUNO LIKE SHE'S SUPPOSED TO!
RANMA DOESN'T LOVE KUNO AFTER ALL!
NO *WAY* SHE CAN WIN THIS!
OOOOO OOOOO
ERRRG...

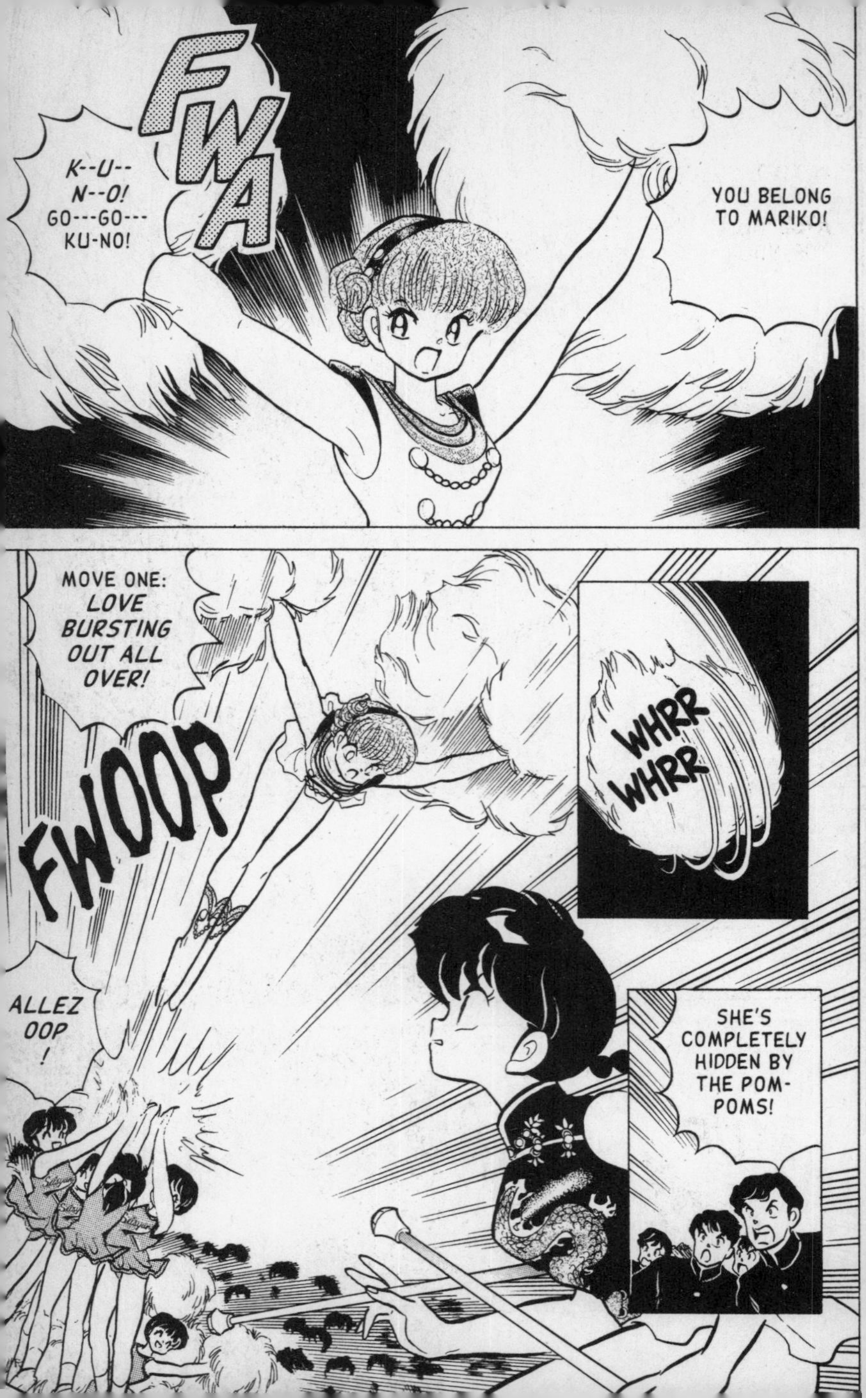

K--U-- N--O! GO---GO--- KU-NO!
FWA
YOU BELONG TO MARIKO!
MOVE ONE: LOVE BURSTING OUT ALL OVER!
FWOOP
WHRR WHRR
ALLEZ OOP !
SHE'S COMPLETELY HIDDEN BY THE POM-POMS!

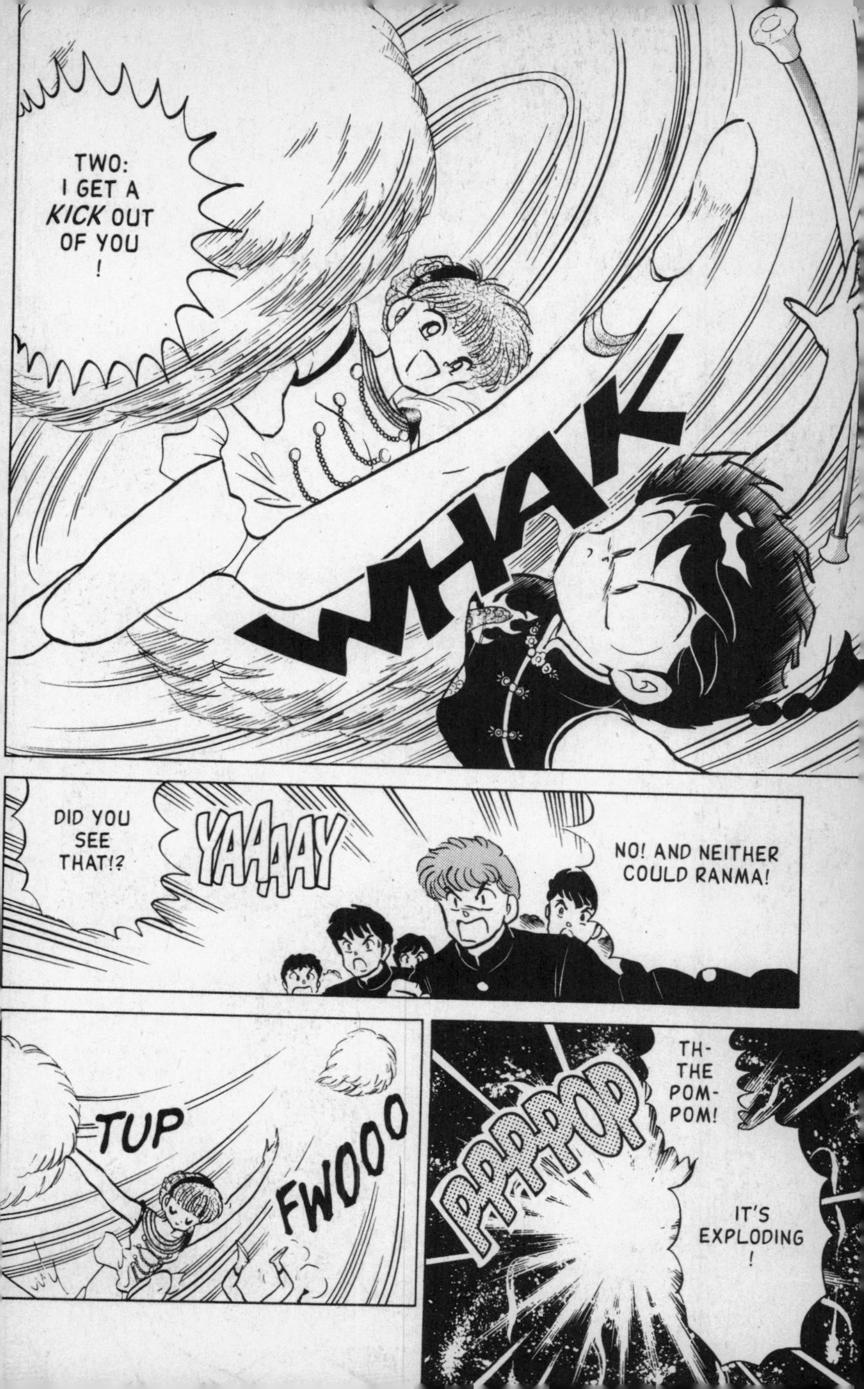
TWO: I GET A *KICK* OUT OF YOU !
WHAK
DID YOU SEE THAT!?
YAAAAAY
NO! AND NEITHER COULD RANMA!
TUP
FWOOO
TH- THE POM-POM!
PAAAPOP
IT'S EXPLODING !

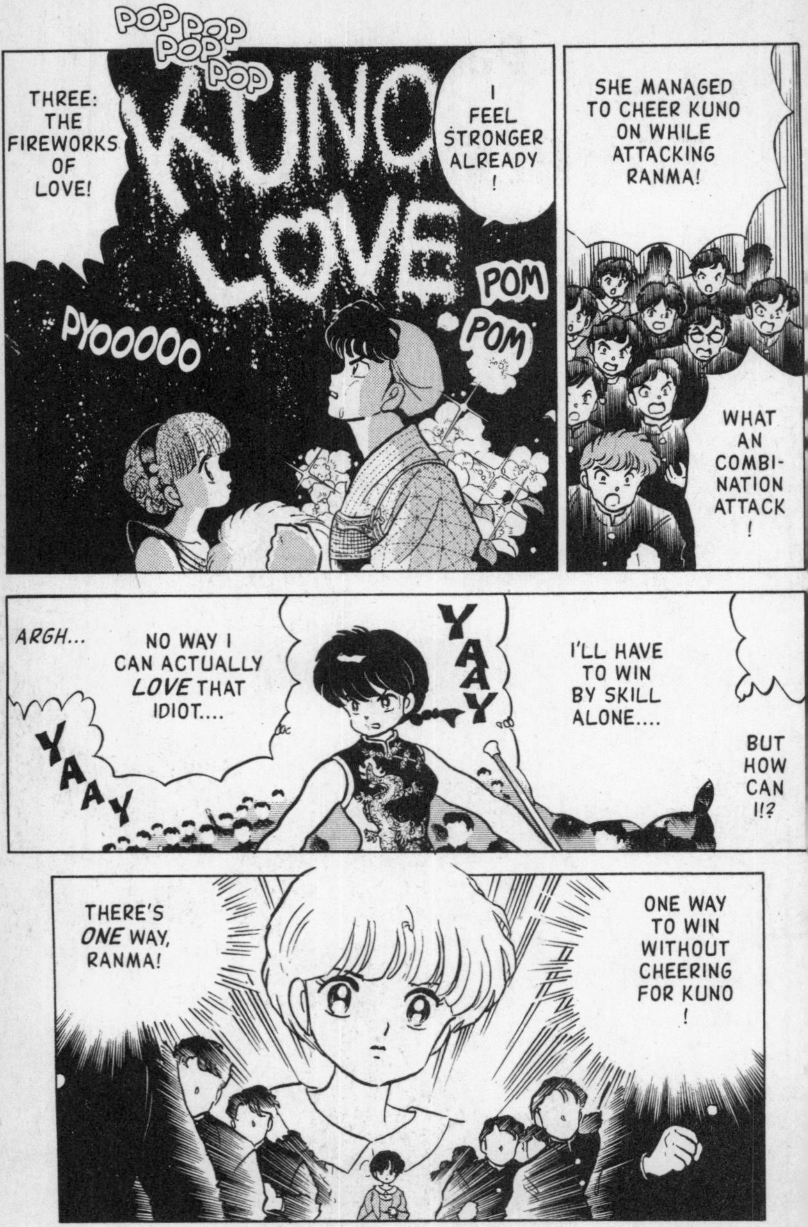
POP POP POP POP
THREE: THE FIREWORKS OF LOVE!
KUNO LOVE
I FEEL STRONGER ALREADY!
PYOOOOO
POM POM
SHE MANAGED TO CHEER KUNO ON WHILE ATTACKING RANMA!
WHAT AN COMBINATION ATTACK!
ARGH...
NO WAY I CAN ACTUALLY *LOVE* THAT IDIOT....
YAAY
YAAY
I'LL HAVE TO WIN BY SKILL ALONE....
BUT HOW CAN I!?
THERE'S *ONE* WAY, RANMA!
ONE WAY TO WIN WITHOUT CHEERING FOR KUNO!

Part 10

EQUALS IN LOVE

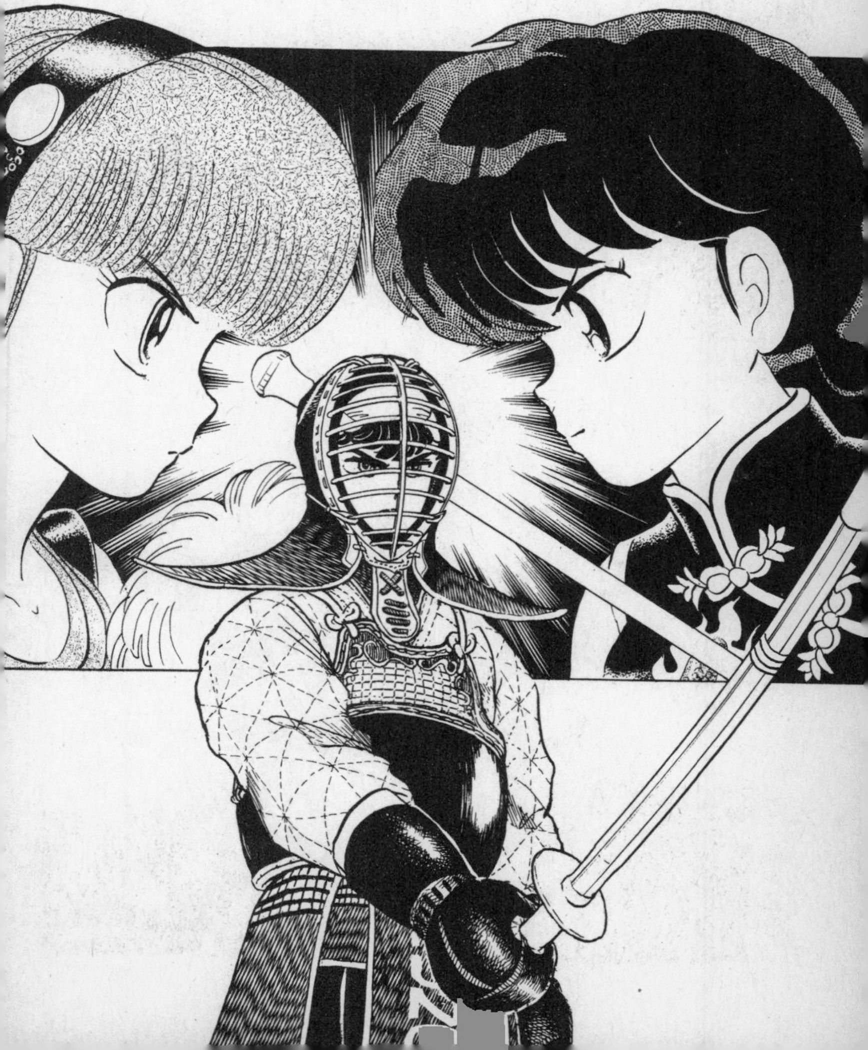

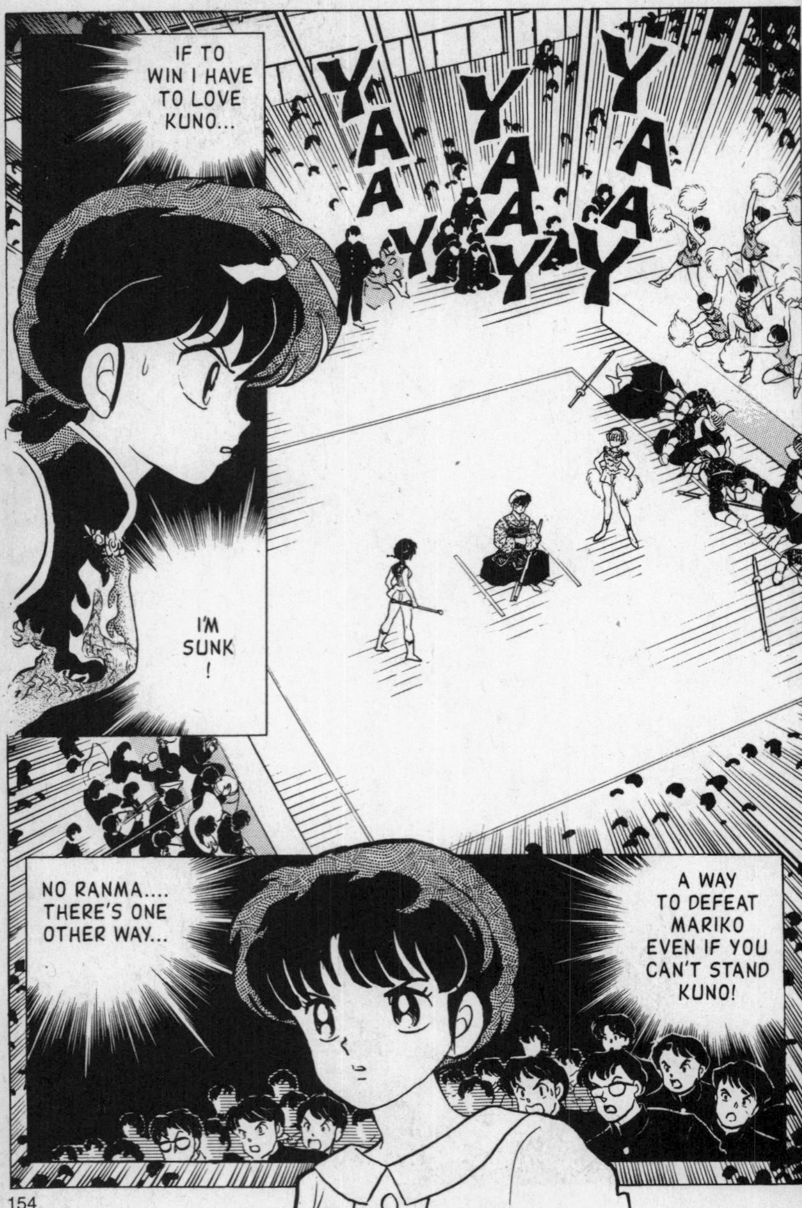
IF TO WIN I HAVE TO LOVE KUNO...
YAAY YAAY YAAY
I'M SUNK !
NO RANMA.... THERE'S ONE OTHER WAY...
A WAY TO DEFEAT MARIKO EVEN IF YOU CAN'T STAND KUNO!

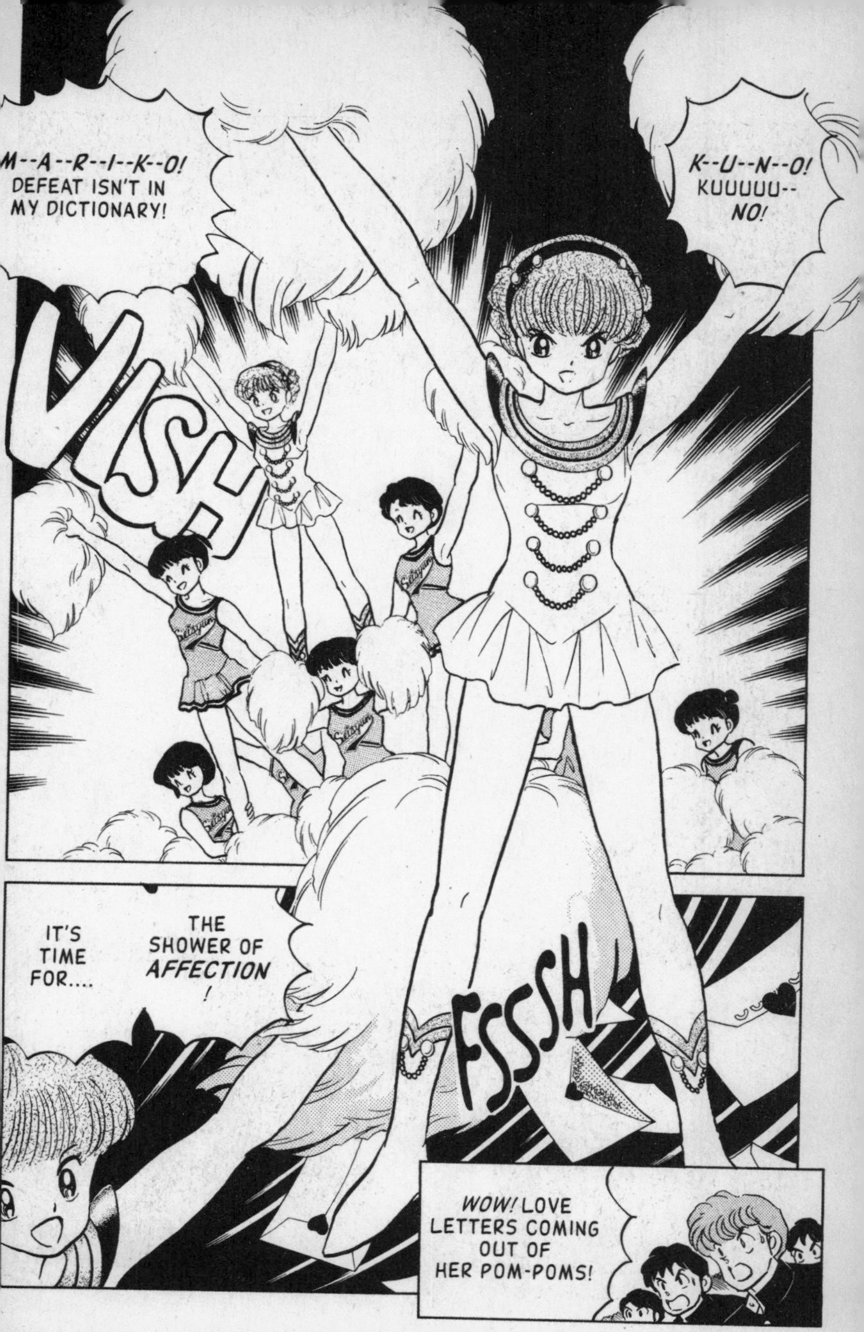
M--A--R--I--K--O! DEFEAT ISN'T IN MY DICTIONARY!
K--U--N--O! KUUUUU-- NO!
VISH
IT'S TIME FOR....
THE SHOWER OF AFFECTION!
FSSSH
WOW! LOVE LETTERS COMING OUT OF HER POM-POMS!

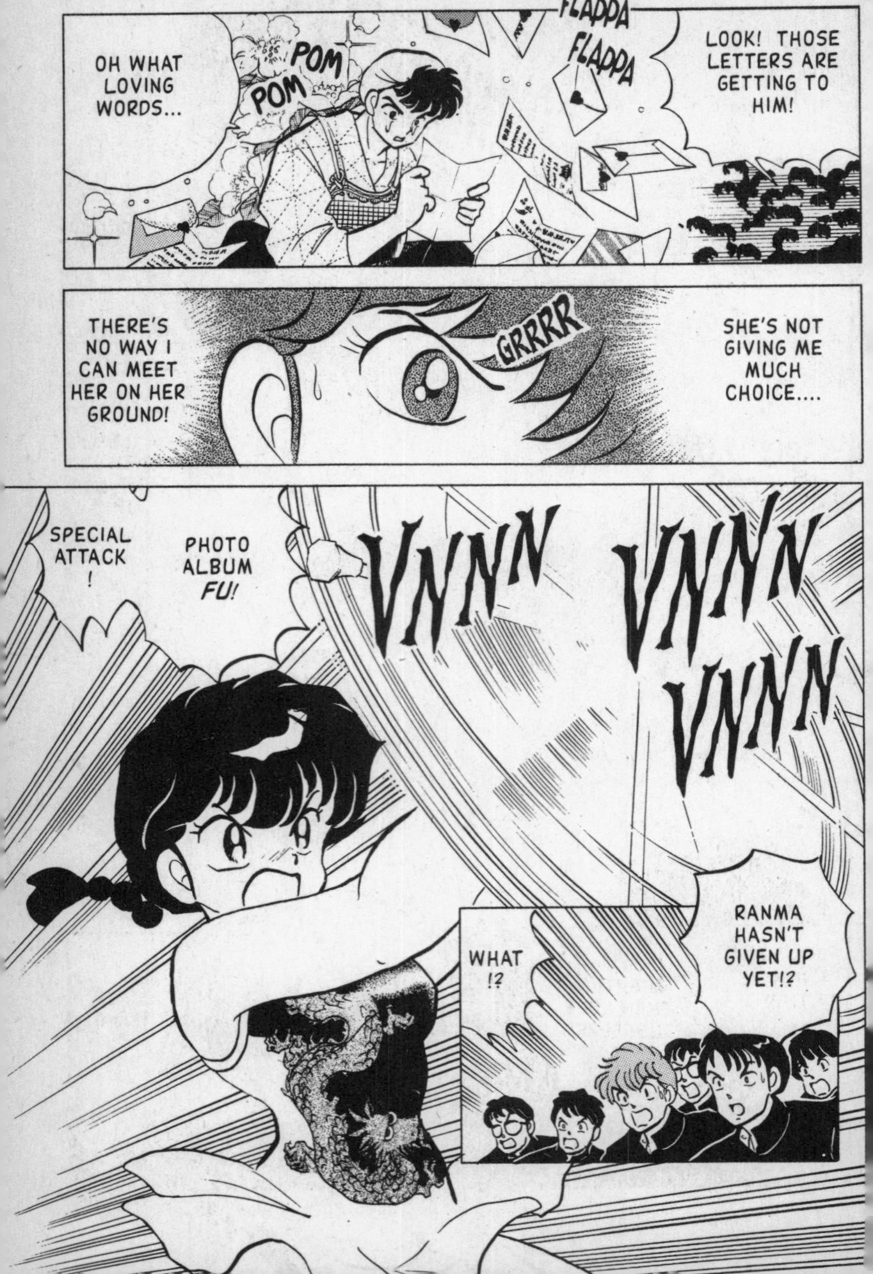
OH WHAT LOVING WORDS...
POM
POM
FLAPPA
FLAPPA
LOOK! THOSE LETTERS ARE GETTING TO HIM!
THERE'S NO WAY I CAN MEET HER ON HER GROUND!
GRRRR
SHE'S NOT GIVING ME MUCH CHOICE....
SPECIAL ATTACK !
PHOTO ALBUM *FU*!
VNNN
VNNN
VNNN
WHAT !?
RANMA HASN'T GIVEN UP YET!?

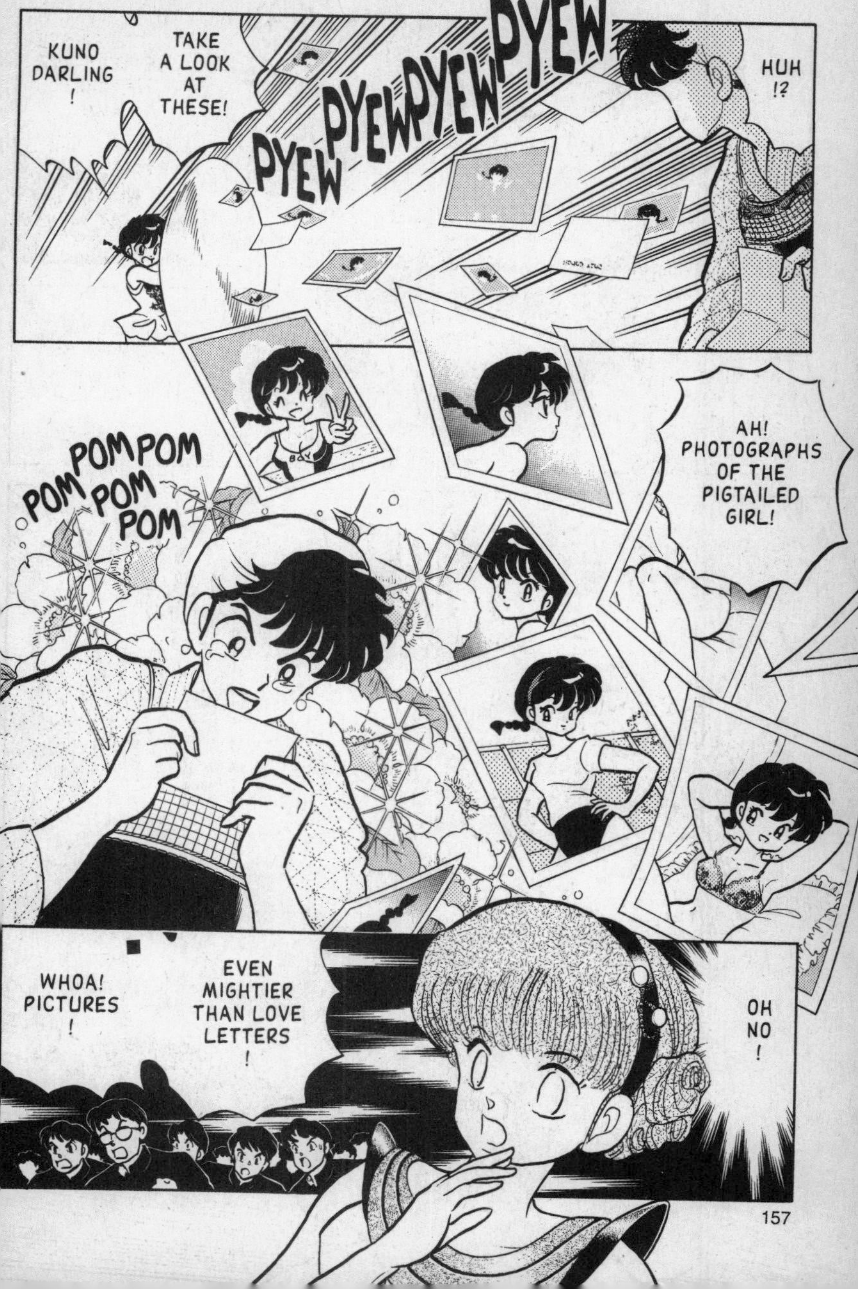
KUNO DARLING!
TAKE A LOOK AT THESE!
PYEW PYEW PYEW PYEW
HUH!?
POM POM POM POM POM POM
AH! PHOTOGRAPHS OF THE PIGTAILED GIRL!
WHOA! PICTURES!
EVEN MIGHTIER THAN LOVE LETTERS!
OH NO!

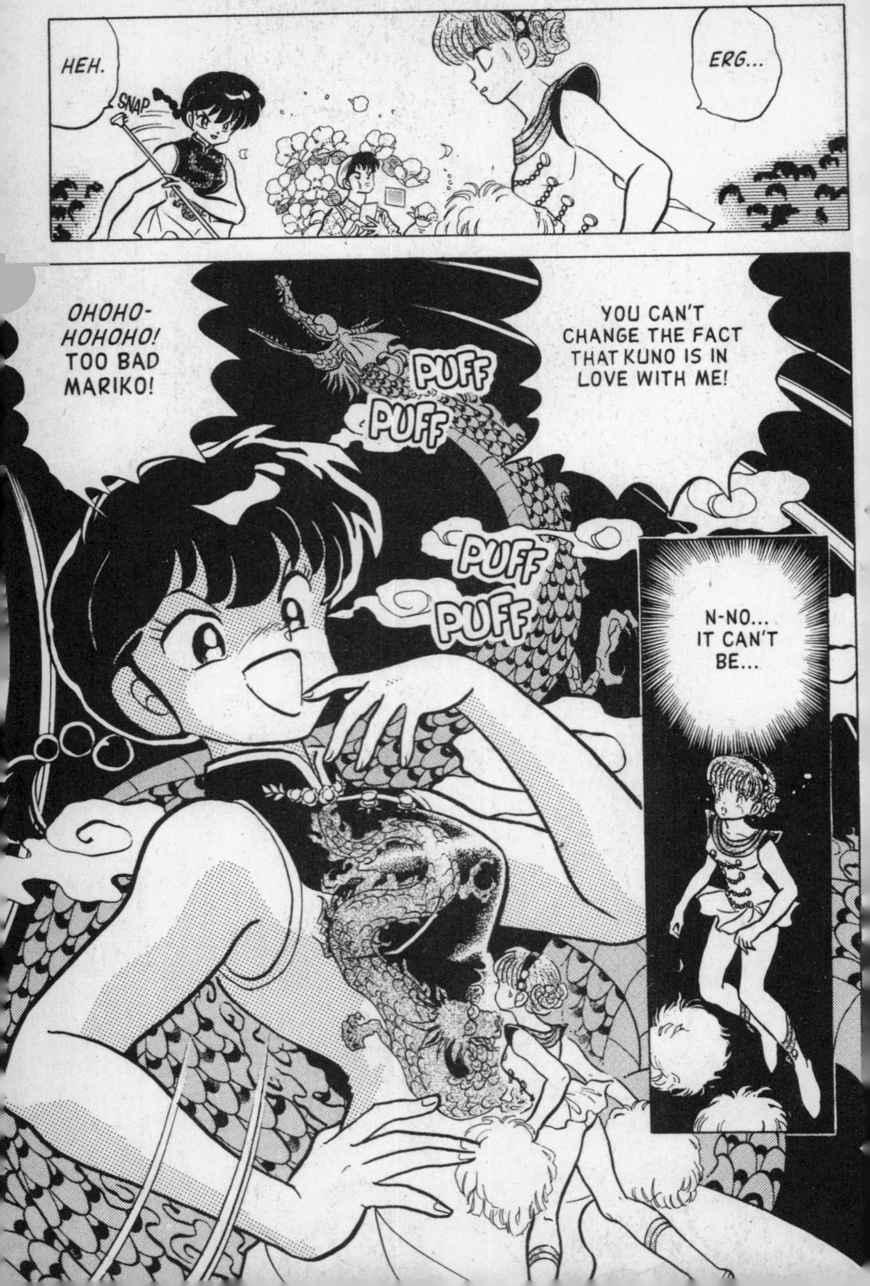
HEH.
SNAP
ERG...
OHOHO-HOHOHO! TOO BAD MARIKO!
PUFF
PUFF
YOU CAN'T CHANGE THE FACT THAT KUNO IS IN LOVE WITH ME!
PUFF
PUFF
N-NO... IT CAN'T BE...

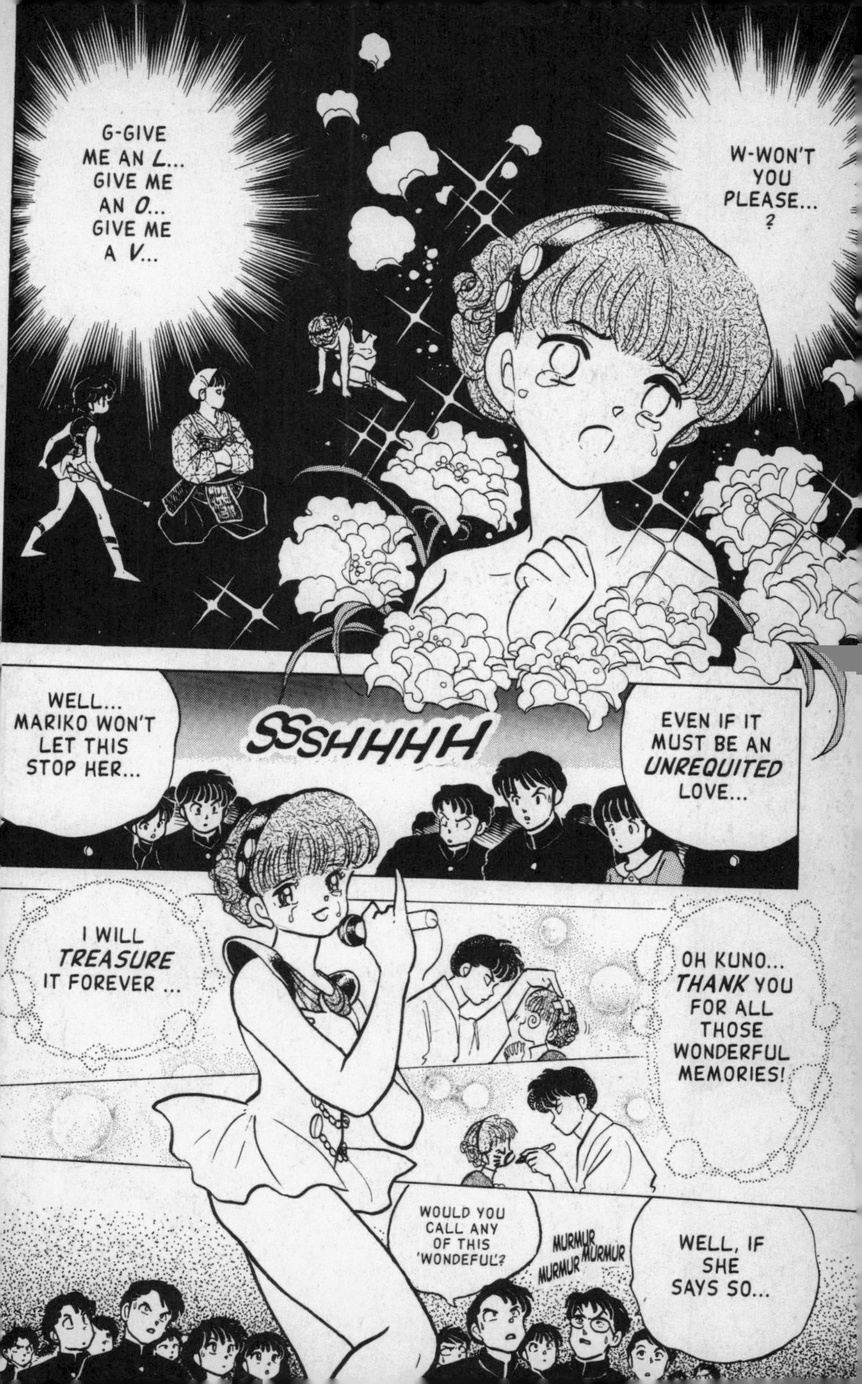
G-GIVE ME AN *L*... GIVE ME AN *O*... GIVE ME A *V*...
W-WON'T YOU PLEASE... ?
WELL... MARIKO WON'T LET THIS STOP HER...
SSSHHHH
EVEN IF IT MUST BE AN *UNREQUITED* LOVE...
I WILL *TREASURE* IT FOREVER ...
OH KUNO... *THANK* YOU FOR ALL THOSE WONDERFUL MEMORIES!
WOULD YOU CALL ANY OF THIS 'WONDEFUL'?
MURMUR MURMUR MURMUR MURMUR
WELL, IF SHE SAYS SO...

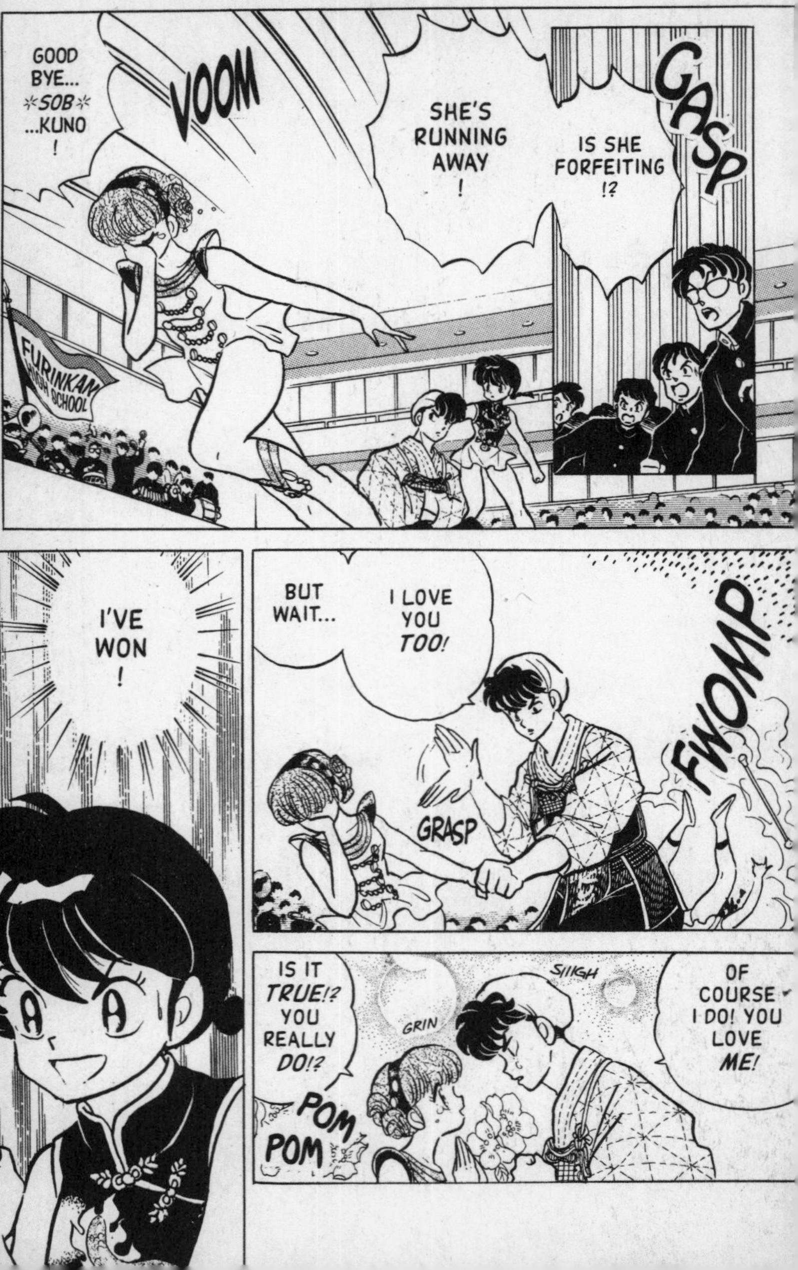
GOOD BYE... *SOB* ...KUNO !
VOOM
SHE'S RUNNING AWAY !
IS SHE FORFEITING !?
GASP
FURINKAN HIGH SCHOOL
I'VE WON !
BUT WAIT...
I LOVE YOU TOO!
FWOMP
GRASP
IS IT TRUE!? YOU REALLY DO!?
SIIGH
GRIN
OF COURSE I DO! YOU LOVE ME!
POM POM

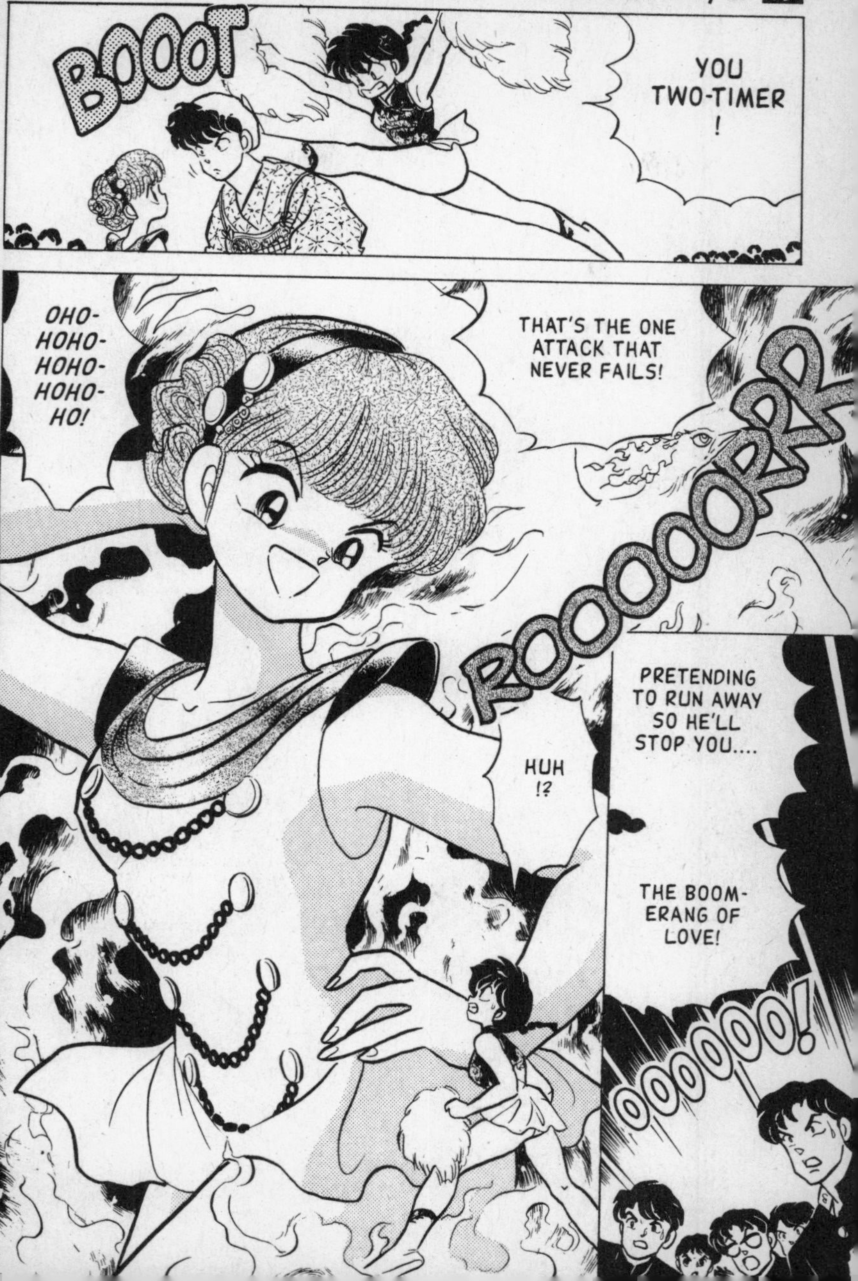
BOOOT
YOU TWO-TIMER!
OHO-HOHO-HOHO-HOHO-HO!
THAT'S THE ONE ATTACK THAT NEVER FAILS!
ROOOOOORRR
HUH!?
PRETENDING TO RUN AWAY SO HE'LL STOP YOU....
THE BOOMERANG OF LOVE!
OOOOOO!

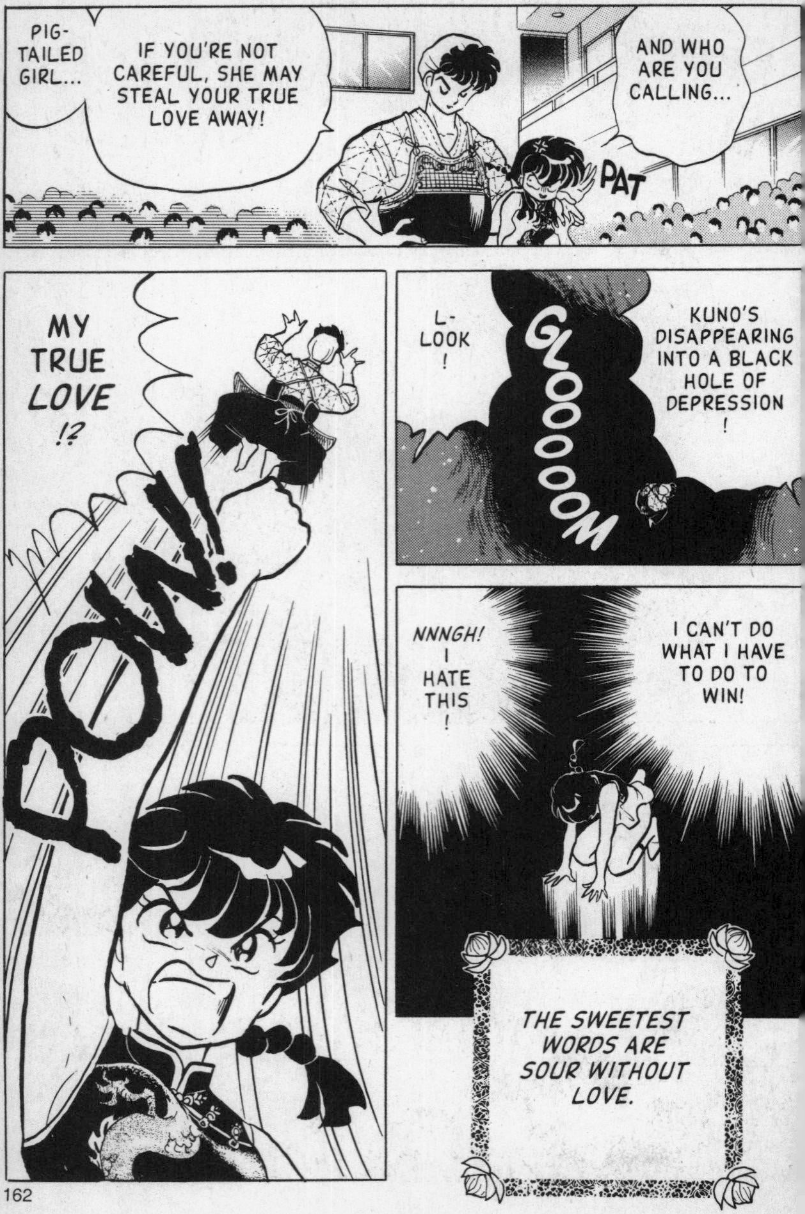
PIG-TAILED GIRL...
IF YOU'RE NOT CAREFUL, SHE MAY STEAL YOUR TRUE LOVE AWAY!
AND WHO ARE YOU CALLING...
PAT
MY TRUE *LOVE* !?
POW!!
L-LOOK!
GLOOOOOM
KUNO'S DISAPPEARING INTO A BLACK HOLE OF DEPRESSION!
NNNGH! I HATE THIS!
I CAN'T DO WHAT I HAVE TO DO TO WIN!
THE SWEETEST WORDS ARE SOUR WITHOUT LOVE.

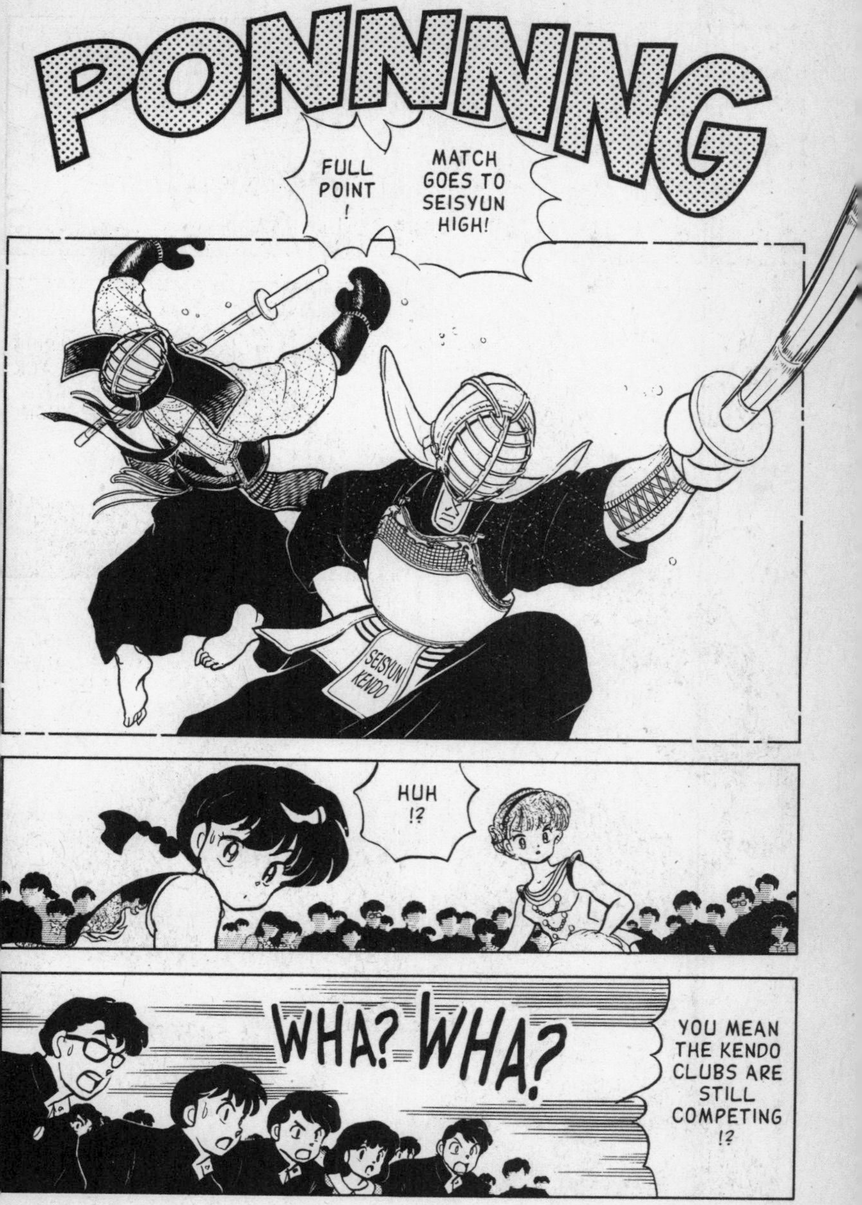
PONNNNG
FULL POINT !
MATCH GOES TO SEISYUN HIGH!
SEISYUN KENDO
HUH !?
WHA? WHA?
YOU MEAN THE KENDO CLUBS ARE STILL COMPETING !?

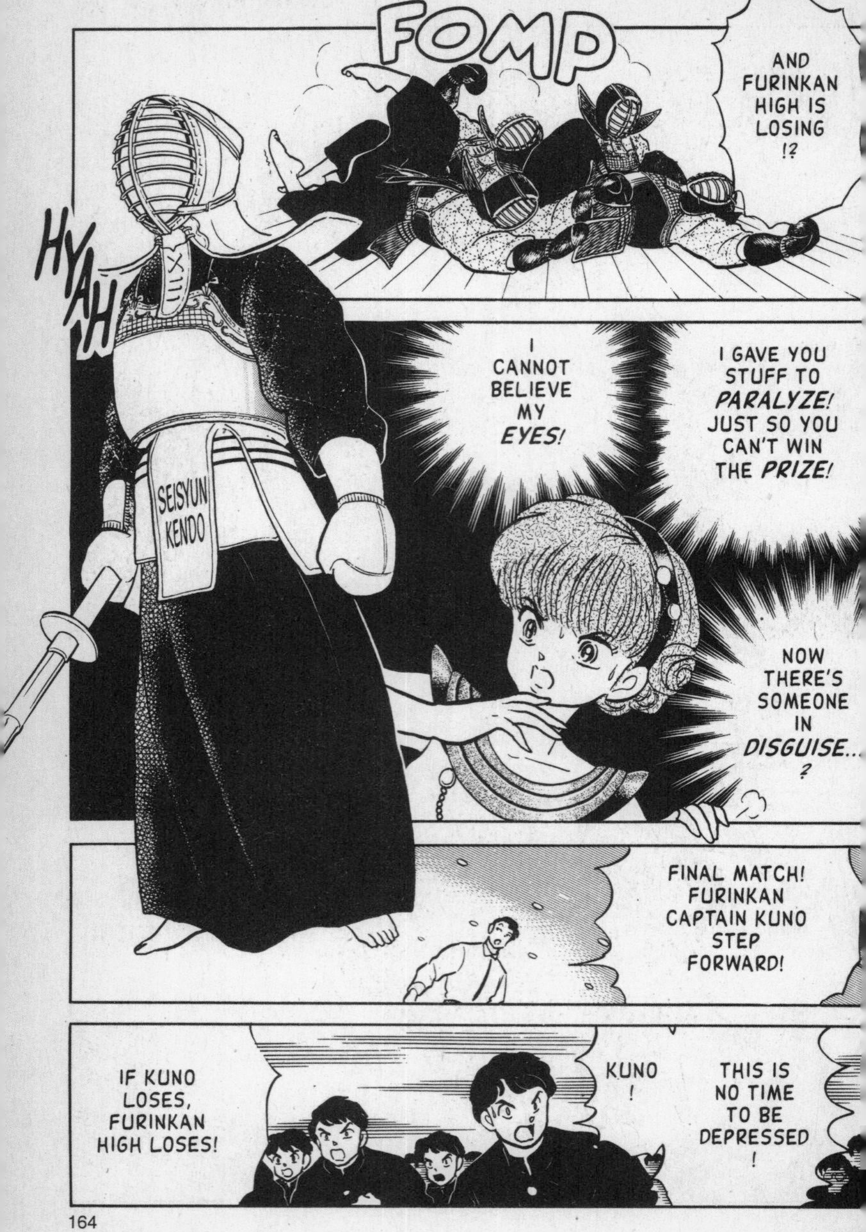
FOMP
AND FURINKAN HIGH IS LOSING !?
HYAH
I CANNOT BELIEVE MY EYES!
I GAVE YOU STUFF TO PARALYZE! JUST SO YOU CAN'T WIN THE PRIZE!
SEISYUN KENDO
NOW THERE'S SOMEONE IN DISGUISE... ?
FINAL MATCH! FURINKAN CAPTAIN KUNO STEP FORWARD!
IF KUNO LOSES, FURINKAN HIGH LOSES!
KUNO !
THIS IS NO TIME TO BE DEPRESSED !

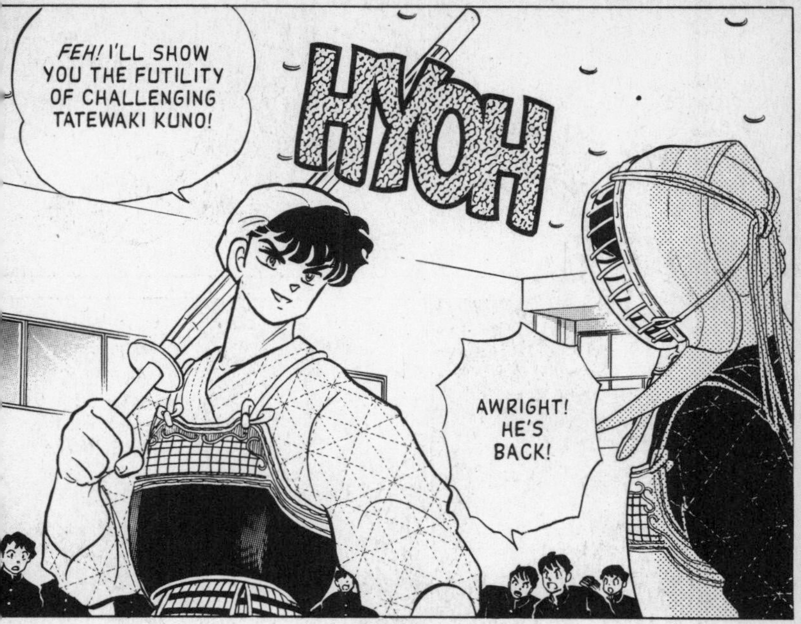
FEH! I'LL SHOW YOU THE FUTILITY OF CHALLENGING TATEWAKI KUNO!
HYOH
AWRIGHT! HE'S BACK!

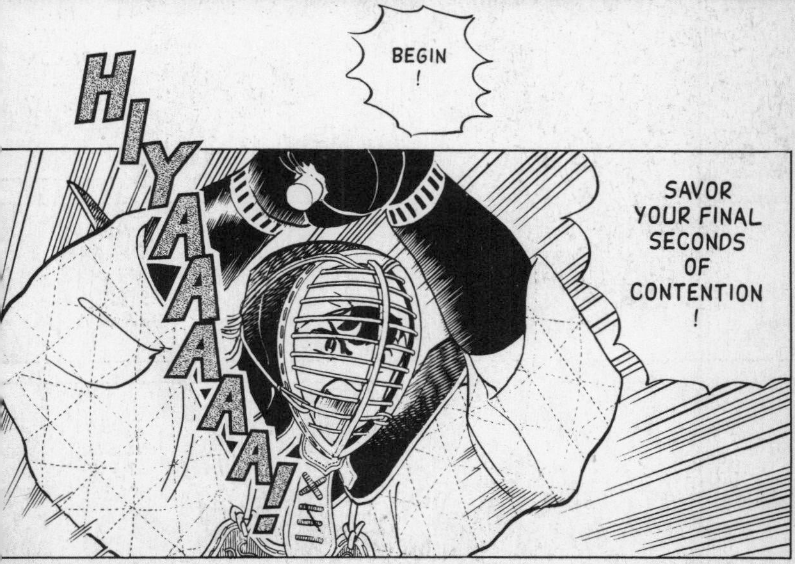
BEGIN!
HIYAAAAAA!
SAVOR YOUR FINAL SECONDS OF CONTENTION!

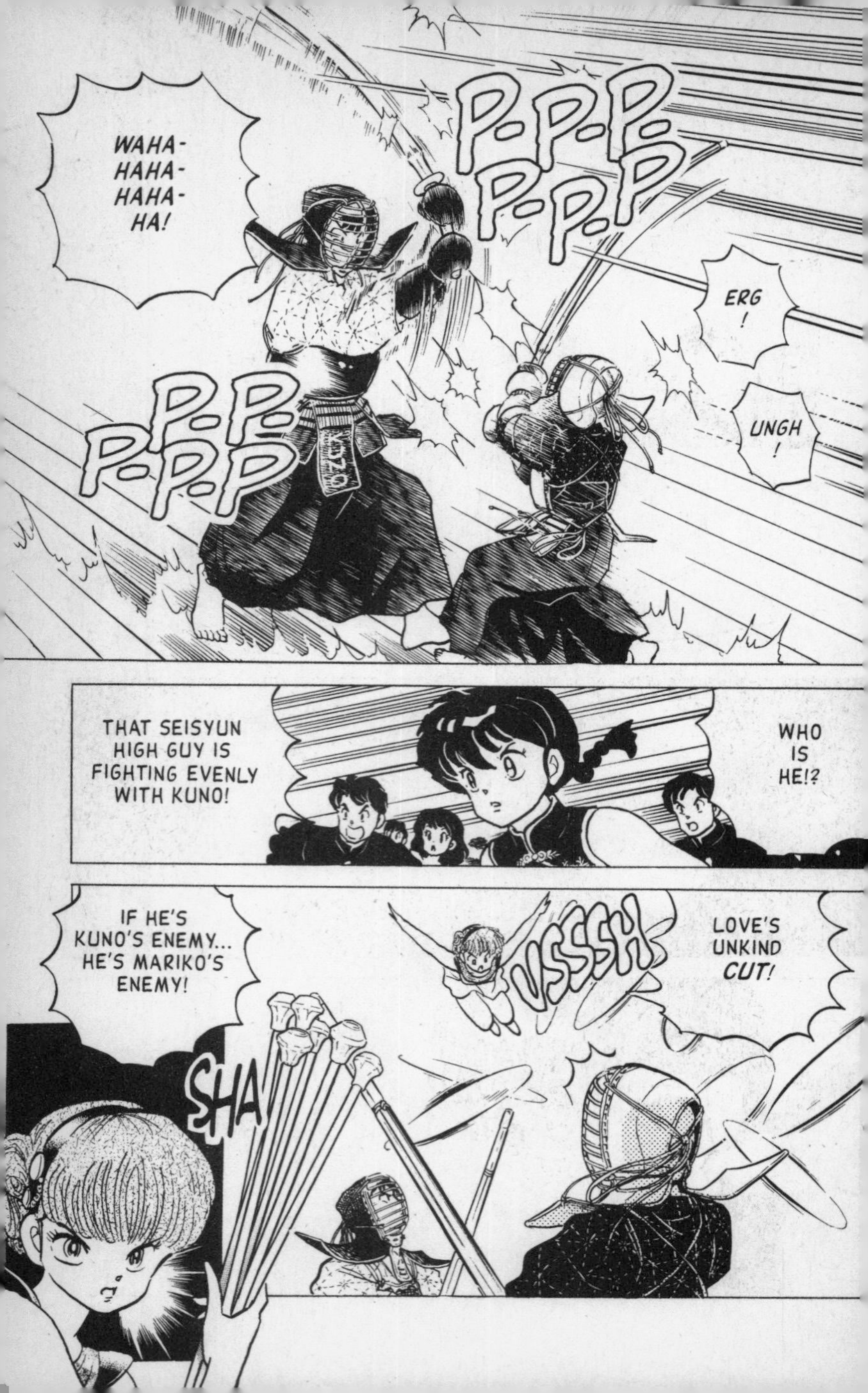
WAHA-HAHA-HAHA-HA!
P-P-P-P-P-P
ERG!
UNGH!
P-P-P-P-P
THAT SEISYUN HIGH GUY IS FIGHTING EVENLY WITH KUNO!
WHO IS HE!?
IF HE'S KUNO'S ENEMY... HE'S MARIKO'S ENEMY!
VSSSH
LOVE'S UNKIND CUT!
SHA

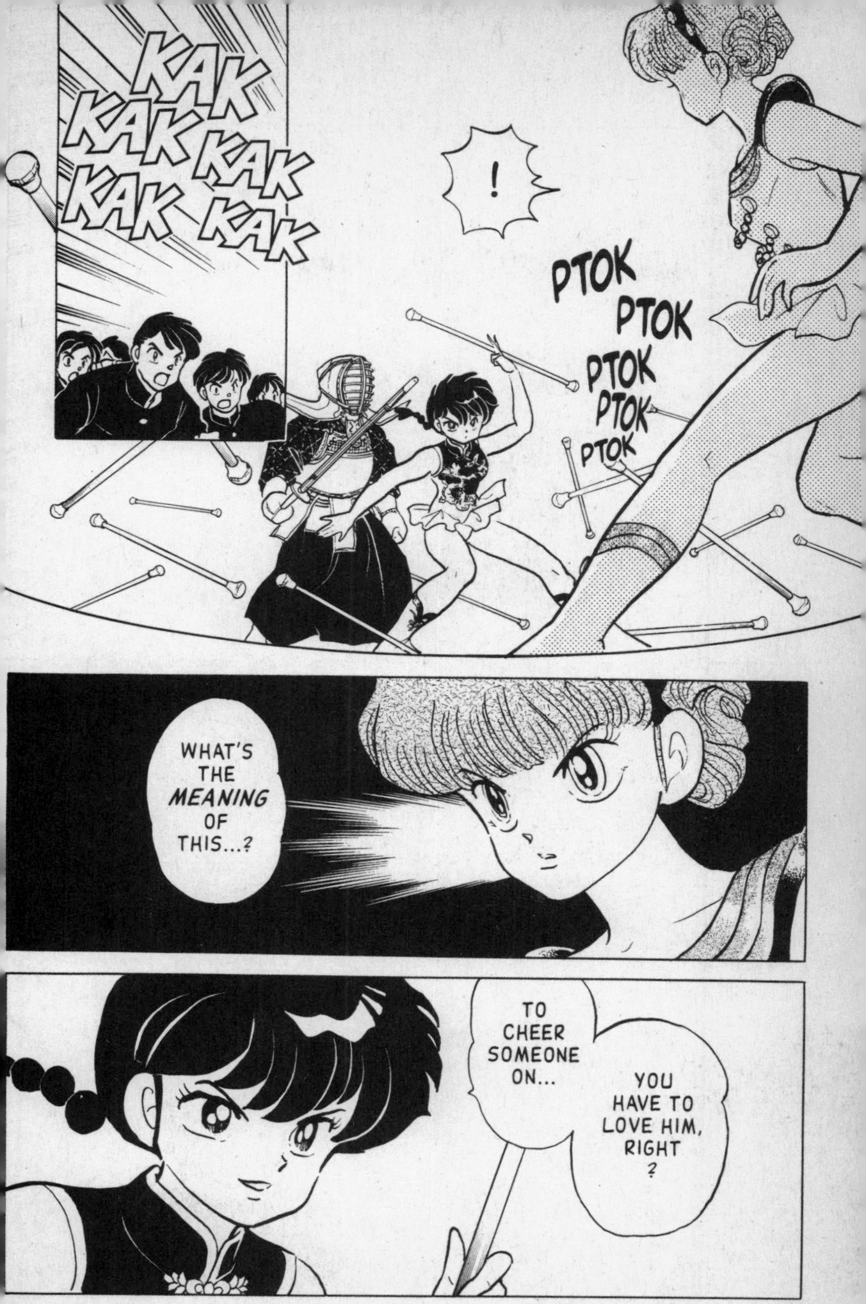
KAK KAK KAK KAK KAK KAK
!
PTOK PTOK PTOK PTOK PTOK
WHAT'S THE *MEANING* OF THIS...?
TO CHEER SOMEONE ON...
YOU HAVE TO LOVE HIM, RIGHT?

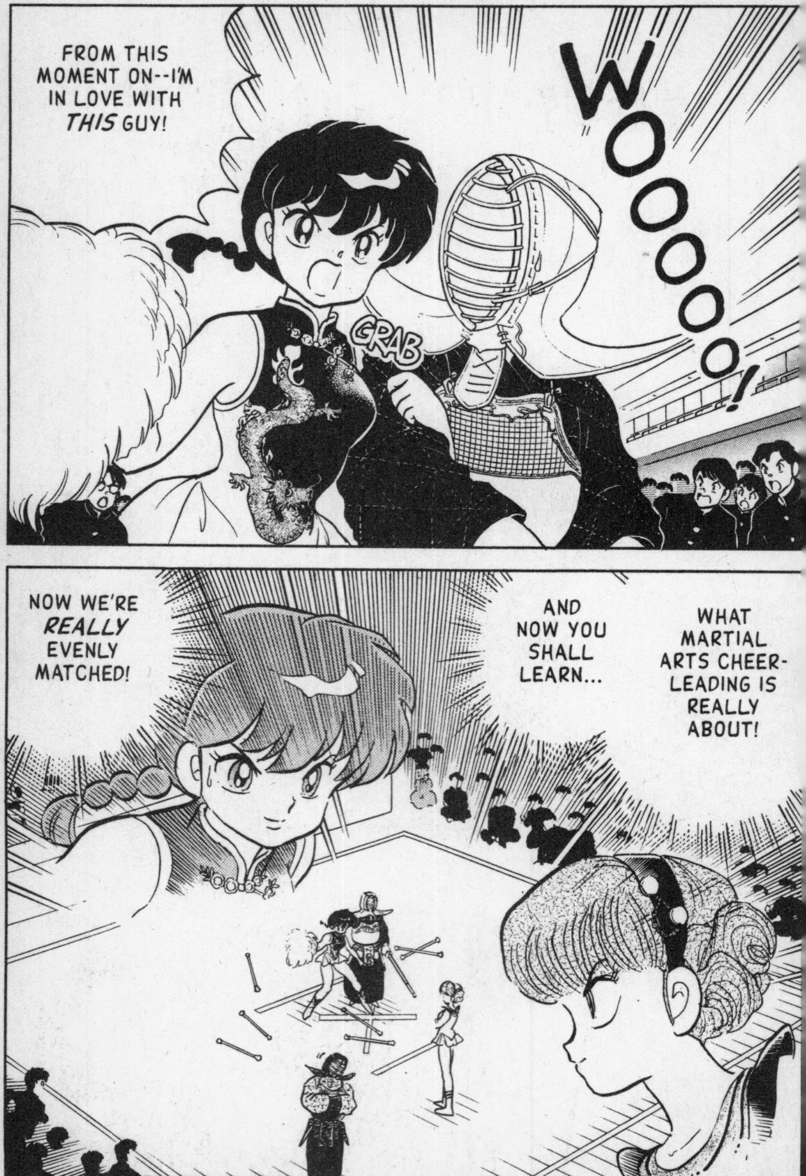
FROM THIS MOMENT ON--I'M IN LOVE WITH *THIS* GUY!
WOOOOOO!
GRAB
NOW WE'RE *REALLY* EVENLY MATCHED!
AND NOW YOU SHALL LEARN...
WHAT MARTIAL ARTS CHEER-LEADING IS REALLY ABOUT!

Part 11

LOVE VS. LOVE

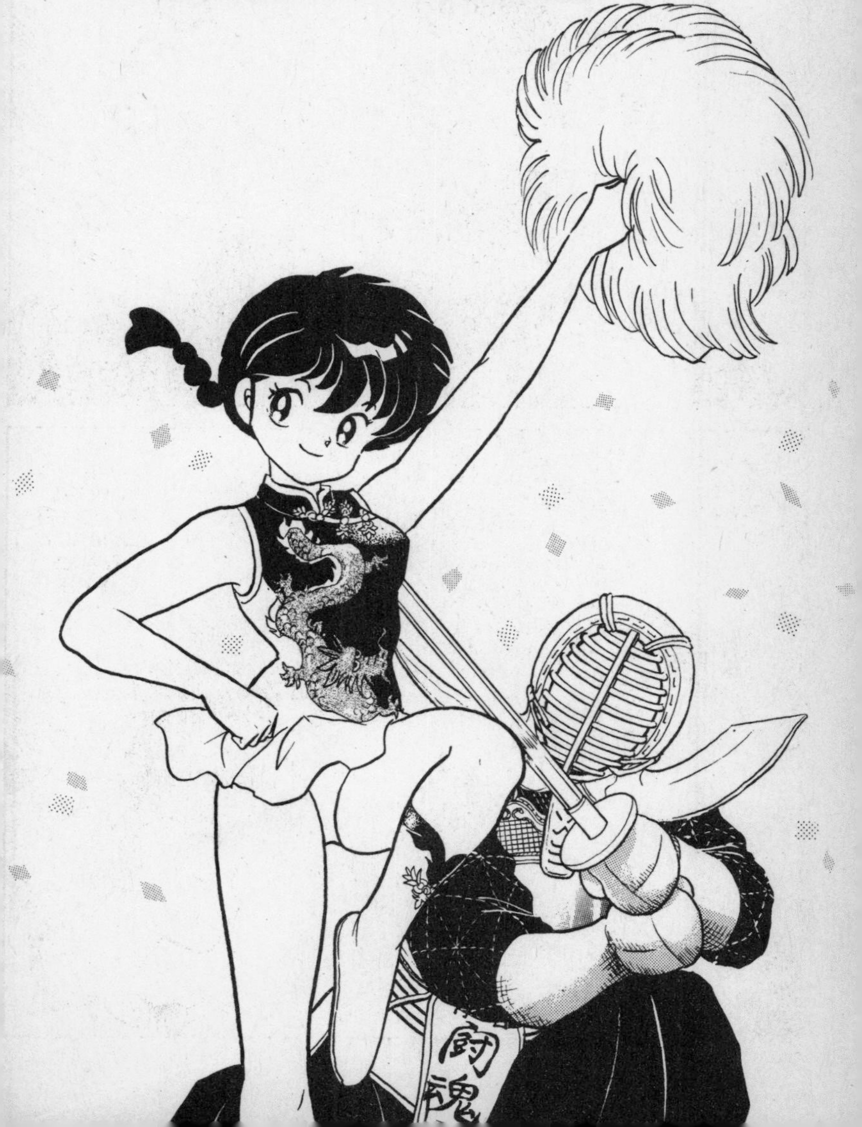
剣魂

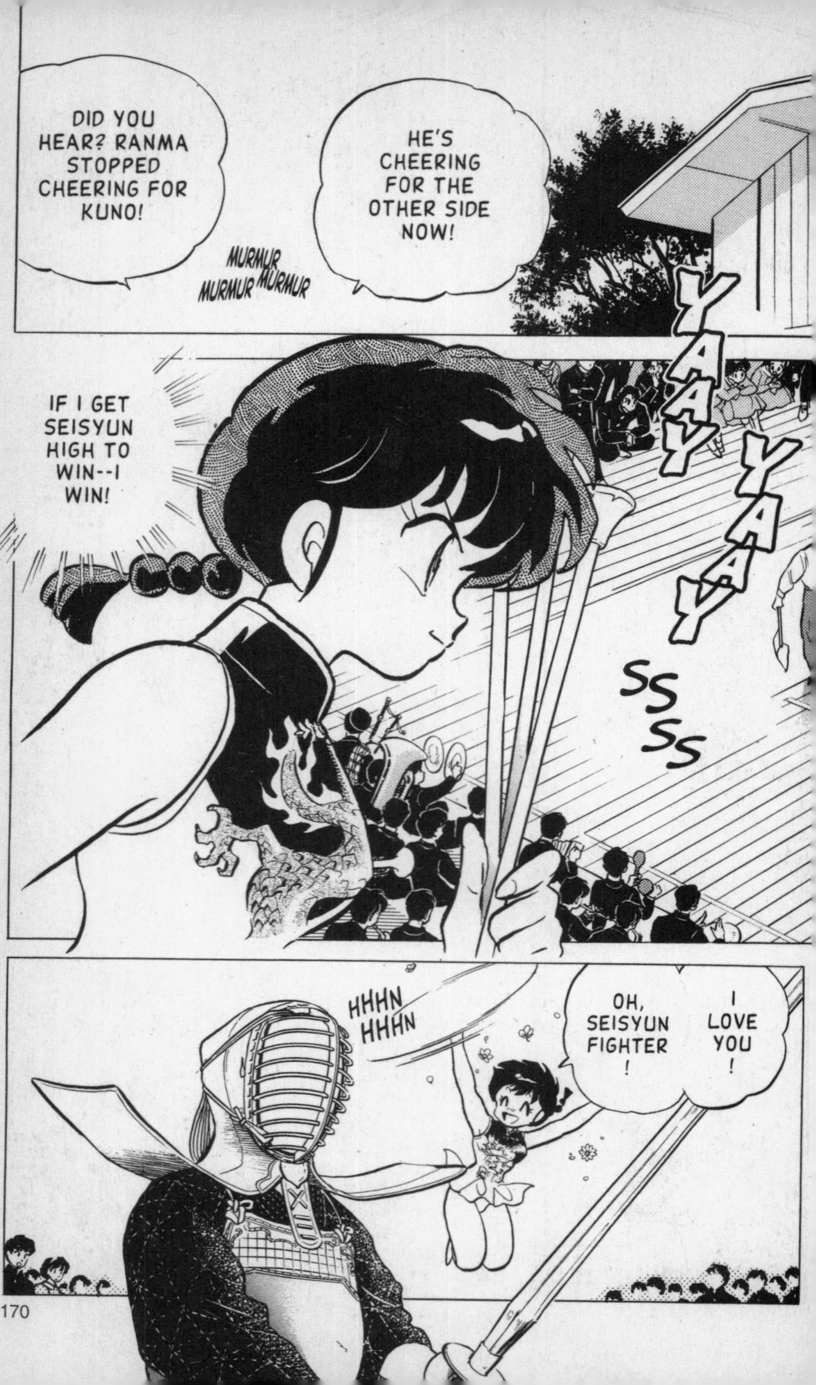
DID YOU HEAR? RANMA STOPPED CHEERING FOR KUNO!
MURMUR MURMUR MURMUR
HE'S CHEERING FOR THE OTHER SIDE NOW!
YAYAYAY
IF I GET SEISYUN HIGH TO WIN--I WIN!
YAYAYAY
SSSS
HHHN HHHN
OH, SEISYUN FIGHTER!
I LOVE YOU!

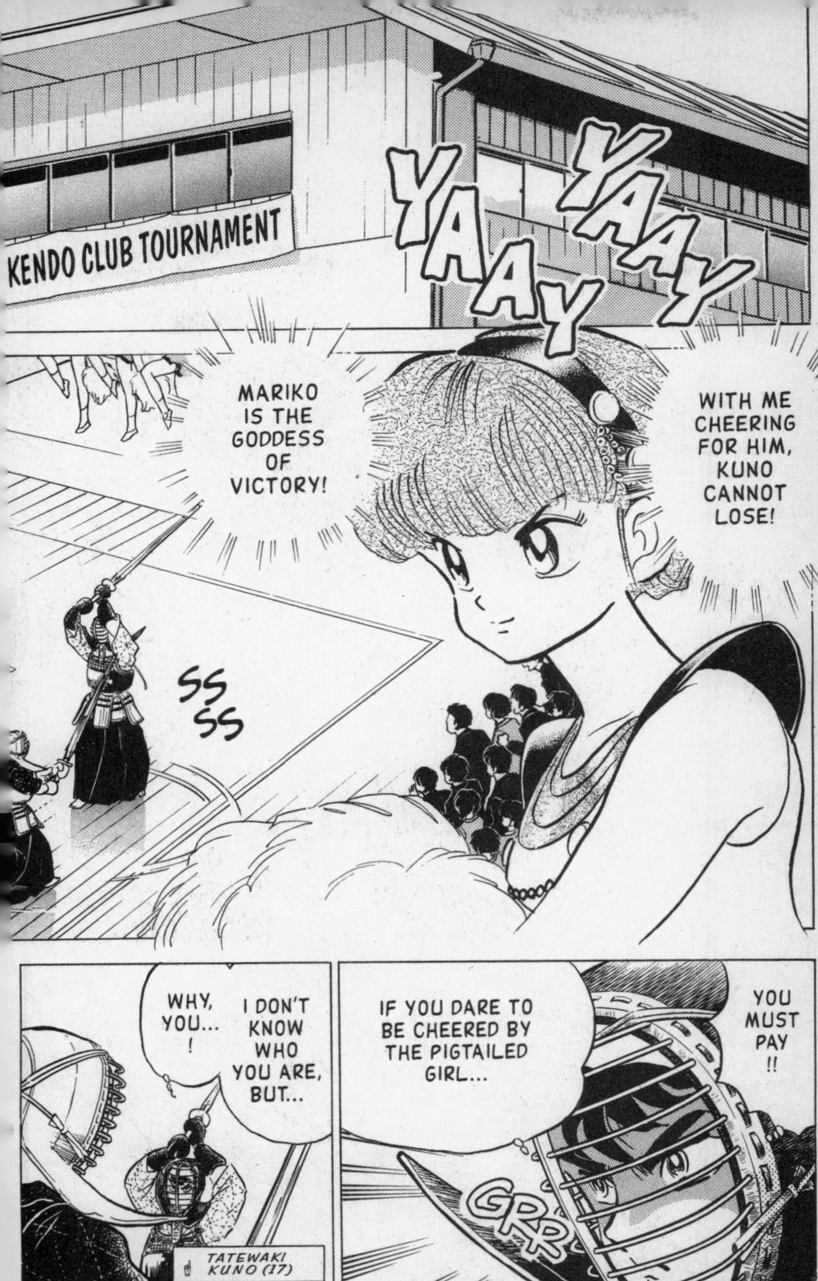

KENDO CLUB TOURNAMENT
YAAAY YAAAY
MARIKO IS THE GODDESS OF VICTORY!
WITH ME CHEERING FOR HIM, KUNO CANNOT LOSE!
SS SS
WHY, YOU... !
I DON'T KNOW WHO YOU ARE, BUT...
TATEWAKI KUNO (17)
IF YOU DARE TO BE CHEERED BY THE PIGTAILED GIRL...
YOU MUST PAY !!
GRR

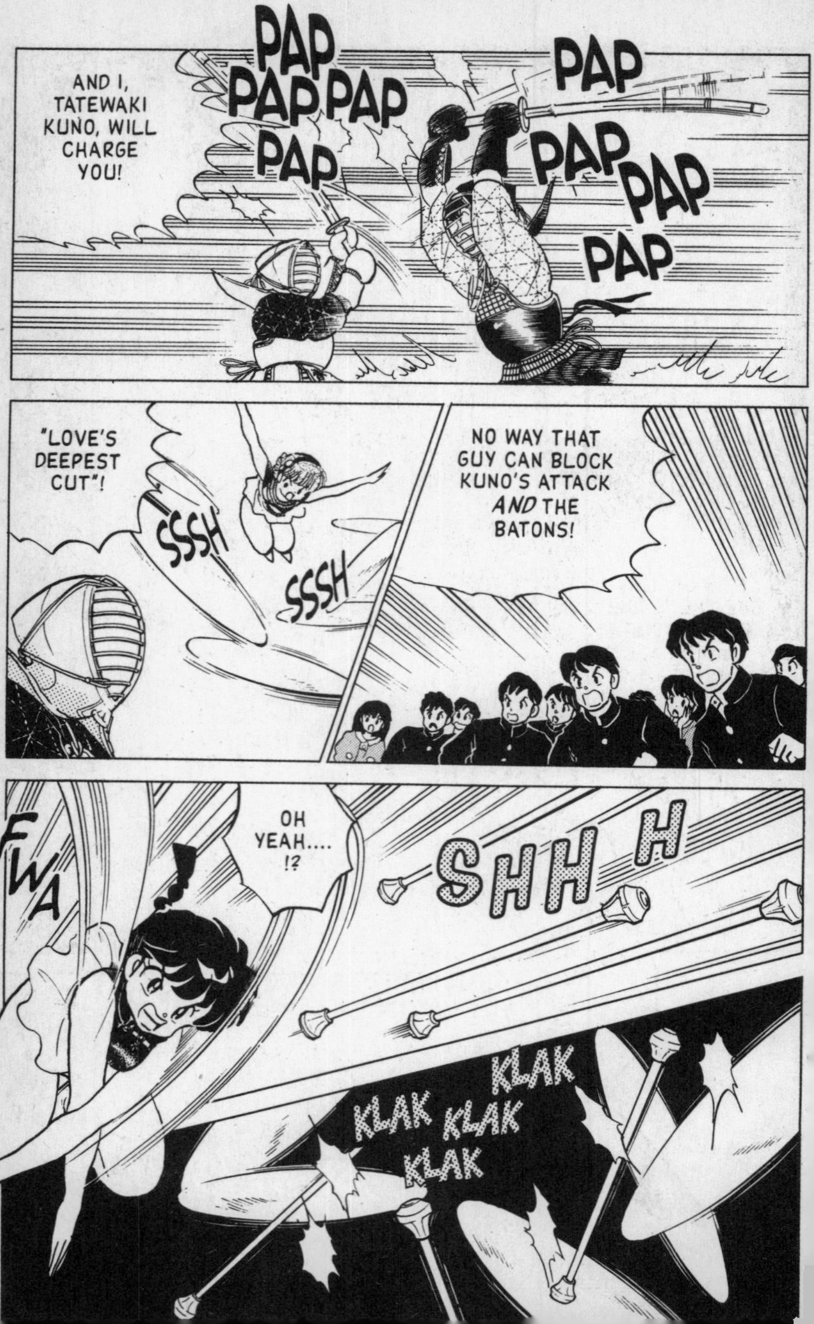
AND I, TATEWAKI KUNO, WILL CHARGE YOU!
PAP PAP PAP PAP
PAP PAP PAP PAP
"LOVE'S DEEPEST CUT"!
SSSH
SSSH
NO WAY THAT GUY CAN BLOCK KUNO'S ATTACK *AND* THE BATONS!
FWA
OH YEAH.... !?
SHH H
KLAK KLAK KLAK KLAK

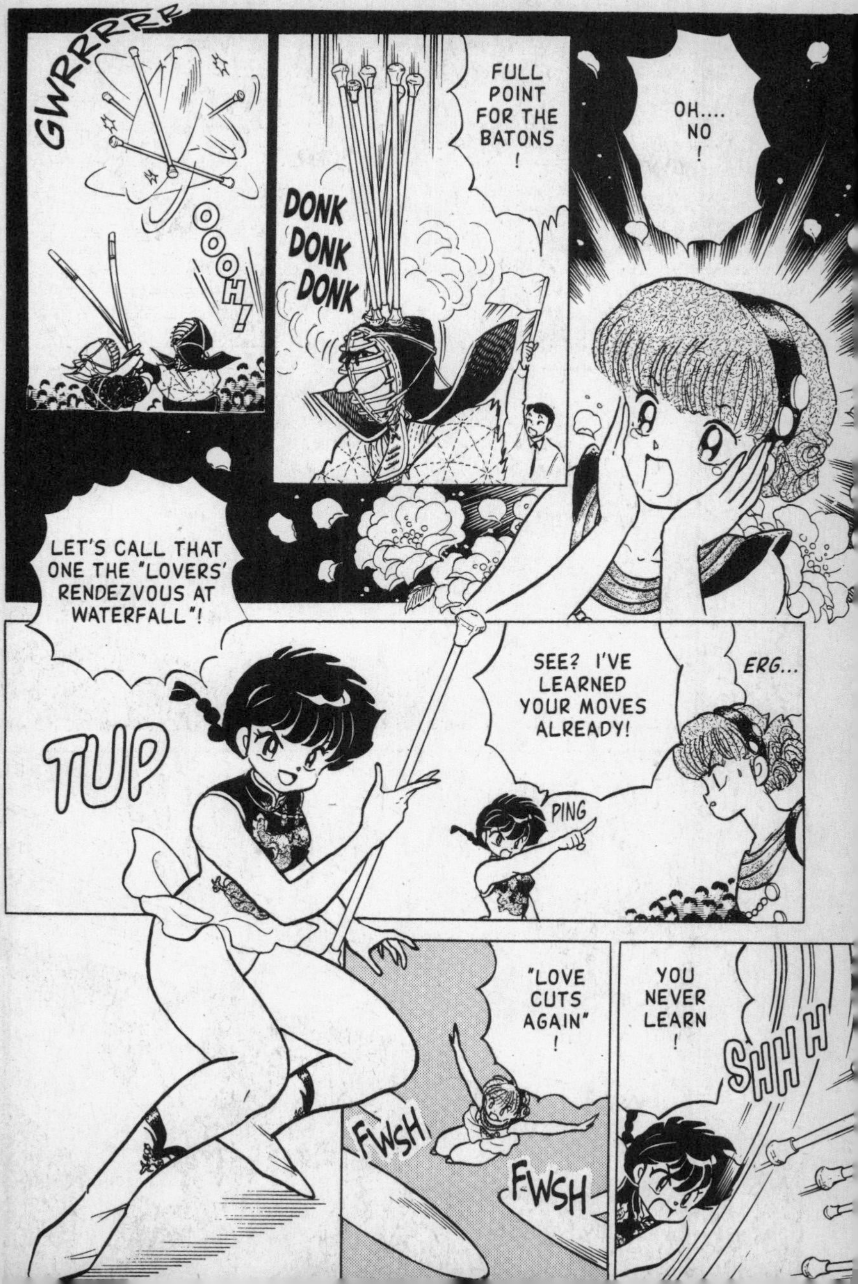
GWRRRRR
OOOOH!
DONK DONK DONK
FULL POINT FOR THE BATONS!
OH.... NO!
LET'S CALL THAT ONE THE "LOVERS' RENDEZVOUS AT WATERFALL"!
TUP
SEE? I'VE LEARNED YOUR MOVES ALREADY!
PING
ERG...
"LOVE CUTS AGAIN"!
FWSH
FWSH
YOU NEVER LEARN!
SHHH

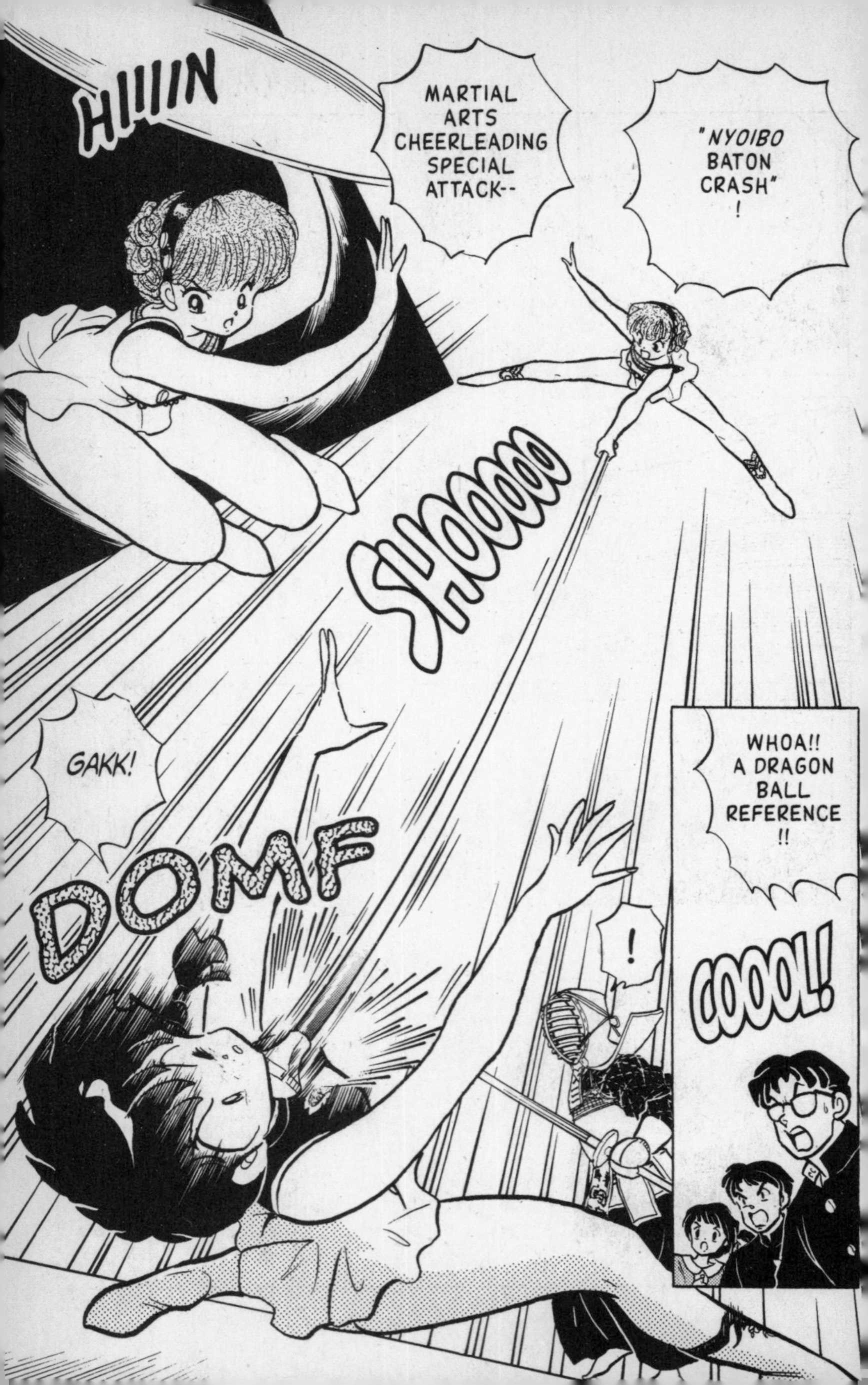
HIIIIN
MARTIAL ARTS CHEERLEADING SPECIAL ATTACK--
"NYOIBO BATON CRASH"!
SHOOOOO
GAKK!
DOMF
!
WHOA!! A DRAGON BALL REFERENCE!!
COOOL!

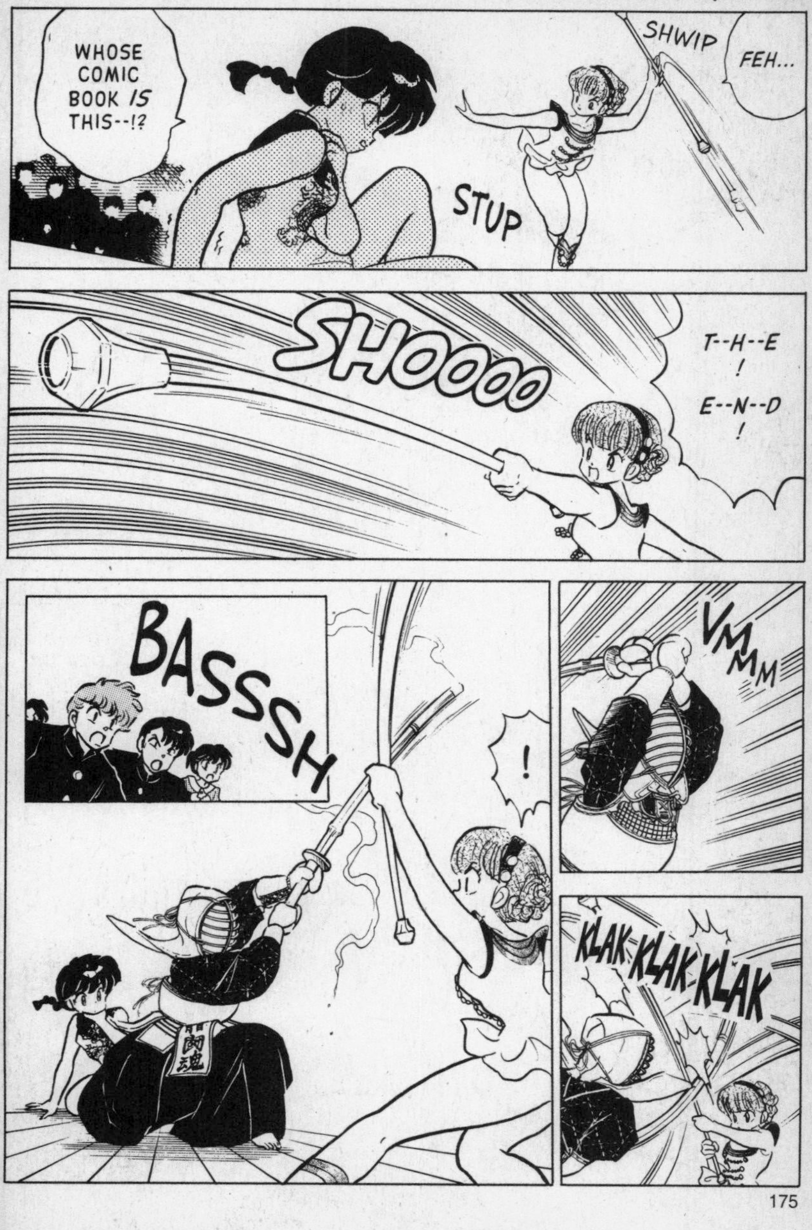
WHOSE COMIC BOOK IS THIS--!?
STUP
SHWIP
FEH...
SHOOOO
T--H--E ! E--N--D !
BASSSH
!
VMMM
KLAK KLAK KLAK

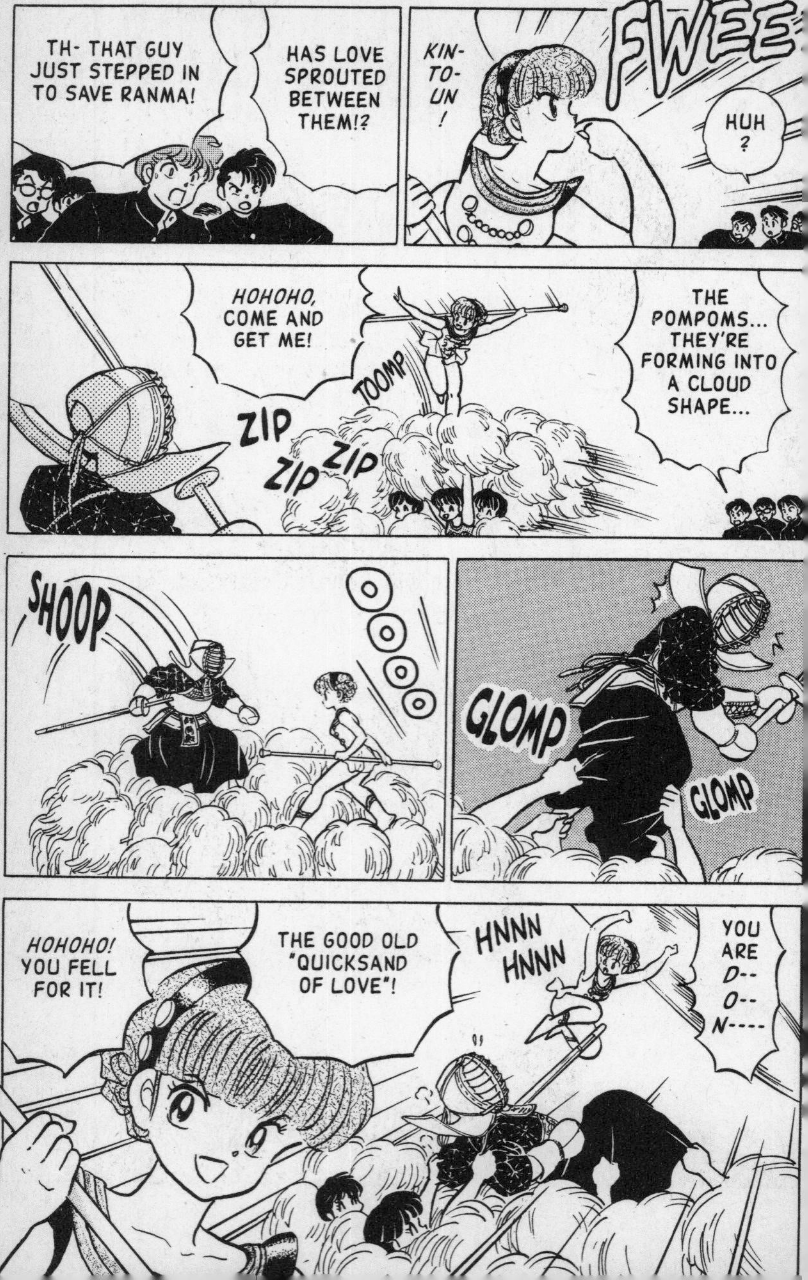
TH- THAT GUY JUST STEPPED IN TO SAVE RANMA!
HAS LOVE SPROUTED BETWEEN THEM!?
KIN-TO-UN!
FWEE
HUH?
HOHOHO, COME AND GET ME!
TOOMP
ZIP
ZIP
ZIP
THE POMPOMS... THEY'RE FORMING INTO A CLOUD SHAPE...
SHOOP
GLOMP
GLOMP
HOHOHO! YOU FELL FOR IT!
THE GOOD OLD "QUICKSAND OF LOVE"!
HNNN HNNN
YOU ARE D-- O-- N----

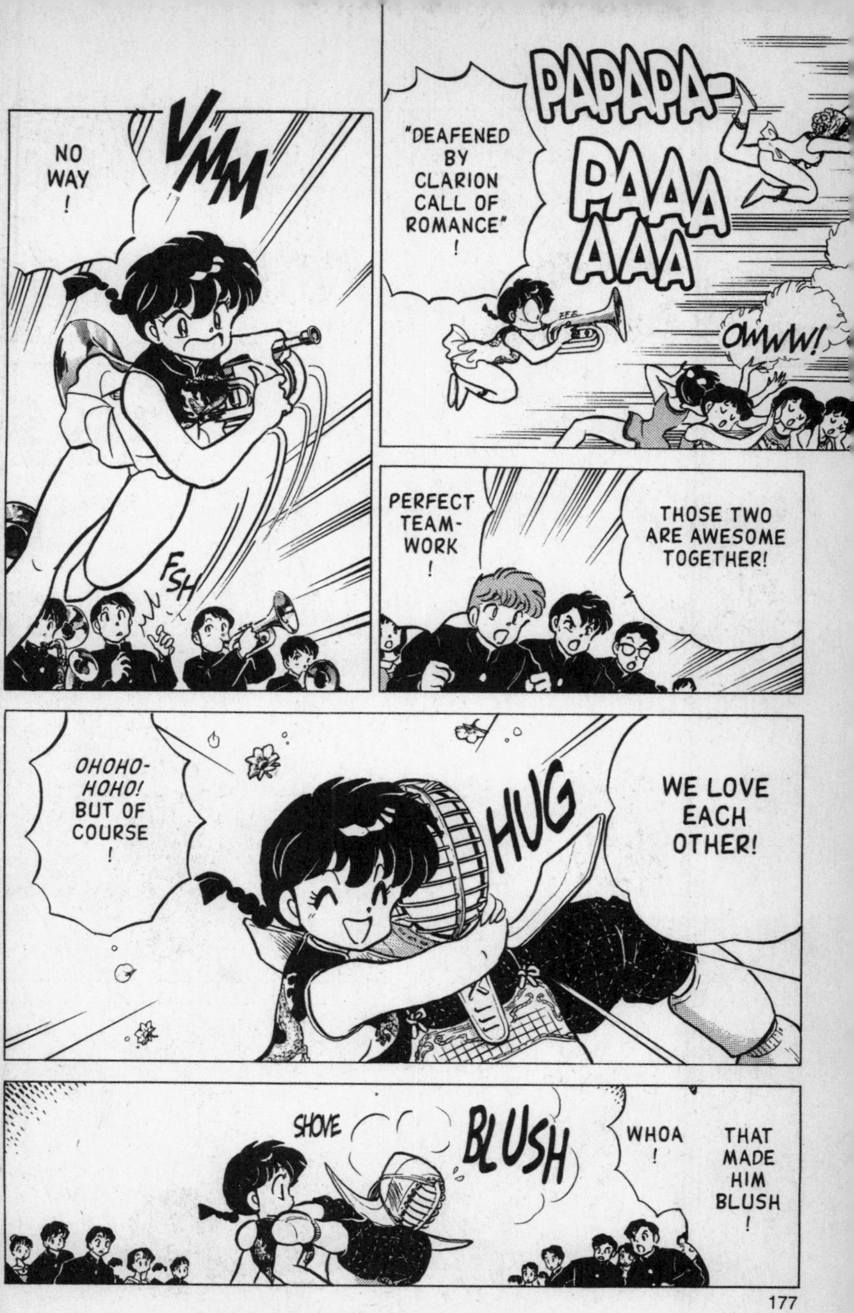
NO WAY !
VMM
FSH
"DEAFENED BY CLARION CALL OF ROMANCE" !
PAPAPA-PAAAAAA
OWWW!
PERFECT TEAM-WORK !
THOSE TWO ARE AWESOME TOGETHER!
OHOHO-HOHO! BUT OF COURSE !
HUG
WE LOVE EACH OTHER!
SHOVE
BLUSH
WHOA !
THAT MADE HIM BLUSH !

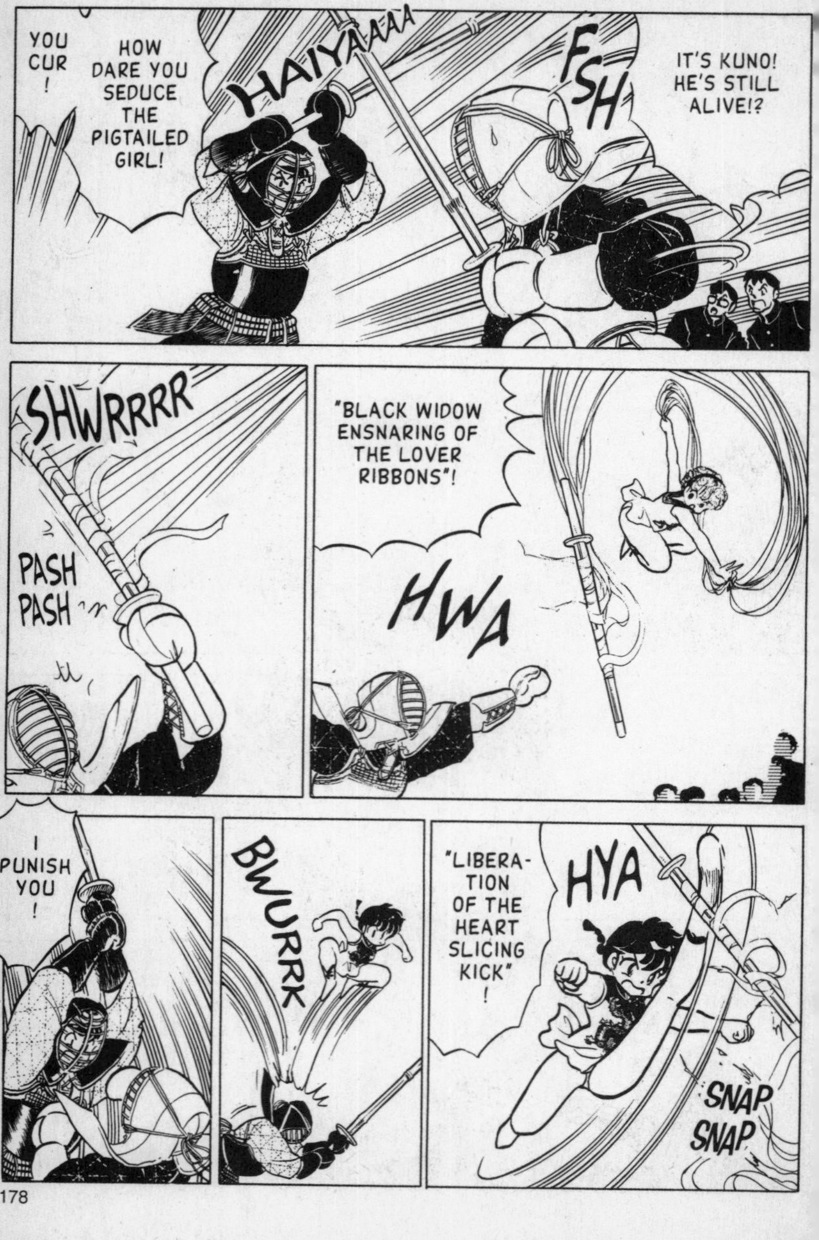
YOU CUR !
HOW DARE YOU SEDUCE THE PIGTAILED GIRL!
HAIYAAAA
FSH
IT'S KUNO! HE'S STILL ALIVE!?
SHWRRRR
PASH PASH
"BLACK WIDOW ENSNARING OF THE LOVER RIBBONS"!
HWA
I PUNISH YOU !
BWURRK
"LIBERA-TION OF THE HEART SLICING KICK" !
HYA
SNAP SNAP

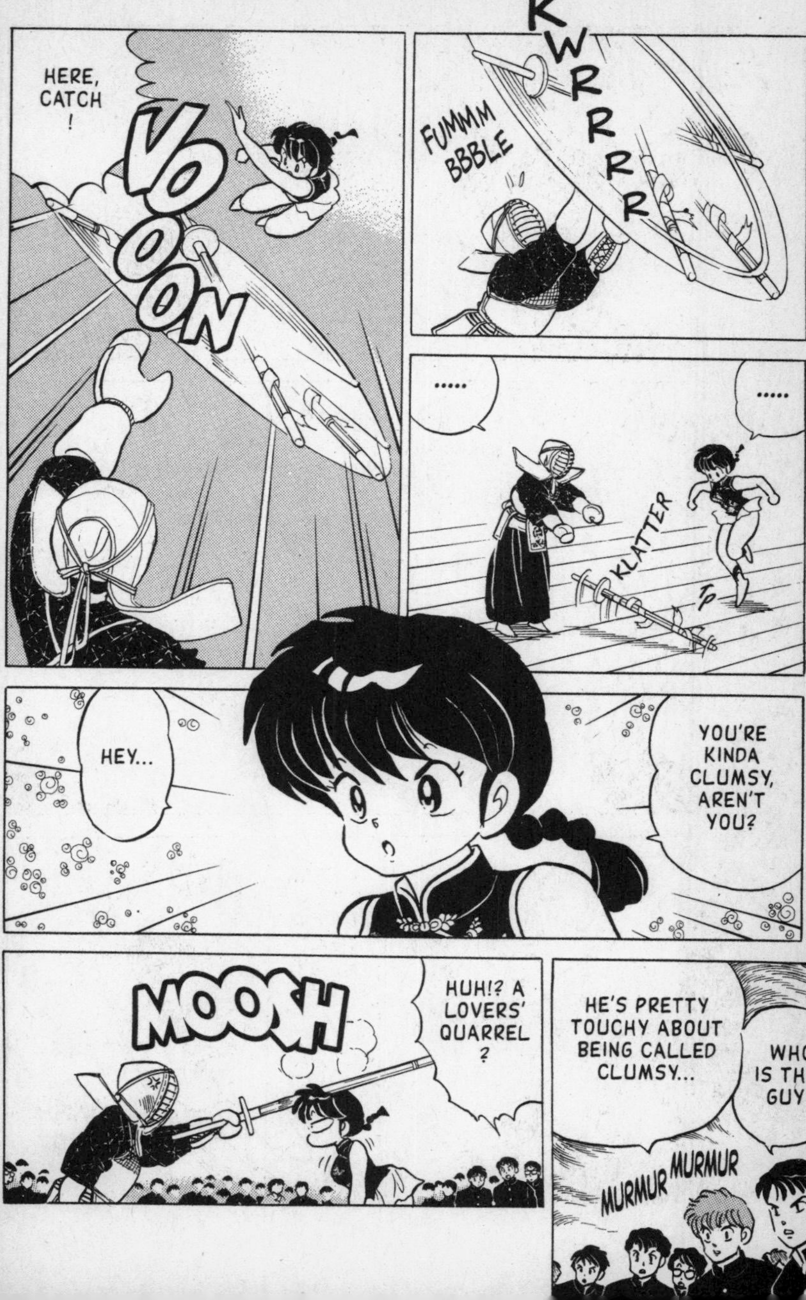
HERE, CATCH!
VOOOON
KWRRRR
FUMMM BBBLE
.....
.....
KLATTER
TP
HEY...
YOU'RE KINDA CLUMSY, AREN'T YOU?
MOOSH
HUH!? A LOVERS' QUARREL?
HE'S PRETTY TOUCHY ABOUT BEING CALLED CLUMSY...
WHO IS THAT GUY?
MURMUR MURMUR

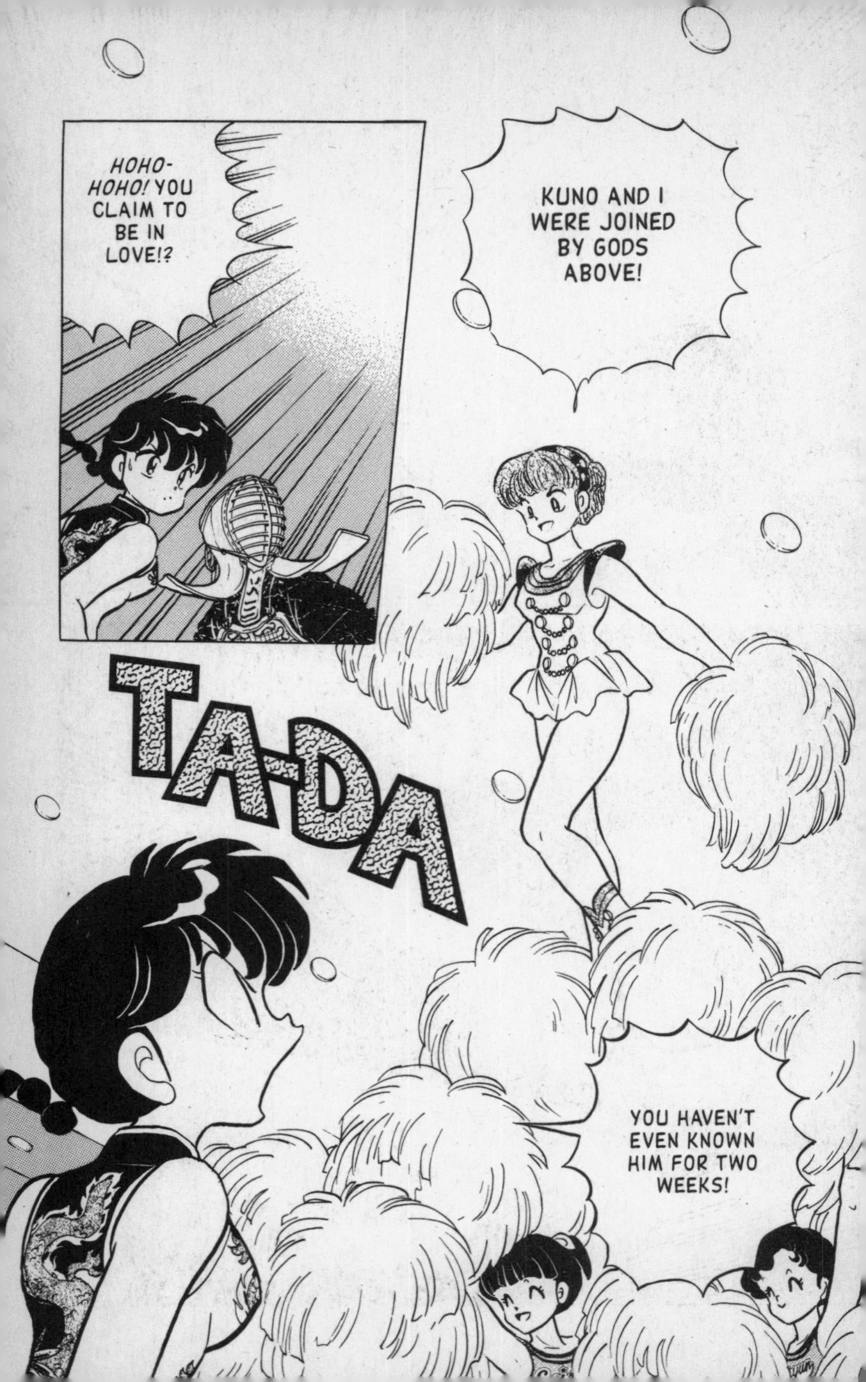
HOHO-HOHO! YOU CLAIM TO BE IN LOVE!?
KUNO AND I WERE JOINED BY GODS ABOVE!
TA-DA
YOU HAVEN'T EVEN KNOWN HIM FOR TWO WEEKS!

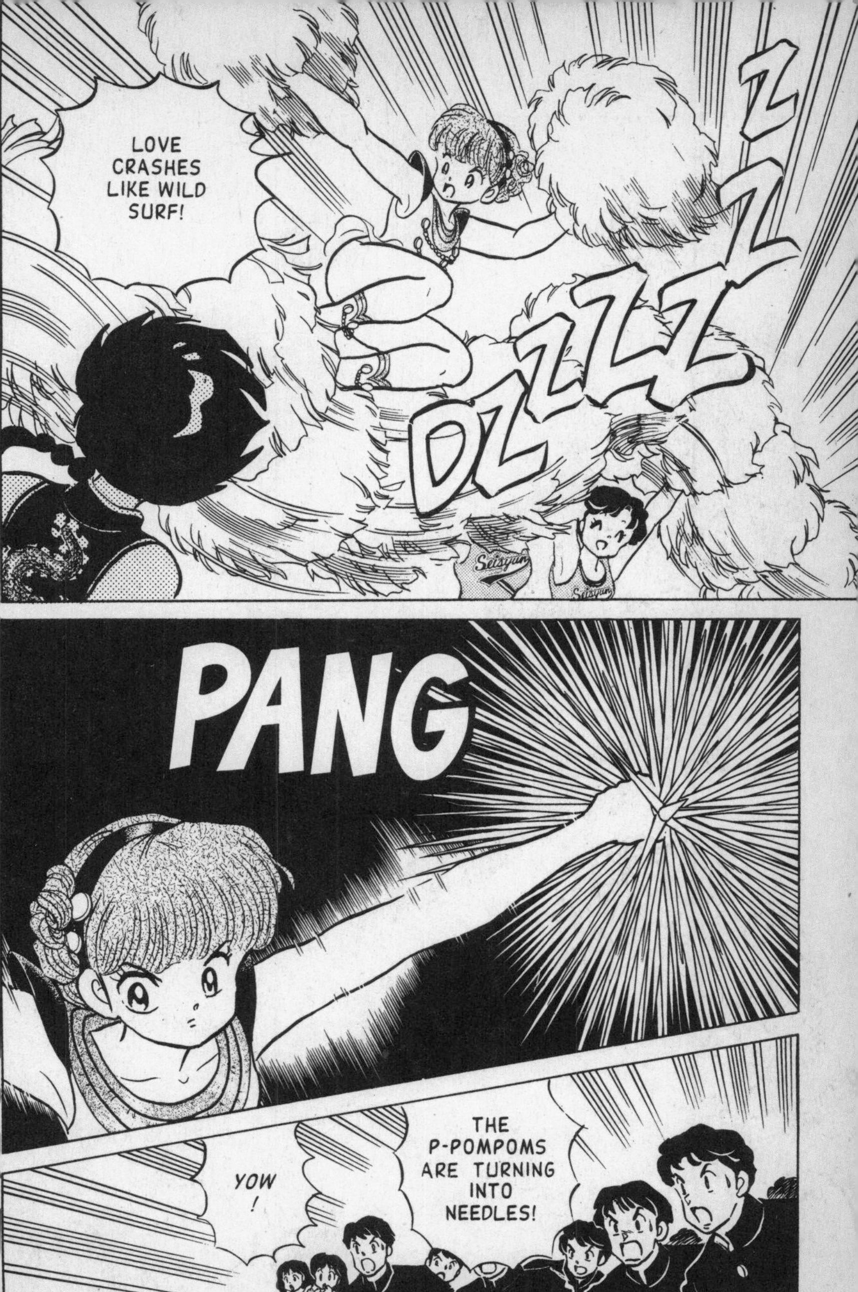
LOVE CRASHES LIKE WILD SURF!
DZZZZZZ
Seisyun
Seisyun
PANG
YOW!
THE P-POMPOMS ARE TURNING INTO NEEDLES!

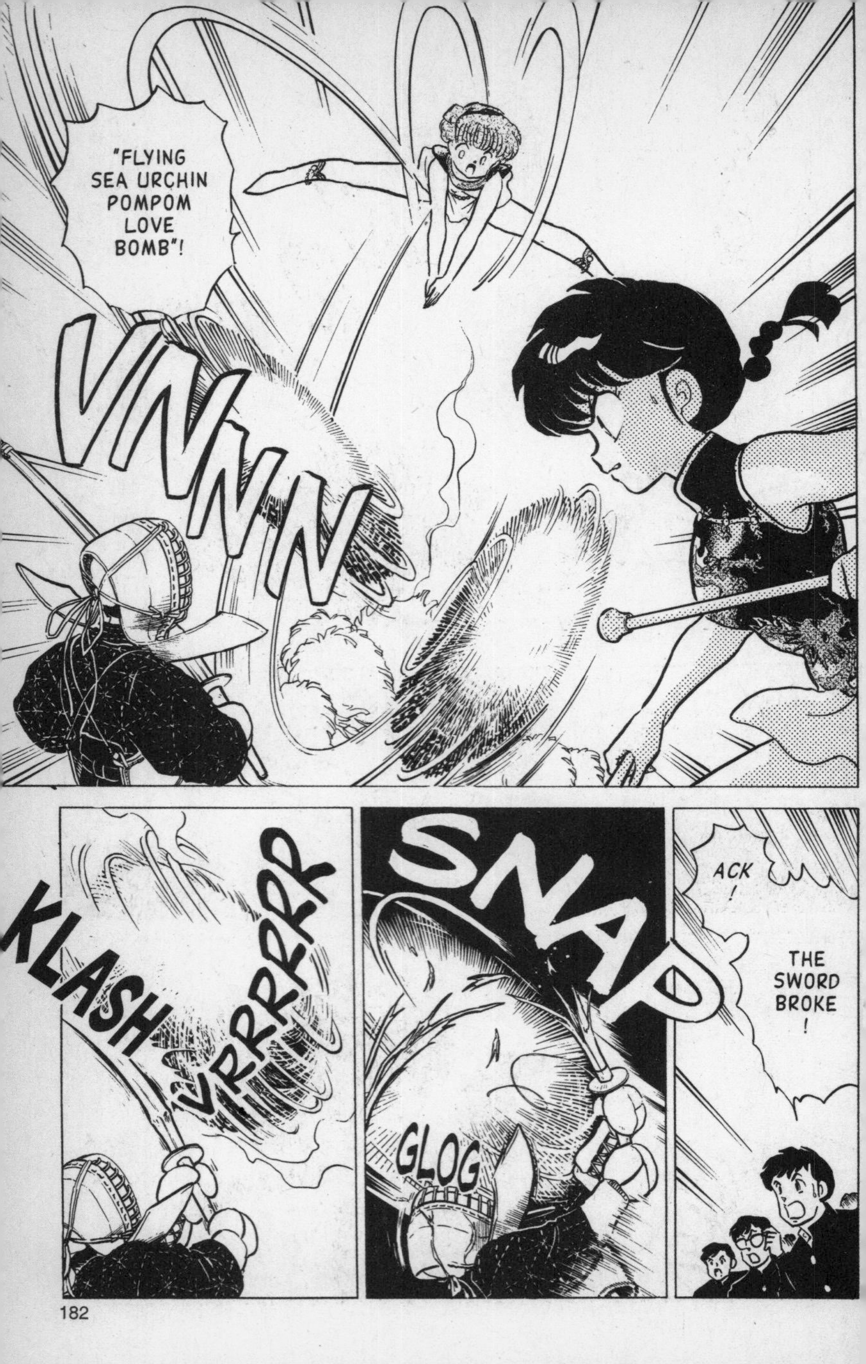
"FLYING SEA URCHIN POMPOM LOVE BOMB"!
VNNNN
KLASH
VRRRRRR
SNAP
GLOG
ACK!
THE SWORD BROKE!

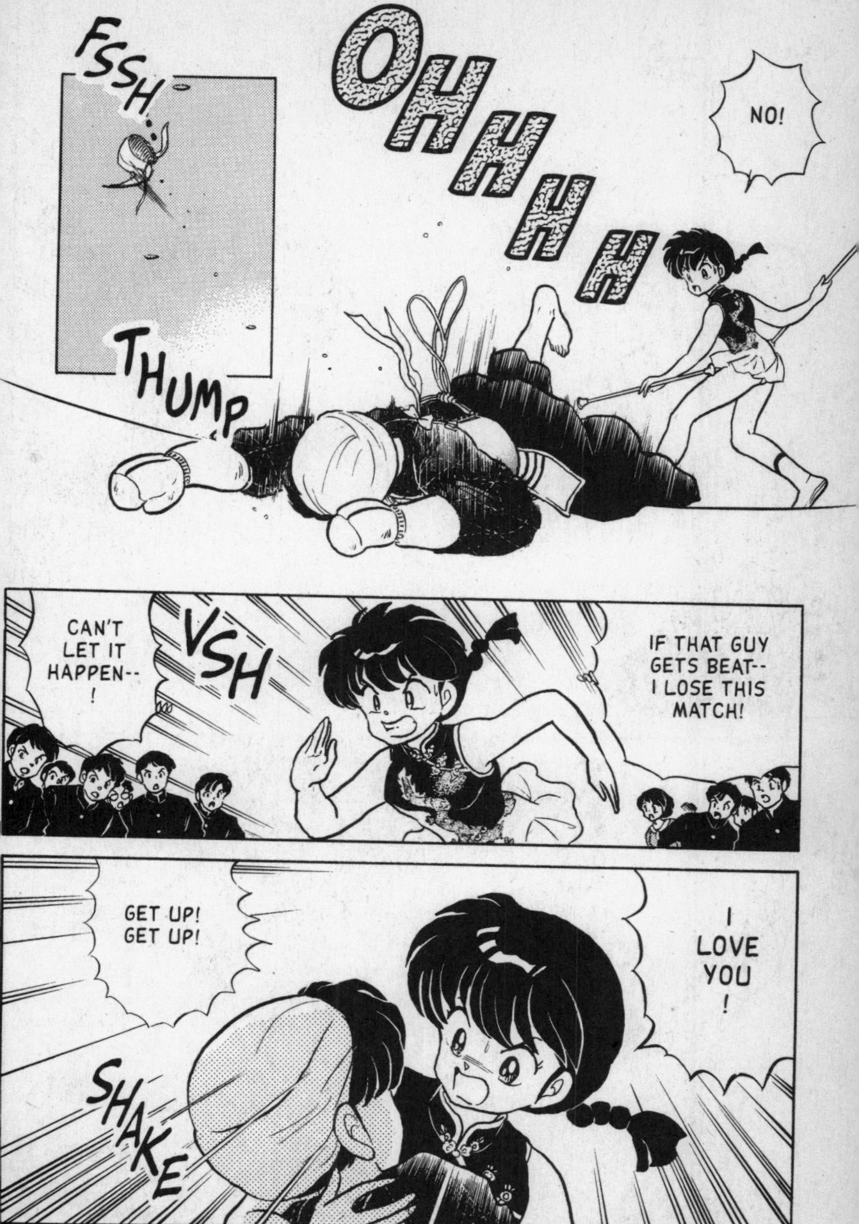
FSSH
OHHHHH
NO!
THUMP
CAN'T LET IT HAPPEN--!
VSH
IF THAT GUY GETS BEAT--I LOSE THIS MATCH!
GET UP! GET UP!
I LOVE YOU!
SHAKE

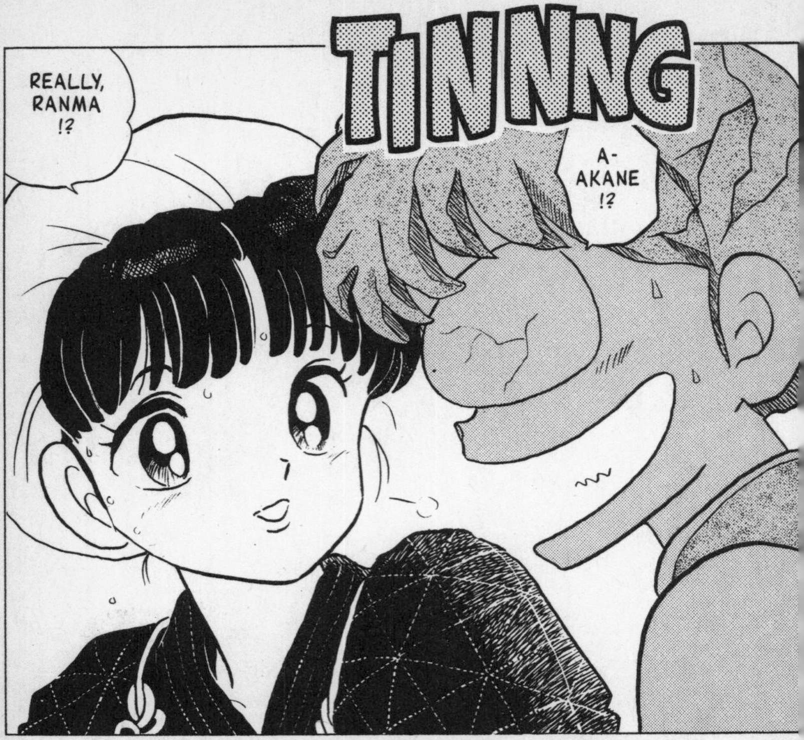
TINNNG
REALLY, RANMA !?
A-AKANE !?

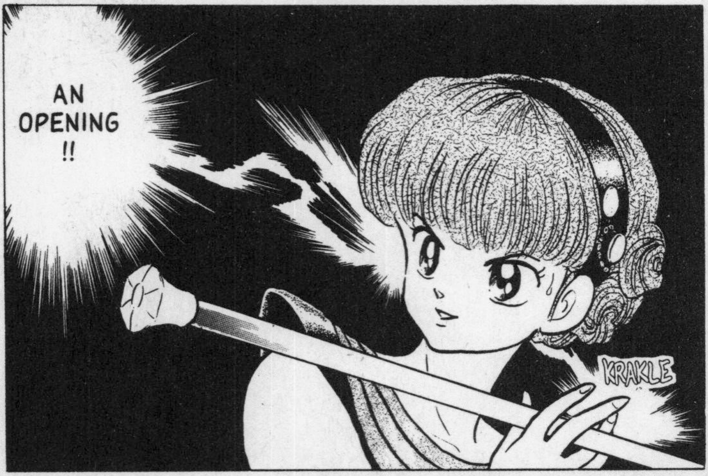
AN OPENING !!
KRAKLE

To Be Continued in Ranma 1/2 Vol. 20

About Rumiko Takahashi

Born in 1957 in Niigata, Japan, Rumiko Takahashi attended women's college in Tokyo, where she began studying comics with Kazuo Koike, author of CRYING FREEMAN. She later became an assistant to horror-manga artist Kazuo Umezu (OROCHI). In 1978, she won a prize in Shogakukan's annual "New Comic Artist Contest," and in that same year her boy-meets-alien comedy series URUSEI YATSURA began appearing in the weekly manga magazine SHÔNEN SUNDAY. This phenomenally successful series ran for nine years and sold over 22 million copies. Takahashi's later RANMA 1/2 series enjoyed even greater popularity.

Takahashi is considered by many to be one of the world's most popular manga artists. With the publication of Volume 34 of her RANMA 1/2 series in Japan, Takahashi's total sales passed one hundred million copies of her compiled works.

Takahashi's serial titles include URUSEI YATSURA, RANMA 1/2, ONE-POUND GOSPEL, MAISON IKKOKU and INUYASHA. Additionally, Takahashi has drawn many short stories which have been published in America under the title "Rumic Theater," and several installments of a saga known as her "Mermaid" series. Most of Takahashi's major stories have also been animated and are widely available in translation worldwide. INUYASHA is her most recent serial story, first published in SHÔNEN SUNDAY in 1996.

COMMENDATIONS

If you enjoyed this volume of Ranma 1/2, then here is some more manga you might be interested in:

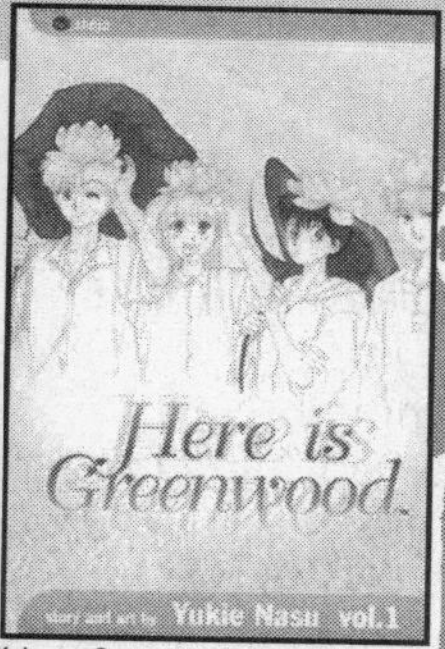
Here is Greenwood
Yukie Nasu vol.1
Koko wa Greenwood © Yukie Nasu 1986/HAKUSENSHA, Inc.

HERE IS GREENWOOD

Perhaps written for a slightly older audience than most of Rumiko Takahashi's work, Yukie Nasu's *Here is Greenwood* is exactly like *Ranma 1/2*, except for the martial arts (none), the wacky hijinks (almost none), and the occasional depiction of the adult relationships among its students. Okay, aside from the fact that they both have male high school students in them, they have nothing in common. But they're both cool!

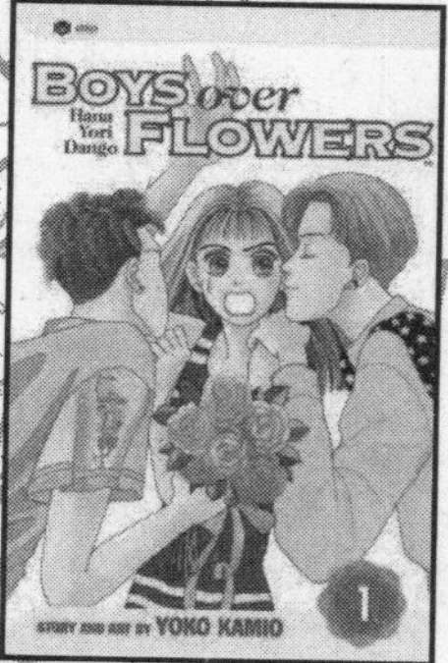
BOYS over FLOWERS
Hana Yori Dango
STORY AND ART BY YOKO KAMIO
1
HANA-YORI DANGO
© 1992 by YOKO KAMIO/SHUEISHA Inc.

BOYS OVER FLOWERS (HANA YORI DANGO)

Another tale of high school life in Japan, *Boys Over Flowers* (or "HanaDan" to most of its fans) is not without its serious side, but overall tends to fall into the "rabu-kome" or "love-comedy" genre.

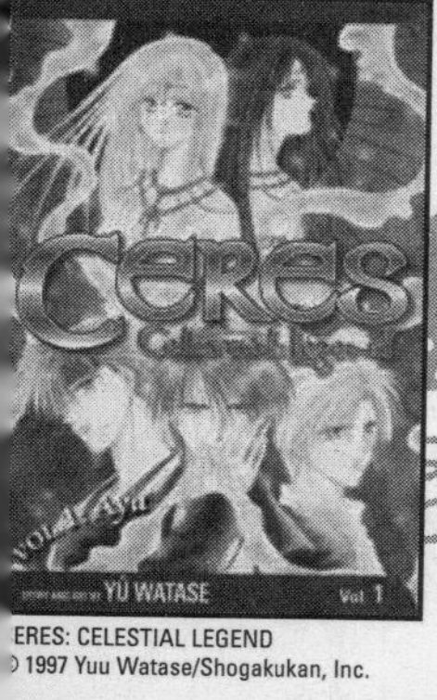
Ceres
YU WATASE
Vol. 1
ERES: CELESTIAL LEGEND
) 1997 Yuu Watase/Shogakukan, Inc.

CERES:CELESTIAL LEGEND

Aya Mikage is a trendy Tokyo teen with not much else on her mind but fashion, karaoke, and boys. But a terrible family secret involving an ancient family "curse" is about to make things a lot more difficult.

LOVE MANGA? LET US KNOW!

☐ Please do NOT send me information about VIZ products, news and events, special offers, or other information.

☐ Please do NOT send me information from VIZ' trusted business partners.

Name: _____

Address: _____

City: _____ State: _____ Zip: _____

E-mail: _____

☐ Male   ☐ Female   Date of Birth (mm/dd/yyyy): ___ / ___ / ___   (Under 13? Parental consent required)

What race/ethnicity do you consider yourself? (check all that apply)

☐ White/Caucasian   ☐ Black/African American   ☐ Hispanic/Latino
☐ Asian/Pacific Islander   ☐ Native American/Alaskan Native   ☐ Other: _____

What VIZ shojo title(s) did you purchase? (indicate title(s) purchased)

_____

_____

What other VIZ shojo titles do you own? _____

_____

Reason for purchase: (check all that apply)

☐ Special offer   ☐ Favorite title / author / artist / genre
☐ Gift   ☐ Recommendation   ☐ Collection
☐ Read excerpt in VIZ manga sampler   ☐ Other _____

Where did you make your purchase? (please check one)

☐ Comic store   ☐ Bookstore   ☐ Grocery Store
☐ Convention   ☐ Newsstand   ☐ Video Game Store
☐ Online (site:_____)   ☐ Other _____

How many manga titles have you purchased in the last year? How many were VIZ titles?
(please check one from each column)

MANGA
- ☐ None
- ☐ 1 – 4
- ☐ 5 – 10
- ☐ 11+

VIZ
- ☐ None
- ☐ 1 – 4
- ☐ 5 – 10
- ☐ 11+

How much influence do special promotions and gifts-with-purchase have on the titles you bu
(please circle, with 5 being great influence and 1 being none)

1 2 3 4 5

Do you purchase every volume of your favorite series?

☐ Yes! Gotta have 'em as my own ☐ No. Please explain: ______

What kind of manga storylines do you most enjoy? **(check all that apply)**

- ☐ Action / Adventure
- ☐ Comedy
- ☐ Fighting
- ☐ Artistic / Alternative
- ☐ Science Fiction
- ☐ Romance (shojo)
- ☐ Sports
- ☐ Other ______
- ☐ Horror
- ☐ Fantasy (shojo)
- ☐ Historical

If you watch the anime or play a video or TCG game from a series, how likely are you to buy the manga? **(please circle, with 5 being very likely and 1 being unlikely)**

1 2 3 4 5

If unlikely, please explain: ______

Who are your favorite authors / artists? ______

______

What titles would like you translated and sold in English? ______

______

THANK YOU! Please send the completed form to:

VIZ media™

NJW Research
42 Catharine Street
Poughkeepsie, NY 12601

Your privacy is very important to us. All information provided will be used for internal purposes only and will not be so or otherwise divulged.